INVISIBLE MEN

THE SECRET LIVES OF POLICE CONSTABLES IN LIVERPOOL, MANCHESTER, AND BIRMINGHAM, 1900–1939

Invisible Men

The Secret Lives of Police Constables in Liverpool, Manchester, and Birmingham, 1900–1939

JOANNE KLEIN

Liverpool University Press

First published 2010 by
Liverpool University Press
4 Cambridge Street
Liverpool
L69 7ZU

British Library Cataloguing-in-Publication data

A British Library CIP record is available

ISBN 978–1–84631–235–9 cased
     978–1–84631–236–6 limp

Typeset by Carnegie Book Production, Lancaster
Printed and bound by Bell and Bain Ltd, Glasgow

Contents

List of Tables

Acknowledgments

This book could not have been written without the generosity and cooperation of the Greater Manchester, West Midlands, and Merseyside Police Authorities. Particular thanks are due to Mr Duncan Broady, curator of the Greater Manchester Police Museum, to Sergeant Patrick Shortt at the Tallyho Police Training Centre, and to Mr Tony Mossman of the Merseyside Police Authority, for their invaluable support and assistance. I also wish to thank the librarians of the City of Manchester Central Library Reserve Room and Local History Department; the City of Birmingham Public Library Local History Department; the Liverpool Brown, Picton, and Hornby Library Record Office and Local History Department; and the Colindale branch of the British Museum Library. A Boise State University faculty sabbatical gave me time to complete a significant portion of this manuscript. Finally, I must thank Anthony Cond of Liverpool University Press for his support and patience, and the Press's entire staff for their hard work.

When deciding to become a police historian, I did not know that criminal justice scholars were such a generous and fun-loving group. I have been fortunate to be welcomed into this 'crime gang'. We share research and share meals, and I would not be the historian I am without them. I cannot name them all, but I particularly wish to thank David Wolcott, Chris Williams, and Jonathan Dunnage, who read this book in manuscript and gave me detailed and valuable feedback. While working on early material for this book, I received assistance from the late David Philips, Eric Monkkonen, and Barbara Weinberger, and I am sorry that I finished too late for them to see the final product. Clive Emsley, Bill Miller, Herbert Reinke, and Haia Shpayer-Makov have been unfailingly supportive. Other members of the 'gang' I wish to thank include Jeff Adler, Lee Beier, Jerry Blaney, Martin Blinkhorn, Marita Boes, Carolyn Conley, Ellen Dwyer, Doug Eckberg, Janet Galley, Mary Gibson, Mark Haller, Barbara Hanawalt, Anja Johansen, Lynn Johnson, Margo de Koster, Paul Lawrence, René Levy, Richard McMahon, Randy Roth, Xavier Rousseau, Eric Schneider, Pieter Spierenburg, Amy Gilman Srebnik, Bob Storch, Jennifer Trost, Klaus Weinhauer, and Martin Wiener, as well as honorary 'gang' member Lucinda McCray Beier. Finally, Mary Beth Emmerichs and I have attended so many 'crime' conferences together that I have lost track, and she has become one of my best friends. Regardless of all the conversations and comments, none of these scholars are responsible for the ways in which I have used their insights in my book.

Personal thanks are due to the 'beer call' gang for keeping me going while completing this book, especially to Ken our leader, Al, Janet, and Linda Marie, to Sandy and Lisa for baseball games and coffee breaks, to Patt, Guen, and Valencia for lunches, and to Donna for endless conversations. Elizabeth and Luis Reina of Liverpool remain my favourite 'partners in crime'. Their entire family, especially their mother Pauline, became my friends, and I will long remember cosy evenings at No 15 with their menagerie of pets. My fabulous brothers – John, Andy, and Paul – gave me the energy to get the final pages written; the company of my sisters-in-law, Maria and Mary, and nieces, Gabby and Hannah, was a welcome refuge from work. Finally, I cannot thank my parents, Don and Anna-Marie, enough for thinking it is great to have a daughter who is a police historian and supporting me all the way.

List of Abbreviations

BAR   Birmingham City Police Annual Reports
BCP   Birmingham City Police
BDRB   Birmingham City Police Disciplinary Report Books
BJSC   Birmingham Minutes of the Judicial Sub-Committee
BOR   Birmingham City Police Orderly Room Books
BPO   Birmingham City Police Orders
BRB   Birmingham City Police Roster Books
BRR   Birmingham City Police Resignation Register
BWCM   Birmingham Watch Committee Minutes
DC   (Desborough Committee) 'Report of the Committee on the Police Service of
         England, Wales, and Scotland', Evidence, 1920, Cmd. 874, vol. XXII, 573
HMI   His Majesty's Inspector of Constabulary
LAR   Liverpool City Police Annual Reports
LCCDR   Liverpool City Police Chief Constable's Disciplinary Reports
LCCO   Liverpool City Police Chief Constable's Orders
LCI   Liverpool City Police Constables Injured
LCP   Liverpool City Police
LDRB   Liverpool City Police Daily Report Books
LHCWC   Liverpool City Police Head Constable to the Watch Committee
LSO   Liverpool City Police Standing Orders
LWCM   Liverpool Watch Committee Minutes
MAR   Manchester City Police Annual Reports
MCP   Manchester City Police
MGO   Manchester City Police General Orders
MPF   Manchester City Police Personnel Files
MWCM   Manchester Watch Committee Minutes
NUPPO   National Union of Police and Prison Officers
PACA   Police-Aided Clothing Association
PC   Police Constable
PP   Parliamentary Papers
PS   Police Sergeant
RIC   Royal Irish Constabulary

Introduction: Invisible Men

> We have most of us known and seen the English Policeman
> crowned and flattered as a Bayard of chivalry and a Caesar of
> efficiency. We may live to see the English Policeman murdered
> like a Russian governor, mobbed like a Pro-Boer, stoned like
> a martyr, kicked like a card-sharper. But we shall not see
> the Policeman treated as an ordinary man, neither better nor
> worse than ourselves. For the ordinary lies, apparently, beyond
> the utmost extravagance of the human imagination.
>
> G.K. Chesterton, 'The Problem of Policemen', 1904[1]

THIS BOOK FOCUSES on the lives of ordinary English constables in the city police forces of Manchester, Birmingham, and Liverpool from 1900 to 1939. What this book is not is a history of police headquarters, criminal investigation departments, and specialized units, or an exploration of government criminal justice policies and legislation except insofar as any of these affected the ranks. Excellent studies have been published on policing as an institution, yet in most of them the constables walking their beats have remained anonymous. Laws were passed and policemen were meant to enforce them; disturbances erupted and policemen were meant to restore order. Constables appear as a category but rarely as individuals. Considering that constables spent much of their time alone, carrying out their duties according to their own priorities, this omission leaves a gap in any analysis of policing. In recent years, this oversight has begun to be remedied. In 1991, sociologist Mike Brogden interviewed retired policemen in a study of policing interwar Liverpool, arguing that policing detached them from their working-class origins and made them effectively classless, a conclusion supported by Barbara Weinberger in her 1995 oral history of English policing from the 1930s to 1960s.[2] The limitation of these

---

1   G.K. Chesterton, 'The Problem of Policemen', *Police Review and Parade Gossip*, 30 September 1904, p. 471.
2   Mike Brogden, *On the Mersey Beat: Policing Liverpool between the Wars* (Oxford: Oxford

oral histories, however, is that the interviews were conducted with retired police officers.[3] This missed the experiences of men who left the force before earning their pensions: over half of constables between 1900 and 1939.[4] Since 1990, more attention has been paid to policemen as workers by historians such as Clive Emsley and Haia Shpayer-Makov, moving away from the argument that policemen lost their class identity.[5] However, no comprehensive history of the experiences of English beat constables has been published.

The purpose of this book is to present a detailed examination of English policing among its lowest ranks and to explore the impact of having hundreds of working-class men more or less on their own enforcing the law. This is a comprehensive occupational study of constables from their joining the force to their leaving it, and of both their work lives and domestic lives. The chapters can be divided into four categories: force expectations and duties; internal force relationships; constables and the public; and domestic life. Each constable had to figure out how to adapt to life in uniform. On duty, they brought the criminal justice system and working-class culture together in unexpected ways, shaping law enforcement through their own notions of what policing meant. They decided what to notice or ignore, and where the line was between professional conduct and neglect of duty. Off duty, some socialized predominantly with other policemen, some kept up civilian friendships, and others did both. Men had long careers, careers cut short by disciplinary offences or health problems, or they left for other opportunities or under pressure from their families. The many who left the force, either by choice or involuntarily, scattered hundreds of former constables across other working-class occupations. Sometimes, constables felt cut off from civilians due to their occupations. Policing strikes and disturbances were perhaps when constables felt their uniforms most, and these events formed a significant part of law enforcement. However, the everyday lives of constables tended towards more trivial incidents, full of cultural and social connections that kept them linked to their class. Police relationships with civilians both on and off the job illustrate that, between 1900 and 1939, constables were a part of ordinary working-class life. They

---

University Press, 1991), pp. 1–4; Barbara Weinberger, *The Best Police in the World: An Oral History of English Policing* (Aldershot: Scolar Press, 1995), pp. 10–13.

3   Brogden interviewed twenty-four retired policemen (*On the Mersey Beat*, pp. 165–7); Weinberger interviewed eighty-five retired policemen (*The Best Police in the World*, p. 4). Both found their respondents through the National Association of Retired Police Officers.

4   See Chapter 10 for details on average lengths of service between 1900 and 1939.

5   See Clive Emsley, *The English Police: A Political and Social History*, 2nd edn (New York: Longman, 1996), pp. 224–47; Haia Shpayer-Makov, *The Making of a Policeman: A Social History of a Labour Force in Metropolitan London, 1829–1914* (Aldershot: Ashgate, 2002). See also Joanne Klein, 'Invisible Working-Class Men: Police Constables in Manchester, Birmingham and Liverpool 1900–1939' (PhD diss., Rice University, 1992).

might remain in the force long enough to become part of police culture but that culture remained linked to the working class.

Police records provide a rich mine of information regarding the thinking and behaviour of constables as well as the lives of civilians who came into contact with them, either through their police work or domestic lives. Not all police records survived from every force but the Manchester, Birmingham, and Liverpool archives together provide a reasonably complete combination of sources, one city filling the gaps left in another. For example, disciplinary report books survive from Birmingham and Liverpool that cover much of 1900 to 1939 though never in complete sets from entire forces. The Manchester City Police kept some personnel files with misconduct investigations and a few handwritten constables' autobiographies; Birmingham City Police saved a list of marriage certificates and a resignation register; and Liverpool City Police has almost a complete set of books listing injuries to constables. All three cities saved complete sets of Watch Committee Minutes, the city authority that dealt with police matters under various Municipal Corporations Acts, but Manchester City Police kept an extra set with supporting documents. In addition, the *Police Review and Parade Gossip*, founded in 1893 as a newspaper for the ranks, gave the police a voice. Both constables and their wives not only read the paper, they wrote letters to the editor expressing opinions on everything from pay and promotion to views on superior officers to domestic life. Finally, annual Inspector of Constabulary reports and Parliamentary papers provide broader information on the state of police forces. Since the working class rarely left behind written accounts of their lives, these sources can recreate not only the everyday lives of constables in depth and detail but also incidents in the lives of many of their friends and neighbours.

This study focuses on the cities of Manchester, Birmingham, and Liverpool, chosen for their similar size with comparable economic histories and police forces that resembled each other in their origins and organization. However, each city also had its own personality and its force its own character, allowing for useful contrasts. During early nineteenth-century industrialism, they were three of England's leading cities, with increasingly crowded populations looking for work in manufacturing, transportation, and the Liverpool dock facilities. They were embroiled in the civil unrest that swept England after the Battle of Waterloo, combining protests over mechanization, unemployment, and electoral reform. Manchester was the site of the 1819 Peterloo massacre where eleven people were killed and hundreds more wounded when the local yeomanry charged a crowd attending a political reform meeting. In reaction to concerns over national disorder, Sir Robert Peel created the London Metropolitan Police in 1829 to be the model of a new English police, its first duty to prevent crime and to preserve public tranquillity without resorting to lethal force.[6] The new police were given ranks and uniforms designed to avoid

---

6   Metropolitan Police, *Instructions to the Force* (London: J. Hartnell, 1829), pp. 1–2.

resembling the military, and were armed with heavy wooden truncheons rather than firearms to avoid any temptations to use them as a standing army. In 1835, the Municipal Corporations Act gave cities the authority to appoint watch committees to manage local police forces.[7] Liverpool was included in this act and refashioned its city watch into a police force in 1836. In the political uproar over Chartist riots, the Municipal Corporation Act was extended to Birmingham and Manchester in 1838 which adopted new police forces by the end of 1839. All three cities modelled their forces on the London Metropolitan Police but local watch committees kept tight control over them. This gave each force its own identity, reflecting the local watch committee and the chief constables they hired. Watch committees had the final say over hiring, firing, discipline, pay, and pensions, though could be internally divided depending on local politics. Chief constables could have more or less power depending on local conditions, and police forces tended to reflect their strengths and weaknesses. Despite the organizational standard of the London Metropolitan Police, each city held on to its own customs. Liverpool, for example, considered its police system satisfactory before 1836,[8] and retained large sections of its 1834 watch instructions well into the twentieth century. By 1901 Liverpool had grown to 685,000 people, Manchester 642,000, and Birmingham 522,000. Birmingham continued to boom, reaching over a million people by 1931, while Liverpool and Manchester grew less dramatically to 856,000 and 766,000 respectively.[9] In the early twentieth century, each city dominated its region – Manchester the northern manufacturing districts, Birmingham the Midlands, and Liverpool the nation's ports, vying with London as the biggest and busiest.

To understand the police forces in these cities from 1900 to 1939, their basic structure needs to be outlined. Birmingham began as the smallest, with 700 men in 1900, but became the largest with 1887 men by 1939, both due to a territorial expansion in 1911 and to the growth of its population. Manchester and Liverpool grew more slowly as their populations expanded. Manchester had 1031 policemen in 1900, and 1511 in 1939; Liverpool began as the largest force, with 1460 men in 1900, and 1821 men in 1939.[10] The lowest rank was constable, rising through sergeant, inspector, chief inspector, superintendent, chief superintendent, assistant chief constable, and chief constable. All policemen up to chief superintendent began as constables and rose through the ranks. Roughly eighty-five per cent of forces were constables, about ten per cent sergeants, and about five per cent in the higher

---

7   Emsley, *The English Police*, p. 37.
8   Emsley, *The English Police*, p. 37.
9   David C. Marsh, *The Changing Social Structure of England and Wales, 1871–1961* (London: Routledge, 2002), p. 73. Birmingham's 1901 total adjusted to 1931 census boundaries was 759,000, Liverpool 711,000, and Manchester 645,000.
10 'Rate of Constables' Pay in English Borough', *Police Review*, 12 January 1900, p. 15; Emsley, *English Police*, pp. 265–6.

ranks.[11] Before the First World War, assistant chief constables and chief constables were frequently appointed from the Royal Irish Constabulary, colonial police forces, and the military; though beginning in the late nineteenth century some men were appointed from English police forces. In the 1920s and 1930s, it became more common for assistant chief constables and chief constables to be career English police officers though appointments from outside the force continued.[12] Despite hopes for promotion, most constables remained constables for their entire career. However, they moved up within the rank of constable in 'classes', sometimes determined by length of service and sometimes by merit; each class brought a pay increase. The number of classes varied from force to force, and over time. Before the war, for example, Manchester had six classes, two long-service classes, and a good conduct class, and after the war, it had eleven classes and two good conduct classes. The higher ranks had similar 'classes' within rank. Sometimes, policemen were reduced in class for disciplinary reasons. Constables up to inspectors were paid on a weekly basis; superintendents, assistant chief constables, and chief constables were paid an annual salary. In addition to their pay, policemen received allowances for boots and rent, and received medical care if injuries and sickness were work-related. Their uniforms were provided and replaced when they wore out or if they were damaged in the course of duty, but policemen had to pay for replacing uniforms lost or damaged through carelessness. Money, called 'rateable deductions', was taken out of their weekly pay to be paid into a pension fund. Once they worked long enough, typically around twenty-five years of service, they could retire on their pensions or men could retire earlier on medical grounds.[13]

Police forces had their own geography. Each force had a main headquarters where the highest ranking officers and their staff carried out administrative duties and often where the force kept its main garage. Eventually, radio and telephone offices tended to be at or near headquarters, and ambulance and motor stations were added at key points. Each city had a specific division that included a variety of administrative departments and criminal investigation. Manchester's division was lettered 'E' before the war and 'F' afterwards, Birmingham's was 'R', and Liverpool's was 'H'. Forces were then divided into geographic divisions. Manchester had four before the war and five afterwards, lettered A to D, and then to E; Birmingham had five, lettered A to E, and Liverpool had seven, lettered A to G. Policemen had a letter on their collars designating their division followed by

---

11   These proportions varied slightly over time, with a slight decrease in constables and increase in sergeants, and from force to force, but the general proportions remained similar.

12   For more on chief constables, see Robert Reiner, *Chief Constables: Bobbies, Bosses, or Bureaucrats?* (Oxford: Oxford University Press, 1991).

13   Length of service required to retire varied from force to force and over time. See Chapters 5 and 10 for more details. In some cases, men resigning from the force could have their rateable deductions returned to them.

their personal number. Each division was under a superintendent. Divisions had varying numbers of station houses supervised by chief inspectors and inspectors, but averaged four to six. In 1908, Manchester's four divisions held twenty-two stations, and in 1923 its five divisions had twenty-four stations.[14] Sergeants were assigned to stations to supervise constables, approximately one sergeant for every ten to fifteen constables. Stations had a public reception area, a charge office, 'lock-ups' for holding prisoners until they could be transferred to court or to more permanent facilities, various offices and interview rooms, and common rooms or canteens where policemen could eat meals and relax. Stations typically had yards where policemen 'paraded' for duty, and most had at least small garages for bicycles, motorcycles, and possibly motorcars. Some stations had classrooms for teaching recruits and for policemen preparing for promotion examinations. Some warehoused lost items found by the police or turned in by civilians, and some had holding pens for stray pets. Some stations had dormitories that housed single policemen and a few had family quarters for resident officers where the wife often served as a police matron for female prisoners. In Birmingham, a few police cottages served as tiny police stations in outlying areas, with the wife taking messages for her husband, a pattern more common in rural forces. The quality of stations varied, with policemen frequently complaining about their poor conditions and watch committees resisting improving them to save money for the rate payers.

The personality of each force was in many ways dependent on the character of its chief constables. Manchester's chief constable, Robert Peacock, took office in 1898 following a significant scandal involving a superintendent running brothels in 'D' division. Peacock's method to return confidence both to the demoralized force and to the city of Manchester was to combine strict discipline with an open approachability. He ended a tradition of detachment between the police and the public, and instead fostered a more neighbourly approach. Peacock tended to be the most responsive and sympathetic of all the chief constables from the three cities studied here and one of the few serving in England before the First World War who began his career as a beat constable. As an example of his leadership style, during a 1911 transport strike, he personally walked the rounds and discovered that many men had been on duty for over twelve hours. He immediately sent a memo to his superintendents insisting that only in the most exceptional circumstances should men be expected to serve such long tours of duty.[15] After his death in 1926, he was followed by John Maxwell, another man who started in the ranks,

---

[14]   City of Manchester, *Police Instruction Book* (Manchester: John Heywood, Ltd. 1908), p. 51; City of Manchester, *Police Instruction Book* (Manchester: Co-operative Wholesale Society's Printing Works, 1923), pp. 76–7.

[15]   MGO, 16 August 1911.

serving as a Manchester policeman from 1901. Maxwell was trained in the Peacock tradition of leadership.[16] Birmingham was under the very different and heavy discipline of Charles Rafter who, more typically for chief constables, came from the Royal Irish Constabulary. He arrived in 1899 and 'took the City Constabulary in hand'.[17] Nothing escaped his attention. Unlike other chief constables, Rafter was caught up in minutiae, like the correct way to salute, the proper care of coat buttons, and how to clean station toilets. Constables complained constantly of unnecessary drill and inspections. His men became so terrified of neglecting their beats under his leadership that he finally had to remind them that they could not refuse public requests that took them off their regular patrols. His force was efficient but inhospitable. Rafter died in office in 1935. He was succeeded by Cecil C.H. Moriarty, his assistant chief constable since 1918 and also from the RIC. Despite these commonalities, Moriarty tempered Rafter's style and was more open to reforms resisted by Rafter but requested by the men.

Unlike Manchester and Birmingham, Liverpool did not have long serving chief constables, creating a gap between the ranks and the chief constable's office.[18] Inconsistent and changing leadership also gave more authority to the city's watch committee than it might have had otherwise. Leonard Dunning, chief constable of Liverpool from 1902 to 1912, was a philosopher.[19] He was one of the few top police officers with national recognition who did not consider that being a policeman was simple or straightforward. Yet, despite his perceptive understanding of police work, he had a difficult time convincing the watch committee to follow his recommendations. He left to become an inspector of constabulary in 1912. From 1912 to 1925, Liverpool was under the leadership of Francis Caldwell, an officer who spent his entire police career working at headquarters, beginning as a junior clerk and moving up through the ranks of the office staff. Since he had never walked a beat, he was unpopular with many constables and had little understanding of police life. Conditions improved under L.D.L. Everett, serving from 1925 to 1931, who started in the ranks in Wiltshire in 1895, and under Archibald Kennedy Wilson, serving from 1931 to 1940, who started in the ranks in Cardiff in 1909.[20] Policemen felt strongly that chief constables should come up through the ranks and have experience walking beats since outsiders could not understand the realities of policing. The 1919 Police Act recommended no one without police experience be appointed chief constable except in unusual cases. However, due to the many

---

[16]   Biographical articles on Peacock and Maxwell were printed in the *Police Review*, 26 November 1926, p. 702; 11 March 1927, p. 182.

[17]   *Police Review*, 23 September 1904, p. 459.

[18]   Liverpool had a 'head constable' until 1919, another example of the city asserting its individuality. For simplicity's sake, he will be referred to as a chief constable.

[19]   Dunning biographical article, *Police Review*, 18 April 1902, p. 186.

[20]   Wilson biographical article, *Police Review*, 5 February 1932, p. 90.

outsiders already serving as chief constables and assistant chief constables across the country, it was some years before this became common practice.[21]

On a smaller scale, superintendents, inspectors and even sergeants could give distinct personalities to divisions and police stations. Having a good senior officer could make the difference between a constable having a decent career or deciding to quit the force. Officers who tolerated slack discipline might be popular in the short run but they got their men in trouble when they transferred to stricter stations or divisions and could create problems with the public. Officers zealous about reporting every broken regulation tended to create hostile atmospheres both with the men reported and with the men above them who had to deal with trivial matters that should have been handled informally. Good officers knew when to give constables advice, when to give warnings, and when to report them. Officers also had to intervene in the more awkward area of constables' private lives. Unlike other working-class occupations, constables were expected to abide by police regulations at all times. They could be punished for their behaviour off duty and for the behaviour of their wives and children if it reflected badly on the reputation of the force. A constable could be called in to speak to senior officers on his choice of public house, if he got a young woman 'in trouble', if a shopkeeper complained about his wife's debts, or if his children upset his neighbours. When domestic problems became serious enough, inspectors and superintendents acted as marriage counsellors and advised couples to get along with each other and with their neighbours. If necessary, they negotiated separation agreements and child support. Adjusting to this level of supervision could be difficult for constables and many left the force rather than put up with it. Senior officers had been constables themselves and good ones helped constables make the transition to police life.

Just as forces were affected by the characters of chief constables and other senior officers, they experienced generational shifts, influenced by Police Acts, decisive events, and new technologies.[22] New constables typically learned more about policing from veteran constables than from their official training and many became good friends, but men recruited under new conditions of service could also create tensions and resentment with often less educated older men. In the late nineteenth and early twentieth centuries, friction existed between men hired before and after the 1890 Police Act which guaranteed police pensions. Even though policing remained paid at unskilled levels, the pension attracted men who had not considered the police an option before. Prior to the 1890s men were more likely to treat the force as a casual job, while after the 1890s more of the men began to see their work as a long-term, skilled career. During the First World War, police pay

---

[21] 'Report of the Committee on the Police Service of England, Wales, and Scotland', Part II, 1920, Cmd. 574, vol. XXII, 53, p. 23.

[22] For more on generational shifts and conflicts, see Chapters 2, 4, and 5.

failed to keep up with inflation, culminating in police strikes in 1918 and 1919.[23]
Parliament created the Committee on the Police Service of England, Wales, and
Scotland in 1918 to investigate why conditions had become so bad that strikes broke
out rather than being corrected by local police authorities. This committee became
known as the Desborough Committee after its chairman, and its work resulted in
the 1919 Police Act. This Act dramatically improved police pay, setting a national
standard at skilled levels. Policemen swore by the 'Desborough Scale' for years to
come. Recognizing that policing had changed, the committee set higher education
requirements, and it called for standardized promotion examinations to discourage
favouritism. While pre-1919, men were proud that their efforts had resulted in this
new Act, they also created a generational shift. Men hired after the 1919 Police Act
were better educated and had not suffered through the hardships leading up to the
strikes, while pre-1919 men might be experienced but could find it difficult to pass
the new promotion exams. During the early 1920s, forces had a high per centage
of young constables hired to replace men who left during the war or were fired for
striking, and not surprisingly this resulted in discipline problems. By the 1930s, this
generation had settled down, and fewer constables were hired since few men left
during the Great Depression. All of these generations of constables were affected
by new technologies. Directing traffic and keeping pedestrians safe took more and
more constables off regular patrol; even constables not on traffic duty were often
called to help at road accidents. After the war, public access to telephones made it
easier for civilians to call the police, and they began to telephone for minor reasons
such as barking dogs and poorly parked cars. Forces began introducing police-box
and pillar systems to handle old duties and new traffic duties as well as telephone
demands. By the 1930s, traffic and telephones began to undermine the tradition
of walking beats. Overall, 1900 to 1939 can be divided into three general periods
– the 1900 to 1919 shift from unskilled to skilled occupation, the 1920s post-
Desborough days, and the 1930s struggles with traffic and telephones.

In 1929, a Royal Commission reminded its readers, 'So many of both the
friends and the critics of the police talk as if police constables were not men.'[24]
This required seeing past the uniform. The public saw a blue uniform and saw a
fully formed police constable. But this impression was often mistaken. The man in
the uniform could be a probationer with a few weeks of training, a veteran with
years of service, or anything in between. Men of similar ages could have vastly
different experience. Civilians thinking simply that this was a constable did not
consider factors such as diversity of personalities, police generations, constables
satisfied with their positions, upset at being overlooked for promotion, or mired in

---

23   See Chapter 5.
24   'Report of the Royal Commission on Police Powers and Procedure', 1928–1929, Cmd.
3297, vol. IX, 127, p. 112.

favouritism networks, constables who were conscientious or doing the minimum to get by. Constables could have good days and bad days just like anyone. Police forces weeded out men unsuitable to be constables but they wore uniforms for months and years before being dismissed or asked to resign. The public could be meeting a constable destined to retire as a superintendent or as a constable, one soon to be dismissed for defaults, or one who would resign in ten years time after deciding he no longer liked the job. The uniform hid the men underneath.

It is important not to romanticize constables, either as 'bobbies' or villains. Police work life was often routine, repetitive, and occasionally farcical. They investigated unusual lights, directed traffic, stopped runaway horses, and loitered in doorways. People handed them found umbrellas, lost children, and stray dogs. They learned to smoke on the job without getting caught, usually resisted the temptation to argue with sergeants, and tried to avoid writing reports. Rather than gun or knife wounds, injuries tended to result from walking mishaps or kicks from drunken prisoners. To combat boredom, constables played checkers with night watchmen and played tricks on each other. The usual shift was not terribly thrilling, but they might face reviving servants suffering from gas poisoning, treating traffic injuries, or recovering corpses from local waterways. They worried about promotion, children, and debts. Many constables came to understand the impact of crime and disorder on ordinary people, as well as the problems facing people living on the fringes of society, in a way that the average person could not. This could separate them from civilian society. But ultimately, the average police constable was trying to do his job without getting into trouble so that he could get paid, hopefully promoted, and retire on his pension. About half left for disciplinary reasons or to return to civilian occupations. A few had to leave or died when their health broke down or from injuries. In Manchester, Birmingham, and Liverpool between 1900 and 1939, around half of police constables made it to take their pensions.

1

Putting on the Uniform

> I, …, declare that I will well and truly serve our Sovereign
> Lord the King in the Office of Constable for the City of
> Manchester, without favour, or affection, malice or illwill, and
> that I will, to the best of my power, cause the peace to be kept
> and preserved, and prevent all offenses against the persons and
> properties of His Majesty's subjects, and that while I continue
> to hold the said Office I will, to the best of my skill and
> knowledge, discharge all the duties thereof faithfully according
> to law.
>
> Manchester City Police Oath of Office, 1901[1]

THE YOUNG MEN taking the police oath of office typically had no clear idea about what kind of job they were in for. Before joining a police force, most held the common working-class perception that police constables were paid a regular wage for walking around doing little more than keeping their eyes open and collaring drunks. Some even considered that policemen duped local authorities into paying them for 'soft' work. Many combined this 'plodder' image with impressions from popular stories by Edgar Wallace, Arthur Conan Doyle, and Arthur Morrison with their mostly dull, stupid policemen but also a few cunning police detectives. Despite these cynical views, working-class families encouraged their sons to apply to the force for its regular wages and chance for promotion. Adding to the force's appeal, young women considered constables to be eligible husbands who could provide for families. The idea that policing paid a steady wage for little effort led to a constant stream of unqualified applicants who believed that they only needed to be tall to be hired. Most did not meet basic police physical and education requirements.

The small number of successful applicants began two types of sometimes contradictory training – formal classroom training and field training. Formal

---

1   MWCM, 1 March 1901, vol. 13, no. 103.

training promoted the official image of policemen as neutral upholders of law and order, an ideal that recruits may have known before but probably had not taken seriously. Police instruction books endorsed the nineteenth-century standard that 'PC X ... is an *institution* rather than a man'[2] and worked to counteract recruits' perception that policing required only that a man have good feet. Recruits soon learned that the 'PC X' standard was as far from life patrolling the streets as their own earlier views. Formal training might teach them basic police duties and force regulations but making it in the force meant picking up informal strategies and unwritten rules from experienced men. Field training could vary dramatically depending on the character of local senior officers and the culture of force divisions. Successful recruits figured out which officers might be strict about enforcing rules and following orders, and which ones would show them how to get around those same rules and orders. The perceptive noticed that good sergeants made good constables, and similarly for poor ones. They learned through watching the older men how each balanced official expectations with what was humanly possible. They took their official duties seriously but carried them out based on their experiences in the streets rather than strictly following regulations. Policemen, out of practical necessity, modified policing in ways that might have little to do with what lawmakers, watch committees, or working-class friends expected.

Police recruits learned that actual policing differed from both official and popular perceptions, but they had to work with a public that did not share that insight. They had been disabused of the working-class notion of policing as a 'soft job' or an Edgar Wallace thriller, but the rest of their class still saw their jobs as easy. They discovered that members of the middle and upper classes might call England's policemen the 'best in the world' but could be thoroughly disrespectful when being issued traffic tickets or chimney fire citations. However aggravating civilians could be, recruits had to avoid creating an adversarial relationship with them. They needed to respond with courtesy to suggestions that expired dog licences be ignored in favour of more critical law-breaking since their work went more smoothly if the public remained cooperative. Belligerence or back-talk created problems not only for their own job prospects but for senior officers who had to handle public complaints and deal with the press. Overall, during their probationary year on the force, recruits learned to balance conflicting expectations from the public and senior officers while carrying out their duties to the best of their understanding. Those unable or unwilling to find that balance left the force before becoming policemen in more than uniform.[3]

---

2   'The Police and the Thieves', *The Quarterly Review* (1856): 171; italics in original.

3   For a long-term perspective on police recruitment and training from 1829 to 1965, see J.P. Martin and Gail Wilson, *The Police: A Study in Manpower* (London: Heinemann, 1969).

The first step in becoming a police constable was applying to a police force. To be qualified for the force in Manchester, Birmingham, and Liverpool, men had to be over age twenty but under age thirty, pass medical and education examinations, present testimonial letters, and promise to obey the conditions of service. Men applied because they were unhappy with their current jobs, they were looking for something with better prospects, or they were unemployed. Many applicants were between age twenty and twenty-five, a time when young men started to think seriously about marriage. Police work had appeal since it was regular rather than seasonal, the need for policemen was unlikely to go away, promotion was possible, and pensions were granted. Men applied to escape fading crafts or bleak occupations, such as Thomas Smethurst who wanted to escape 'the life of a miner earning his living in the bowels of the earth'.[4] Robert Mark applied to Manchester out of boredom with working as a clerk at a carpet manufacturer, considering his qualifications to be that he was 'well built, fit, good at games and not entirely stupid'.[5] George Fancourt lost his job at age twenty after six years working as a motor mechanic. His fiancée, no doubt wanting him in steady employment so they could marry, encouraged him to apply to Birmingham.[6] Some applicants knew someone connected to policing, or liked the uniform. John Tanner applied because 'a chum of mine was the son of a policeman, and an uncle, a Guardsman, was a policeman, and I thought he seemed very smart and I was jealous of his appearance'.[7] A few had fathers or brothers in the police.[8] Others applied more casually, considering employment in the force simply because they were tall, such as Harry Daley who figured that he could leave on a month's notice if he did not like it.[9] Similarly, many applied because friends and families encouraged them to try it. Even though a 'candidate with any sprinkling of common sense ... will say that it has been his ambition to be a Police officer', applicants' primary motivation was the pay and steady hours for what they thought was straightforward work.[10]

---

4   Thomas Smethurst, 'Reminiscences' (Greater Manchester Police Museum: unpublished manuscript, 1922), p. 11.

5   Sir Robert Mark, *In the Office of Constable* (London: Collins, 1978), p. 16.

6   George Fancourt, 'The Police Service of George Frederic Fancourt: Birmingham City Police 1929–1960' (Milton Keynes: Open University Police Archive, n.d.), p.3; 'Interview with George Frederick Fancourt Who Served in the Birmingham City Police from 1929 to 1961' (Milton Keynes: Open University Police Archive, 1986), p. 1.

7   DC, Evidence, question 4731, John Tanner, Bristol City Police, p. 231.

8   Birmingham City Police Constables' Marriage Certificates, 1900–1927.

9   Harry Daley, *This Small Cloud: A Personal Memoir* (London: Weidenfeld and Nicolson, 1986), p. 77.

10   *Police Review and Parade Gossip*, 22 July 1938: 78; see also *Police Review*, 15 July 1938; 58. Arguments that policemen were attracted to the job due to authoritarian or deferential personalities are not supported by research. See Reiner, *Chief Constables*, pp. 55–6; Shpayer-Makov, *The Making of a Policeman*, pp. 63–4.

Due to force age minimums, applicants had held jobs for five to ten years already and so were working class through their work experience as well as by upbringing.[11] Policing was usually a second or third job. Applicants came from typical working-class occupations, and came from jobs similar to those held by their fathers.[12] Similar to other English forces, each city had a steady stream of unskilled labourers, agricultural workers, and shop assistants as well as a wide variety of artisans, such as bakers, smiths, and carpenters. In spite of police perceptions that soldiers made poor policemen since they were trained to work in units rather than alone, a few applied every year, as did sailors. The occasional musician applied, hoping to play in police bands, particularly the acclaimed Birmingham band.[13] Occupations varied from city to city. Manchester tended to get more men from textile industries, Liverpool from mining areas, and Birmingham from the nearby Cadbury plant. Manchester had a steady trickle of postmen, firemen, and constables apply into the 1930s while Birmingham had few after the early 1920s. Occupation lists from Manchester and Birmingham show that Manchester consistently attracted a slightly higher class of applicant, especially before 1914. This could be due to their better reputation as a force but also to poorer employment prospects in Manchester. More overseers, salesman, shopkeepers, and clerks applied to Manchester before the war while Birmingham attracted more waiters. Both cities show similar shifts after the war. Applicants from textile, mining, and steel industries became less common as these industries became less dominant. Similarly, coach trimmers, blacksmiths, porters, and servants were gradually replaced by salesmen, wireless operators, electricians, and chemists. Grooms and carters disappeared, supplanted by motor mechanics and lorry drivers. Clerks, teachers, and students showed up in greater numbers. In the 1930s, a few 'boy clerks' from Birmingham police headquarters applied, often sons of policemen. Yet despite the 1919 Police Act's higher education standards, the basic pattern of previous occupations did not shift significantly. Changes reflected national economic transitions and improved education rather than policing attracting a different kind of applicant.[14]

---

11   See also Robert Reiner, *The Blue-Coated Worker: A Sociological Study of Police Unionism* (Cambridge: Cambridge University Press, 1978), p. 152.

12   For a detailed analysis of recruitment, see Clive Emsley and Mark Clapson, 'Recruiting the English Policeman c. 1840–1940', *Policing and Society* 3 (1994): 269–86. Birmingham, Liverpool, and Manchester generally follow the patterns that they found for the 1900–1939 period. Birmingham City Police Constables Marriage Certificates, 1900–1927, show that the occupations of fathers of policemen and their wives followed the same patterns as their sons and sons-in-law.

13   See Shane Ewen, 'Civic Identity and Police Leisure in Birmingham during the Inter-war Years', *International Journal of Regional and Local Studies* 2nd ser., 1:1 (2005): pp. 51–4.

14   Occupational patterns primarily based on Manchester City Police roster cards and Birmingham City Police roster books, 1900–1939. Similar records from Liverpool no longer exist.

Applicants rarely looked far from home when choosing a force, wanting to remain close to family and friends and possibly to a young woman on whom they had their eye. The vast majority of recruits came from regions immediately surrounding the city, and then from a widening geographic circle.[15] Manchester took applicants from the city itself, citing the advantage of men who knew local conditions; Birmingham and Liverpool did not due to concerns over conflicts of interest. Yet Birmingham had a steady flow of recruits born in the city and its suburbs, possibly men no longer living in the city but still with connections there. In Manchester and Birmingham, rosters show that slightly under half of recruits were from the cities themselves and the counties immediately around them. In Manchester, another fifth came from the next ring of counties out. In Birmingham, about quarter came from southern England, including London.[16] Liverpool had about a third of recruits from Ireland, Scotland and Wales, Manchester around a quarter, and Birmingham around fifteen per cent. Irish recruits came from all counties but somewhat more from western ones; the Welsh came from every corner of Wales. Scottish recruits rarely came from far north of Glasgow and Edinburgh, hardly surprising since most Scots lived in that area. From 1900 to 1916, Liverpool annual reports reported a steady decline from around thirty-seven to thirty per cent of Irish, Welsh, and Scottish constables. Irish recruits averaged 271 a year, Scottish 252, and Welsh 124. Birmingham had much lower per centages, dropping from only around fourteen to twelve per cent before the war. Their Irish recruits averaged seventy-two a year, the Welsh thirty-six, and Scottish only seven.[17] Since most men applied to forces closer to home, these low numbers were not unexpected. The small decline in constables from outside England in both cities could be a result of better employment options closer to home. After the war, Birmingham went from twelve to nearly nineteen per cent non-English constables by 1939, the economic depression apparently making men more willing to look further afield for jobs. This increase was primarily Welsh and Scottish; Welsh recruits doubled from forty-eight to 110 and Scottish skyrocketed from twenty-eight to 156.[18] Manchester rosters show a similar increase in men from Scotland and Wales, particularly southern Scotland.[19]

---

15   See W.J. Lowe, 'The Lancashire Constabulary, 1845–1870: The Social and Occupational Function of a Victorian Police Force', *Criminal Justice History* 4 (1983): 41–62, Carolyn Steedman, *Policing the Victorian Community: The Formation of English Provincial Police Forces, 1856–80* (London: Routledge and Kegan Paul, 1984), Emsley, *The English Police*, and Shpayer-Makov, *The Making of a Policeman*. All found recruit ages, occupations and places of origin similar to those in my period and cities. My three forces had the occasional recruit from outside the United Kingdom, mostly from the British Commonwealth and British colonies, but they were statistically insignificant.

16   Manchester City Police roster cards, Birmingham City Police roster books, 1900–1939.

17   LAR, 1900–1916; BAR, 1900–1910.

18   BAR, 1923–1939.

19   Manchester City Police roster cards, 1919–1939.

The number of Irish constables dropped steadily after the war with the appearance of an independent Ireland. In general, around seven out of ten recruits were English, and roughly half lived within a county of the force to which they applied.

Thousands of men applied to the police every year, but most did not have adequate reading and writing skills or were not physically fit enough to be recruited. The fundamental problem was that police wages, however steady, did not attract many suitable applicants. Before the war, police pay was pegged to unskilled labour levels. Watch committees kept pay as low as possible to save the rate payers money and did not comprehend that pay scales dissuaded qualified men from applying. The 1919 Police Act increased wages but also the minimum qualifications. Seeing only a consistent pattern of more applications than openings, watch committees avoided the problem. In addition to neglecting pay, they refused to adopt recruitment strategies beyond advertising in local papers and by word of mouth in mining and agricultural areas, traditional recruiting grounds but less so after the war. In 1934, an article in the *Police Journal* lamented, 'Little endeavour has been made ... to attract young men to the service; it has been left to the would-be recruit to take the first step.'[20] Watch-committee thrift aggravated senior officers who needed decent recruits and instead wasted their time weeding through stacks of applications searching for the few qualified men.

Men who made the initial cut soon got hints of how strange life in the police could be, including misguided economy and interest in their private lives. Even though few applicants qualified, these scarce men were told to pay their own travel expenses to the city for medical and education exams. This could mean asking for time off if employed, jeopardizing a man's current job, while men without jobs did not necessarily have the money. Police suggestions that applicants be allowed to take exams at their home police force were never tried, perhaps for fear of losing direct supervision of the exams.[21] Watch committees would not pay travel expenses, an early sign of how frugality could come into conflict with effective policing. If applicants passed the exams, the force investigated their credentials, including the character of their wives if married. This was a clue that men should expect interference in their domestic lives for the purpose of preserving the reputation of

---

[20] Clifton Reynes, 'The Police as a Career: A Review of the Past, with Suggestions for the Future', *Police Journal* 7:3 (1934): 319. See also Peter Joyce, 'Recruitment Patterns and Conditions of Work in a Nineteenth-Century Police Force: A Case Study of Manchester 1842–1900', *Police Journal* 64:2 (1991): 140–50.

[21] Metropolitan Chief Constable J.W. Olive recommended to the Desborough Committee that men be able to take these exams through their local police force but his idea was never implemented (DC, Evidence, questions 753–8, p. 46). Even though recruiting improved after the war, this part of the process continue to annoy potential and actual policemen. In 1938, 'PC Gee' revived the idea that applicants be able to take examinations through the force where they lived to save themselves an unnecessary trip. (*Police Review*, 15 July 1938, p. 58) See also Shpayer-Makov, *The Making of a Policeman*, pp. 52–4.

the force. If applicants passed these obstacles, they might be rushed into training or they might have to wait until an opening appeared, sometimes for months, before being called. They could make it all the way to being recruited into the force only to be dismissed if discovering lying or exaggerating on their application.[22] Arnold Scull nearly lost his appointment to Manchester when he gave false information in his application, stating that he was single since he thought that Manchester did not hire married men. Only after an appeal by his older brother, who was already a Manchester constable, and by his wife did he keep his position.[23] Many men dropped out at various stages of this lengthy process, unable or unwilling to put up with it.

Between 1900 and 1914, police forces experienced increasing difficulties in finding recruits since stagnating police wages failed to attract suitable men. Young men from agricultural areas or declining trades who typically joined the police instead found better-paid options or choose to emigrate.[24] In 1905, Liverpool decided to accept men half an inch under the regulation height of five foot ten to fill immediate vacancies[25] and in 1907, Birmingham began accepting recruits under their twenty-one-year age minimum.[26] Liverpool Chief Constable Dunning lamented, 'The number of men, who have to be discharged within their probationary period as being unlikely to make good policemen, shows that we are not able to pick and choose as we used to.'[27] These disappointing recruits wasted valuable training time and resources. When the Birmingham City Police expanded into new districts in 1911, they needed three hundred additional constables but kept falling short of their authorized strength by up to seventy men. In 1913, Chief Constable Rafter urged men going home on leave to take recruiting papers to show to their friends, hoping that constables knew who would suit the force.[28] When the Police (Weekly Rest Day) Act went into effect in 1914, the shortage of

---

22   Hugh Coyle gave 'false information respecting his previous career' (BPO, 15 January 1900, p. 116); William Walker lied about his ability to ride a horse and service in the Horse Artillery (Birmingham City Police Conduct Book, 19 March 1902, p. 199). Frank Trevor put 'an untruth on his application form' (BPO, 20 April 1910, p. 247).

23   MPF, PCB 100 Arnold Scull, appointed April 1932.

24   HMI Leonard Dunning, former Liverpool Chief Constable, complained that 'emigration has stripped bare some of the best recruiting grounds' ('Inspectors of Constabulary report for year ended the 29th September 1913', PP 1914 (193) lxvii, 663, pp. 4, 55).

25   LHCWC, 15 May 1905, p. 141. Liverpool Chief Constable Leonard Dunning did not 'suggest a permanent lowering of the standard'. Despite this change, the average height of Liverpool constables only dropped from 5 feet 10.9 inches in 1904 to 5 feet 10.75 inches in 1905. From 1900 to 1915, average heights ranged between 5 feet 10.5 inches and 5 feet 11 inches (LAR, 1900–1915). From 1902 to 1910, Birmingham constables averaged 5 feet 10.5 inches every year (BAR).

26   BAR, 1900–1914.

27   LAR, 1907, p. 7.

28   BPO, 8 April 1913, p. 417.

recruits became even more urgent as forces scrambled to find men to cover beats now empty one day a week.[29] But young men with the necessary qualifications continued to ignore the police.

Already undermanned, the war depleted force strengths with men leaving for military service or to better-paying war industries. Birmingham and Manchester were unable to recruit new constables, with Birmingham dropping from 1164 constables in 1914 to 658 in 1918, well below their authorized strength of 1233.[30] In Liverpool, 1300 men resigned voluntarily between 1914 to 1918 and around 300 military reservists left for France. This loss was only partially offset by bringing in around 700 recruits, most in 1915 and 1916. By 1916, Liverpool reported that it had 861 men serving in the military, though it is unclear if these were reservists or men who had resigned to join the war effort.[31] What is clear is that all three forces fell significantly below authorized strengths as the war continued. At the same time, police wages failed to keep pace with war inflation, encouraging more men to resign. To cope, forces urged men to defer retirements and pensioners to re-enlist; not only were fewer constables patrolling, the ones who remained were no longer young.

When the war ended, police forces hoped that better pay and conditions established by the 1919 Police Act would attract good applicants and restore the number of constables to authorized strengths.[32] They needed to replace men who had left for the armed services and not returned, either through death, injury, or inclination, to replace men who had found jobs in war industries, and to replace men fired for striking in Liverpool and Birmingham in 1919.[33] The higher wages attracted high numbers of applicants. But again, most men had to be rejected since not only had wages increased, but so had education requirements. Birmingham had 1200 applications between November 1918 and mid-1919 but found only sixty suitable recruits.[34] Forces had little choice but to take risks since they needed to get constables on the streets as soon as possible, even knowing that borderline recruits cost money to train, caused problems internally and with the public, and rarely stayed. Manchester lost a third of the recruits it hired in 1919 and 1920 within three

---

[29]   See Shpayer-Makov, *The Making of a Policeman*, pp. 53–4.

[30]   BAR, 1914–1918. Manchester City Police roster cards show only one recruit during the war; unfortunately, their annual reports for the war years were missing from the Greater Manchester Police Museum and from the Manchester Public Library.

[31]   LAR, 1914–1918.

[32]   This act was based on the recommendations of the 1919 Committee on the Police Service of England, Wales, and Scotland, known as the Desborough Committee after its chairman.

[33]   The 1919 Liverpool City Police Strike, and more limited London, Birkenhead, and Birmingham City Police Strikes, took place during the Desborough Committee's investigations and contributed to their final recommendations. The strikes are discussed in Chapter 5.

[34]   DC, Evidence, question 10,008, Chief Constable Rafter, BCP, p. 460.

years.[35] Liverpool was particularly desperate, and was forced to bend its standards. In 1919, 969 men were fired for striking, 264 resigned voluntarily, and 288 retired out of an authorized strength of around 2000. They interviewed 3952 applicants and hired 1814 of them over the next year, an unusually high acceptance rate. However, 309 of these hastily recruited men had to be let go almost immediately. From 1919 to 1921, a substantial proportion of constables in all three cities were young, newly trained, and transitory.[36]

Despite police efforts to improve the image of the force as a profession rather than merely a job, problems finding recruits continued through the 1920s. In 1924, around ninety per cent of applicants nationally were turned away for failing the education test, and most of the remaining men failed the physical examination. Only five out of 100 applicants might be suitable, and perhaps only one or two had the personality to make it through probation.[37] From 1924 to 1929, Liverpool averaged 5000 applicants a year but only ninety recruits, less than two per cent.[38] Birmingham Assistant Chief Constable Moriarty estimated that only 3.4% of men applying between 1919 and 1927 remained long enough to become police officers.[39] The actual number of constables in Birmingham stayed nearly 100 below the number of authorized constables between 1919 and 1929.[40] This failure to find recruits reflected the continuing disparity between popular images of policing by potential applicants and the actual requirements of the job, a public-relations failure never successfully corrected.

Only during the 1930s economic depression did forces have less trouble attracting suitable recruits but could not keep many of them once the economy improved. Manchester was able to accept nearly fifteen per cent of applicants in the 1930s[41] and men kept applying even when the national government lowered recruit pay from seventy to sixty-two shillings per week in 1933.[42] Manchester Chief Constable Maxwell complained in 1937 that 'great difficultly is being experienced in obtaining suitable recruits', but in 1939 Manchester recruited twenty per cent

---

35   Manchester City Police roster cards, 1919–1920.

36   LAR, 1921, p.2. In 1920, 1437 members of the Liverpool police force had twelve months of service or fewer.

37   'Inspectors of Constabulary report for year ended the 29th September 1923', PP 1924, (19) xii, p. 5.

38   LAR, 1924–1929.

39   Cecil C.H. Moriarty, 'The Making of an English Policeman', *Police Journal* 2:1 (1929): 8.

40   BAR. The shortage of constables led to a serious shortage of sergeants. From 1921 to 1934, Birmingham averaged only 162 out of 191 authorized sergeants.

41   MAR, 1931–1939.

42   'Report of the Committee on Police Pay (New Entrants)', 1932–33, Cmd. 4274, vol. XV, 379. In 1935, the *Police Review* wanted the 'Revised Rates of Pay for New Entrants' scrapped so that police forces could attract a decent standard of recruit, fearing to lose advances made in the status of the occupation (*Police Review*, 12 April 1935, p. 354).

of the men who applied.[43] Birmingham finally had enough constables to meet their authorized strength in the 1930s until they expanded by 250 men in 1937 when the economic recovery was beginning.[44] Only Liverpool continued to struggle; an average of 4000 men applied every year but only eighty qualified as recruits, still around two per cent.[45] Chief Constable Wilson complained that the 1933 pay decrease had dissuaded 'a good type of young man' from applying.[46] Police work only seemed attractive to quality recruits when other options were not available. After the Second World War, Manchester lost a quarter of the constables who had joined in the 1930s to the postwar economic boom even though many had ten to fifteen years' experience and were well on the way to earning their pensions.[47]

The men who successfully negotiated recruitment received an instruction book that presented policemen as impartial upholders of legal authority, moral examples of respectability, and preservers of English civilization. They were to 'bear in mind that, to be thoroughly efficient, your character as a Police Officer as well as in private life should be above reproach'.[48] Well aware of the low opinion most recruits had of police work, police authorities presented them with these rousing images as a counteractive measure. In order to impress on them the unique position of policemen in English society, recruits read a glowing vision of the origins of police forces. Liverpool and Manchester instruction books gave stirring accounts of modern policemen carrying on traditions of preserving the King's Peace that came from the Anglo-Saxons, Shire Reeves, and the Statute of Winchester.[49] Prevention, not detection, was the '*true aim of a police system*',[50] inherited from these 'recognisable beginnings of the present system of the prevention of crime'.[51] After praising the ancient roots of preventive policing as a uniquely English institution, appealing to the men's patriotism, the books informed recruits that they were a proud part of the 'New Police', founded in the nineteenth century to replace crippled, drunk, and corrupt watchmen. While recruits might be sceptical

---

43   MWCM, 11 March 1937, vol. 207, no. 80; MAR, 1939, p. 22.

44   BAR, 1930–1939.

45   LAR, 1930–1938.

46   LAR, 1933, p. 7.

47   Manchester City Police roster cards, 1929–1939.

48   Manchester Constabulary Force, *Constables' Guide* (Manchester: Henry Blacklock and Co., 1898), p. 9.

49   In an address to the Chief Constables' Association, Edward Shortt, K.C., M.P., traced police history back to the 'frank pledge' and King Alfred, emphasizing how English police forces were superior to those of the continent (Chief Constables' Association Annual Reports, 12 May 1916, pp. 17–18). See also Reynes, 'The Police as a Career', pp. 292–320.

50   *Liverpool City Police. Instructions* (Liverpool: C. Tinling and Co., 1903, 1911, 1926 editions), p. 6 in each edition, emphasis in original.

51   City of Manchester, *Police Instruction Book* (Manchester: Co-operative Wholesale Society's Printing Works, 1923), p. 12.

of these visions, so counter to their previous opinions, it was a gratifying image nevertheless. Few minded their new jobs being portrayed as part of a noble national tradition. However, a careful reader could find contradictions in these books. In spite of the emphasis on prevention of crime rather than detection as a policeman's goal, the number of indictable crimes solved was used to illustrate efficiency. Told that their 'true aim' was prevention on page six, they were told that their primary duty was 'the detection and suppression of crime' on page thirteen.[52] Recruits were left on their own to reconcile these statements.

Once this heroic history was introduced, instruction books defined the qualities of the 'New Police' in relation to the public. They emphasized that policemen needed to maintain public support in order to maintain the law. 'Let your conduct towards all persons, of whatever rank or class, be marked by kindness and civility.'[53] A constable must inspire public confidence; 'Without it he is only a big man with a stick, and only one against a thousand' instead of 'the handy man of the Constitution'.[54] Fostering this image was not simply a matter of pride but of practical necessity:

> To him, in their time of trouble, the members of the public look; and if, when an accident or other incident of a trying nature has occurred, the police officer preserves an unruffled bearing, and displays a calm confidence, combined with promptitude of action and initiative, he will be rewarded by the cordial respect of the public, and, as far as may be necessary, their hearty co-operation.[55]

Recruits might have wondered how to measure 'as far as may be necessary' when counting on cooperation, reminding them of the popular view that it was disagreeable to be 'mixed up' with the police. This distinction between public respect and public cooperation warned recruits of the difficulties they faced balancing public support and law enforcement. Instruction books stressed that a good relationship between policemen and the public was crucial but insisted that this relationship be established with as little contact with the public as possible. Recruits were told to keep a professional distance from the public, including not speaking to them except as part of their duties. Policemen were prohibited from outside work and banned from membership in or contributions to political parties and societies. After 1919, they were forbidden membership in or contributions to unions. These constraints were meant to prevent ties that might hinder their ability to enforce the law impartially. The problem of how to develop a relationship

52 *Liverpool City Police. Instructions* (1903, 1911, 1926), p. 13 in each edition.
53 Manchester Constabulary Force, *Constables' Guide* (1898), p. 11.
54 *Liverpool City Police. Instructions* (1903, 1911, 1926), p. 8 in each edition.
55 City of Manchester, *Police Instruction Book* (1923), p. 12.

with the public without crossing an invisible line into too much contact was left to recruits to unravel.

Disreputable behaviour undermined public confidence, as well as hindered internal efficiency, and therefore was firmly condemned in instruction books. While on the job, a constable must not leave his beat, fail to report or disclose evidence, or divulge police matters to anyone, not even his wife. He must not use unnecessary violence against any person, be absent without leave, be late for duty, or feign sickness. He could be disciplined for insubordination, tyrannical conduct, drunkenness, and abusive language. Entering a public house or smoking while in uniform could lead to dismissal. Bribes and gratuities, especially from publicans, were forbidden. In his personal life, a constable could not move to another residence, apply for another situation, or get married without permission from the chief constable. While off duty, he must avoid frequenting public houses, the society of betting men, and neglecting to pay his debts. These were just a few of the expectations presented to recruits.[56] While some regulations were straightforward and practical, such as arriving for work on time, recruits were left to themselves to figure out the nuances of 'abusive language', 'unnecessary violence', and 'insubordination'.

Finally, recruits were cautioned that policing required that they devote their entire time to the police force. Policing was not a job but a way of life. Instruction books reassured them that submitting to discipline even while off duty did not reflect poorly on their manhood or self respect.[57] This encouragement was necessary because the list of official expectations was formidable. A policeman must be honest and truthful, fair, civil, good tempered, and smart in appearance. He must devote himself to his education. He renounced rights to found property and he was prohibited from collecting tips. In order to avoid conflicts with civilians over law enforcement, he was to follow orders without comment or thought. 'Your duties and powers are correctly described: it is not for you to either approve of or find fault with them.'[58] On the other hand, he was expected to exercise discretion and make sound judgments in how he carried out those duties. In private life, both he and his family lived where the chief constable directed, maintained respectable behaviour, and knew only respectable people. In the interests of good health, he lived a sober and clean life with healthy recreation.[59] Finally, the recruit made a declaration before a magistrate to serve the King's Peace faithfully. Following these conditions made recruits part of 'a bond of mutual trust and co-operation'.[60]

---

56   *Liverpool City Police. Instructions* (1903, 1911), pp. 19–29, (1926), pp. 18–34. The 1926 edition included changes in procedure for discipline cases instituted by the Desborough Committee in 1919.

57   *Liverpool City Police. Instructions* (1903, 1911, 1926), p. 15.

58   *Liverpool City Police. Instructions* (1903, 1911, 1926), p. 4.

59   City of Manchester, *Police Instruction Book* (1923), p. 13.

60   *Liverpool City Police. Instructions* (1903, 1911, 1926), p. 15.

Presenting such an ideal policeman set the bar high; while senior officers never expected their men to match such an ideal, hopefully it rubbed off on recruits enough to create good constables.

Police forces taught policemen to treat their uniforms as symbols of the institution they represented. They were expected to keep their hair cut to regulation length and present a clean-shaven face, with possibly a neatly trimmed moustache.[61] If their uniforms were shabby and their grooming careless, or if they acted in a heedless manner, they undermined public respect. Recruits learned how to care for their uniforms, including proper brushing, cleaning, and mending of helmets, coats, trousers, gloves, and boots. To insure that uniforms were cleaned regularly and in good condition, forces required uniform inspections about every four months. Men whose uniforms were damaged, wrinkled, or dirty could be fined in addition to restoring their uniforms to good order. But while training stressed the centrality of the uniform, recruits picked up a more mundane attitude from experienced men. They heard complaints that inspections injured their image by requiring policemen to make a spectacle of themselves carrying their belongings through the streets.[62] As if to confirm this ludicrous potential, two Liverpool constables crashed their bicycles after inspections when their suitcases got caught in the wheels.[63] Recruits heard the common complaint that making constables responsible for the care of uniforms was simply to save watch committees money by not providing cleaning or repair services. Men argued that it was hard to be proud of their uniforms when watch committee economies led to poor quality or poorly designed uniforms. Manchester in particular was notorious for their poor uniforms. They kept changing firms to find one that could supply decent quality at a low price and finally settled on a military tailoring firm.[64] Cheap uniforms did not merely look bad, they were uncomfortable and even a health risk. The dye for a batch of Liverpool trousers kept giving men leg rashes.[65] Manchester helmets leaked water, forcing men to work with wet hair on rainy days.[66] Being expected

---

61   Chief Constable Rafter inquired of his men why the smart appearance they had presented at a recent government inspection had not been maintained. The men's hair was too long and untidy; they were unshaven, and their trousers were wrinkled and baggy at the knees (BPO, 22 August 1901, p. 512). Beards were not allowed in this period. Regulations regarding moustaches varied.

62   For an excellent satire of Birmingham's uniform inspection, see 'Pat O'Rafferty', *Police Review*, 25 May 1906, p. 244.

63   LCI, 4 April 1929, PCG 88 Stabb, broken arm; 15 April 1930, PCF 237 O'Donoghue, skinned knee, sprained thumb.

64   MGO, 28 August 1928.

65   LCI, 25 July 1926, PCD 76 Roberts, PCG 210 Gibson; November 1928, PCA 217 Wappett.

66   The helmets finally had to be specially treated to make them waterproof (MGO, 7 November 1930).

to keep uniforms in good order when cost-cutting provided inferior uniforms reinforced police perceptions that watch committees were hypocritical and made men less likely to care for uniforms. For recruits, this was an early lesson in how watch committees demanded ideal policemen while paying as little as possible.

While looking the part no doubt gave recruits confidence, even the best uniform could not make up for a lack of understanding of their fundamental duties. Despite high expectations of police behaviour, watch committees put economy before efficiency and recruits found their training to be deficient and brief. Before the 1919 Police Act, men typically got a few weeks of training much like that described by Manchester P.S. Seaman:

> In the morning I go to the court, listen to cases and the way evidence is given and so forth, and afterwards I go and take up scholastic studies. It may be three weeks that I am occupied at that, and later I get turned out on a beat. I get about three nights, under present conditions, with an officer or three different officers, and the result is when I am turned on to a street without much knowledge of the law, I am expected, nevertheless, to deal efficiently with all that turns up. This is impossible.[67]

This practice was consistent with both watch committee perceptions and working-class views of policing as unskilled labour. Recruits were in for a rude shock when turned out on their beats alone. They generally spent the next year on probation learning their jobs on their feet. They might be required to take additional classes during the first year or they might have to study on their own time for examinations they needed to pass at the end of their probation. Their general suitability was also reviewed by their senior officers. They were then promoted to regular constable, their probation might be extended for three or more months, or their services were dispensed with as unsuitable for the force.

While most recruits felt unprepared when first on their beats, Birmingham's training was better than most since Chief Constable Rafter, a demon of efficiency, pressured his watch committee to fund it. On his arrival in Birmingham in 1899, Rafter

> found that the Police Sergeants could not instruct or ask questions in Police Duties, nor could constables answer them in the way I had accustomed to hear [in the Royal Irish Constabulary]. Since then I have established a good school of instruction, and our method of teaching is systematised and much improved.[68]

---

67   DC, Evidence, question 3231, p. 171.
68   Chief Constables' Association Annual Reports, 30 May 1918, p. 19.

Training involved six weeks to two months of instruction before doing any street duty, and six additional months of evening classes. Each week, recruits spent twelve hours in school, eleven hours at drill, eight hours on patrol, six hours in court, one hour at ambulance school, and two evenings in structured study time. In 1905, three hours a week at the gymnasium and another evening of study were added.[69] The city soon had the best penmanship of any force.[70] But Birmingham was an exception. Even in Birmingham, nearly thirty per cent of their time was spent on drill. While this hardened the men physically and bonded them as a group, men pointed out that drill was never used in police work and led to drinking since men retired to a pub afterwards and complained.[71]

Chief constables recognized that recruits needed better preparation, but convincing watch committees of this was a battle even for men such as Rafter. When the Desborough Committee convened in 1918, chief constables hoped that parliament could improve training through national legislation. The committee, agreeing that training was deficient, recommended universal adoption of a one-year probationary period with improved two-month courses of instruction followed by an hour of instruction a day for the probationary period.[72] Voluntary classes changed into part of basic training, including police duties, court attendance, and literary topics. Subjects included English, composition, dictation, arithmetic, civics, and general knowledge. Local information was necessary since a constable 'will be called upon to answer many locality questions from passers-by, particularly from travelling motorists'.[73] They received instruction in gymnastics, jiu-jitsu, or boxing, and every policeman had to be certified in ambulance work and swimming.[74] The detested drill remained as well. The new system did provide better training but problems continued as watch committees fought to keep expenses low. Robert Mark remembered training in 1937 Manchester as spending 'most of each day dictating laws, orders and regulations to be painstakingly copied in longhand and learned each evening'. He never learned shorthand since

---

69   DC, Evidence, question 6206–8, Inspector Frederick Walsey, BCP, p. 299; BPO, 2 March 1901, p. 369; December 1905, Birmingham City Police: Duties of Recruits.
70   *Police Review*, 23 September 1904, p. 459.
71   *Police Review*, 18 October 1901, p. 496; 25 October 1901, p. 508; 1 November 1901, pp. 519–20; 8 November 1901, p. 532. Some even argued that drill, which Rafter required of everyone, was a plot to reduce the number of pensioners by killing off men before retirement.
72   Chief Constables' Association Annual Reports, 31 May 1918, p. 15; 'Report of the Committee on the Police Service of England, Wales, and Scotland', Part II, 1920, Cmd. 574, vol. XXII, 539, p. 7; 'Inspectors of Constabulary Report for Year Ended the 29th September 1923', PP 1924, (19) xii, 65, p. 13. Most forces already had one-year probationary periods. The larger cities were expected to share their training facilities with surrounding smaller forces.
73   Cecil C.H. Moriarty, 'The Police Recruit', *Police Journal* 2:3 (1929): 459.
74   Moriarty, 'The Making of an English Policeman', pp. 3–4.

the test simply involved copying a model answer provided by the instructor.[75] Two Liverpool recruits remembered spending their first day of training emptying spittoons at police headquarters and another recalled spending much of his training scrubbing floors.[76] Before the war, men were rushed into the job without a basic grasp of the law or their duties; after the 1919 reforms, instruction tended to consist of repetition of essentials.

Due to inadequate official training, recruits acquired their most practical job training from experienced policemen encountered both formally at work and informally in police canteens and living quarters. Veterans could provide positive examples of exercising discretion and good judgment but also bad habits such as how to 'skulk' or smoke without getting caught. Working beats with their fellow policemen introduced recruits to a policing that was not the unskilled job they anticipated when they applied. For men who stayed in the force, this insight began to detach them from working-class attitudes towards policing. At the same time, they did not become the neutral institutions of their instruction books. Once on the streets, recruits realized that policemen could not be the ideal described in their classes. Enforcing every law and regulation was not only physically impossible, it was not appropriate in every situation. They needed to judge when and if to act regardless of injunctions to carry out their duty without question. Lack of constant supervision required men to make major and minor choices based on their own evolving perception of what policing meant. Members of the public could encounter constables with widely different notions of their proper duties depending on their time in the force and their individual experiences.

From the day they showed up for training, recruits thinking that policing was an easy way to earn a wage were shocked by how wrong their perceptions had been. Even though they were the select few to make it through the application examinations and interviews, each group of new recruits quickly lost members who suddenly realized what they were in for. The 'burden of individual discretion and responsibility placed upon a constable is much greater than that of any other public servant of subordinate rank' and it could prove to be too much for young men not expecting it.[77] After one day of parade work, John Southern left, stating that the police was 'different to what he has been accustomed to'[78]; after four days William Knapton 'considered himself unsuitable for Police Service'[79]; and after a week, Gwilym Williams decided that he was 'unable to assume responsibilities of

75   Mark, *In the Office of Constable*, pp. 19–20, see also 'Interview with George Frederick Fancourt', pp. 2–3; Fancourt, 'The Police Service of George Frederic Fancourt', p. 2.

76   Brogden, *On the Mersey Beat*, pp. 21–3.

77   'Report of the Committee on the Police Service of England, Wales, and Scotland', Part I, 1919, Cmd. 253, vol. XXVII, 709, p. 8.

78   BRR, 29 July 1931, PCE 185 John Edward Southern.

79   BRR, 23 May 1933, PCC 66 William Leonard Knapton, four days' service.

a Police Constable'.[80] John Bell stuck it out for a year and decided that policing simply did not interest him any longer.[81] Some recruits were homesick or did not like city life, leaving after a few days or months to return home. Stanley Martin was so eager to be gone that he 'announced his intention of not returning' and left without bothering to resign.[82] PC McClelland got drunk first and left Liverpool to go home, never to be seen in the city again.[83] Not all recruits resigned voluntarily during their training. Senior officers and schoolmasters observed whether men were likely to become efficient constables and tried to weed out unlikely candidates as quickly as possible to save money on unnecessary training.[84] Some recruits struggled in the class room and were let go.[85] Others failed examinations on their police duties, first aid, general education, or swimming.[86] Although recruits had been screened for suitability, some simply could not make it through training, even with its many deficiencies.

Recruits struggled to remember a bewildering variety of rules that did not always make sense based on their previous work experiences. Some rules were not surprising, such as arriving for duty on time. However, young men unused to working night shifts could still find this a challenge. They slept through their alarms and they dashed to work without breakfast, such as PC Hanson who fainted at training school after twelve days on the force since he had got up too late to

---

80   BRR, A 247 Gwilym Harrison Williams, eight days' service, 5 June 1930. PCE 93 Charles Wm H. Lawrence, three months' service, 'Considers himself unsuitable' (BRR, 20 April 1934); PCD 243 Arthur Jack Thorogood, six months' service, 'Does not like the work' (BRR, 11 August 1934).

81   BRR, PCE 191 John Bell, one year's service, 17 August 1936.

82   BPO, 7 May 1935, p. 23689. PCD 119 Paul Macdonald, ten days' service, 'to return to Bath' (BRR, 10 April 1932); PCD 205 Horace Joffre Lowe left after one day 'to return home' (BRR, 18 February 1937); PCE 44 Leslie A.K. Harris, two months' service, 'Dislike of City' (BRR, 5 September 1937).

83   PCD 99 McClelland, probationary, drunk on duty, 'absenting himself from duty without leave on the eight following days', fined £2 by Stipendiary Magistrate for withdrawing from force without permission of chief constable (LDRB, 10 May 1912).

84   Rafter 'wishes to impress upon the Superintendents and the Schoolmaster the necessity of eliminating from amongst the recruits and Probationary Constables those not likely to become efficient at the earliest possible moment after the fact has been established … it is a matter of extreme importance that the finances of the Police Department should not be frittered away'. It cost £50–60 to put recruits through the two months' training, and more in pay and allowances (BPO, 14 November 1927, p. 13530).

85   'Recruit 9048 (PC 85 C) John Foulkes, is reported on as having made little or no progress in his education, or his knowledge of Police Duties; and that he is not likely to make an efficient Constable' (BPO, 25 September 1919, p. 1174).

86   PCD 260 John Robinson, 'This man had already been punished for gross irregularities and now has failed to pass the educational examination' (BPO, 21 April 1922, p. 4937); PCA 96 Cyril Alan Randall, four months' service, 'Failure to swim' (BRR, 4 November 1939).

eat.[87] Relying on his landlady to wake him rather than an alarm clock, Robert Orr was still late after she confused fire drill day with ambulance class day.[88] Few constables made it through their early careers without being late to work once or twice. Staying home from work due to illness seemed reasonable to recruits but now they had to remember to report themselves as too sick to parade and to see the divisional doctor to be declared sick officially. No doubt some worn out by new responsibilities, night duty, drill, and schooling just wanted to stay in bed for a day. But not following procedures could have dire consequences. Men neglecting to see the doctor could have their leave stopped or face fines; men lying about being ill in order to skip work could be fined or fired.[89] Senior officers visited sick men to check on their progress, and caught men not at home when supposedly in bed.[90] Recruits faced rules unlike any they had encountered before. If policemen wished to move, their new residence had to be approved. PC Felstead could not understand why he had to fill out forms since he wanted to move in with another police constable. After being ordered by his superintendent to 'give the necessary particulars he replied "Well that is all bloody red tape."'[91] The police force was a bureaucratic organization with a chain of command and regulations. Recruits might grumble but they needed to learn how it worked to get through their probationary period successfully.

Recruits who survived the initial weeks of training began work as probationary constables. While they might continue taking classes, they now took responsibility for a beat of their own. A beat generally followed a set pattern and had 'points' where constables were expected to be at specific times. Sergeants visited probationers to check on their progress but the men were on their own much of the time. Just getting around their beats undamaged could be harder than men anticipated. In 1920s Liverpool when two-thirds of constables had under three years' experience, the number of constables getting injured from falls, bicycle crashes, dog bites, and other accidents more than doubled compared with before the war.[92] While the

---

87   MPF, 15 February 1932, PCC 174 William James Hanson, appointed 3 February 1932.
88   MPF, 22 December 1927, PCE 35 Robert Alexander Rankin Orr, appointed October 1927, fined one shilling.
89   PCA 106 Charles Frederick Pretty, joined March 1907, 'Not parading for duty at 5.45 a.m. November 4th, then reporting himself sick, and failing to see the Divisional Surgeon before he resumed duty at 5.45 a.m. November 5th. This being the second occasion on which he acted this way. Leave stopped till further orders' (BRB, 7 November 1907).
90   PCB 168 Alcock, probationary, '(1) Absent from duty on the plea of sickness on the 11th inst. and not at home with visited. (2) Cause to be sent a telephone message with the intention of misleading his officers. Fined 10/-' (LDRB, 16 July 1915). PC Thompson, probationary, 'Habitually making false statements for the purpose of obtaining time off, during the past eleven weeks. To Resign Forthwith' (MGO, 23 October 1919).
91   LDRB, 19 July 1921, PCD 118 Felstead, fined twenty shillings.
92   LCI, 1907–1929.

pattern of a beat might look simple on paper, probationers found that if they hurried to get to points on time, they could be in trouble for missing signs of problems, yet if they took the time to be observant, they could be in trouble for being late to points. Much of their night work involved checking that doors of businesses were secure so they needed to learn the location and type of each door and its locking mechanism. For two nights in a row, Ernest Lamb failed to notice that doors on his beat were unlocked and that one business had been robbed. He was ordered 'to attend Instruction School one hour daily in own time for further instructions in police work'.[93] Learning to judge what was important, particularly to a local senior officer, also took time. Eight Liverpool probationers made the same mistake of not reporting that a young girl was wandering alone one night and each got six extra months of probation.[94] Probationers might agree with experienced constables that 'to work round the beat by a certain fixed route to a definite time-table is inefficient, is irksome and mechanical, and not in the best interests of the public'[95] but they needed to determine how far they could deviate from their pattern without creating problems for themselves. Sergeants, inspectors, and superintendents who had worked beats themselves might know that working a beat should be flexible, but they also had to answer to senior officers. In Birmingham, flexibility was frowned upon by Rafter who insisted that beats be followed exactly as designed.[96] Manchester probationers were fortunate in Chief Constable Peacock who had begun his career walking a beat and understood that exceptions could be made to general rules.[97]

The most common problems for probationers were keeping on their feet, staying awake, and remaining focused for their entire shift, particularly on night duty. The temptation to take a break or even a nap was strong, but the price of getting caught could be high. John Dean was caught reading a newspaper one morning and was fined half a crown; Matthew Cumberland was found 'skulking in a Cabman's shelter' on a cold February night and lost three months' leave.[98] Young officers could get led astray by older men, as PC Ashton learned after he joined PC Love in game of cards while on duty, only to be dismissed.[99] Since probationers

---

93   MGO, 12 January 1934; also fined ten shillings.
94   LDRB, 20 December 1914. Four other constables were punished as well.
95   DC, Evidence, question 3111, PC James Magee, Leeds City Police, p. 165.
96   'A great number of cases have recently come before Orderly Room in which Constables have neglected to work their Beats in accordance with instructions. In the cases of young Constables this undoubtedly arises, in many cases, from want of appreciation of the seriousness of the work in the Police Department and the duties that they are employed to perform' (BPO, 21 January 1922, p. 4569).
97   City of Manchester, *Police Instruction Book* (1908), pp. 110–11.
98   MGO, 31 August 1911, probationer John Dean; BRB, PCB 132 Matthew Cumberland, joined December 1903, 27 February 1904.
99   LDRB, 22 February 1913, PCD 153 Ashton, dismissed; PCD 237 Love, five years, fined twenty shillings.

were new to their jobs, they did not always come up with convincing stories for neglecting their duty. After missing his point, PC Woodcock unwisely told his sergeant, 'I have been chasing roughs ... but I have nothing to report.' When asked to explain why, in spite of heavy rain, he was quite dry, Woodcock amended his story to standing in the doorway of a chip shop while watching the disturbance. His probation was extended for three months.[100] Probationers did not always make good choices about their lax behaviour. While on duty at the polls, PC Goodwin took advantage of a quiet period to sit down with 'his hands in his pockets, his legs stretched "right out" and his helmet pushed to the back of his head'. Since his actions were so public, he earned a reprimand and no doubt a reminder on proper posture while in uniform.[101] Sergeants often handled problems with probationers informally, since their job was to provide training and correct mistakes. Unless a sergeant was rigid or the transgression severe, probationers would not be reported unless they kept repeating the same problems. If a sergeant reported every minor default, his inspector and superintendent would not thank him for wasting their time, regardless of regulations.

While probationers continually faced temptations to neglect their duty, doing so with the help of alcohol was particularly an issue before the war when working-class drinking in general was more prevalent.[102] Probationers drank on duty to stay warm on cold winter nights, such as Edwin Walden found sleeping and 'under the influence of drink in a cab' in November[103] and they drank to cool down on hot summer evenings, such as when Benjamin Hibbard was 'found in bed at Edward Rd Sub-Station under the influence of drink' in July.[104] Older constables might lead their younger colleagues astray, even arranging to meet for a drink together while on duty.[105] PC Roxborough lost his position after being found singing a suggestive song in the kitchen of a woman considered 'unfit for constabulary company' along with three other constables.[106] Probationers did not have the experience to hide drinking as successfully as their older colleagues. They got so

---

[100] LCCDR, 27 August 1927, PCC 120 Woodcock.

[101] MPF, 1 November 1930, PCC 115 Herbert Goodwin, joined March 1930.

[102] For more information, see A.E. Dingle, 'Drink and Working-Class Living Standards in Britain, 1870–1914', *Economic History Review* 2nd ser., 25:4 (1972): 608–22.

[103] Birmingham City Police Conduct Book, 15 November 1901, PC 281 Edwin Walden, appointed April 1901, called upon to resign, p. 186.

[104] Birmingham City Police Defaulters Books, 6 July 1905, leave stopped for six months, p. 145.

[105] Probationers Saycell and Sprague (nine months), to resign after arranging to meet PC Taylor (nine years' service) at a shop for the purpose of drinking. Taylor dismissed (MWCM, 28 November 1900, vol. XII, p. 76).

[106] LDRB, 14 November 1914, PCD 85 Roxborough, probationary, 1 default; PCD 210 Atkinson, one year's service, fined 20/-, PCD 166 Reeves allowed to resign, and PCD 218 Forshaw, two years' service, two defaults, reprimanded and transferred, for being present.

drunk that they missed duty due to hangovers or they got drunk while off duty but were still intoxicated when they showed up for parade.[107] PC Davies managed to break any number of rules, including being out drinking while on the sick list, missing ambulance class, and showing up for work drunk.[108] While older men caught drinking were generally sent home to sober up and perhaps fined, nearly all probationers caught drinking on duty were dismissed or ordered to resign. It was one thing to take up drinking on the job but quite another to begin the job that way. Problems with drinking throughout the force decreased dramatically after the war due to changes in overall working-class drinking habits, though it still could end the career of probationers.

Combined with the stress of working beats without taking harmful missteps, probationers found it challenging to endure supervision from sergeants and other senior officers. Small problems turned into large ones if they over-reacted to inquiries about their work. Young men could be quarrelsome when they knew that they had made mistakes and were embarrassed about being found out. Found chewing gum on duty and reprimanded by his sergeant, PC Fred Bolton made the ill-advised reply, 'I would think you are trying to take the piss out of me.' He may even have remarked when told that he would be reported, 'You can please yourself, I shan't wriggle.'[109] Probationers needed to avoid the temptation to talk back to senior officers, however provoking they might be. PC MacPherson forgot to acknowledge his sergeant's instructions at parade and 'when asked by the Sergeant 'Did you hear what I said to you?' replied 'Of course I did, do you think I am deaf.'[110] But what could seem like a harmless wisecrack elsewhere could get a man disciplined for insubordination, particularly if said in front of witnesses, a lesson PC Jones needed to learn. When Sergeant Gough asked to see his notebook to check his work, Jones replied, 'What the bloody hell do you want with my notebook: you saw it this morning ... I will take my coat off to you & I will knock the shit-pot out of you.' He then took off his coat and helmet and assumed 'a threatening attitude towards the Sergeant'. He was suspended for five days and fined fifty shillings.[111] That these men were fined rather than fired suggests that senior officers were sympathetic to their frustrations. But habitual insubordination was not tolerated and such men were let go. Taking out their frustrations on the few employees lower than them could be just as disastrous: twenty-year-old PC Wheeler lost his job after

---

[107] LDRB, 12 March 1915, PCE 360 Goosey, probationary, drunk on duty 10:20 pm and absent without leave the next day, dismissed.

[108] Birmingham City Police Defaulters Books, 2 April 1904, PCE 28 Charles Robert Davies, joined December 1903, to resign, p. 183.

[109] BPO, 12 May 1938, p. 29706; BOR, 12 May 1938. He was fined ten shillings. Bolton denied making these remarks.

[110] LDRB, 22 February 1921, PCB 234 MacPherson; fined twenty-five shillings.

[111] LDRB, 9 Dec. 1919, PCD 191 Jones, probationary.

being rude to a woman who cooked and cleaned at the station house.[112] However much constables might complain among themselves about rules and duties, they were wise to keep grievances to their own level.

Probationers had to become accustomed to dealing with the public in their new roles, finding a balance between law enforcement and establishing a good relationship. Most probationers erred on the side of being too friendly. Even though their instruction books told them to keep a distance from the public, experienced men taught them that learning the normal patterns of their beats was the best way to uncover abnormal activity. But probationers were still learning how to frame their meetings with civilians as professional conversations rather than as chattiness or gossip. More of a problem for forces were probationers prone to violence. Young men could be impatient; this was compounded by probationers insecure in their duties and uncertain how to respond when challenged by civilians. The young constables in Liverpool in the 1920s suffered twice as many injuries inflicted by prisoners and crowds than did constables before the war.[113] Constables who routinely resorted to physical force or assaulted prisoners gave forces a bad reputation. When John Forster kicked a prisoner, he was quickly told to resign.[114] Even fighting while off duty and out of uniform could damage a probationer's career. After PC Davies got into a fight at a public house on his own time, he had to pay a twenty-five-shilling fine.[115] Similar to problems with drinking, it is not surprising that senior officers got rid of probationers already showing tendencies to resort to violence too easily.

Young women met on the job caused another dilemma for probationers. Tall and fit young men looking smart in their new uniforms could attract women looking for men with steady jobs. But this could be ruinous for men who did not exercise good judgment in how they responded to the attention. Neglect of duty while spending time with civilians was more serious than idling alone, and men consorted with women at their peril. Even cat calls that men might consider an innocent indulgence could get them fired.[116] Gossiping with women reinforced the stereotype of policemen frittering away their time chatting up shop girls and servants, and was discouraged with fines and probation extensions.[117] But, not

---

[112] BOR, 28 January 1938.

[113] LCI, 1907–1929.

[114] MGO, 2 April 1914, allowed to resign.

[115] LDRB, 30 August 1921, PCD 121 Davies, probationary, 1 default.

[116] 'Probationary Constable E 203 Allison Gray's services are dispensed with forthwith … a complaint having been made that he shouted at two women who were proceeding to the Hospital at 3.10 a.m. remarks which were of an improper character' (BPO, 29 July 1929, p. 15626).

[117] PCF 80 Nash, probationary, fined fifteen shillings for idling his time with a women (LDRB, 12 April 1921); Probationary Constable C 233 Carr Enos Cauling, gossiping with a

surprisingly, some men could not resist the temptation offered by friendly women. Infractions often occurred late on Saturdays, a time reserved for socialising. PCs Maddox, James Daly and Percival Jump were each caught acting in an 'indecent manner' with young women while on duty on Saturday nights and all were dismissed, one in 1915, one in 1923, and one in 1938.[118] While normally their off-duty courting was not a problem, a disapproving parent could end a romance by complaining to the constable's senior officer. In these cases, sergeants gave their men advice and perhaps warned them to be careful if the young woman was under eighteen. While being caught courting during work hours ended careers, being discovered in compromising circumstances with married women or prostitutes even when off duty led to quick dismissals.[119] Not even the domestic life of the few married probationers was excluded from consideration. Men who mistreated their wives, at least in public, were called in to explain themselves and then fired.[120] Policemen were supposed to protect the public, not get a reputation for leading women astray or harming women, on or off duty. Similar to other discipline issues, veteran constables might not be dismissed for similar offences, but probationers already in trouble with women were quickly let go.

The most profound change that probationers had to accept was that their private lives were just as regulated as their work lives. This concern over their off-duty conduct separated policemen from other members of the working class. Most were single and, regardless of their personal inclination, many were expected to live in 'singlemen's quarters' with other single officers.[121] On the surface, official quarters were not unlike living in lodging houses, all of which had rules regarding noise, hot water and bathrooms, curfews, and visitors. But now they were being supervised by their employers, not by landladies. Men found that housing in police

woman while on duty in uniform, probation extended three months (BDRB, 11 June 1922, p. 99).

118 LDRB, PCE 251 Maddox, probationary, 16 July 1915; BPO, 28 May 1923, Probationary Constable E 138 James Daly, p. 6385; BRB, PCE James Joseph Daly; BPO, 3 December 1936, Probationary Constable E 271 Percival Taylor Jump, p. 26566.

119 PCE 208 Leedale, probationary, entered a water closet with a married woman while on duty. Dismissed (LDRB, 5 September 1913); Probationary Constable A227 Stanley Bates was dismissed after being found off duty walking arm in arm with a known convicted prostitute and thief (BPO, 3 November 1922, p. 5627; BDRB, p. 116).

120 PCD 145 Mooney, four months, 'Found to be unfit for the force by reason of his conduct towards his wife etc. Services dispensed with' (LDRB, 27 December 1912); PCC 105 Ashcroft, one month, drunk on duty, 'turned his wife out of the house & used filthy language to her while in the street, same date. His services be dispensed with' (LDRB, 30 April 1915).

121 'Single men must reside in the Station House unless they have permission from their Superintendent to reside elsewhere' (BPO, 19 November 1937, p. 29224) During housing shortages after the First World War, Manchester housed about 500 single men at the Alexandra Park Aerodrome in converted buildings, used previously for married policemen (MGO, 17 February 1921).

dormitories under the watchful eyes of resident officers was another way to train them to be a credit to the force. Lengthy lists of rules were posted in the mess room or charge office.[122] To ensure obedience, a sergeant made daily inspections and superintendents made monthly visits to see that conditions met regulations, including checking their cupboards for offensive or improper articles. Single men were the first to lose off-duty time when crises occurred since police forces used quarters not only to keep an eye on their junior members but also to provide a reserve in emergencies. Visitors were not allowed in the dormitories and only allowed in the station house to transact business. This meant that men with civilian friends had to meet elsewhere. However, rules against 'frequenting public houses' could make this difficult. Not surprisingly, constables often socialized with each other, especially since they shared the same unsociable hours. Men not living in quarters were sent to pre-approved lodgings, sometimes run by retired policemen or their widows. These, too, were subject to regular inspections.

Forces used police dormitories to teach probationers good habits and the need to present a positive image at all times. Not only did men learn how to maintain their uniforms, men were expected to clean their quarters. They had not imagined that cleaning would be part of their new jobs but soon they polished floors, cleaned fire grates, aired out mattresses, polished brass bath and sink taps, caught rats, and cleaned blue station lamps. Generally, a cleaning room was set up for brushing clothing and boots, and another designated for bicycles.[123] Bedrooms were expected to be tidy by afternoon inspection. This included having beds made up according to force protocol and having clean uniforms stowed properly in their cupboards.[124] Cleaning could be just as hazardous as walking beats, with probationers constantly injuring themselves, skinning knuckles, falling down stairs, and slipping on soap.[125] Requiring cleanliness and actually getting

---

[122] Unless otherwise noted, singlemen's quarters rules and regulations are from BPO, 19 November 1937, pp. 29223–5.

[123] 'It must be distinctly understood that no boots must be cleaned in any portion of the Police Station except the boot room. Boots also must not be left lying about the Station, but placed in the proper place viz:- the boot room' (BPO, 29 March 1913, pp. 413–14; 8 October 1918, p. 259).

[124] BPO, 22 July 1917, p. 94. Dirty uniforms were only allowed in the cleaning room. PCD 199 Alfred Joseph Wright and PCD 223 Herbert Jarvis were cautioned for having dirty boots in their rooms (BPO, 29 March 1913, p. 413).

[125] BPO, 14 May 1914, order to clean brass bath and other taps, p. 130; LCI, 31 January 1906, PCH 101 Sweeting skinned knuckles while polishing the floor; 16 August 1907, chunk of marble mantelpiece fell on PCG 167 Hudson's foot while cleaning out a grate; 13 August 1910, while cleaning the day room, PCG 105 Hunt slipped on a piece of soap, tripped over a form, and fell onto an iron boot last, fracturing two ribs; 2 September 1911, carrying bed ticks down stairs, PCD 229 Brown caught his foot and fell to the next landing, spraining his chest; 28 May 1920, PCC 162 McLaughlin was bitten on the hand by a rat which he caught in

it were two different matters. Constables persisted in having messy bedrooms and in not storing their uniforms correctly. They left their boots anywhere and stacked their bicycles in the hallways. Even though only safety matches were allowed to prevent accidental fires, men persisted in leaving marks on walls from striking non-safety matches against them. They continued to smoke in their bedrooms.[126] Men were fined for having dirty rooms, and often had to pay for repairs, such as repainting walls, but these measures seemed to do little to turn young men into paragons of cleanliness.[127] They probably realized that authorities were reluctant to fire hard-to-find probationers over their difficulties in learning orderly domestic habits.

An unintended lesson that probationers learned from police quarters was that the economies that hampered their training also affected their housing; this reinforced a growing scepticism that watch committees thought that good policemen were worth paying for. Constables could be housed in old buildings that they were expected to keep clean and ventilated. Forces even used living in often spartan conditions as a punishment.[128] Inspectors of Constabulary repeatedly issued orders that station dormitories be updated.[129] Old station houses could make living conditions hazardous and even deadly. In Liverpool, the son of a resident inspector died of diphtheria in 1901, and a resident sergeant's daughter became ill with scarlet fever in 1905, both caused by defective drainage and poor sanitation.[130] Into the 1930s, men complained that they were forbidden to marry at an early age and yet

---

the station school room; 6 January 1928, PCB 190 Stone fell off a ladder while cleaning the station lamp.

126   BPO, 18 May 1903, p. 436. An order stating that 'no matches are to be permitted ... unless they are safety matches' made four months earlier had not been followed (BPO, 7 January 1903, p. 328). Another order showed that men persisted in smoking and not using safety matches (BPO, 27 April 1904, p. 162). Smoking was forbidden in bedrooms for safety reasons and due to usually poor ventilation but men often had to be reminded 'that the habit of men smoking in their bedrooms ... is to be discontinued' (BPO, 7 January 1903, p. 328).

127   PCD 116 Martin Quigley was fined a day's pay for having a dirty bedroom and had to pay for repair of his bed (BPO, 3 July 1907, p. 97). PCE 274 William Alford was punished for having dirty linen in his bedroom (BPO, 10 June 1926, p. 11370).

128   After PC Saunders struck his landlord, he was directed to live at a police station in order to put him under the strict observation of a station officer (BPO, 31 October 1912, p. 298).

129   'Inspectors of Constabulary report for year ended the 29th of September 1905', PP 1906 (127) xlix, 1, p. 97; '... September 1906', PP 1907 (128) xxxi, 1, p. 94; '... September 1909', PP 1910 (106) lxxv, 587, p. 69; '... September 1910', PP 1911 (64) lxv, 175, pp. 72, 87; '... September 1933', PP 1933–1934 (26) xiv, 711, p. 13; '... September 1938', PP 1938–1939 (83) xiv, 317, p. 20; also 'Report of the Royal Commission on Police Powers and Procedure', 1928–1929, Cmd. 3297, vol. IX, 127, p. 22.

130   LWCM, 10 June 1901, pp. 102–3; LHCWC, 11 September 1905, sergeant compensated for medical expenses and apartment rent paid until drainage repaired, pp. 308–9. The stations were condemned as residences until the sanitation systems were rebuilt.

the quarters they were required to live in were 'so cheerless and comfortless as to incite to matrimony at the first chance'.[131] In 1933, HMI Allan agreed that young constables were rushing into matrimony to escape the poor food and conditions in singlemen's quarters.[132] The goal of moulding young constables into good officers through constant supervision at station houses was undermined by economic compromises that instead taught them that watch committees gave their budgets higher priority than the police force.

Just like Birmingham had the best training school due to the efforts of Chief Constable Rafter, they also had the best police quarters. But even though Birmingham was commended for having superior accommodations for single men, 'a plan which not only provides a reserve for emergencies, but is also of great advantage to the men themselves',[133] Birmingham men had to live under the heavy hand of their chief. He was a terror for proper cleaning and frequent inspections, habitually giving detailed instructions on the proper way to clean in formal police orders, such as preventing corrosion of water closet pans by using oxalic acid.[134] He expected dormitory rule infractions to be reported officially unlike Manchester and Liverpool where supervising officers handled problems locally. Neither of the other cities included breaking of dormitory rules in their official disciplinary records. Men caught not acting as Rafter commanded could face harsh penalties. A month shy of completing his probationary year, PC Wakefield had his probation extended by three months for failing to clean a wall after he accidentally spat on it, missing the spittoon.[135] The constant stream of petty offences indicates the difficulties probationers faced adjusting to such strict supervision. Probationers in Liverpool and Manchester also broke rules but these were handled at the local station rather than at headquarters and rarely made it into the records.[136]

The wife and family of a resident officer might live in police quarters,[137] and women, often police widows or police relatives, came in to do cleaning

---

[131] *Police Review*, 9 March 1934, p. 176.

[132] 'Inspectors in Constabulary report for year ended the 29th September 1933', PP 1933–1934, (26) xiv, 711, p. 13. Years of service required before giving permission to marry varied from force to force, some requiring as many as four years' service.

[133] 'Inspectors in Constabulary report for year ended the 29th September 1912' PP 1913 (76) lii, 663, p. 107.

[134] BPO, 1 March 1907, p. 10.

[135] BRB, 4 February 1926, PCC 161 Albert Arthur Wakefield, joined March 1925, probation extended three months; BPO, 4 February 1926, p. 10880.

[136] The activities of Liverpool probationers can be deduced from injuries reported in the Injuries to Constables books. Very occasionally, a constable might be cautioned for breaking dormitory rules in Manchester and Liverpool.

[137] Apartments typically contained 'a sitting room and combined kitchen and scullery ... two bedrooms and a bathroom' (LCCO, 5 March 1936) If there was no resident, an officer was assigned to monitor the station.

and cooking.[138] These women could fill the roles that landladies often served for single men, officially or unofficially. Their personalities could have a huge impact on dormitory life and introduce probationers to the intricacies of rank and internal frictions. One sergeant's wife who cooked and cleaned at a station treated constables with contempt, much to their annoyance.[139] Usually wives were not allowed to do cooking, cleaning, mending, or errands for constables to prevent contact that could lead to accusations of favouritism or discrimination. This did not stop another sergeant's wife from cooking dinners for single men at a set charge per meal. She was paid a weekly allowance by the men, but was ordered to cease the practice once news of it spread.[140] These prohibitions could leave single men in a bind since they did not have the usual landlady to look after them and most had no local family. Constables improvised by using station cleaners to run errands, do mending, or do other favours for them, especially if the constable was on night duty and needed the day for sleeping. These women were continually reminded that they were under no obligation to run errands for the men, and were instructed not to accept commissions unless the money necessary was paid in advance.[141] Problems occasionally arose when a woman bought groceries or sundries for a constable who then could not pay for them. The tendency to act as helpers for the constables continued, however, since it was customary for domestics at lodging houses to run these kinds of errands for single tenants. Regardless of the rules, constables rarely had any other options when they needed errands run.

Once probationers became accustomed to life in quarters, they made themselves at home rather than remain on their dignity twenty-four hours a day. Like other duties, they learned through experience and from older men which dormitory regulations they could ignore and which they should follow. Respecting rules that could be verified during inspections made sense, but they often ignored behavioural rules they did not like. Regulations that affected the comfort of everyone tended to be given more attention than those that did not. Understanding the need for sleep

---

138 Though the men were expected to make their beds and keep personal belongings orderly, cleaners kept station public areas clean, scrubbed floors and emptied rubbish bins. Men on night duty were expected to be out of their rooms by 3:00 pm so the rooms could be cleaned and ventilated and other men were not allowed in their rooms during the daytime until 4:00 pm.

139 *Police Review*, 27 May 1910, p. 250. While not allowed to be station domestics, wives generally acted as searchers of female prisoners, an example of an official tendency to treat wives as auxiliary policemen. They were paid a flat fee and usually an extra fee for each prisoner searched since the number of female prisoners could vary from twelve per station to well over 1000 annually (LWCM, 19 March 1900, pp. 94–5). In a request for resident officer applicants, it added that the wife would 'perform the duties of a female searcher' (LCCO, 5 March 1936).

140 BPO, 30 July 1927, p. 13130.

141 BPO, 20 November 1919, p. 1417.

for men on night shifts, they usually kept quiet; an equal desire for a social life kept them out after the midnight curfew. Constables continued to burn gas lights during the day time, hang uniforms in the day rooms instead of in their cupboards, cut up the tables with knives, and tamper with the key holes of their lockers. In the recreation rooms, they tore the bagatelle tables, broke the cue sticks, and ripped up the periodicals to light their pipes.[142] In a rare Manchester comment on behaviour in the dormitories, Chief Constable Peacock reminded the men that 'the Recreation Rooms attached to Police Stations are provided by the Watch Committee free of cost and for the use of members of the Force only'.[143] Apparently, constables had been having friends over regardless of the rules. Probationers continued to act like young men, and resident officers overlooked minor infractions just as sergeants did with minor problems working beats. The existence of so many trivial rules may even have added zest to otherwise mundane activities, like using a prohibited match.

The attempt to create good habits worked to some degree since most constables wanted to keep their jobs, but rules that put a cramp on men's recreation were often broken, sometimes with the connivance of resident officers. A common indoor pastime was card-playing even though gambling and therefore card-playing, was prohibited, both to prevent disputes over winnings and to keep men from losing their wages. In Birmingham, men found playing were fined half a crown or a crown.[144] But cards were such a normal activity that a Manchester probationer caught playing in the dormitory argued that he 'had not the slightest idea of the offense I was committing by doing so'.[145] Enforcement of rules against card-playing was left to the resident officer and not all agreed with the rule.[146] PS Finding sometimes hosted constables in his police cottage kitchen next door to the singlemen's quarters 'for the purpose of gambling by playing cards'.[147] The relaxed disposition of a resident officer was one way that strict obedience to rules could be circumvented. But

---

[142] BPO, 27 April 1927, pp. 161–3.

[143] MGO, 22 February 1912.

[144] PCD 103 Harold Gray, PCD 160 Herbert Brown, PCD 223 Albert Hammond, and PCD 242 George Dovey were found playing cards in the kitchen of the singlemen's quarters at 3:30 am (BDBD, 21 December 1922, each fined 2/6d., pp. 36–7; BPO, 21 December 1922, p. 5847). PCD 112 William Quinn and PCD 220 Wilfred Hamblett were caught gambling with cards because they had the mess room light on after midnight (BOR, 22 November 1928, fined 5/-; BPO, 22 November 1928, p. 14784).

[145] MPF, 3 December 1920, PCC 191 Thomas Osbaldiston, appointed October 1920, cautioned.

[146] BPO, 11 December 1913, p. 23. While on the sick list, two constables passed time playing cards in the mess room.(BPO, 3 March 1915, PCB 83 Alfred Hemming, reduced, PCB 128 Arthur E. Revill, leave stopped, p. 473).

[147] BDRB, 23 April 1921, PSE 11 George Finding, reduced, p. 27; PCE 151 Cuthbert William Toft, PCE 84 Thomas Victor Marsh, PCE 152 Edward Thomas Harrison, also charged with absence from quarters after midnight, cautioned, pp. 28–9; BPO, 20 April 1921, p. 3513.

probationers needed to sum up their superiors carefully. A sergeant caught six men gambling at cards in a station bedroom one Sunday afternoon and four of them got the usual fines. But two men refused to stop playing, challenging the sergeant's authority in front of witnesses. Both were dismissed for insubordination.[148]

The regulation probably broken most often was curfew. Men not on duty were expected to return to quarters by midnight when the lights were put out to ensure that they got enough sleep. But men in their twenties were not likely to obey curfew if an evening's entertainment was going well. It prevented going out after a show and some girlfriends were not impressed that their men had to be in by midnight. Probationers out together were more likely to miss their deadline; two constables at a party were late getting back, another pair was out late carousing at the New Year, and three stayed out until nearly 3:00 am.[149] Perhaps none liked to suggest getting back to quarters in time in front of each other and come across as a killjoy. The strictness of enforcement depended on the resident officer. Only eight minutes after midnight, PC Collins had to use a skeleton key to get into the already locked door of quarters and was ordered to resign after he was caught, but most officers were a little more lenient, having been probationers themselves once.[150] Most caught breaking curfew had their probation extended rather than more serious punishments.

Staying out late could compensate for rarely being allowed to spend the night away from quarters to visit family or friends. Resident constables acted as police reserves so forces preferred to keep absences limited. Probationers almost never obtained leave for holidays since everyone applied for it. Generally, probationers followed this rule since being absent without leave almost always ended in dismissal. The men who risked it tended to have other discipline problems as well, suggesting that they did not have the temperament for the job. PCs Kitson and Latham spent Christmas night away from quarters without permission but Kitson was already in trouble for not repaying money he borrowed from fellow constables and Latham had neglected his duty and behaved poorly when giving evidence in court.[151] PC Parsons

---

148 BDBD, 27 February 1921, PCD 182 Frank Light, PCD 230 Arthur Edward Wickstead, to resign for refusing to stop; PCD 148 George Percival Arnus, PCD 99 John Craig, PCD 41 William Bourne, fined 5/-; PCD 126 Bruce Frederick Waugh, cautioned, pp. 4–6; BPO, 3 March 1921, p. 3302.

149 LDRB, 22 February 1921, PCD 222 Geraghty, probationary, returned to quarters 2:00 a.m., lied about another constable at party, fined 20/-. BPO, 27 January 1926, PCE 275 Edward Baker, PCE 277 William George Ette, also interfered with a motor car and got into 'unseemly' dispute with people regarding car, reduced, p. 10851. BOR, 13 August 1931, PCD 145 William Ette, cautioned, PCD 102 Kendrick Davies, cautioned, PCD 278, probation extended three months.

150 BPO, 20 November 1929, PCA 244 James Collins, to resign, p. 16062.

151 Birmingham City Police Defaulters Books, 25 December 1900, PCE Anthony Kitson, joined February 1883, also borrowed money from policemen and contracted outside debts, to resign, p. 165; BPO, 22 January 1901, p. 345; 2 January 1903, PCD 35 James Latham, also loitering, giving unsatisfactory evidence, to resign, p. 322.

also had multiple problems. He was absent from quarters and from the city without permission, got into a fight at a public house while away, and lied about his injuries, saying that they came from a suitcase falling on his hand.[152] Men with legitimate leave could get into trouble for not getting back on time, or for using leave for purposes other than those approved. PC Milloy had permission to stay out one night to visit a specific address but was dismissed when he was discovered at a different house carrying on an affair with a widow.[153] Men who went on to have long careers in the force might get back late from an evening out once or twice but realized that they were less likely to get away with disappearing for an entire day without being noticed.

Despite all the rules and supervision, life at singlemen's quarters tended to be like life anywhere where young men shared living space. They tried to keep quiet since constables were sleeping at nearly all times, but sometimes commotions broke out when excited young men forgot themselves, shouted, and banged doors.[154] When in a hurry to go on duty, they borrowed each other's belongings, not always asking first. PC McHale took another constable's bootlace after his own broke, and another man took a rain cape after forgetting his own in a shop.[155] Food was taken from each other's cupboards when a constable could not be bothered or was unable to go out and buy his own.[156] Money left in garments hanging on doors had a way of disappearing but chief constables agreed that the men had only themselves to blame for being careless with valuables.[157] They kidded around and

---

[152]   BRB, 4 January 1934, PCA 139 Arthur Kenneth Parsons, joined January 1932, discharged; BOR, 4 January 1934. He also failed to inform the force that he had purchased a motorcycle. PCD 219 Arthur Jordan spent night away from quarters without permission; next day on duty he snuck back into quarters to take a nap after losing previous night's sleep (BPO, 22 February 1912, leave stopped, p. 114). PCB 112 Frank Langton was absent overnight without permission (MGO, 20 August 1926, to resign).

[153]   BRB, 26 February 1936, PCC 170 Robert Irvine Gilmour Milloy, joined April 1932, unmarried; Birmingham City Police Defaulters Books, 12, 26 February 1936, PCC 170 Milloy; BOR, 20 February 1936; BPO, 26 February 1936, p. 25043.

[154]   When PCD 47 Henry Whittaker and PCD 267 William Henry Griffin shouted and banged doors one midnight, they earned severe cautions and the animosity of men on morning shifts (BDBD, 18 May 1935, p. 150).

[155]   BPO, 21 June 1900, PCB 63 Richard McHale, leave stopped, p. 209; 17 October 1901, p. 552. The wool capes were expensive to replace. Rafter issued an order against borrowing after complaints had been made that items were being taken without the owner's permission. He warned that future instances would be treated as stealing (BPO, 22 June 1900, p. 210).

[156]   PCA 169 Robert Dyer took a loaf of bread belonging to another man (BPO, 11 June 1904, leave stopped, p. 257). PCA 131 Neville Rushton, four years' service, found the food of PCA 130 Frederick Thompson on a window ledge in the parade room and took it without permission (BOR, 5 March 1936).

[157]   BPO, 19 November 1934, p. 22936. PCD 214 Harold Frederick Selby borrowed £5 from a constable without paying it back and broke into another constable's locker to search for valuables (BDBD, 2 October 1924, nothing missing from locker, to resign, p. 62).

bickered with each other. Food fights erupted in the mess hall, such as when PC Cullmane threw bread around, and PCs Harris and Butts threw potatoes at each other.[158] They played practical jokes, sometimes damaging property or throwing bedding around. Rafter issued orders against practical joking, annoyed that they were 'again on the increase in the Force', and sometimes had to separate men to different dormitories.[159] They challenged each other to friendly fights, which could get out of hand. PC Fitzsimmons cut his head open in a wrestling match with another constable, and PC Little fractured his jaw while 'indulging in horse play' with PC Barker.[160] Police forces hoped that housing probationers at stations would turn them into good police officers but they remained young men.

The proportion of probationers who survived long enough became police constables gradually increased from 1900 to 1939 as pay and conditions of service improved. Before the First World War, around a third of Manchester constables did not make it beyond three years of joining, either leaving on their own, asked to resign, or dismissed. After the 1919 Police Act, men leaving within three years dropped to about a quarter and during the Great Depression to about fifteen per cent. But after the Second World War, many men who had joined in the 1930s left once better opportunities presented themselves.[161] Of those probationers who did not make it, many lost their jobs due to their inability to pass examinations, to carry out their duty correctly, or to follow force regulations. A few unfortunate men died, often in traffic accidents.[162] But others left voluntarily.[163] They got homesick, their families did not like them being so far away, or they did not like the work. After

---

[158] Birmingham City Police Disciplinary Book 'D' Division, 16 November 1901, PCE 38 David Cullmane, joined April 1900, leave stopped, transferred, p. 149; 29 June 1904, PCE 29 John Walter Harris, joined February 1894, PCE 134 Edwin Bennett Cutts, joined February 1902, cautioned, pp. 42, 259; BPO, 2 July 1904, p. 278. Potato-throwing was mentioned again in 1911 (BPO, 23 February 1911, p. 452).

[159] BPO, 23 February 1911, p. 451. PCC 31 Eli Stanton and PCC 35 William Leighton damaged a felt hat belonging to PCC 166 Michael Jennings while playing a practical joke (BPO, 23 February 1911, Stanton, severely cautioned, Leighton, leave stopped, paid 4/- to replace hat, p. 452). PCD Herbert George Richard Lipscombe and PCD 209 Frank Jarvis lost leave and were cautioned for practical joking. They were separated with Jarvis sent to live at other quarters (BRB, 14 March 1914, Lipscombe, joined September 1913; BPO, 14 March 1914, p. 95).

[160] LCI, 18 March 1912, PCH 267 Fitzsimmons, cut head; 10 November 1922, PCH 172 Little, 'Con pulled Con Little's head under his arm with a jerk'. Emsley outlines life at quarters, including horseplay, in *The English Police*, pp. 193–4.

[161] Manchester City Police roster cards, 1900–1939. For more on length of service, see Chapter 10.

[162] BRR, 25 June 1931, PCD 273 Joseph Shipton, one year's service, 'Died in Hospital as the result of a motor cycle accident'; 17 August 1936, PCC 49 Ronald George Dawding, five months' service, 'Died from injuries received in accident when riding m/cycle'; PCC 260 John Kirkby, four months' service, 'Died in Kenyon Street Police Station'.

[163] For a more detailed exploration of men leaving the force voluntarily, see Chapter 10.

experiencing force conditions, some men decided that their old jobs were not so bad after all. Walter Hunt decided to return to working in insurance and Thomas Exelby went back to working as an engineer for the merchant service.[164] Probationers persisted in applying for other situations without asking for permission, no doubt thinking that their desire to leave the force could lead to internal problems, particularly if no other job materialized.[165] Some probationers liked policing but preferred to join forces closer to home or where promotion was more likely.[166] A few emigrated, such as PC Flannagan who left for the Malay States and PC Stephenson who joined a colonial force.[167] Despite all efforts to screen applicants, train recruits, and supervise probationers, only actually working a beat could decide which men were willing or able to become fully fledged constables.

During the probationary period and beyond, the ideal of the neutral upholder of the law turned into something else when combined with real working-class men concerned with earning a regular wage and living a decent life. In spite of the mismatch between policemen as paragon and the actual policemen on the streets, the reality of working-class policemen worked reasonably well. The contradictory layers of official and unofficial training, the contrary pull towards an ideal and towards working reality, resulted in an amalgamation more appropriate to the realities of policing than the mythical 'PC X'. Most policemen appreciated enough of the ideal to feel a responsibility to uphold their oath of office and the reputation of the police force. Being the personification of justice could be a rather attractive idea. Yet their working-class roots and habits remained, making them more suitable for their jobs and tolerable to members of working class, among whom they primarily worked and lived, than if they had become neutral institutions.

---

[164] BRR, 27 May 1930, PCE 274 Walter Holman Hunt, two months' service, resigned at own request; 9 May 1930, PCC 315 Thomas Harold Exelby, six months' service, resigned at own request.

[165] Two probationers fined 10/- for 'applying for other situations without first obtaining the permission of the Chief Constable' (MGO, 28 March 1901). Order to halt this practice, BPO, 15 November 1906, p. 521. PCD 196 George A. Lockyer had to resign after 'making application for a situation without obtaining permission' (MGO, 23 April 1921) PCC 68 W. Dean, probationary, had to resign after applying to join another police force without permission (MGO, 23 October 1919). PCA 241 Charles R. Miles was allowed to resign after applying for the Royal Air Force without permission (MGO, 26 September 1935).

[166] BRR, 23 January 1931, PCA 129 Frederick Edward Smith, ten months' service, resigned at own request 'to join another police force nearer to his home'; 25 March 1938, PCD 295 James Graham Arthur, ten months' service, at own request, 'To join Glasgow Police'; 10 April 1938, PCB 254 George Thomas Nalty, eleven months' service, at own request, 'To join Southport Police'; 16 April 1939, PCC 23 Edward Brynmoor Williams, six months' service, at own request, 'To join Metrop Police'.

[167] BRR, 5 November 1931, PCE 149 Edward John Woulfe Flannagan, five weeks' service, at own request; 13 July 1932, PCA 141 Henry Stephenson, twenty-five weeks' weeks' service, at own request.

2

Multifarious Duties

Universal to almost all expressions of opinion about the
duties which the police ought to perform or ought not to
perform there is one prominent feature, a remarkable want of
knowledge of the duties which the police actually do perform.
Leonard Dunning, Chief Constable, Liverpool, 1909[1]

THE DAILY LIFE OF POLICE CONSTABLES did not consist of walking
about doing little, nor were constables the perfect neutral ideal or part
of a police thriller. While policemen received public attention for their actions
during disturbances and strikes, or for dramatic rescues of people and animals,
the vast majority of their work was routine. They walked their beats, checking
the security of doors, and talking with neighbours. They directed traffic, stopped
runaway horses, and fished people out of rivers and canals. Civilians handed over
lost children and property, and stray dogs. The law-breaking they discovered
tended to be minor thefts, miscellaneous violations of public order, and traffic
infractions. Priority was given to obvious dangers such as fires and to duties easily
checked by their senior officers. Injuries were generally minor and rarely heroic.
Constables were kicked, bitten, and pelted with missiles; they fell off their bicycles,
off walls, and down stairs. Remaining calm while handling suicides or dealing with
victims of road collisions required not thinking about particulars too much. Some
duties gained policemen respect; others did not. The same action could win them
praise from some individuals and scorn from others. Most duties, however, were
unnoticed and unsuspected, accounting for the low working-class opinion of the
job and for why watch committees undervalued them.

In spite of perceptions of civilians and recruits that constables patrolled to
discourage crime, policemen actually carried out a baffling variety of activities that
appeared to have little to do with lawbreaking. Some duties were clearly tied to crime
prevention, such as when they discovered insecure doors or windows, informed the

---

[1] LAR, 1909, p. 71.

owners, and secured the premises. Many tasks related to keeping public streets and walkways safe. Constables cleared both an assortment of obstacles and dangers. One constable climbed a lamp post to detach broken telephone wires crossing a street and blocking pedestrians;[2] another climbed up onto a roof to remove a loose brick threatening to fall on passersby.[3] They impounded horses found straying, unfit for work, or with drunk drivers, as well as unattended handcarts, coal wagons, and other vehicles. Constables protected school children crossing busy intersections and were 'instructed to see that children do not expose themselves to unnecessary risks'.[4] They took lost children, wandering lunatics, and stray pets to the nearest police station. They rescued people unintentionally locked into buildings, poisoned by gas, and trapped by fires. They examined dead bodies found on their beat and sent them to the mortuary.[5] They performed first aid. The growing popularity of football and holiday spots increased time required for the 'shepherding of crowds'. As telephones became more common, policeman found themselves summoned more and more often for minor problems such as noisy neighbours, children's pranks, or cats up trees. All of this came under the broad heading of public safety, not an explicit part of their oath of office but an increasing proportion of their duties.

Other duties were difficult to associate with crime prevention or public service. Many involved enforcing a variety of government regulations, in many cases acting as inspectors. Policemen issued licences to marine store dealers, peddlers, and pawnbrokers after making inquiries into each application. They registered and inspected common lodging houses. Birmingham constables on duty at amusement venues such as cinemas and dance halls were expected to 'nightly inspect all Lavatories, see that they are kept clean and in working order, they will also examine exits, see they are in order and un-obstructed'.[6] Liverpool constables were ordered to keep an eye out for leaflets that the Home Office wanted them to confiscate, such as 'Get Ready for the Revolution' and 'British Workers – What are we going to do?'[7] They served poor rate summonses and executed poor rate distress warrants, duties policemen disliked for making them unpopular with the public. Much to their own annoyance since it made them feel like errand boys, they had to hand out government circulars and sell tickets to police charity events. In one example, circulars concerning evening classes had to be distributed to the 'houses of Artizans or persons likely to make use of the Schools'.[8] Manchester policemen sold tickets to an Ambulance Review, distributed invitations to Old Folks' Treats,

---

2   LCI, 24 February 1908, PCA 120 Kormos.
3   LWCM, 23 July 1900, pp. 293–4.
4   MGO, 21 November 1913.
5   LCI, 16 November 1919, PCE 116 Cassin.
6   BPO, 31 January 1900, p. 131.
7   LCCO, 15 August 1919, p. 242.
8   BPO, 27 August 1902, p. 197.

and handed out tickets to the Lord Mayor's Christmas Charities.[9] Inspectors of Constabulary expressed alarm at governments using policemen to attend to weights and measures, food and drug acts, explosive acts, swine and cattle licences, sheep dipping, local taxation duties, election supervision, and other miscellaneous tasks.[10] But local governments with regulations to enforce found policemen to be more convenient and cheaper than hiring inspectors.

The growing use of motor vehicles added more laws to enforce, public safety problems to resolve, and regulations to follow. Traffic created frictions between policemen, the driving public, and pedestrians, and between policemen handy with cars, those left on foot patrol, and those working hazardous new traffic points. Regulating intersections, stopping speeders, protecting pedestrians, and removing obstructions took up a growing share of constables' time and energy. To cope with these new responsibilities, men were pulled off of regular beats to create traffic and communications departments. Men spent their shifts directing traffic at busy intersections. Telephone exchanges were set up and motorcycle policemen appointed to respond to emergencies quickly. Instead of hiring men to cover regular beats left empty by policemen moving into these new positions, watch committees introduced police-box or pillar systems. Where practical, men patrolled on bicycles to allow fewer men to cover larger areas.[11] The men left on regular beats had more territory to cover and no longer had opportunities to perform appealing, specialist tasks now handled by separate departments. New technical skills that policemen hoped would bring them professional status were being segregated, creating an internal caste system. While new technology improved criminal investigation, it began to erode the quality of traditional beat policing as policemen became busier and stretched thin.[12]

---

9   MGO, 1 June 1901, 15 June 1911; for example, MGO, 6 December 1913, 10 December 1925, 14 December 1927. The practice was common enough by the 1930s that organizations in Birmingham were asking if they could use policemen to sell tickets. This finally convinced the chief constable to stop the activity (BPO, 22 November 1935, p. 24,596).

10   'Inspectors of Constabulary report for year ending the 29th September 1909', PP 1910 (106) lxxv, 587, p. 3; '... September 1912', PP 1913 (76) lii, 663, p. 4; '... September 1917', PP 1917–18 (173) xxv, p. 4.

11   Between 1911, when the Birmingham City Police amalgamated with Aston Manor, Erdington, Yardley, and other outlying districts, and the First World War, each constable was responsible for around thirty-two acres and 640 people. Even with new departments that pulled men off the streets, the 1930s had similar figures, around thirty-one acres and 630 people per constable. This meant fewer men actually walking street beats (BAR, 1911–1914, 1930–1939).

12   For more information on the decline of beat policing, see Joanne Klein, 'Traffic, Telephones and Police Boxes: The Deterioration of Beat Policing in Birmingham, Liverpool and Manchester between the World Wars', in *Policing Interwar Europe: Continuity, Change and Crisis, 1918–1940*, ed. Gerald Blaney. London: Palgrave Macmillan, 2007, pp. 216–36.

Having too many duties to carry out all of them, each constable decided which laws and regulations warranted his time and energy. Conscientious probationers may have tried to fulfil the surprising variety of tasks expected of them but they soon learned that no one could follow every order in a normal working day.[13] Not only that: enforcing every law made them unpopular with the public.[14] Constables had to prioritize their duties to what was practical and avoid unnecessary conflicts over trivial matters. They might enforce laws they otherwise overlooked during special campaigns against violations such as prostitution or youthful smoking, but they asserted their own priorities as much as they could. Obvious crimes and emergencies got attention since ignoring them could jeopardize their jobs. Catching thieves rewarded constables with mentions in the press and recognition from senior officers; it was also gratifying to protect people they knew from their beats. Constables tended to ignore a multitude of public order laws unless they involved public danger or hazards. Having no dog licence could be disregarded, but dangerous dogs could not. Not only did seemingly trivial public order laws not deserve precedence over preventing crimes such as theft, but enforcing some of them would leave constables despised by civilians. Offences such as obstructing footpaths, jostling, shouting, or using indecent language were handled on a case-by-case basis, getting attention only if someone complained or if someone was clearly being bothered. Chimney fires were difficult to overlook but constables did not always issue citations after they had warned occupants. Over time, constables developed a sense for when activities crossed a line and required attention, a line which could be quite different in different neighbourhoods or for individual constables.

About two-thirds of constables patrolled at night, and their primary activity was 'milking' doors – checking that locks on their beat were properly fastened. Buildings that required special attention were called lock-ups, usually warehouses and businesses. Owners left a key at the local police station so that constables could get inside if necessary. Constables gave this duty attention since they could get into trouble if they missed an unlocked door later found by another constable, or worse, if an open door they missed was linked to a burglary. Householders also informed local police if they were going out of town so that attention could be given to their homes. Chief Constable Dunning complained that lock-ups and houses were

---

13   For the nineteenth century, Carolyn A. Conley found that young constables tended to be overly strict but seasoned officers allowed 'normal if strictly illegal practices as long as no one was bothered'. *The Unwritten Law: Criminal Justice in Victorian Kent* (Oxford: Oxford University Press, 1991), p. 37.

14   Robert Reiner noted 'the casual recognition of the way the system relies on policemen *not* enforcing the law in the technically proper way' since this would overload the judicial system and alienate the public. *The Blue-Coated Worker: A Sociological Study of Police Unionism* (Cambridge: Cambridge University Press, 1978), p. 109, emphasis in original.

being left protected only by latches rather than watchmen, a practice 'encouraged no doubt by modern systems of insurance against loss by burglary',[15] and giving constables more work. According to annual reports, Liverpool constables found about ten insecure premises every night from 1900 to 1939; Birmingham and Manchester constables found nearly twenty.[16] During the war, even though numbers were lower with fewer constables to check doors, Chief Constable Caldwell wrote in frustration, 'The fact that last year over 2,000 premises were found insecure during the night time and for which special police protection had to be provided, shows a state of carelessness with regard to property which should not exist.'[17] The constable finding an unlocked door had to alert a nearby constable, usually on the next beat; one of them was left on guard while the other reported to the station. Owners had to be tracked down to check that nothing was amiss and to secure the building. All this left other premises unprotected and two beats vacant.

While checking locks, constables stayed aware of strange lights, unusual noises, and traces of illegal entry. Investigations of abnormal occurrences could lead to the discovery of lawbreakers stealing lead piping, stripping metal off roofs, breaking into warehouses and shops, or cracking open gas and electric meters. Breaking glass was sure to get a constable's attention. After hearing a window shatter, PC Ross found a broken shop door and a man inside. The solitary Ross persuaded the burglar that he had the building surrounded and convinced him to surrender.[18] A constable finding a burglar at a jewellers' shop used a similar ruse, running back and forth from the front to the back blowing his whistle and yelling that the building was surrounded. The burglar jumped from a window, threw a dustbin at the constable and ran away, only to be caught a few blocks away.[19] A less energetic constable, hearing noise from a lock-up shop, kept watch while another constable went to the station for the keys. They captured the man inside in possession of ninety-three paint brushes and sheets of gold leaf.[20] Constables often found another policeman before approaching potentially dangerous criminals. While examining the back of a jewellers', PC Coffey heard a noise and saw that the padlock on the shutter was broken. Looking in, he saw a man taking jewellery from the window display. He got help, threw open the shutter, and captured the thief in spite of a blow from the

---

15   LAR, 1903, p. 15.

16   LAR, 1900–1938; BAR, 1903, 1913, 1916–1927, 1929–1939; MAR, 1901, 1902, 1904, 1906, 1907, 1909, 1911, 1913. While it is possible that Liverpool constables were less adept at finding insecure doors, or that Birmingham and Manchester businesses were more careless at locking up, the difference in numbers probably reflects how each force determined what counted as insecure premises. Overall, average numbers of insecure premises found do not change dramatically between 1900 and 1939.

17   LAR, 1916, p. 2.

18   MWCM, 1 July 1936, vol. 202, no. 53.

19   MWCM, 27 April 1939, vol. 222, no. 76.

20   MWCM, 29 July 1909, vol. 44, no. 96.

thief's pry bar.[21] A hotel robbery was prevented when a constable found a window with the putty removed. He told his sergeant, and they caught the burglars on the way out.[22] But more careful burglars who left no outside signs and exercised caution regarding noise and lights were unlikely to be bothered by a constable.

Familiar with the regular occupants of their beats and with their normal patterns, constables scrutinized strangers and strange behaviour. They caught men carrying housebreaking tools at night, but also children stealing letters from post-boxes and coins from automatic machines. In the 1930s, Manchester and Birmingham had a rash of cases where thieves stole milk bottles from house steps, leading to constables stopping anyone carrying milk bottles soon after the delivery truck came by.[23] The first step was generally talking to the individual. One man simply replied, 'I stole it' when PC Warwick asked him about a bag of coal.[24] Spotting a stranger rolling a cask down the street, PC Gainham asked him where it came from. The man told him to mind his own business. This naturally made Gainham suspicious and the cask was identified as stolen.[25] A constable seeing anyone running, especially while carrying something, was likely to stop them. Two constables stopped a man running with something in his hand and found that he had a lady's watch. When they did not believe his story that he was catching a train, he gave them the watch and asked them to let him go, without success.[26] A common form of theft was stealing goods displayed outside shops or off trucks, such as when constables caught two men with a roll of bacon and another with rabbit skins, both lifted from stationary trucks.[27] Houses, particularly their front entry ways, were vulnerable. PC McConnell arrested Elizabeth Wickinson for taking two shawls from a house[28] and PC Whittaker caught Elizabeth Bradshaw with a gold-topped umbrella stolen from an entry.[29] HMI Leonard Dunning frequently complained that shopkeepers created their own problems by displaying goods outside shops within easy reach of thieves and a constant temptation to the poor, and that householders

---

21   *Police Review and Parade Gossip*, 13 April 1922, p. 177.

22   MWCM, 13 October 1901, vol. 16, no. 7.

23   MWCM, 1935, vols 191–5; Fancourt, 'The Police Service of Fancourt', p. 5; 'Interview with George Frederick Fancourt', pp. 6–7. During an epidemic of burglaries, the postal workers union complained that their members were being stopped at night by constables who had flooded the district in an effort to catch the culprits. To solve this problem, postal workers began carrying membership cards to prove that they were indeed postal workers (BPO, 27 March 1934, pp. 21957–8).

24   MWCM, 10 November 1900, vol. 13, no. 7.

25   MWCM, 8 April 1901, vol. 14, no. 44.

26   MWCM, 24 September 1900, vol. 12, no. 24. Perhaps he would have been more successful in his bribery attempt if only one constable had been present.

27   MWCM, 23 December 1902, vol. 18, no. 20; 6 January 1930, vol. 137, no. 7.

28   MWCM, 7 June 1900, vol. 11, no. 4.

29   MWCM, 30 September 1901, vol. 16, no. 7.

left their homes vacant and protected only by common latch locks, trusting that constables would protect their property from their own carelessness.[30]

Policemen were often part of a modern 'hue and cry', chasing lawbreakers first seen and pursued by civilians.[31] In a typical example, PC Morgan was walking his day beat when he heard cries of 'stop thief' and saw a man running with something in his hand. He caught hold of him and a woman came up and accused the man of stealing her purse. When the man was searched he was found to have not only her purse, but two others and a necklace.[32] Most chases involved such petty thieves, with dozens of examples every year. In a more modern and dangerous version of this kind of pursuit, PC Dixon responded to shouts of 'police', and found several people trying to drag a drunken man from behind the wheel of his car. Hearing Dixon shout that he was a police officer, the man broke free and started the car. Dixon jumped on the running board. The man cried 'I bloody well know who you are – but I am not stopping for you', and speeded off in a zig-zag pattern down the street, striking out at the constable. Dixon's leg was hit by a passing tram car but he managed to keep his grip. The car was finally stopped by other drivers blocking the road.[33] In this case, the constable needed the public to end the chase as well as begin it.

Constables risked accidents every time they went on duty, suffering three injuries from common mishaps for every two caused by crowds or prisoners. In Liverpool from 1907 to 1918, a constable got into an accident every third day. After the war, the many young constables were twice as accident prone, one getting hurt two out of three days.[34] While dramatic injuries and deaths did occur, most were mundane and even absurd by-products of the beat. Just walking, a major part of a constable's life, was a hazard owing to bad lighting, weather, and the poor condition of streets and walkways. Constables stumbled and skidded over boxes, orange peels, and tramlines. Losing his way during a heavy fog, PC Short blundered into

---

30   'Inspectors of Constabulary report for year ended the 29th of September 1918', PP 1919 (38) xxvii, 671, p. 3.

31   Petty theft of clothes, food, coal, money, and other valuables made up the majority of crimes dealt with by policemen. David Philips found a similar willingness of the working class to use the justice system to prosecute thefts that affected them. His descriptions of petty thefts of clothing, food, and so on, were similar to those I found, even to the laments against shopkeepers leaving items out in ways tempting to steal. *Crime and Authority in Victorian England: The Black Country, 1835–1860* (London: Croom Helm, 1977), pp. 127–9, 177–218. See also Emsley, *The English Police*, p. 229, and Joseph Fowler, 'From a Convict to a Parson' (Greater Manchester Police Museum: unpublished notebook, 1912), duty lists.

32   MWCM, 13 October 1901, vol. 16, no. 7.

33   MPF, 2 October 1929, PCD 90 Philip Dixon, appointed May 1923. Dixon received seven stitches on his leg and a £2 reward.

34   LCI, 1907–1929; 1937–1939. Injuries caused by crowds and prisoners are addressed in Chapter 6.

a stack of timber, breaking his nose and injuring his back.[35] PC Parry broke his collar bone slipping on a cooked potato.[36] While patrolling an icy quay, PC Brown lost his footing and fell into the river.[37] PC Wright collided with a lamp post during the war blackout and cut his nose, 'owing to darkness'.[38] PC Charters got crushed against a door in a rush of dock workers eager to be home.[39] The high winds off the Mersey River were a special hazard in Liverpool. Constables were constantly blown off their feet and off their bicycles. Trying to close the gates of the South Docks, PC Byron had them blown out of his hands and was struck in the face.[40] Even without wind, constables continually caught their hands and feet shutting the dock gates. Accidents resulted when constables tried to do too much on their bicycles. PC Irving tried to close a set of gates without getting off his bicycle, [41] and PC Poston tried to hold a prisoner in one hand and his bicycle in the other.[42] Both ended up falling over their bicycles.

When duty required climbing walls and across roofs, constables injured themselves due to fatigue, clumsiness, and simple bad luck. Constables investigating strange lights and unusual sounds were forever spraining their ankles and scraping their hands attempting to scale walls. Security spikes were particular hazards. PC Delaney, trying to discover why a shop light was on,[43] and PC Winstanley, searching for the source of excessive light during the war,[44] both tore their hands on spikes. Young constables over-estimating their abilities seemed prone to more severe injuries. PC Rogers managed to pull a coping stone on top of himself while investigating noises, fracturing his right leg, puncturing his left leg and fracturing both feet.[45] Getting into chases across rooftops could lead to disaster. PC Evans fell through a roof while chasing a burglar and was severely injured. To add insult to injury, the watch committee had to pay to repair the roof.[46] PC Wilson and PS Morgan unsuccessfully tried to get an insane man off a roof. The man kicked the sergeant off a ladder and pelted the constable with bricks until he fell as well. Both men had multiple injuries.[47] While such serious injuries were rare, most constables suffered a mishap or two at some time in their career.

---

35   LCI, 17 December 1916, PCE 141 Short.

36   LCI, 8 October 1903, PCB 171 Parry.

37   LCI, 4 December 1925, PCC 221 Brown. He was successfully rescued.

38   LCI, 18 November 1916, PCG 53 Wright.

39   LCI, 10 December 1904, PCE 128 Charters.

40   LCI, 11 June 1928, PCE 252 Byron.

41   LCI, 21 July 1919, PCG 70 Irving.

42   LCI, 16 December 1919, PCG 161 Poston.

43   LCI, 4 November 1903, PCD 67 Delaney.

44   LCI, 28 April 1916, PCB 251 Winstanley.

45   LCI, 18 March 1921, PCG 188 Rogers.

46   BJSC, 25 March 1925, PC Evans, p. 43.

47   LCI, 7 May 1923, PCB 143 Wilson, PSB 32 Morgan.

If nothing demanded their immediate attention, bored constables found ways to break the monotony of routine. Policemen discovered a surprising variety of ways to liven up their work. On a slow July night, a constable and sergeant stopped by a shop to play on automatic machines,[48] and at 5:35 one June morning, a startled superintendent discovered PC Crawford with his helmet in his hand, singing and dancing.[49] After the war, the many young Liverpool constables either faced senior officers without a sense of humour or had a gift for absurd behaviour. They introduced unnecessary flourishes into salutes to members of the city council, the watch committee, anyone in uniform, and visiting dignitaries, and were ordered to stop it.[50] One Liverpool constable, coming out from refreshments with his colleagues, 'all bored to death, waiting to go round again, flings his cape round his shoulder, took his helmet off, and started dancing down the road, throwing flower petals about'.[51] Some mischievous constables took linoleum doormats from the steps of houses and switched them around during the night.[52] Filling out paperwork and writing reports was one of the more dreary activities constables faced. Birmingham policemen livened this up by using extravagant language in place of simple statements of facts, much to the annoyance of Chief Constable Rafter.[53] Liverpool required a standing order warning them against 'the waste of time and stationery by the use of exaggerated headings and of unnecessary blank lines'.[54] Most efforts to relieve the tedium of routine were harmless but every now and then a constable got carried away. Manchester PC Chorley made friends with Thomas Green, a watchman with a fear of the supernatural. Chorley decided to have a bit of fun on his rather dull suburban night beat by scaring Green. Putting white paper over his uniform and helmet, Chorley cried out in a high-pitched voice, 'Oh Master, Oh dear, come here.' His scheme worked so well that Green hired a man to sit with him and the neighbourhood was 'in a state of terror'. Finally, a few men arranged to wait up to catch the ghost and Chorley was dismissed for 'behaving in a manner unbecoming of a Police Officer' due to the public nature of his misbehaviour.[55]

---

48 MGO, 13 July 1923, PCD 121 Albert V. O'Neill, PSD 7 Earle Nuttal, fined 2/6d.

49 LCCDR, 6 June 1930, PCE 96 Crawford.

50 LCCO, 25 October 1921. Soon afterwards, Manchester constables had to be reminded to start saluting when appropriate (MGO, 8 April 1927).

51 Brogden, *On the Mersey Beat*, p. 59.

52 Brogden, *On the Mersey Beat*, p. 59.

53 BPO, 11 July 1922, p. 19,600.

54 LSO, March 1912, p. 3.

55 MWCM, 9 January 1908, PCB 188 John Chorley, seven years' service, 1 default, vol. 38, no. 18. He wrote to the committee begging to be given another chance on account of his wife and five young children but without success. He wrote, 'I can only say in defence for doing such a foolish thing, I acted on the impulse of the moment, never thinking how serious my fun was going to end to me, and that it would cause people to complain of my conduct.'

Paying attention to obvious crimes, emergencies, and suspicious events was an easy call for constables to make but they were also expected to maintain public order. Clearly disruptive behaviour needed to be halted, similar to obvious lawbreaking, but many of these orders were ignored if no one seemed bothered. Constables developed their own set of priorities on what constituted a public order problem. They often distinguished between people doing business and people just being noisy, especially when neighbours found businesses such as peddlers or musicians beneficial. PC Hewitt left alone a hawker obstructing a walkway, and PC Taylor allowed a woman to sell flowers contrary to the Shops Early Closing Act.[56] Travelling musicians provided entertainment in working-class neighbourhoods. PC Ryan must have had fond memories of organ grinders since he twice got into trouble for allowing them to play even after householders complained, once when he was new to the force and again twenty-one years later.[57] Constables were expected to check that bands had permission to beg in the streets but few did.[58] No prosecutions took place for shouting false news to sell papers in 1900, and Rafter had to re-issue the order, insisting that constables make the necessary arrests.[59] Constables often ignored noise on holidays such as Guy Fawkes Night and Christmas. On New Year's Eve, PC Chambers was ordered to remain outside St Clement's Church to prevent revellers from singing and shouting during midnight watch services but he decided not to bother. While each constable had his own noise standard, no doubt many did not even register the normal clamour of neighbourhood life.

Complicating enforcement of public order was the fact that constables dealt with more than one public. Some liked a quiet and orderly city, while others enjoyed a little noise and liveliness. Disciplinary actions filed against constables for public order problems were more likely to come from civilians than from senior officers. Certain individuals seemed to thrive on complaining about noise or obstruction of walkways and wrote letters to local police stations accordingly. Senior officers did not have time to worry about every law and expected constables to exercise good judgment on what to ignore and what to give attention to. Constables had to determine which public they were dealing with when deciding to act. A common grievance was with groups of young men standing on street corners. They may have 'earned the condemnation of all respectable citizens' but working-class boys and

---

[56]   MGO, 30 October 1914, fined 2/6; LDRB, 28 August 1934, PCE 123 Taylor, fifteen years' service, one default, reduced.

[57]   Birmingham City Police Defaults Books, 1 October 1901, PCE Luke Ryan, joined January 1900, lost three months' leave; PC Ryan later ignored Harold Rollison's request to remove an organ grinder from his street (Birmingham City Police Disciplinary Book 'D' Division, 1 January 1923, pp. 37–8).

[58]   MGO, 25 July 1901.

[59]   BPO, 26 February 1900, p. 144.

teenagers picked up social and job information at these gatherings.[60] Constables such as Harry Daley remembered their own participation in such groups when they were younger.[61] Ignoring the law against obstructing street corners could get a constable in trouble with certain civilians and with particular senior officers. One Liverpool constable came up with his own arrangement for getting out of this dilemma. He explained,

> I used to go round and there'd be crowds of people standing at the corners by the pub, leaning against it. If I got a new beat, I'd go round the beat and say 'Get to the kerb!' and they'd move to the kerb reluctantly. As soon as I had gone they were back. So I got fed up with this. So I used to say to each crowd 'Look, when you see me or see my Inspector, move to the kerb and stay there. What you do after I've gone, I couldn't care less.' … I didn't use to curse or swear at them … the Chief Inspector walking down on a Saturday morning in full regalia and one of these fellows would nod and they'd always walk to the corner, and the Chief wouldn't say anything about it because they were on the corner and not causing any obstruction.[62]

Manchester PC Fred Wright had a similar arrangement with men on his beat.[63] The letter of the law was observed without actually enforcing the law and no one got into trouble. Similar strategies kept complaints down and minimized the inconvenience for people who lived more public lives.

A surprising number of public order rules involved children, 'unruly' children offending a great many letter-writers with strict standards of proper childhood behaviour. These orders were usually ignored as long as children were not in danger. Constables stopped children from playing near railway lines or busy streets, and tried to stop the dangerous practice of boys swinging on the back of moving vehicles. But they were less strict regarding orders to keep 'May dressing' and 'May Queen' parties of children out of the centre of town, though there was 'no serious objection to their parading the back streets in their own localities'.[64] An order to arrest adults sending children to fetch beer or supplying beer to children in unsealed containers produced no prosecutions, and no doubt some constables sent their own children on such errands.[65] Manchester school principals complained that

60   Robert Roberts, *The Classic Slum: Salford Life in the First Quarter of the Century* (Harmondsworth: Penguin, 1974), pp. 155–7.
61   Daley, *This Small Cloud*, pp. 22–5, 66–9.
62   Brogden, *On the Mersey Beat*, pp. 98–9.
63   MPF, 15 March 1933, PCC 118 Fred Wright, joined March 1930; full account given on pp. 92–4.
64   MGO, 12 October 1900; MGO, 22 April 1914; 17 July 1914.
65   BPO, 2 May 1909, p. 10.

policemen had relaxed their efforts to prevent children from buying and smoking cigarettes.[66] One constable must have enjoyed raiding gardens as a boy since he twice failed to take the offence seriously. The Rev. John Quinlan complained that he had sent for the constable to stop four young lads from loitering in and around his garden and stealing apples but the constable treated the boys sympathetically and had to be compelled to take them to the station. The constable had done something similar a year earlier regarding another illegally entered garden.[67] Constables could have different opinions about what deserved their attention. Asked by PC Everitt to help him clear a street of boys playing football, PC Siddon declined, not considering the game to be a problem.[68] As with other public order situations, constables acquainted themselves with expectations for children on their beats and adjusted their responses accordingly.

A growing number of police duties had nothing to do with preventing crime or maintaining public order. Since constables were present on the streets already, difficulties that required immediate attention tended to be handed to them for solution. People asked them for directions and for lunch recommendations. Constables took charge of lost children, property, and animals, and they offered advice to married couples, parents, and children. They rendered first aid in homes, at businesses, and on the streets. They rescued people and animals from waterways, buildings, and fires. Their public services responsibilities proliferated with the spread of the telephone, as more and more of the public decided that calling the police was the simplest way to resolve a problem, regardless of its relationship to law and order. Reflecting this change, the 1923 edition of the Manchester Police Instruction book stressed that, 'Each constable is a public servant in the fullest sense of the term, not merely to the individual but to the community as a whole.'[69] This statement did not appear in the 1908 edition. At the same time, the *Police Review* shifted from referring to the police 'force' to the police 'service', recognizing that a fundamental shift had occurred.

Not certain where to go, those who found property and those who lost it turned to the police force. Lost property grew as a problem along with the increase in public transportation. Instead of handling lost property themselves, public transportation companies had tram, omnibus and cab drivers turn over to the police umbrellas, gloves, handbags, brief cases, books, spectacles, hats, and other odds and ends that passengers left behind. Lost items handed in to Birmingham rose steadily from 3,540 in 1900 to 6,165 in 1920 and then skyrocketed to 29,818 in 1929, and 59,310 in 1939.[70] All of it had to be labelled and stored until recovered by

---

66   MGO, 12 January 1916.

67   LCCDR, 2 August 1934, PCG 139.

68   BPO, 5 May 1906, PCC 31 John Hy Siddon, leave stopped, p. 371.

69   City of Manchester, *Police Instruction Book* (1923), p. 13.

70   BAR, 1900–1939. Miscellaneous items included an artificial leg, a barrel of oysters,

owners; after three months, finders could reclaim items. About a quarter of items were never claimed and had to be stored and disposed of somewhere. By the 1930s, owners reclaimed only about a quarter of their possessions, dropping by half from before the war. When Chief Constable Moriarty took over in 1935, he made it easier for finders who now regained about half of items. Sifting through this mountain of stuff, verifying ownership, and organizing storage took an enormous number of man hours for something not clearly a police responsibility.

A child lost on a police beat was a duty difficult for constables to ignore. Both civilians and constables came across lost children, and children sometimes handed themselves over constables or walked into stations. Not all children wished to be found but constables could not leave them to wander the streets alone, leading to the occasional foot race. Lost children were taken to the local station, and their parents identified and notified. Policemen had to entertain, feed, and comfort children until collected. Between 1900 and 1914, Liverpool police stations hosted around ten children every day. After the war, numbers declined to around five children a day.[71] Birmingham also dropped by about half, from around six a day to about three.[72] Stricter school attendance enforcement took children off the streets, and schools themselves were improving, both as buildings and in curriculum, making children less likely to skip.[73] Also, since policemen were increasingly occupied with traffic or given extra beats, fewer were available to handle lost children.

While lost children could be classified as an emergency, neighbours also reported neglected or abused children to policemen. Constables investigated and sent any confirmed reports to the National Society for the Prevention of Cruelty to Children. This was not policing in a traditional sense but rather a modern social service. In one case, a neighbour pointed out three children, aged six, three and two, to PC Fowler. His investigation found that the parents spent every day begging, and that the children were 'badly neglected by want of food & clothing, as their parents was continually out drinking from a early hour in the morning until late hours at night'. The elder boy 'stated that neither he nor the younger children had, [sic] had anything to eat that day as they had no bread in the house'. The entire

---

barrister's robes, birds, bookmakers' charts, bottles of spirits, Christmas puddings, coffin plates, crates of soap, false teeth, firearms, footballs, a glass eye, gramophone records, horses bridles, a human skull and arm bones, kettles, legs of mutton and pork, perambulators, roller skates, a sun dial, teddy bears, telephones, a tiller of a boat, and wireless sets.

71 LAR, 1900–1938. Before the war, Manchester police found an average of twenty-two children a day; numbers for after the war are unavailable (MAR, 1901, 1902, 1904, 1906, 1907, 1909, 1911, 1913).

72 BAR, 1900, 1903–1905, 1913, 1919–1939.

73 G.A.N. Lowndes, *The Silent Social Revolution: An Account of the Expansion of Public Education in England and Wales, 1895–1965* (Oxford: Oxford University Press, 1969), pp. 127–89. See also Stuart Maclure, *A History of Education in London, 1870–1990* (London: Allen Lane, 1990).

family slept on one verminous mattress.[74] Two constables who wrote full accounts of such cases both deplored the alcoholism that contributed to the terrible state of the children. Constables also kept a look out for children eligible for help from Police-Aided Clothing Associations (PACA). Each child's situation was investigated, often by a constable, and clothing given out from a police clothing depot.[75] While neglected and needy children clearly demanded attention, it was not an obvious police matter and investigating cases took constables away from other duties.

While not as important as coping with lost and neglected children, constables also responded to reports of lost or stranded pets. Stray dogs and cats had to be captured, brought to the station and looked after until their owners, if any, could be notified. Dogs and cats not claimed were destroyed or moved to other premises. Constables handling strays were constantly scratched, bitten, and knocked over. While stray animals could be a public nuisance, the police seemed to be left coping with them because they took care of other lost belongings. In 1919, Birmingham stations did not have adequate food or kennels for the volume of stray dogs and could not get Chief Constable Rafter to respond to the problem. Fed up, policemen allowed Mrs Blanckensee, secretary of 'Our Dumb Friends League', access to a station to inspect the conditions of the dogs. Learning that they were dependent on the charity of policemen for scraps of food, she approached several superintendents who accepted her offer to supply the dogs with biscuits, meal, drinking troughs, and pens. Several hotels offered to allow her to collect scraps to make dog food. She sent a letter to Rafter outlining this program. Since it reflected poorly on the force, he protested that they were quite capable of keeping the dogs properly and inquired into who had let the woman into a station. Only then did he ask superintendents if it were true that the dogs were not properly fed and official steps were taken to remedy the situation.[76] In the end, the stray dogs and cats got proper care which was the main concern of the policemen.

Constables rescued pets, even though rescues had little to do with public order and more to do with public relations since rescues tended to attract sympathetic crowds and newspaper coverage. One daring Manchester sergeant made it into the newspapers after being lowered by a rope from a window overlooking the River Irwell, risking a fall into it, to save a cat wedged between a pipe and the wall of a factory.[77] It was difficult to ignore a distressed cat or dog, especially if appealed

---

[74]   Fowler, 'From a Convict to a Parson', p. 104. Thomas Smethurst described an equally neglected group of children in *'Mems.'*, pp. 127–31. Policemen generally had a weak spot for children, leading to sometimes contradictory behaviour. Brogden described a constable who casually clobbered a prostitute but kept candy in his pockets for children (*On the Mersey Beat*, pp. 101, 110).

[75]   For more on the PACA and other police service activities, see pp. 215–20.

[76]   BPO, 8 February 1919, pp. 503–4.

[77]   *Police Review*, 14 September 1928, p. 724.

to by a similarly distressed child, but constables also received rewards from the Royal Humane Society and other like minded organizations. PC Grisdale received a Silver Medal from the National Canine Defence League after saving a dog swept down a river onto the footings of a bridge. The frightened dog bit him five times before the constable could secure him.[78] Bites and scratches from scared pets were a normal part of rescues. A cat PC Herald freed from the rafters of a house severely scratched him, and an Airedale rescued from a dock by PC Liston bit the constable on the face.[79] Trapped pets even tempted senior officers into rescues such as when Liverpool Inspector Butcher saved a puppy from a canal while out on an inspection patrol.[80]

The heroic rescues of pets dropped in number after the tragic death of Manchester PC Tom Jewes in 1933. According to the local grapevine, an ex-boxer, William Burke, had arranged with a friend to 'frame' a kitten's rescue from the River Irwell and take a collection from the crowd. After stranding the kitten near Victoria Bridge, Burke went down a rope to a nearby ledge, caught the kitten, and tried to carry it back up with him. The kitten, frightened by Burke, fell into the river, and returned to the ledge. Burke tried again but slipped and fell into the river. PC Jewes heard shouting, ran to the river, and jumped in to rescue the man. Burke struggled with him and both men disappeared under the surface. A bystander went down the rope after them but could not find either man. Eventually they were discovered drowned. The kitten was rescued by policemen recovering the bodies and taken to a cats' home. The route of Jewes' funeral procession was lined by an estimated 20,000 people, bringing central Manchester to a standstill.[81] Jewes died attempting to rescue the man rather than the kitten but, after this, policemen were prohibited from putting their lives in danger to save pets by order of both police forces and the Royal Humane Society.

In 1877, the St John Ambulance Association was created, and by around 1900 passing the St John Ambulance examination in first aid became mandatory in most police forces. The 1899 Liverpool annual report already stressed the shift from complete police ignorance of first aid in 1879 to the systematic training of all policemen.[82] The public began to expect police assistance in emergency medical situations not only for street accidents but also at businesses and homes. For many, no other realistic option existed if they could not afford to call in a doctor. Besides applying first aid, these cases required that constables keep the injured calm and control spectators. The numbers of first aid cases increased steadily, and the

---

[78]   MWCM, 14 March 1932, PCA 285 Grisdale, vol. 159, no. 2.

[79]   LCI, 1 March 1937, PCF 68 Herald; 13 July 1923, PCE 178 Liston.

[80]   LCI, 10 June 1926.

[81]   *Police Review*, 23 June 1933, p. 468; Duncan Broady, *The Police! 150 Years of Police in the Manchester Area* (Manchester: Archive Publications, 1989), p. 18.

[82]   Quoted in *Liverpool City Police. Instructions* (1903), p. 14.

situations became more diverse. Before the war, Manchester constables attended to nearly 3000 first aid cases a year, Birmingham constables handled around 1550 cases, and Liverpool constables handled around 770. In the 1920s, this increased to 3200 a year in Birmingham and to 4500 in the 1930s. Liverpool saw an increase from 900 to 1500 for the same years.[83] In 1929, Manchester handled 10,131 calls for ambulances and this number nearly doubled by 1931.[84] The differences between the three cities may have been a result of how actively each city supported first aid or simply how cases were counted, but what is clear is that numbers kept increasing, doubling in Liverpool and tripling in Birmingham. With civilians turning to the police with growing frequency, first aid became another element of a constable's responsibilities.

First aid cases tended to involve minor wounds, sprains, and ailments, but policemen were also called upon to apply tourniquets, treat poison cases, and improvise treatments under stressful conditions. Constables rarely had access to first aid kits and improvised with what they found nearby. One constable called in for internal haemorrhaging grabbed ice from an ice cream vender to stop the bleeding,[85] and another scraped whiting from a ceiling to treat a case of spirit of salt poisoning.[86] Both adults and children regularly called constables into their homes to give aid. Treating women with burst varicose veins was a frequent task, constables having to intervene before the women bled to death. The yards of working-class houses provided special hazards, such as when a child was pulled apparently dead from a well. PC Hooper was summoned and revived the child with artificial respiration.[87] Cooking disasters, falls down stairs, sudden illnesses, and other domestic misfortunes sent people scrambling to find a constable. In one case, a twelve-year-old girl scalded herself while home alone looking after her younger siblings. She later explained, 'there being no one else in, I ran from the house and saw a police officer and told him what had happened'. Getting supplies from a grocer, PC Chatham bathed her legs with bicarbonate of soda, bandaged them with his handkerchief, and gave her tram fare home.[88] The introduction of gas lighting into homes increased the number artificial respiration cases, which could take anywhere from half an hour to five hours of work. Men walking their

[83] MAR, 1902, 1906, 1908, 1911; BAR, 1900–1911, 1913–1939; LAR, 1900–1938.

[84] MAR 1929, 1931.

[85] BAR, 1910, p. 33; *Police Review*, 24 June 1910, p. 299.

[86] BAR, 1909, p.34.

[87] BAR, 1906, p. 27.

[88] MPF, 25 December 1938, PCA 217 Walter Chatham, appointed February 1936. Florence, age twelve, was at home looking after a two-month-old baby, a two-year-old, and Harry, age eleven, while her father was visiting her mother in the hospital. The grocer gave her a cup of tea with rum in it and a bag of fruit as a present. Harry followed her and was impressed by the attentions of Catham and the grocer. It was not clear who was watching the other children.

beats could face frantic householders or landlords with an unconscious person on their hands. It was not unusual for servants, usually girls, to be found unconscious in their beds from gas poisoning. Constables sometimes treated people too poor to afford professional medical care, and forces were willing to give or lend money for a doctor if the alternative was to let someone die. In one case, a constable found a woman in a dangerous condition after an accident at home. Since she was alone, he called a doctor. Because the woman was 'in poor circumstances', the watch committee agreed to pay the doctor's fee.[89]

The most gruesome cases tended to be at businesses or connected with traffic. Individuals rarely came out well in accidents involving machinery. Constables could be asked to cope with traumatic injuries such as a man whose arm was torn off by a mill band,[90] a youth who severed fingers in a press machine,[91] and a woman badly scalded by boiling lacquer.[92] After a siphon of carbonic acid gas exploded in the City Arcade, shattering the bones of an employee, PC John Barrier applied bandages and splints to save the man's leg.[93] The most disturbing injuries involved traffic and trains. PC Scotson had to stop the bleeding of a man whose leg had been crushed under a vehicle, severing arteries, and another constable was called to help a railway constable who had been run over by a train, losing his left leg and right foot.[94] Accidents involving children were especially upsetting. While directing traffic, PC Sebborn was told that a boy had fallen onto a railway bed and had his neck across the electric rail. Sebborn stood on his rubber traffic mackintosh, grabbed the boy's clothes, and pulled him clear. He applied artificial respiration but the boy was already dead.[95] While many men never saw anything worse than cuts and scrapes, they had to be prepared for such crises, a prospect most had not considered when joining the force.

Constables were often the first to discover fires, particularly at night or early in the morning. Their knowledge of local conditions could save lives since they knew whether or not a building was occupied. When two constables found a shop on fire at 2:00 am, they knew that two women lived above the shop. They tried to awaken them by banging on the door. They finally broke a window with their truncheons, climbed in, and brought the women out.[96] Being familiar with the types of businesses could also prevent disaster. Noticing a smell of fire, PC Walters traced it a furniture store. Next door was a shop that stocked inflammable paint.

---

89   LHCWC, 19 June 1905, fee 7/6, p. 185.
90   BAR, 1907, p. 25. He stopped the bleeding and saved the man's life.
91   BAR, 1913, p. 33.
92   BAR, 1911, p. 34.
93   BAR, 1911, pp. 32–3.
94   BAR, 1913, p. 34; 1911, p. 34.
95   *Police Review*, 17 January 1938, p. 10.
96   MWCM, 3 February 1900, vol. 10, no. 18.

He warned a girl working late to leave before anything exploded and called the fire brigade.[97] Similar to first aid cases, fires could call for improvisation. PC Roberts, hearing screams at 6:40 am, discovered smoke coming from a bedroom window. Unable to get up the stairs due to heavy smoke, he found an ice-cream cart and climbed up its canopy to get into the window. He rescued the three occupants with the help of the gathering crowd.[98]

When not rescuing the public from accidents and fire, constables were fishing them out of rivers, canals, ponds, and the Liverpool docks. HMI Dunning remarked in 1914, 'the recognition of knowledge of the right way to rescue a drowning person ... as a desirable, almost a necessary, qualification in a policeman, is another indication of the growing habit of the public to look for help from the police in every form of trouble'.[99] Policemen had training in basic lifesaving and swimming, but dangers from exposure and their heavy uniforms made jumping into water hazardous. Jumping in alone could endanger the constable rather than help the victim. Liverpool PC Tiernan dove into a dock to rescue a woman but efforts by bystanders to pull them out failed when a line repeatedly broke. Tiernan swam to a lower section of wall but by then had been in the water for twenty minutes and was exhausted with cold. Luckily the night shift arrived and PC Harrington jumped in to help. All three people were finally pulled out with ropes and chains.[100] Lifesaving could be called for in bizarre circumstances. When a water main burst, it undermined the floor of a shop, throwing a woman and three children into the flooded cellars. Two constables pulled them out, saving them from drowning.[101] More typically, constables responded to cries for help from victims or bystanders, and could pull people to safety without entering the water.

Preventing and restoring attempted suicides, committed by means of poison, hanging, drowning or cut throats, were emergencies that could tax all a constable's diplomatic and physical skills. Men tended to choose cutting their throats or gas poisoning, while women inclined towards drowning or gas poisoning when contemplating suicide. Suicides did not always appreciate being stopped. James Mason severed a gas pipe during the night and tried to suffocate himself. PC Gameson helped revive him and sat with him while another constable went for help. Mason suddenly leapt for two razors and tried to cut his own throat. Gameson struggled with him and got the razors away from him briefly, but severely cut his hands. Mason got onto the constable's chest and held him by the throat with one

97   MWCM, 2 April 1935, vol. 192, no. 7.
98   MWCM, 5 January 1928, vol. 120, no. 80.
99   'Inspectors of Constabulary report for year ended the 29th of September 1914', PP 1914–1916 (209) xxxii, 187, p. 64.
100   *Police Review*, 10 January 1936, p. 38. Tiernan received the King's Police Medal for bravery.
101   MWCM, 5 February 1900, vol. 10, pp. 7–8.

hand and kept trying to cut his own with the other. Gameson managed to blow his whistle and was finally rescued, and Mason was stopped from killing himself.[102] Others were glad for their rescues. After her mistress berated her for breaking a glass that had been a wedding present, a domestic servant tried to kill herself by inhaling gas from a bracket. PC Fowler revived her to both mistress and servant's relief.[103] Thomas Smethurst prevented a man he knew from jumping off a bridge while the worse for drink because he was out of work and in debt. The man lived to find a new job.[104] Often, these attempts were complicated by domestic disputes. PC Bailey heard a woman screaming and found Elizabeth Lyons standing in the street at three in the morning. She asked him to go home with her since she had been quarrelling with her husband. John Lyons told the constable that his wife had thrown his supper at him, dish and all. Since it was a domestic situation, Bailey advised them to make it up. Shortly afterwards, he saw Mrs Lyons in the street again, heading towards the Rochdale canal. He followed, joined by Mr Lyons. Seeing her jump into the water, Bailey jumped after her, and after a struggle, succeeded in getting her out. While on the tow path the woman broke free, crying out, 'I want to die.' A doctor who had heard the constable's whistle finally calmed the woman down.[105] These cases could draw not only on a constable's first aid skills and his knowledge of his beat, but on his ability to remain calm when coping with desperate individuals and their distressed friends and families.

At the same time that public service duties demanded a larger share of a constable's attention, fewer constables were available to provide it. By the 1920s, traffic duty pulled men from regular beats to cope with the growing volume of vehicles. Traffic duty often received priority since traffic jams and crashes required immediate attention. Manchester frankly admitted that superintendents had 'to rob beats to provide men for traffic control'. In one division alone, eleven points required a constable to control traffic for twelve hours a day.[106] In Liverpool, traffic direction and control required around 300 men a day by 1929, about fifteen per cent of their policemen.[107] First aid and rescues had their positive sides for constables; traffic did not. It took men off beats, and they were rarely replaced; it was one of their more hazardous duties; and it created ill will from a public still learning to follow traffic directions. Automobiles, busses, and lorries competed for space with trams, bicycles, pedestrians, and a still large number of horse-drawn wagons

102 *Police Review*, 25 June 1909, p. 311.
103 Fowler, 'From a Convict to a Parson', p. 4.
104 Smethurst, *Reminiscences*, pp. 387–93.
105 MWCM, 5 February 1900, vol. 10, no. 16. Since attempting to commit suicide was a crime, she was brought to the station and charged. 'In answer to the charge, she replied "I intended to do it."'
106 City of Manchester, *Reports Relating to the Police 'Box' System*, 1927, pp. 1, 12.
107 LAR, 1929, p. 13.

and handcarts. Bicyclists, including policemen on duty, had collisions with other cyclists, cars, dogs, children, horses, and just about anything else that found its way into the roadway. Pedestrians and bicycles slipped on steel tram rails, and the wheels of bicycles and wagons kept getting stuck in them. One spooked horse bit the constable helping to free his wagon.[108] Confused and distracted pedestrians needed help safely navigating intersections. Constables had to keep all this traffic flowing in a safe manner. They ticketed unsafe drivers, they rescued people involved in wrecks, and they educated school children about safe traffic habits. Pedestrians, bicyclists, and drivers needed time to adjust to the increase in moving objects and to new traffic rules. For the first time, traffic brought the middle and upper classes into contact with policemen as lawbreakers rather than victims of crimes. These new offenders proved to be just as troublesome to constables as the more conventional variety.

A major traffic duty was 'points', directing traffic at intersections. Policemen always had directed traffic in busy areas but before the war the numbers involved were small. By 1918, a handful of traffic constables was no longer adequate, and an expanding number of constables were assigned to traffic-related duties instead of to regular beats. Many of these points stationed men on raised platforms in the middle of intersections but often constables simply stood in the road. To make their hand signal more visible, they wore white gloves which the men disliked and which they had to keep clean. Some had to wear unpopular white uniforms. Men directing traffic were constantly hit by passing vehicles. Their extended arms were frequent targets, such as when a passing tram hit PC Bishop's arm and knocked him down.[109] Men were trapped between vehicles passing too close to each other. PC Nelson ended up in the hospital after being crushed between two lorries[110] and PC Keeble got jammed between two horse-drawn wagons.[111] Others were crashed into by careless drivers, even by bicyclists. A lorry pinned PC Park against an electric standard.[112] PC Dutton was rammed from behind by a tram.[113] Simple fatigue made traffic duty risky. Manchester's Chief Constable Maxwell commissioned a study of traffic duties in 1928 and learned that most constables suffered from nervous strain if kept on point duty for any length of time. The fumes from passing vehicles undermined the men's health, already susceptible to respiratory ailments.[114] This study convinced Manchester to invest in automatic traffic signals. Both the need to preserve manpower and the hazards involved made their adoption a welcome

---

108 LCI, 3 June 1919, PCA 240 McKeown.
109 LCI, 26 June 1922, PCA 72 Bishop.
110 LCI, 12 October 1908, PCA 84 Nelson.
111 LCI, 15 December 1926, PCE 284 Keeble.
112 LCI, 3 September 1919, PCA 158 Park.
113 LCI, 23 January 1937, PCD 228 Dutton.
114 MWCM, 13 September 1928, vol. 126, no. 16.

change. Traffic signals became common in the 1930s though some particularly challenging intersections continued to be manned by constables

While everyone needed to learn safe traffic habits, police forces turned their attention particularly towards children. Children without traffic sense endangered both themselves and others. Small children were difficult for drivers to see, and constables had to be ready to haul children out of the paths of motorcars, tramcars, wagons, and bicycles, sometimes hurting themselves instead. PC Quillian pulled a child clear of a tram but the tram hit Quillian, dragging him and dislocating one thigh and breaking the other leg.[115] PC Power moved two children from the path of a bicycle, but was himself knocked down, fracturing his skull.[116] Children panicked in traffic. A boy pulling a handcart, thinking that he was in danger from a tram, let go of the cart and ran away. The cart rolled into the street, colliding with PC Pierce and spraining his ankle.[117] Constables were assigned as school crossing guards. This mostly involved stopping heedless vehicles and preventing children from walking into traffic but, like any duty, constables had to be ready for the unpredictable. While working as a crossing guard, PC Yardley saw a horse galloping towards him with broken reins flapping behind it. He managed to grab the horse's head and stop it before it reached the children.[118] Manchester PC Fowler became known as 'the children's friend' for patrolling a busy intersection near seven schools from 1928 to 1933. 'Each day I keep my eye on about 1,100 children who cross at this junction, and I'm pleased and proud today that during my five years there has never been an accident to a child.'[119] After the war, policemen began visiting schools every year to teach children safe road habits. In 1933, Manchester initiated a 'Safety Week' to teach road dangers and 'safety first' principles to elementary school children. By 1938, they were visiting over 200 schools a year.[120]

In the midst of the growing volume of motor vehicles and trams, streets still included horse-drawn wagons and vans. Stopping runaway horses was not a new part of traffic duty but it became more frequent with faster and noisier vehicles frightening horses still used for hauling. This crisis could not be ignored. Bolting horses endangered everyone around them, even more so if still pulling their loads. Catching these animals was one of the more dangerous duties constables faced, and it was rare for a constable not to be hurt. Accounts of constables stopping horses

---

[115] LCI, 2 December 1903, PCD 57 Quillian.

[116] LCI, 21 April 1904, PCA 176 Power.

[117] LCI, 17 April 1924, PCH 172 Pierce.

[118] *Police Review*, 24 February 1928, p. 160.

[119] PC7 Joseph Fowler retirement clipping, c. 1933, Greater Manchester Police Museum catalogue number 2723. For a photograph of school children presenting Fowler with gifts after his retirement, see Duncan Broady and Dave Tetlow, *Images of England: Law and Order in Manchester* (Stroud: Tempus, 2005), p. 61.

[120] MAR, 1929, p. vii; 1935, p. iv; 1937, p. 5; 1938, p. 52.

usually included how far the constable was dragged. In one case, the clanging bells of a fire engine frightened a horse pulling a heavy load of lumber. PC Ewan, who was directing traffic, grabbed the reins and was dragged eighty yards before he brought the horse to a standstill.[121] Not surprisingly, constables sprained ankles and broke bones. They skinned their hands grabbing at reins, and were kicked by rearing horses. They risked being crashed into and run over by the horse's load. Fatalities were unusual; constables were more likely to be permanently disabled since their legs were so vulnerable to injury if they were dragged far.

Adding to the confusion of city streets, loose livestock had to be chased down and captured nearly every week. Butchers ran animals through the streets on the way to their shops, and panicked animals often got away, providing a little excitement for witnesses.[122] In one thrilling chase, a constable and a sergeant pursued a loose bull in a newspaper van until the constable could throw his cape over its head and run it down a passage.[123] Constables rarely escaped cuts and bruises while corralling cattle. PC Millward jammed his wrist between a cow's horn and a wall after it escaped into a house, PC McKay skinned his knuckles removing a cow from a rear entry way, and PC Kirby strained his arm holding onto an escaped cow he cornered at the Pomona Garage.[124] When 'a drove of eighteen bullocks ran amok in Leeds St.', three constables were jammed against a wall, butted on the arm, and accidentally struck by a baton.[125] Sheep also could be troublesome but at least they were small. Panicked livestock qualified as both a traffic hazard and public order mayhem.

The increasing use of policemen for public service duties such as first aid, lost property and traffic control rather than their traditional crime prevention began to cause comment by both policemen and the public. Already in 1906, policemen complained that police forces treated them like convenient machines.[126] Chief Constable Dunning declared in 1908:

> Person, property, and the public peace are best protected by a sufficient system of patrol by police both in uniform and plain clothes, but it is this very duty which is being continually reduced, not only by the adoption of duties unconnected with it, for which men have to be specially detailed, but also

---

[121] MWCM, 14 January 1925, vol. 106, no. 34. The constable's action prompted numerous people to write the chief constable recommending him for his bravery, and he was awarded the Watch Committee Medal for Bravery.

[122] Robert Roberts remembered cattle being run to butcher shops in town, including a weekly 'mad bull' or escaped animal (Roberts, *The Classic Slum*, pp. 114–15).

[123] LCI, 15 March 1926, PCA 237 Rigby, PSA 11 Jones; *Police Review*, 16 April 1926, p. 234.

[124] LCI, 14 February 1904, PCD 300 Millward; 31 October 1904, PCC 156 McKay; LCI, 7 February 1928, PCA 127 Kirby.

[125] LCI, 5 June 1926, PCD 146 Angell, 78 McGregor, 199 Jones.

[126] *Police Review*, 1 June 1906, p. 261.

by assigning to 'the man on the beat' all sorts of odd jobs which divert his attention from his proper duties.[127]

HMI Terry agreed; 'It is a serious question whether any more miscellaneous work can be put upon the police without destroying their efficiency for the performance of their more primary duties.'[128] While policemen always complained that they had too much to do, they had some excuse in light of their growing number of duties that had little direct connection to crime prevention or public order.

During the First World War, when forces were well below authorized strengths, the fighting added more tasks to be carried out with fewer men. Policemen were lent to the army as drill instructors. Deserters from the armed forces were picked up and returned to the camp. Policemen were expected 'to protect and assist soldiers' wives in order to guard them from any conduct which may lead to the loss of their allowance, and possibly to the ruin of their married lives'. They guarded munitions factories, impressed horses, protected public works, and posted a wide variety of war-related notices. They captured escaped German prisoners. Men with an agricultural background were borrowed for spring ploughing and sowing.[129] Even Robert Roberts, who was rarely sympathetic to the police, noticed that the 'depleted police forces, manned mostly by elderly officers and "specials"' were 'burdened with new regulations every week'.[130]

The increase in duties continued in the 1920s and 1930s on top of the burdens imposed by traffic. Inspectors of Constabulary encouraged police forces to use telephones, cars, motorcycles, and bicycles to help men keep up.[131] While telephones were meant to direct police attentions more efficiently, instead they added to the demands on police time. Manchester acquired an exchange-board phone system in 1922.[132] In 1928, members of the public called over 3000 times; in 1929 this had quadrupled to nearly 12,000 calls.[133] By 1930, people were phoning

---

127 LAR, 1908, p. 18.

128 'Inspectors of Constabulary report for year ended the 29th September 1909', PP 1910 (106) lxxv, 587, p. 3; '... September 1917', PP 1917–1918 (173) xxv, 823, p. 4.

129 BWCM, 20 January 1915, p. 142; BPO, 30 August 1915, misconduct included excessive drinking, neglecting children and 'otherwise', p. 530; BPO, 30 August 1917, p. 152; 14 March 1917, p. 583; 2 April 1917, p. 594; BWCM, 4 April 1917, p. 265. A full description of war duties is found in 'Inspectors of Constabulary report for year ended the 29th September 1914', PP 1914–1916 (209) xxxii, 187, pp. 1–4.

130 Roberts, *The Classic Slum*, p. 206.

131 'Inspectors of Constabulary report for year ended the 29th September 1922', PP 1923 (55) xii, pt. 2, 267, pp. 6–7; Chief Constables' Association Annual Report, 12 June 1935, pp. 18–19; '... September 1935', PP 1935–1936 (43) xiv, 339, p. 5; '... September 1932', PP 1932–1933 (46) xv, 283, p. 6.

132 MGO, 11 August 1922.

133 MAR, 1928, p. vi; 1929, p. vi.

in their business rather than coming in personally or finding a beat policeman. The convenience in calling led to an increase in non emergency calls, such as noisy parties. Civilians blamed the diversion of policemen from crime prevention to traffic for the persistence of burglary and housebreaking even though, ironically, the beat policemen they missed were often busy investigating their own calls regarding barking dogs and miscellaneous activities 'about which there had been complaints'.[134] The police had so many new duties to perform that HMI Dunning suggested that the public be reminded that they, too, had a responsibility to 'set the law in motion'.[135] In 1926, a Liverpool superintendent took an early retirement, feeling that he was getting too old to handle the 'exacting demands of duty, and the enormous amount of legislation which in these days has to be assimilated'.[136] The Chief Constables Association agreed with him; 'there is little doubt that during the past twenty-five years the multitudinous responsibilities that have been placed upon Police Officers have made their duties much more onerous than was the case years ago'.[137] The image of policemen mainly spending their time walking a beat was increasingly out of date.

Police forces had to find a way to continue patrolling traditional beats while coping with traffic and telephone calls. Cities began giving two beats to a single policeman or leaving beats vacant due to shortages in manpower. Even with help from new technologies such as traffic lights, Inspectors of Constabulary warned that traffic collisions were increasing at such a rate that police responsibilities to protect life on the roads were more urgently required than protecting property.[138] Either more policemen were needed or some other authority had to take over the plethora of duties that overwhelmed policemen to the detriment of their original crime prevention and public order duties. But both of these alternatives cost money. Frequent reminders from Inspectors of Constabulary to

---

[134] 'Inspectors of Constabulary report for year ended the 29th September 1929', PP 1929–1930 (69) xvii, 1, p. 5; '... September 1930', PP 1930–1931 (40) xvi, 813, p. 10.

[135] 'Inspectors of Constabulary report for year ended the 29th September 1924', PP 1924–1925 (2316) xv, 177, p. 10. Dunning wrote in 1922, 'the duties of the police ... have been largely extended in answer to the demands of the ratepayer, who is more and more ready to call for a policeman to protect him from dangers other than those of crime, from something which he does not like because it interferes with his comfort and the social amenities, to perform some act of municipal service, to aid schemes of charity or social betterment, or to collect and supply information on which the private person may require on seeking a civil remedy for wrong where the criminal law gives none' ('... September 1922', PP 1923 (55) xii, Pt. 2, 267, p. 7).

[136] *Police Review*, 8 March 1926, p. 178.

[137] Chief Constables' Association Annual Report, 18 June 1931, p. 14.

[138] 'Inspectors of Constabulary report for year ended the 29th September 1924', PP 1924–1925 (2316) xv, 177, p. 11; '... September 1931', PP 1931–1932 (36) xii, 639, p. 8; '... September 1936', PP 1936–1937 (75) xiv, 695, p. 5.

watch committees to hire more men indicate that watch committees were not following the advice.

To solve the problem without expanding police manpower, watch committees invested in police-box and pillar systems in the late 1920s and early 1930s. The box system sounded good on paper. Policemen did not have to follow a fixed route and time was saved by not requiring duty parades. They could be summoned easily to call their stations by a flashing blue light on top, and sergeants could keep track of their men by recording 'check-ins' from the box telephones instead of walking their territory. But while the boxes saved time by doing away with parades, they isolated men who could go on duty, patrol for eight hours, and retire without seeing another policeman. Manchester Chief Constable Maxwell complained that the system did not allow for satisfactory contact among members of the rank and file.[139] As beats were made longer to cover manpower shortages, men became more concerned with getting to their next check-in on time than with patrolling. The schedules, complained one constable, did 'not permit him to examine thoroughly the houses, windows, shops and back passages on his beat'.[140] After his sergeant told him to get moving, PC Graham replied in frustration, 'I suppose you are like a good many more. You think I can run round the beat.'[141] Another sergeant had to be reminded that 'a too rigorous insistence upon the making of points at definite times made the working of beats automatic and therefore useless'.[142] Even worse for policemen, watch committees used the boxes as a way to save money on manpower and to postpone building new police stations. The Manchester watch committee requested a force reduction which the Home Office declined, considering that 'with regard to the extension of your Police Box scheme ... [and] your proposal to reduce the strength of your force ... it would be better to postpone any formal reduction of your authorized establishment for the present'.[143] Overall, the boxes did little to resolve the central manpower problem.

Manchester was one of the first cities to adopt the boxes, primarily for economic reasons. Their stations were old and the boxes were cheaper than renovations or building new ones. Manchester's watch committee had a reputation for penny pinching, and the city became heavily dependent on the box system. The floors of their boxes measured four feet by four and a half feet, and the walls were six and a half feet tall. The box contained a desk, stool, telephone, ambulance box, and electric stove. If the area had a bicycle beat, the bicycle sometimes had to be stored in the box as well. Police circulars on stolen articles and missing persons, daily orders, pawnbrokers' bills, and police gazettes tended to accumulate. Lost

---

139 MAR, 1936, p. 42.
140 *Police Review*, 2 May 1930, p. 324.
141 LCCDR, 13 May 1929, PCC 208 Alan Graham.
142 LCCDR, 23 May 1933, PSB 17 Irving, no charge framed.
143 MWCM, 20 December 1928, vol. 129, no. 34.

and found property, including dogs, added to the clutter. When the boxes were first introduced, the men were expected to take their meal breaks in them. Unlike stations, the boxes had no lavatories. Finding alternatives could be awkward, especially for the night shifts. Police-box instruction books showed a lack of faith in the constables. Men had to ring in at nine specific times during their eight hours of duty. At first, the constable had to note in the day journal which box he would go to next, but after protests this was changed to informing the police operator if he was working his beat to the left or to the right. Circulars were initialled to prove that the men had seen them and messages from headquarters recorded in the journal. When a constable wrote a report at a box, he had to inform headquarters as he began writing and record the time in the journal. When he had completed the report, he had to inform headquarters and record that fact in the journal. Sergeants were to check that the time taken was not excessive.[144] Combined with the longer beats they now had to patrol, all of this created a deep loathing for the police boxes among policemen.

Police-box restrictions undermined morale and encouraged insubordination. Constables quickly developed strategies to weaken the strict regime. They found ways to sit in the boxes for longer than allowed. When answering a summons to call headquarters, constables waited until they were ready to leave the box before they turned off the blue light, providing an excuse to be in the box legitimately. They did not use the heating stoves or internal lights excessively to prevent sergeants from noticing that the box had been used for a long period. A box located near several beats became a common meeting place for constables.[145] The men were warned that if any idling in the boxes occurred, the system of fixed-point beats would be revived but since this would require hiring more men, watch committees had a hard time making this threat convincing. In 1936, the Manchester Police Federation protested against the cramped conditions of police boxes and requested that other arrangements be made. Under pressure from Chief Constable Maxwell as well, the watch committee finally changed the box system in some divisions to a police pillar telephone system and built three new section houses for refreshment purposes.[146]

Most cities eventually adopted police-box systems and all came to rely on telephones. Liverpool resisted boxes at first, having an extensive system of substations. In 1928, Chief Constable Everett insisted that they did not need what he

---

144 From Manchester City Police, *'Police Box' System. Reorganization of the 'C' Division* (Manchester: Henry Blacklock and Co., 1929), pp. 32, 35; Manchester City Police, *'Police Box' System Instruction Book. 'C' Division* (Manchester: Henry Blacklock and Co., 1931), pp. 36, 51; *Manchester City Police Telephone Pillar System 'B' Division* (Chief Constable's Office, January 1938), p. 5.

145 R. Howard, 'The Tardis', *Journal of the Police History Society* (1990): 98–100.

146 MGO, 11 February 1936.

called 'the huts' but they put in a system of police call boxes.[147] Constables took out
their frustrations for having to call in check ins by slamming the doors of the call
boxes. This both disrupted the phone signal at the Switch Room and damaged the
phone cords. The problem became bad enough that the chief constable had to issue
general orders in 1929 and 1930 insisting that 'the door must not be *slammed*'.[148] By
1930, their watch committee began shutting substations and installing a box system.
Birmingham avoided 'the huts'. Under Rafter's leadership, they combined their
network of substations with police cottages that served as tiny stations. By 1933,
they had linked these to a telephone pillar system tied to police headquarters and
to each other. Similar to the boxes, the pillars had blue lamps that flashed to inform
policemen on the beat to call the station.[149] Constables there found a creative way
to protest the excessive reliance on telephones in place of direct contact with other
officers. When using public telephones, they were expected to pay two pennies and
be reimbursed, or to inform the operator that it was a police call so that the force
could be charged. The men never seemed to have two pennies, a circumstance
Rafter found difficult to believe, leading to enormous paperwork for the telephone
company. Regardless of the system adopted, a fundamental modification in policing
had taken place. In addition to constables now having to phone in their 'points',
both the boxes and pillars had telephones accessible to the public to enable them
to call for police assistance.[150] Rather than their usual patrolling, constables were
now often reacting to telephone calls. The ready access to telephones undoubtedly
improved public safety. But the ease of telephoning created a new habit of calling
the police for trivial complaints, consuming police time.[151]

Policemen fought the tendency to use boxes and telephones to decrease
manpower, insisting that mechanization be used as an aid to the policeman, not as
a substitute for him. They considered that the constable's personality was crucial
in establishing rapport with the public. Inspectors of Constabulary agreed that
police boxes and pillar systems were no substitute for the personal attentions of
constables to the fundamental duties of protecting lives and property.[152] They

---

147   LAR, 1928, p. 18.
148   LCCO, 13 October 1930; 9 October 1929, emphasis in original.
149   BPO, 20 September 1933, pp. 21,145–21,146.
150   BWCM, 5 May 1937, report no. 2, p. 5; BPO, 21 July 1939.
151   A 1973 study disclosed that social services made up over half of the calls to police forces
even though policemen tended to see criminal investigation as 'real' police work. The public
explained that 'it just seemed quicker and easier to call the police than anyone else'. The
study listed roles policemen played for which they had no formal training: veterinarian, mental
welfare officer, marriage-guidance counsellor, home help, welfare worker, accommodation
officer, and friend and confidant. The researchers were surprised at 'the incredible diffuseness
of the policeman's role', requiring 'basic shrewdness and humanity'. See Maurice Punch and
Trevor Naylor, 'The Police: A Social Service', *New Society* 24: 554 (1973): 358–61.
152   'Inspectors of Constabulary report for year ended the 29th September 1937', PP 1937–

continued to insist that police strengths needed to be increased, not decreased, as the development of speciality skills, such as wireless operators, mechanics, and photographers, tended to remove more men from general patrol.[153] The 1928–1929 Royal Commission on Police Powers and Procedure also disagreed with attempts to cut force strengths, concluding, 'Under present circumstances the Police are in danger of being overburdened with duties … if the imposition of new burdens on the Police continues, their number must be adequately and proportionally increased.'[154] By 1937, while new departments created new opportunities for advancement within police forces, it left 'the skimmed varieties for the consumption of the rest of the force'.[155] HMI Frank Brook warned,

> There is a danger that this specialisation may leave the ordinary patrol man with the odds and ends of police work. He may come to regard himself as merely a 'beat-walker' waiting for something to turn up, or a 'property-trier,' and I regard it as imperative that this should be counter-acted by giving all suitable men an opportunity of bearing a share in those duties which may be regarded as of greater interest and of greater value.[156]

Instead of technology helping policemen carry out their duties, it created new classes of specialized policemen and left the beat constables with more to do and less time to do it.

In spite of efforts to stay focused on traditional beat policing, policemen now carried out a growing proportion of public service duties. They grappled with the explosion of traffic duties and telephone calls while trying to carry out their regular rounds. HMI Leonard Dunning lamented that the English had grown out of the habit of policing themselves, hoping that they would learn to 'rely upon their own powers for the protection of themselves and their property instead of leaning on the police'.[157] The Desborough Committee shared his concern, observing that most people had forgotten that 'the citizen is still bound, at the direction of a magistrate, or on the appeal of a constable, to take his part in the preservation of the peace

---

1938 (53) xiv, 521, p. 5.

[153] For examples, see 'Inspectors of Constabulary report for year ended the 29th September 1931', PP 1931–1932 (36) xii, 639, p. 6, and '… September 1933', PP 1933–1934 (26) xiv, 711, p. 6.

[154] PP, 'Report of the Royal Commission on Police Powers and Procedure', 1928–1929, Cmd. 3297, vol. IX, 127, p. 82.

[155] F.T. Tarry, 'Mechanization as an Aid to Police Duties', *Police Journal* 6:2 (1933): 212; *Police Review*, 19 January 1934, p. 36.

[156] 'Inspectors of Constabulary report for year ended the 29th September 1938', PP 1938–1939 (83) xiv, 317, pp. 10–11.

[157] 'Inspectors of Constabulary report for year ended the 29th September 1918', PP 1919 (38) xxvii, 671, p. 3; also LAR, 1903, p. 15, 1904, p. 15.

and suppression of disorder'.[158] Civilian carelessness with their property as well as their now love of calling the police may have been a tribute to their good opinion of the police force but created more work than constables could manage. It is ironic that while policemen were performing more public service duties, changes brought about by traffic and telephones removed policemen from their beats. The policeman that people looked to for help was the policeman they met on the streets and there were fewer of them to be found. While it may not have been realized until the 1950s and 1960s that the relations between the police and the public had become harmfully distant, the seeds of this problem were being sown during the interwar period.

---

[158] 'Report of the Committee on the Police Service of England, Wales, and Scotland', Part I, 1919, Cmd. 253, vol. XXVII, 709, p. 4.

3

Discipline and Defaulters

Absent without excuse; Arrest, failure to; Arrest, unlawful;
Assault on Public; Beats, improper working; Beats, leaving too
soon; Dishonest practices; Disobedience of orders; Disorderly
conduct; Documents, losing; Drunkenness; Drinking offences;
Falsehood; Females; Gambling; Gossiping; Insubordinate
conduct; Incivility to public; Late for duty; Malingering;
Neglect to do some duty; Premises, not examining; Prisoners,
escape; Prisoners, not searching; Reports, failure to make;
Sleeping on duty; Smoking; Uniforms, damage; Untidiness;
Miscellaneous.

Categories of Disciplinary Offences,
Birmingham City Police, 1927[1]

T HE POLICE CONSTABLE who carried out his duties without question existed
only in fiction and police instruction books. Actual constables sidestepped
orders to make their jobs less irksome, ignored orders they considered unfair, and
made mistakes. Many infractions remained undiscovered or unrecorded; police
memoirs usually related at least one instance when a default went unnoticed.[2] One
new constable remembered senior men telling him the locations of safe places
to 'skulk in' and smoke, of peep shows, and of night watchmen with coal fires.
Though taking advantage of this information, he was never caught.[3] All constables
broke rules at some point in their careers if only because, humanly speaking, no
one could perform every single duty. Complicating their lives, the line between

---

[1]   BDRB, 11 March 1927.
[2]   PC Thomas Smethurst remembered not only falling asleep while manning the station
on the night of Queen Victoria's Diamond Jubilee but also locking the door so no one would
disturb him. He admitted that 'Had it occurred under ordinary circumstances, it would have
been considered a very serious thing' (Reminiscences, pp. 162–4).
[3]   Mark, In the Office of Constable, p. 22; served in Manchester City Police; no defaults in
surviving records.

exercising discretion and committing defaults was never stable. The same decision could be viewed as good judgment by one senior officer and as a violation by another. Some handled discipline more informally, giving unofficial warnings and advice to constables committing minor infractions. One sergeant found a constable making pancakes in a bakery in the middle of the night but never reported the incident, having made pancakes at the same bakery when he was a constable.[4] Other sergeants, often newly minted ones, could plague the ranks, reporting every minor infraction. PC Cole got reported for ripping up a pawnbrokers' bill for backing buttons he was sewing onto his traffic coat,[5] and PC Carson got in trouble for spilling water in a police box, and throwing tea leaves onto the footpath.[6] Superintendents and inspectors did not appreciate overly conscientious sergeants since official reports had to be followed up; they also set the divisional reputation for strictness or leniency and expected sergeants to follow suit.[7] Tolerance for some offences changed over time, and probationers were treated more strictly than veterans. While useless, violent, corrupt, or criminal policemen existed and might thrive in some settings, men whose judgment was too far removed from force standards were usually weeded out quickly. The majority of defaults were minor. Most constables had few if any infractions on their records, especially after the First World War.

Two basic types of defaults reached the record books: lack of action and too much action.[8] Police duties required constant attention to police regulations. Following this path was difficult, especially at three or four in the morning, common times for constables to be caught neglecting their beats. Neglect of duty cases accounted for seventy to seventy-five per cent of reported disciplinary offences for the entire period in Manchester, Birmingham, and Liverpool, with only a slight dropping-off in the late 1930s.[9] They covered any situation where constables failed to patrol their beats in the designated manner or failed to perform duties such as writing reports correctly. Constables who did not notice an insecure premise or who sat down on the job made up a high proportion of such defaulters. Alcohol-related offences made up a sub-category of neglect of duty, and typically both charges were made against imbibing constables. Less frequently, constables defied authority, with both good and bad intentions. Around twenty to twenty-five per cent of defaults included excessive actions of some kind, either against other policemen or against

---

4   Brogden, *On the Mersey Beat*, pp. 54–5.

5   MPF, 10 August 1931, PCB 222 George Frederick Cole, appointed July 1930.

6   MGO, 2 April 1931.

7   A senior police officer observed in 1990 that, once filed, a disciplinary charge could not be ignored, but that later the charging officer would be warned not to waste everyone's time on trivial offences.

8   Conflicts with the public are addressed in Chapter 6, gossiping with the public in Chapter 7, offences involving women in Chapter 8, and police domestic problems in Chapter 9.

9   LDRB, 1900–1901, 1905–1939; BDRB, 11 March 1927.

the public. These could occur when constables reached the end of their patience or took their discretion too far. Constables talked back to senior officers out of frustration or when they considered officers to have overstepped their authority. They took too much initiative, either resisting or overstepping force expectations. They invented duties to create a law and order that they considered to be fair. Police corruption made up a final though small part of this defiance of police orders. This varied from activities not considered wrong by the working class such as perks to serious but rare cases of burglary and extortion. Temptations to use the police uniform for illicit purposes faced constables every day though most decided that resisting paid them better than giving in. A final fraction of offences involved women; in Birmingham from 1921 to 1926, about three per cent of charges involved 'females'.[10] Rather than dramatic scandals, however, most police defaults involved minor failures to live up to expectations.

From 1900 to 1939, while neglect of duty charges consistently made up a majority of disciplinary cases, they shifted from a predominance of alcohol-assisted neglect to a majority of plain neglect. From 1900 to 1914, nearly half of defaulters were found drinking or drunk on duty, taken to the station to sober up, and sent home. Every year, the first week of January found a dozen men up on charges of being drunk and staggering from too much holiday cheer. Nevertheless, the rate of drinking was slowly declining. In 1889, just before the 1890 Police Act began attracting better recruits, one in eleven Liverpool constables was charged with drinking; this dropped to one in twenty by 1894 and to one in fifty in 1911.[11] The number of total defaults decreased at a similar pace. By 1910, when most pre-1890 men were gone, drinking cases dropped to about the same level as neglect charges without drinking. In 1913, HMI Eden noted with satisfaction, 'Convictions for drunkenness have certainly on the whole decreased very much in the last ten or twelve years.'[12] This decline reflected both a police generation shift and a change in working-class culture, where drinking and drunkenness were no longer so prevalent.[13] During the war, neglect with drinking made up about forty per cent of cases and without drinking around thirty-five per cent. The total number of defaults dropped by half, reflecting the decrease in personnel.[14] A higher

---

[10]   BDRB, 11 March 1927.

[11]   LAR 1911, p. 6.

[12]   'Inspectors of Constabulary report for year ended the 29th September 1913', PP 1914 (193) lxvii, 663, p. 3.

[13]   A.E. Dingle found that expenditure on drink declined while expenditure on tobacco increased. His conclusion was drink was more a response to than a cause of squalid living conditions. If applied to the interwar period as well, this would help explain the decline in police drinking in a period with relatively good pay ('Drink and Working-Class Living Standards in Britain', pp. 611, 621, 622).

[14]   LDRB, 1914–1918.

proportion of constables were older men and retirees, men less likely to be caught making foolish mistakes under lax wartime supervision.

After the war, defaults persisted in their decline. Working-class drinking continued to moderate and the 1919 Police Act generation, with its higher education standards, began replacing prewar constables. From 1920 to 1925, total defaults rose from the wartime lows but not to prewar levels. As well as a sign of the restoration of normal police numbers, this increase was largely due to the high per centage of young men learning their jobs. But a reversal had occurred. Before the war, drinking default rates mirrored total default rates. Now, neglect without drinking followed the overall default rate while drinking continued its steady descent. Plain neglect charges jumped to nearly sixty per cent of total defaults in the 1920s and drinking charges dropped to twenty per cent. Policing improved as drinking declined; drunken constables were less common and time was freed to focus on beat duties being carried out properly. Constables began to exercise greater care before endangering their futures in the force, creating an overall atmosphere of better behaviour. The total number of defaults declined rapidly after 1925 as the postwar recruits gained experience, particularly in Liverpool where three-quarters of the force was appointed in 1919 and 1920. During the high unemployment of the 1930s, many constables were older with families, so committing defaults was not worth risking. A slight rise in Liverpool defaults in the early 1930s reflected the end of the 1920s recruitment lull and new recruits again on the streets. But in 1939, Liverpool Daily Report Books listed only four defaults, excluding cautions.[15] Along with the steady fall in disciplinary cases, fewer constables were dismissed or forced to resigned due to misconduct. Before the war, nearly twenty constables a year were dismissed and ten a year asked to resign in Liverpool. In the 1920s, this dropped to thirteen, and in the 1930s to five, but now with two-thirds being asked to resign and a third dismissed.[16] This shift reflected a lessening in the severity of even career-ending offences as well as a willingness to give ex-constables a better chance to find new occupations. 1920s Birmingham matched Liverpool's rate of removals; most defaults were punished by fines, reductions in pay, or cautions.[17] Not only were fewer defaults being committed, the defaults that did get punished were rarely serious enough to end careers.

The handling of discipline varied from city to city, both in strictness and style, due in large part to the character of chief constables. Robert Peacock's General Orders in Manchester were matter-of-fact and avoided the discourses on school attendance, gossiping, and betting favoured by Birmingham's Charles Rafter in his

---

15   LDRB, 1900–1901; 1905–1939. Cautions and 'lateness' did not count as defaults.

16   LAR, 1900–1939.

17   BDRB, 11 March 1927.

Police Orders. When John Maxwell succeeded Peacock in 1926, he gave orders more in the Rafter style regarding saluting officers, gossiping on traffic duty, and similar concerns with their public image. When Cecil Moriarty succeeded Rafter in 1935, his orders did not have the same hectoring tone as Rafter, taking on a more professional polish. Liverpool's chief constables fell between the two, not lecturing but occasionally giving a homily in response to troubling disciplinary offences. The frequent changes in Liverpool's leadership, especially in a force notorious for its favouritism, gave less consistency and assurance to disciplinary actions, tending to vacillate from severe penalties to leniency for similar offences. Not surprisingly, Liverpool policemen felt the least confidence in their senior officers. Birmingham men resented Rafter's patronizing tone while Manchester men were generally satisfied with Peacock but at least the two men were consistent.

Levels of penalties varied, with Manchester typically having less severe penalties than Birmingham and both more lenient than Liverpool. Manchester's moderation resulted from having two chief constables who began their careers as beat constables and who understood the problems and resentments caused by fines and pay reductions that could seem out of proportion to offences. Robert Peacock set the tone for the twentieth century. When he was hired in 1898, his primary consideration was improving the force's morale after a corruption scandal in 'D' Division.[18] After years of favouritism and watch committee interference in shielding 'D' division officers, Peacock made restoring the trust of his men with a fair disciplinary system a top priority. In Birmingham, unlike the other two forces,

---

[18] See Eric J. Hewitt, *A History of Policing in Manchester* (Manchester: E.J. Morton, 1979), pp. 96–102. Briefly, from 1882 to 1896, Superintendent Bannister made Manchester's 'D' Division notorious for its intrigues with disorderly houses. He owned brothels in his division and protected them from prosecution with the assistance of Sergeants Cubberly and Bloomfield. Inquiries into the brothels in 1893 and 1895 only resulted in Bannister being reprimanded. The watch committee had appointed him against the wishes of the chief constable and it refused to act until PS Stephens helped constables collect evidence against Bannister in 1897. Division inspectors denied that anything was wrong and constables assumed that inspectors were aware of the real situation. See *In the Matter of an Inquiry re the Efficiency and Discipline of the Manchester Police Force. Before J.S. Dugdale, Esq., Q.C., Commissioner. At the City Sessions Court, Minshull Street, Manchester, On May 24th, 25th, 26th, 27th 28th, 29th, and June 14th, 15th, 16th, 17th, 18th, 1897. From the Shorthand Notes of Mr. Frederick William Baber, York Chambers, 27, Brazenose Street, Manchester* (Manchester: John Heywood, 1897). The chief constable resigned after the scandal, and Peacock was hired to restore morale and regain public trust. Into 1900, rumours declared that police witnesses against Bannister were being mistreated by the force. These rumours were strongly denied since nine of twelve witnesses had been promoted (*Police Review and Parade Gossip*, 9 February 1900, p. 66). A condition of Peacock's appointment forbade him to investigate past conduct of members of the force which meant PSs Cubberly and Bloomfield were not disciplined for their role in the scandal (*Police Review*, 7 April 1905, p. 163). Charges of scandal and tyranny were made against Peacock in 1905 by a city councillor but none of the charges were substantiated (*Police Review*, 7 April 1905, pp. 163–5).

Rafter relied heavily on stopping leave or stopping pay instead of on fines before 1919. He may have believed that losing leave weighed more heavily on men than paying a fine or, alternatively, that losing leave or pay was easier for families to bear than having to pay ten or twenty shillings immediately. Overall, Birmingham's penalties were higher than Manchester's by about five shillings. In Liverpool, the watch committee's obsession with economy encouraged higher fines than other forces, and frequent changes in chief constables gave them less authority over the committee to discourage this practice. Penalties for neglecting duty provide an example of force variations. Before the war, Manchester men were fined half a crown to ten shillings; after 1919, the top fine increased to twenty shillings. Birmingham stopped leave for two- or three-month periods or stopped one to two days pay before the war, the equivalent of about five to fifteen shillings, and gave five to twenty shilling fines afterwards with a few forty shilling fines in the late 1930s. Liverpool's neglect fines ran from five to twenty shillings prior to 1919 and from five to forty subsequently, nearly double the other two forces.[19] These heavy penalties, combined with inconsistent enforcement of discipline, contributed to Liverpool's chronic problems with malcontent.

Each city had its particular obsessions. Only Manchester had a systematic scale of fines for lateness, sixpence for every thirty minutes up to 1920, then for each fifteen minutes from 1921. Liverpool and Birmingham had few lateness defaults listed, presumably since sergeants handled minor offences, but fined those reported officially from five to twenty shillings. Birmingham was strict about gossiping, frequently stopping men's leave until further notice before 1919 and giving ten to twenty shilling fines afterwards.[20] The penalties for drink-related offences were far heavier in Liverpool than in the other two cities, even considering their overall higher fines. Typical fines ran from ten to twenty shillings before the war and thirty to forty shillings afterwards. All three cities cracked down on drinking in the 1920s. Peacock adopted a policy of dismissing men found drinking on duty to make it clear to young constables that the offence was not acceptable. For consistency with moderate penalties, Manchester was the best choice for a new constable unless prone to tardiness.

The shift from constables commonly drinking on duty in 1900 to tolerably sober constables in the 1930s ranks as the most fundamental change in police discipline. Before the war, drinking at work was accepted as standard practice for many working-class men, and some workshops allowed beer for employees on the

19   MGO, 1900, 1901, 1910–1913, 1914–1937; BPO, 1900–1939; LDRB, 1900–1901, 1905–1936; LCCDR, 1923–1939; LCCO, 1918–1922, 1926–1931, 1933–1939; for this and following paragraphs. See also Emsley, *The English Police*, pp. 235–41
20   Liverpool also had high fines for gossiping, giving 5/- to 20/- fines before the war and 5/- to 30/- following. Manchester had the lowest fines, stopping 2/6s. for gossiping before and 5/- to 10/- after the war.

premises.[21] Some constables had worked at such places before joining the force or had friends or family who did. In 1875 the entire Birmingham force defended their right to drink ale on duty in order to perform their duties properly.[22] The watch committee did not agree but drinking remained such a normal part of prewar life that some constables were found drunk on a regular basis. In 1900, PC Tinsley missed eight days of work 'through illness caused by drink', and in 1905, PC Wasley was reported for being 'continuously drunk for some time'.[23] A young PC Crennell was caught drunk on duty three times in three years; fortunately for his employment prospects, Chief Constable Dunning allowed him to resign instead of dismissing him 'as an act of kindness, as the man was not strong'.[24] The 1898 Manchester Constables Guide even advised men that, 'Experience has proved that coffee is better adapted for keeping the body warm and comfortable in cold and wet weather than spirits or beer.'[25] Many men preferred the second option. Finding a drink was rarely a problem. Licensees regularly left beer bottles for policemen on doorsteps so they did not have to enter public houses in uniform.[26] PCs Robertson and Edwards went so far as to take off their uniforms while on duty in order to enter public houses and drink ale.[27] Members of the public often offered constables drinks, mostly on holidays or to celebrate special occasions, but also during bad weather. Some constables carried flasks 'for medicinal purposes'. Drinking offences were generally accompanied by charges such as neglect of duty, sleeping on duty, absence from the beat, gossiping, insubordination, or fighting. Before the 1919 Police Act improved their conditions of service, low pay provided constables with little incentive to avoid risking their jobs over something that seemed unremarkable to many.

Conspicuous drinking at any time undermined the force's efficiency and damaged the reputation of the force. Due to expectations that constables be ready for duty at all times, drinking charges included not only being 'under the influence' or on licenced premises while on duty, but also drinking off duty. But constables considered their off-duty recreation as their own business and resented interference in their domestic habits. Enjoying a round or two of drinks at the local pub was too

---

21   Roberts, *The Classic Slum*, p. 123.

22   Steedman, *Policing the Victorian Community*, p. 108.

23   LDRB, 19 September 1900, PCC 153 Tinsley, joined January 1890, reduced; MWCM, 5 January 1905, vol. 26, no. 82; resigned on report. PCC 153 Tinsley had to 'resign forthwith' on 6 November 1900 for being 'absent from duty without leave 2nd to 4th inst.'(LDRB, 6 November 1900).

24   LHCWC, 13 March 1905, PCC 83 John James Crennell, joined February 1901, p. 63.

25   Manchester Constabulary Force, *Constables' Guide*, p. 9.

26   This practice continued into the 1960s according to police officers I spoke to in 1990, and quite probably long thereafter.

27   LDRB, 11 May 1907, PCD 98 Robertson, eleven years' service, five defaults, dismissed; 16 April 1918, PCC 91 Edwards, twenty years' service, three defaults, reduced two classes.

much a part of working-class culture to be given up. Generally, forces overlooked thin an long an men did not draw attention to themselves. The off duty PC Parker made the mistake of being intoxicated in uniform and then being rude to fellow tram passengers by refusing to wait in line.[28] Constables also needed to be careful that their off-duty beer was out of their system by the time they paraded for duty rather than showing up in a 'muddled condition'.[29] Besides drinking at pubs, the families of constables often fetched beer from public houses to drink at home, regardless of whether or not licensing laws were being observed. This was a common practice, and no doubt most constabulary families were never caught or reported for it. The wife of PC Welburn had the misfortune of meeting a conscientious on-duty constable after she got a jug of beer from a public house after licensing hours to take home to her husband. When he challenged her, she threw the beer into his face, making clear her opinion of licensing restrictions.[30] Constables needed to exercise care that their off-duty drinking did not affect on-duty responsibilities, but they persisted in enjoying their off-duty time on their own terms. The incongruity of constables breaking licensing laws did not seem to bother them.

The Christmas and New Year holidays were the least sober time of year. People offered constables celebratory drinks, often whisky and wine, even when constables came to the door to tell occupants that neighbours had complained about noisy parties. Every December, chief constables issued warnings against getting carried away by 'holiday spirits', hoping that 'the men will preserve their self respect and character during the coming festive season'.[31] In order to stop holiday drinking in Manchester in 1911, Peacock began a reward policy, giving every division that avoided alcohol charges during the holidays four hours off duty per man when duty permitted. But few divisions had met the challenge when the policy was reviewed in 1921.[32] The orders of Birmingham's Charles Rafter illustrate a persistent pattern of good years and bad years of Christmas cheer. On 12 December 1902, he announced that 'any further Constables becoming drunk on duty are to be suspended'.[33] He made good on his threat and the holiday drinking list was unusually long.[34] In 1904, no men were reported for drinking around Christmas, and on 21 December 1905, Rafter hoped 'that they will retain

---

28   MWCM, 27 August 1908, PCA 205 William P. Parker, fined 10/-, vol. 40, no. 176.

29   MWCM, 13 June 1901, PCC 86 Robert Roberts, twelve years' service, eleven defaults, to resign, vol. 14, no. 69.

30   MWCM, 29 October 1903, PCA 3 William Welburn, fourteen years' service, seven defaults, reduced three classes, vol. 22, no. 103. Welburn was charged with 'aiding and abetting' his wife, and she was fined five shillings for throwing the beer. The landlady was fined 40/- and costs for selling beer after hours.

31   MGO, 21 December 1911.

32   MGO, 31 March 1921.

33   BPO, 23 December 1902, pp. 308.

34   BPO, 2 January 1903, p. 322.

that good reputation they earned last Christmas'.[35] But on 27 December 1906, he again regretted the number of men reported for drunkenness, adding that 'people who offer drink to Police Officers ... are not their true friends'.[36] After Christmas in 1908, he expressed his satisfaction that the men had stayed relatively sober over the holidays.[37] Early in the war, Rafter was disgusted at the number of men reported for alcohol offences, considering it 'extremely unpatriotic', and he did 'not intend to palliate any further cases of this kind'.[38] On 24 December 1915, he congratulated the force for keeping sober.[39] Birmingham police managed to behave themselves for the rest of the war.

Yet in spite of the general drop in working-class drinking after the war, to be found drunk and staggering occurred regularly around Christmas time until the 1930s. In 1920 and 1921, Rafter warned constables to avoid persons who 'think it is an act of kindness to the Officer doing duty on the Beat outside in the cold and inclement weather, to wait for him and give him various drinks'.[40] Penalties became harsher, with more men dismissed for alcohol defaults. Manchester did not initially reinstate its prewar reward system, Peacock making it clear that men found drunk would be immediately suspended from duty. In 1922, he added, 'The Chief Constable hopes that at this time when employment is so scarce, members of the Force will, in their own interests, as well as in the interests of their wives and families ... refrain, when on duty, from taking intoxicating drinks.'[41] The following year, he had to repeat this warning.[42] After his death in 1926, Chief Constable Maxwell sent out a Christmas appeal for policemen to honour Peacock's efforts to 'raise the reputation of the Manchester City Police to a very high standard', and brought back the prewar reward system.[43] Ignoring this special plea, PC Feuring got drunk on Christmas Eve and threatened a cab driver.[44] Despite this setback, Maxwell kept the reward system, finding it useful in getting the men to police each other.[45] Maxwell's 1932 January orders included 'an appreciation of the

---

35   BPO, 21 December 1905, p. 278.

36   BPO, 27 December 1906, pp. 560–1.

37   BPO, 7 January 1909, p. 518.

38   BPO, 20 May 1915, p. 544.

39   BPO, 24 December 1915, p. 137.

40   BPO, 24 December 1920, p. 3031. 'NEW YEAR'S EVE ... The Householders are very much inclined to call in Police Officers from their beats and offer them intoxicating liquor. This is natural when persons are enjoying themselves and hear the Police Officer in the cold on his beat outside' (BPO, 31 December 1921, p. 4490).

41   MGO, 15 December 1922.

42   MGO, 20 December 1923.

43   MGO, 22 December 1926.

44   MWCM, 6 January 1927, PCA 56 Horace Feuring, eighteen months' service, dismissed, vol. 114, no. 70.

45   MGO, 20 December 1927; 20 December 1929; 2 January 1930.

splendid response … to his appeal for sobriety'[46] and in 1933, he gave his men a day off, instead of four hours, when the entire force had a clear holiday record.[47] By the 1930s, reported holiday drinking had effectively disappeared, a combination of changing working-class habits, police fears of unemployment, and perhaps civilians less able to afford being so generous with their spirits.

When charged with intoxication, constables came up with an excuse or mitigating circumstance to explain away alcohol-related symptoms. These claims rarely if ever worked.[48] Medicinal excuses were common and changed little over the years. In 1901, an inebriated PC Philpotts explained that he had been unwell 'and had carried some brandy about with him in his pocket, which had taken effect upon him'.[49] Twenty years later, PC Banks, suffering from a slight attack of malaria, drank some whisky 'thinking it would make me sweat which is necessary for that complaint, and not being accustomed to taking whiskey, it had the unexpected effect complained of'.[50] Constables caught after accepting holiday spirits often claimed that they had been drugged.[51] War veterans used their military service to explain away drinking. In 1921, PC Sohl related that he had been gassed in the trenches, 'and that causes me to always speak hoarse, and which is most likely, to make me look doubtful, and probably had a lot to drink'.[52] This story did not convince anyone. PC Bramley got into trouble after meeting up with an army pal after duty. He failed to tell his wife where he was and she telephoned his station to ask why he was not home. Dismissed for being drunk off duty in uniform, he petitioned for reinstatement, telling how he had entered the army at age fourteen in 1914 and served the entire war in the trenches. His war service combined with his clean seven-year record in the force got him reinstated at a reduced class.[53] Senior officers did make mistakes. Finding PC Gaffney too sick to ride his bicycle, Inspector Lloyd and PS Humphrey accused him of being drunk. The force doctor examined him and found him to be suffering from 'gastric disturbance', and not in fact too much alcohol.[54] Generally speaking,

---

[46] MGO, 2 January 1932.

[47] MGO, 6 January 1933.

[48] Peacock issued an order that in cases of drunkenness on duty, 'no excuse can be accepted' (MGO, 21 September 1921).

[49] MWCM, 20 June 1901, PCA 151 Mark Philpotts, twenty-two years' service, eight defaults, to forfeit two merit badges, vol. 14, no. 81.

[50] MPF, 25 June 1922, PCC 88 Richard Banks, appointed May 1919, reduced three classes.

[51] MGO, 20 December 1900; 23 December 1915.

[52] MPF, 13 August 1921, PCB 156 John Sohl, appointed November 1913, excuse not accepted, reduced two classes.

[53] MWCM, 17 October 1928, PCD 243 Wilfred Leslie Bramley, vol. 127, no. 15. He would later have domestic problems that led to an investigation. See pp. 281–2.

[54] MPF, 1 December 1936, PCD 184 Frank Gaffney, appointed September 1930. Gaffney complained of stomach pains which he attributed to the dense fog.

inebriated constables were better off telling the truth and hoping for sympathetic treatment. Senior officers had heard the excuses too many times already.

While constables might value their jobs enough not to be caught drinking, everyone yielded to the occasional temptation to sit down for a few minutes or to skip checking a few doors. Neglect of duty was the most common offence committed by constables, and remained so even as drinking declined. One of the more common misdeeds was lateness to shift parade or classes. The typical schedule of two months on night shifts and one month on day shifts made it easy for men to oversleep. Similar excuses for tardiness appeared again and again on disciplinary report sheets and no doubt many were perfectly true. Men forgot to release the catch on the alarm, alarm clocks failed to ring, men slept through alarms, and clocks stopped or were not wound properly. Single men at lodgings often relied on landlords or ladies to help them wake up, a system that sometimes broke down. Men cut themselves shaving, family emergencies kept constables awake past their bedtimes, and men misplaced parts of their uniforms. They missed trams and buses, or trams were delayed by inclement weather and accidents; bicycle chains broke and tyres punctured. They misread or forgot to read daily duty sheets, showing up at the wrong time.[55] It was an unusual constable who never arrived late for parade, though his infraction was not always reported. Every now and then, an otherwise decent constable just could not get himself to work on time. Appointed in 1919, PC Doodson was reported late to parade forty-three times by 1925, and twenty-two more by 1931. He must have had worthwhile qualities because he was not fired. He promised to mend his ways and managed to reach his pension. PC Brooks had similar problems.[56] Habitual lateness typically resulted in reduction in class or dismissal in all forces. Constables also had to be on time for classes, inspections, and other official events. When late for life-saving class, PC Barton tried to bluff his way by explaining that he had already been in the water and dressed again. He was unable to explain, however, why his hair and swimsuit were dry.[57] Constables could be just as challenged as anyone else in getting places on time.

Once constables made it on duty, they skulked, idled, and slept. Except in the livelier parts of town, walking a beat for eight to ten hours with only meal breaks could induce boredom and fatigue. Men found many refuges to sit out a cold or dull stretch of time. PC Gorton was found in a bakehouse, PC Bailey riding a tram car, and PC Villiers sitting in a watchman's hut smoking.[58] During

---

55   MPF, 1900–1939.

56   MPF, PCE 86 George Doodson, appointed May 1919. PCE 83 Eli Frederick Brooks had twenty-seven lates between 1925 and 1929 and forty-one by the time he retired in 1947 (MPF, appointed January 1922).

57   LCCDR, 14 June 1922, PCA 196 Barton, 'given benefit of the doubt as to his intention to deceive Sergt'.

58   BPO, 29 November 1900, p. 318; MGO, 28 March 1901; BPO, 20 June 1901, p. 475.

bad weather, constables found it difficult to resist temptations to take shelter. PC
Richards knew where to find a concealed key for a potting shed, and entered 'same
for the purpose of skulking'.[59] Smart constables had a good excuse ready. Found
in the Droylesden Cooperative Stores at 4:39 am, PC Evans explained that he had
been washing pots from supper and using the lavatory. He added, 'My use of the
lavatory is, in my opinion, contributory to my good health and not to be neglected.'
He was advised to take less time washing up.[60] When not skulking, men 'idled
their time'. PC Jones watched a football match, PC Dean was early to his point
and read a newspaper, and PC Chetwood was discovered coming out of the Grand
Turk bath house, 'his presence there not being required in the execution of his
duty'.[61] PC Lesley was found in the Metropolitan Theatre, PC Smith in the Prince
of Wales Theatre, PC Fox in a picture palace, and PC Cutler at a picture house.[62]
After taking a person to the hospital, one constable spent five and a half hours
waiting until the patient was admitted. Chief Constable Moriarty responded, 'It
is understood that this is not an isolated case … If cases of long delay at Hospitals
come under notice, Superintendents will enquire into the matter.'[63] Idling could
easily turn into napping. Not surprisingly, most men caught sleeping were on night
duty. At four on a July morning, PC Jones took a nap on the lawn in front of a
house, and a cab proprietor was surprised to find PC Foxcroft asleep in his harness
room at 1:30 am.[64] Idling, skulking, and sleeping tended to be handled on a case-
by-case basis. A constable with a clean record or a young constable still getting
used to the schedule usually got off lightly while men with a history of defaults
faced heavy fines and class reductions.

   Many men caught skulking, idling, or sleeping were found in pairs, talking
each other into unofficial breaks.[65] This was a double offence, since it not only left

---

59   BRB, 21 September 1903, PCB 180 John Luther Richards, joined July 1901, deprived of
merit stripe.
60   MPF, 8 November 1922, PCE 50 Norman Leslie Evans, appointed April 1920, fined 5/-.
A Birmingham police order in 1929 stated that in the last year fifty-seven men had suffered
stomach complaints ranging from ulcers to diarrhoea. Eight were seriously ill and two died.
'Most, if not all of this sickness, is due to constipation, which is caused by neglect of the
individual concerned' (BPO, 1 November 1929, p. 15980).
61   LDRB, 10 March 1911, PCE 145 Jones, four years' service; MGO, 31 August 1911; BRB,
18 July 1922, PCB 101 George Albert Chetwood, joined May 1913.
62   BPO, 24 September 1908, p. 424; BPO, 6 February 1913, p. 384; MGO, 19 December
1913, 2 February 1929.
63   BPO, 8 March 1939, p. 30429.
64   BRB, 18 July 1919, PCE 204 Thomas F. Jones, joined September 1907, leave stopped one
day, later dismissed for striking; MWCM, 2 November 1905, PCD 158 William Foxcroft,
fourteen years' service, seven defaults, to resign, vol. 28, no. 21.
65   Men committed other defaults in pairs, but neglect charges were the most common.
Evidence of constables committing defaults in pairs and frequently in company with civilians
contradicts Mike Brogden's argument that constables were so isolated that they 'carried a

two beats empty, but usually two beats close to each other. One long afternoon, PCs Culsham and Brown idled their time playing cards in a dock shed;[66] bored one December morning, PCs Nixon, Williams, and Ablewhite skulked in a stable.[67] On cool nights, napping together was one way to keep warm. PC Evans and another constable were found sleeping in a warehouse doorway at 3:45 am, though Evans tried to convince his sergeant that he was investigating an insecure door.[68] PCs Goode and Fensone managed to sleep through a burglar alarm going off near their shared doorway.[69] Preferring more comfortable surroundings, PCs Hatfield and Falconer napped together in easy chairs in the lounge of the Midland Hotel early one November morning.[70] The numerous cases of men neglecting their duty together show that they found ways to spend time with each other, despite the beat system being based on constables patrolling alone.

Most idling constables were found on or near their beats; more serious was abandoning their beats altogether. Men had legitimate reasons to be off of their beats, such as escorting prisoners or responding to emergencies; absences unrelated to their duties almost always involved constables impatient to go off duty or take meal breaks. Men went to the boundary of their beats nearest to the station to wait for their relief man or left their beats assuming that their relief would get there. After seeing too many such defaults in 1905, Rafter declared,

> If any further cases of men leaving their beats, or neglecting to work their night beats occur, the Chief Constable will be compelled to send them before the Committee with a recommendation for a reduction. This is too serious to be lightly dealt with. Constables seem to be too careless on this respect.[71]

A year later, Rafter had to warn men to stop going 'to the extreme front of their beats, near the Station, before they are relieved' since thieves were committing crimes after watching constables leave. He concluded, 'The police are in fact being watched by the thieves and not watching them.'[72] This practice became less frequent

---

mobile Panopticon' with them, and that constables were unable to seek collective solutions to collective problems (*On the Mersey Beat*, pp. 36–7, 163).

[66] LDRB, 28 April 1925, PCC 109 Culsham, five years' service, PCC 158 Brown, four years' service, fined 15/- each.

[67] LDRB, 18 December 1934, PCC 133 Nixon, thirteen years' service, two defaults, PCC 278 Williams, fourteen years' service, and PCC 51 Ablewhite, thirteen years' service, found 7:26 am.

[68] BPO, 11 October 1900, p. 280, leave stopped indefinitely and fined one day's pay for lying about his presence.

[69] BWCM, 29 September 1913, p. 55, Fensone cautioned and Goode's promotion deferred.

[70] BPO, 28 November 1930, p. 17406, fined 10/- each.

[71] BPO, 7 October 1905, p. 210.

[72] BPO, 15 November 1906, p. 521.

but it never stopped. As late as 1937, PC Barlow left his beat 'without authority' to take refreshments 'to which he was not entitled',[73] After the war, traffic posts, a difficult duty requiring standing in one place for long periods, were repeatedly abandoned. PC Clark left his traffic post for a meal break without waiting to be relieved. When asked who had relieved him, he replied, 'A228', an unfortunate choice since A228 had been with the sergeant the entire time.[74] PC Lindup left his traffic post because he was cold only to have a lorry sink into an excavation while he was gone. Rafter had 'not encountered a more gross and deliberate breach of duty for a considerable time'.[75] Most men were not this unlucky, managing to sneak off duty a little early without mishap.

A few reckless constables removed themselves from duty altogether, taking leave to which they were not entitled. Obtaining official leave could be difficult, even more so if constables wanted time off for specific dates such as birthdays or family gatherings. So they deceived officers to obtain leave, they left the city without permission, or they lied to extend legitimate leave. In a typical case, PC Ricketts asked for two hours of compensation time for attending an ambulance course, hoping that no one would notice that he had missed the class.[76] Even if constables received leave, they needed extra permission to leave the city since off-duty constables were considered a reserve force. On two occasions, PC Owen got leave to nurse his ill mother; on both occasions he used the time to leave the city instead.[77] When men did have permission to leave town, they were required to give addresses to their superintendents in case they were needed for emergency duty.[78] Wanting to enjoy his leave uninterrupted, PC Harcourt took annual leave and forgot to inform anyone of his whereabouts.[79] In order to stretch annual leave for a week or more, a number of Birmingham constables sent in medical certificates claiming illness towards the end of their leaves.[80] Since men were making false statements to their senior officers, they rarely got off lightly. PC McPherson lied 'with a view to obtaining a rotation leave day to which he was not entitled'[81] and PCs Tinsley and Fowler took unauthorized weekends.[82] PC Clark took advantage of special plain-clothes duty to disappear from the city for

---

[73]   MGO, 14 May 1937, PCC 37 Barlow.

[74]   MPF, 3 February 1926, PCA 51 David Peattie Clark, appointed November 1919.

[75]   BPO, 17 November 1927, p. 13535.

[76]   BDRB, 23 March 1921, PCD Edward S. Ricketts, fined 5/-, p. 24.

[77]   BPO, 24 August 1914, p. 254. He was warned that he would be dismissed if it happened again.

[78]   BPO, 11 August 1922, p. 5309.

[79]   BPO, 19 August 1926, p. 11633.

[80]   BPO, 4 September 1912, p. 249.

[81]   MGO, 17 December 1926, PCA 276 John McPherson.

[82]   LDRB, 6 November 1900, PCC 153 Tinsley, joined January 1890; 8 August 1908, PCG 157 Fowler, five years' service.

a morning.[83] All of these men were ordered to resign. But frustrated with not getting leave when they wanted it, men continued to make false statements and sneak out of town. PC Fancourt recalled leaving Birmingham without permission to take his wife on a visit to Dudley Castle without being caught.[84]

Malingering on the sick list was another way to neglect duty, either stretching a legitimate illness into extra days or feigning illness altogether. The most common reason to linger on the sick list was badly needed time off. Receiving one rest day in seven was not fully implemented until after the First World War, so feigning or exaggerating sickness was one of the few ways to get a break. In 1909, Birmingham reported problems with an 'enormous amount of sickness since 1892' and adopted strict rules regarding men habitually on the sick list.[85] Watch committee economics sometimes tempted constables to malinger. Under pressure from constables angry at having a shilling deducted from their pay for every sick day, in 1897 the Liverpool watch committee agreed to stop deducting the shilling but only for sick days over a week. They created an artificial epidemic as men stretched sick leave to at least eight days. In 1901, the chief constable convinced the committee to stop deductions for even a day's illness since men stretching out sick leave cost the city more in replacement constables than they saved in deducting pay for short illnesses.[86] Men sometimes faked illness to avoid unpopular duties. PC Pierce shammed illness to avoid station reserve duty and PC Sharpe exaggerated sickness to evade first day watch.[87] To excuse unsatisfactory performance on his beat, PC Oakes feigned a 'rupture'.[88] Misbehaviour on the sick list was also frowned upon. Men were supposed to get well, not risk missing more days through treating sick leave as regular leave. Yet while on the sick list, PCs Hemming and Revill were found gambling and playing cards after midnight[89] and PC Hawkins was found playing cards in the bar of a public house.[90] Not only did PC Morgan sneak off to the Empire Music Hall when on the sick list, he presented himself on stage during the performance and, not surprisingly, got caught.[91] Police authorities considered

---

83   BRB, 22 September 1937, PCE 285 William Henry, joined April 1931, two awards, married, one child, to resign.

84   'Interview with George Frederick Fancourt', pp. 19–20.

85   BPO, 24 March 1909, p. 559. For example, one man with twenty-four years' service had 367 days illness from varicose veins, and another with twenty-two years' service had 686 days from bronchitis and chest ailments.

86   LWCM, 29 April 1901, pp. 280–4. Sick days per year increased from 9497 in 1897 to 13,043 in 1901.

87   BRB, 25 February 1925, PCD 42 James Pierce, joined April 1923, to resign; BOR, 2 January 1936, PCC 61 Edward Everard Sharpe, five years' service.

88   BDRB, 8 August 1921, PCC 213 Charles Oakes, p. 41, transferred.

89   BWCM, 1 March 1915, p. 152.

90   BPO, 25 April 1901, p. 410, lost leave and put on six months' probation.

91   BPO, 27 February 1904, p. 116, Morgan lost leave and was transferred.

improperly reporting on the sick list to be a serious offence, requiring the cost of a replacement constable, visits from the force surgeon, and paying an unproductive constable's wages. Taking too many sick days was bound to be noticed, leading to days being added to the service required before retirement.[92] But similar to workers anywhere, constables persisted in calling in sick when they did not feel like working that shift.

One duty constables hoped to avoid through irregular leave was paperwork. For most, filling out forms and writing reports was a new requirement not typical for working-class employment. Constables neglected reports, both by not writing them and not writing them correctly. They constantly had to be reminded to record the visits of sergeants as required, and sergeants reminded to check that their visits had been properly noted in constables' notebooks.[93] In a typical case, a constable found an open door, had a resident secure it, and did not report the matter since it seemed trivial. Unfortunately for him, a witness told the proprietor that the constable had tried to break in.[94] While no doubt prewar constables avoided paperwork with the same dedication as their postwar colleagues, chief constables began to crack down on poor record-keeping in the 1920s and 1930s. While this was partly due to higher expectations for constables after the 1919 Police Act, it was mainly a result of the prevalence of traffic. Constables displayed 'considerable laxity' and 'gross carelessness' in noting down accurate or necessary details in street collisions, including registration numbers of vehicles which were incorrect half of the time.[95] To the embarrassment of forces, people calling at police stations to get particulars on accidents sometimes discovered that the constable present had filed no report. In one case, a constable did not bother to report that a bicyclist had knocked over a woman since she appeared unhurt. When her husband called the station to get the bicyclist's name, the constable had not taken down the information.[96] Rafter issued orders on the correct way to report occurrences in 1921, 1923, twice in 1925, 1927 and 1931, and still could not get men to report every event.[97]

---

[92] 'PCE 31 Patrick Slattery having been on the sick list for 15 days for a trivial cause, and having been 18 times on the sick list, totally 256 days during the last 10 years, making a total of 30 times sick with a total number of 395 days sickness during his service … the Watch Committee decided to … add 15 days on to the time he will have to serve for pension … as the Committee consider that he has been malingering' (BPO, 1 October 1919, p. 1207). Similar cases appear in the Birmingham order books.

[93] For examples, see LCCO, 31 August 1934; 15 October 1936.

[94] BPO, 20 August 1925, p. 10239. 'Next day the Proprietor of the premises called at the Police Station and informed the Reserve Officer that a man had told her that on the previous night he had seen a Policeman trying to break in … the neglect of duty on this occasion exposed the Constable to the risk of a very serious charge being brought against him.'

[95] MGO, 29 October 1920.

[96] BPO, 24 September 1927, p. 13300.

[97] BPO, 20 August 1925, p. 10239; 24 September 1927, p. 13300; 14 July 1931, p. 18323.

PC Eldridge refused to report a collision between a motorcar and motorcycle even after his sergeant had ordered him to do so.[98] Faking reports to save the trouble of doing them properly was also tempting. PC Dolphin regularly forged the signatures of policemen at the foot of reports to avoid the bother of tracking the officers down.[99] Policemen considered filling out reports to be so tedious that a popular joke related that if a road accident took place in front of a police station while the men were parading for duty, within two minutes no policemen would be within hailing distance.

Normally, constables avoided paperwork. One exception was reports on their own conduct in first aid cases and rescues since men might receive rewards and merit stripes for showing special skill and bravery. A few constables gave into the temptation to inflate their roles in rescues or even invent rescues altogether. When constables asked for recognition for drowning rescues, senior officers began to check stories after finding misstatements regarding the depth of water in order to make rescues appear more dangerous. Constables omitted details to make their actions more important. PC Hammond stated that he alone assisted at a traffic accident, forgetting to mention that a nurse had been present.[100] Constables exaggerated actions in runaway horse cases, PC Jones reporting that he stopped a horse that stopped on its own before he could catch up with it,[101] and PC Donnelly claiming that he stopped a horse when he had done nothing at all.[102] Because constables were often rewarded for particularly bold rescues, men got themselves into trouble for taking too active a role in soliciting award nominations. One constable was reprimanded for asking a person to recommend him to the Royal Humane Society for saving someone from drowning.[103] A creative constable forged a letter from a witness commending him in a first aid case. The chief constable noticed the similarity in handwriting, however, and sent the letter and a sample of the constable's writing to the Criminal Investigation Department for investigation.[104] Constables considered many reports to be busy work with no serious purpose except to monitor their behaviour. It is perhaps not surprising that the reports that did get attention and got constables into trouble were those where constables saw a benefit in it for themselves.

---

[98]   BDRB, 17 September 1922, PCE 262 Thomas Eldridge, p. 296.

[99]   BPO, 18 June 1924, to resign, p. 8507.

[100]   BDRB, 12 November 1927, p. 95, PCA 190 William Hammond, given benefit of doubt and not charged.

[101]   LDRB, 14 July 1905, PCF 100 Jones, nine years' service, dismissed, changed to reduction to lowest class.

[102]   BPO, 13 May 1904, p. 180.

[103]   BPO, 30 November 1910, pp. 384–5.

[104]   Birmingham City Police Superintendents Reports and Confidential Letters, 12 March 1907, outcome unknown, p. 303.

Just as constables resisted becoming model pen-pushers, attempts by police forces to get them to behave with proper decorum did not meet with universal success. Men generally followed orders to keep uniforms clean, but getting them to stand up straight was more difficult. Reminded that they were in the public eye, Manchester men were ordered to stop walking around 'with their hands engulfed in their overcoat pockets ... [a] very undesirable and slovenly habit'.[105] Birmingham constables were reprimanded for 'wandering about on beats in an irresponsible manner with their mouths open'.[106] Liverpool policemen were warned to stop lolling in the witness box with their arms spread across the sides, instead of standing properly at attention.[107] Manchester Chief Constable Maxwell deplored the unseemly and undignified practice of men running and jostling each other when dismissed from duty in order to board tram cars, leading to one constable being knocked down and his uniform damaged.[108] Liverpool policemen were ordered not to chew tobacco or gum while in uniform, and Birmingham's Rafter had been shocked to see a constable chewing gum during the two minutes' silence on Armistice Day.[109] Constables had to be urged to stop using slang. Rafter disliked the phrase to 'run in' people instead of to take a person 'into custody' since the phrase originated among 'the corner boys'.[110] Orders not to smoke or gossip were ignored since constables did not consider these to be detrimental to policing. Two constables fined ten shillings for gossiping with each other argued that they had been discussing a recurring problem with rowdy youths, not simply chatting.[111] Constables resisted constant reminders from chief constables to behave with dignity, ignoring finicky regulations that seemed pointless or even counterproductive to good policing.

Smoking in uniform was a particular sin, regardless of whether or not the constable was on duty, since it looked sloppy and suggested that the constable was not alert. Men on night duty kept having to be reminded that smoking rendered them inefficient since anyone could smell the tobacco, not to mention see the lit cigarette.[112] In 1900, after a constable was seen smoking a pipe, Rafter warned his policemen that these cases would no longer be dealt with leniently.[113] Twenty years later, policemen reported for smoking in uniform still maintained that it was a general practice, especially among band members.[114] In 1936, Rafter again had to

---

105   MGO, 18 March 1927.

106   BPO, 7 November 1928, p. 14,734.

107   LCCO, 2 August 1922.

108   MGO, 8 April 1927.

109   LCCO, 3 September 1919, p. 266; BPO, 4 February 1926, p. 10,881.

110   BPO, 15 October 1901, p. 549.

111   MPF, 28 January 1930, PCA 147 Edward Cassidy, appointed February 1927.

112   BPO, 25 March 1920, p. 1966.

113   BPO, 5 April 1900, p. 162.

114   BPO, 15 October 1920, p. 2755.

remind men to stop smoking after finding a man smoking a cigarette on duty.[115] But policemen preferred their tobacco to obeying the order. To continue smoking, men perfected the skill of invisible smoking, cupping their hands around the lit cigarette to hide the glow. Many simply hid. PCs Myatt and Anderson were both cautioned for being in lavatories smoking while on duty.[116] Orders might lessen the amount of smoking on duty but the habit was too ingrained for men to quit.

While neglect of duty made up the majority of defaults, a persistent twenty to twenty-five per cent of cases involved more active resistance to police regulations. These cases roughly divided into insubordination against senior officers and constables exceeding their duties. Insubordination involved constables talking back to senior officers, occasionally escalating into physical assault. It sometimes included constables ignoring orders out of belligerence rather than from a legitimate use of discretion. The constant appearance of insubordination both over time and throughout careers suggests that any constable could be overwhelmed with frustration with strict sergeants, with friends promoted over them, with problems at home, or with a myriad of other aggravations. Constables exceeding their duties were more difficult to categorize. Their intentions often began as good, trying to help the vulnerable against perceived injustices or carrying out rough justice. But these actions could end in constables breaking the law themselves or getting themselves entangled in civil matters where they did not belong. In the worst cases, constables could slip into tyrannical habits, enforcing their particular vision of law and order.

Insubordination in the form of 'speaking in a disrespectful manner' was the most common form of striking back. Defiant words were nearly always provoked by a specific remark from a senior officer on how the constable was working his beat, accounting for why any constable might succumb to the temptation. Constables particularly disliked being rebuked in front of civilians since this damaged their image and made their jobs harder. Sergeants received most of the abuse, since they were the officers who most often caught constables committing an error or who gave constables orders that they might not want to follow. The amount of 'lip' constables gave sergeants refutes any notion that they were cowed by their immediate superiors. Charges often included constables challenging the sergeant to report them. For example, 'On his attention being called by Sgt to certain entries in his memo book he (Con) said "You can report it if you think fit. I'm not afraid of you or anyone else in the Division."'[117] When PS Hanlon criticized PC Green's demeanour, Green replied, 'I wont be spoken to like a dog. If youve

---

[115] BPO, 20 February 1936, p. 25,015.

[116] Birmingham City Police Disciplinary Book 'D' Division, 12 February 1921, PCD 207 Robert Myatt, p. 3; 17 April 1928, PCD 236 Ernest Anderson, p. 99.

[117] LCCDR, 2 January 1925, PCA 170 Dempsey, fined 10/-.

got anything to say, stick it on paper.'[118] Constables rarely confined themselves to one remark. Another common reaction was to question the sergeant's tone. PC Halen told PS Bird, 'The next time you speak to me Sergt, speak decently. I am having no Prussianism.'[119] While constables assigned as acting sergeants might have come in for special abuse because of the fragility of their authority, constables gave acting sergeants the same treatment they gave full sergeants. Asked why he had not responded to Acting PS Watson's signal, PC Thomas replied, 'I did not hear your stick, I was working my fucking beat, that is all I know, and I admit I am 5 minutes late on this point. You can fucking well report me for that if you like.'[120] When handed a report against him by his acting sergeant, PC Jessop tore it into pieces.[121] Most insubordination was simply straightforward rudeness in response to criticism of their beat work.

Some constables took insubordination a step further, accusing sergeants of inventing charges to look like conscientious officers or, more seriously, of unfair practices. Failing to work his beat to his sergeant's satisfaction, PC Calland replied, 'Well, get it on paper & I will explain my movements. You are on the look out for a case.'[122] PC Hone believed that his sergeant was singling him out for special attention. After the sergeant asked him about the time of a crime, Hone retorted, 'I have two PCs to say it was 10.50 pm, you are trying to make a case of idling my time against me, the same as you have done with others. It is not the first time you have tried it on me.'[123] Constables accused sergeants of bullying them and abusing their authority. Found absent from his post, PC Douglas told PS Cronin, 'You are after me since I came down here. You are harassing me. Its the likes of you that is making all the men resign.'[124] Officers who were too strict could get on constables' nerves. Birmingham's PS Cockbill was a 'by the book' type who came in for regular abuse. After he found PC Toon sleeping in a hut, Toon accused him of saying, 'I shall dog you and watch you round your beat, and see if you go to the Watchman's hut again.'[125] Nine years later, PC Blyth told the now Inspector Cockbill, 'I know my job – you can report what the hell you like Mr. Cockbill, who the hell are you.'[126] Constables threatened to retaliate with charges of their own though they

---

[118] LDRB, 26 April 1932, PCG 156 Green, twelve years' service, three defaults, fined 10/-.

[119] LCCDR, 30 May 1927, PCH 292 Halen, admitted, cautioned.

[120] LCCDR, 8 November 1923, PCC 102 Thomas, cautioned.

[121] LDRB, 7 February 1928, PCH 253 Jessop, four years' service, fined 20/-.

[122] LCCDR, 2 December 1924, PCD 239 Calland, resigned voluntarily.

[123] LDRB, 28 June 1921, PCC 63 Hone, one year's service, fined 30/-.

[124] LCCDR, 30 September 1927, PCA 212 Douglas, cautioned.

[125] BPO, 11 January 1923, p. 5926, PC Toon to resign.

[126] BRB, PCC 276 David Edley Blyth, joined October 1926, reduced; BOR, 4 February 1932; BPO, 10 February 1932, p. 19037.

rarely followed through. Accused of gossiping, PC Watkins answered, 'You report us and I will bring that other thing up against you. I am getting out of your section this time anyway.'[127] PC Banks got himself into trouble after throwing away the supper of PS Dodds. A month later, Dodds accused him of being late to a point. Banks replied, 'Its fucking vindictiveness and spite. I know that you have been after me for years, Dodds, you and a few more have been after me.'[128] Banks clearly saw this as the latest act in a feud and he was transferred to another division to separate him from Dodds. Despite the insolence of these men, few had to pay more than a small fine or received a caution. More serious accusations got a constable reduced in class but men were rarely fired. Senior officers remained sympathetic to the occasional outbreak, having come up through the ranks themselves.

On rare occasions, a constable accused of insubordination succeeded in getting the sergeant charged with oppressive conduct. Superintendents took note as to whether any of their men developed bad habits, and a sergeant continually provoking insubordination was probably creating his own problems. After PC Bainbridge was reprimanded for talking back to PS Mathinson, further investigation found Mathinson guilty of abusive and insulting language to five constables over the previous two and a half years.[129] PS Stephenson lost his temper at PC West and shouted at him in front of a crowd, adding, 'You know West, when I was a young PC and the Sergeant used to get on to me, I said "Fuck the Sergeant, or bugger the Sergeant."' Despite being found guilty of oppressive conduct, two weeks later Stephenson was hassling West again. West was finally moved to another division.[130] Transferring men to separate them was a common option. After being accused of insubordination, PC Kirkwood was given the benefit of the doubt when PS Lowe was charged with tyrannical conduct. However, Kirkwood was also transferred away from Lowe.[131] Sergeants with a pattern of overbearing conduct could finally find themselves back at a constable's rank and at the mercy of sergeants.

While most insubordination charges give minimum information on circumstances, usually from the sergeant's point of view, one detailed 1933 Manchester case provides a constable's perspective on an exchange. It includes many of the typical patterns found in other cases. PC Wright thought that he was doing his duty based on his personal knowledge of regular routines after three years of service. In his statement, he described how he had set up a common arrangement between constables and regulars on their beats:

---

[127] LDRB, 13 March 1923, PCG 106 Watkins, three years' service, fined 20/- and transferred.

[128] MPF, 9 April 1933, PCD 88 Richard Banks, appointed May 1919, reduced three classes.

[129] LDRB, 13 June 1908, PCG 129 Bainbridge, thirteen years' service, one default, reprimanded; PSG 10 Mathinson, seventeen years, transferred, promotion postponed.

[130] Birkenhead Disciplinary Report Book, 11, 23 May 1925, pp. 170, 172.

[131] LCCDR, 13 February 1922, PCD 305 Kirkwood, PSD 10 Lowe.

three men are in the habit of talking to each other, for about five minutes three or four times a week, they are friends and Chadwick (24) and Livesey (18) take leave of Trainer (27) at this corner when they have been together. I have spoken to these three men previously asking them not to stay long, so as not to be too vindictive, and they have complied with my request.

Wright was about twenty-three years old so could sympathize with these friends. This kind of agreement was fairly ordinary. He continued,

[A]t about 11–0 pm I noticed these three men on the corner … I went to try the door near them. I did not speak to them and passed them, knowing they would only be a few moments longer. As I had passed them about fifteen yards I heard a stick knocking, on looking round I saw Sergeant Turnbull coming toward me, he moved these men from the corner … he said to me 'What's the idea of not moving those men?' I replied 'Well Sergeant they would only be there about five minutes' Sergeant Turnbull then said 'You know, no wonder they give policemen Raspberries when you don't move them.' I then said to him 'But Sergeant they are only saying good-night' He said 'How do you know?' I told him I was on this beat for a month and had spoken to them not to be long previously … Sergeant Turnbull then said 'If you're trying to be funny, you are being funny with the wrong one.' these words raised in anger towards me, I said 'I don't think I am being funny Sergeant!' He then said 'You're getting big ideas into your head!['] these words were also raised and a number of people were passing, these people noticed the Sergeant's agitation and appeared to be watching us both.

I then said to Sergeant Turnbull 'I don't care for the way you are shouting at me Sergeant before these people, If I have done wrong in any way you report me not shout at me.['] Those were the only words spoken by me. Sergeant Turnbull then appeared to lose his temper, and shouted 'All right I'll report you! You will be reported for neglect of duty.['] I said 'Right Sergeant' he then said 'I think you are being insolent!' I replied 'I am not Sergeant, I am speaking civilly and I expect the same back.['] Sergeant Turnbull then walked away from me, making no further statement. He had gone about ten yards when he knocked his stick again. I went to him and he said 'You will also be reported for insolence'. I said 'All right Sergeant'.[132]

Turnbull not only reported Wright for insolence and neglect, he reported him for slovenly appearance for having his hands in his pockets. Wright denied all the charges. He felt that he had been doing his job properly and resented being

---

[132] MPF, 15 March 1933, PCC 118 Fred Wright, joined March 1930.

accused of neglect, especially in public. Turnbull's comments seemed out of proportion to the situation and he must have been aware that such arrangements were common. But once the two men began such a public exchange, neither could back down easily. That Wright could write such an unflattering description of his sergeant suggests confidence in his version of events. Perhaps Turnbull was an insecure new sergeant or had a poor reputation as a sergeant. In the end, Wright was only fined five shillings, getting the benefit of the doubt from senior officers. Turnbull was probably given advice on how to supervise his men without creating such acrimony.

Rarely, frustrated constables assaulted senior officers, usually with a quick punch to the face. Many of these men had been drinking, with fewer inhibitions against venting their hostilities. Startled by his sergeant who found him drunk and asleep, PC Smith took off his belt and threatened to 'knock out the brain of PSC 9 Francis Taylor'.[133] PC Allibone and PC Handley were so ferocious in their drunken attacks on sergeants that they were bound over by magistrates.[134] Some attacks resulted after constables discovered that sergeants had reported them for disciplinary offences. PC Smallwood's sergeant accused him of improperly working his beat; he attacked the sergeant two days later when he discovered that the sergeant had filed an official charge.[135] Attacks could be a final sign of distress for constables unable to cope with policing. When coming off night duty, a sergeant reprimanded PC Bowcott for failing to work his beat properly. Bowcott 'called a Sergeant out of the Station, became very excited and hysterical and commenced swinging his arms about and struck the Sergeant in the eye with his fist. After a time the Constable calmed down and expressed his sorrow for the blow'. Bowcott had served two years in the force; this encounter convinced him to quit. He left the city, sending a telegram saying, 'I have decided not to bother any further in the matter.'[136] Similar to insubordination, constables were rarely dismissed for these attacks which were rarely serious. Even PC Handley remained on the force, shown leniency due to his nearness to retirement age.

A step beyond insubordination was refusing to obey direct orders. While many of these refusals were fleeting and minor, similar to insubordination, they also included major upheavals with constables defying all authority. Yet even these constables tended to calm down soon after they exhausted their outrage. Defiance had a wide variety of motives. It might be distaste, such as when PC

---

133 BDRB, 26 December 1922, reduced, p. 124; BRB, 10 January 1923, PCC 214 George Smith, joined February 1901.
134 BPO, 24 November 1909, dismissed, p. 160; LDRB, 10 May 1912, PCB 113 Handley, eighteen years' service, initially dismissed, changed to reduced to probationary class.
135 MGO, 17 June 1927, PC Smallwood, fined 20/-.
136 MWCM, 6 February 1930, PC Bowcott, two years' service, vol. 137, no. 24; MGO, 7 February 1930. He did not show up for his next parade and was dismissed.

Thomas refused to clean station windows and PC Barton refused to clean up the constables' kitchen.[137] PC Wearing could not face destroying a diseased cat and tried to chase the cat away.[138] It could be fatigue at the end of a shift. Coming off his beat and told that a sudden death needed attention, PC Roddan 'continued on his way ... saying "I don't want your job at this time in the morning" & went away'.[139] Ten minutes later in response to the same sudden death, PC Dodd replied, '"Oh well, I don't want to know anything about it. You havent told me" & went away.'[140] In more extreme cases, men refused to do duty at all. After seven years' service, PC Wright suddenly had had enough of night duty and refused to parade. He was warned that he would be sent to prison unless he returned to duty. Wisely not pushing the matter any further, he did.[141] Angry at his sergeant for accusing him of being off his beat, PC Finch went to the station and resigned after being ordered not to do so. He changed his mind about resigning, was fined ten shillings, and continued his career.[142] Even though failure to obey a direct order might appear to be a serious offence, most instances were sudden flare-ups that quickly died down. Men were cautioned or fined, given some advice, and put back to work.

A more urgent problem for police forces than insubordination was constables who exceeded their duty to recreate policing as they saw fit since this directly involved the public.[143] They overstepped their orders, carried out orders incorrectly, or even made up orders. They acted against legal acts and resorted to rough justice. Every constable exercised discretion, judging what required their attention and what was better to ignore. While all constables ignored minor illegal acts, some constables succumb to the temptation to enforce laws that did not exist but which they thought should exist. Liverpool Chief Constable Dunning described this dilemma; 'A policeman, working largely as he does on the seamy side of life, comes across many things which lie outside the legitimate scope of his duties, many which he would like to see within that scope, many wrongs which the law

---

137 BPO, 25 August 1911, lost one day's leave, p. 569; LDRB, 21 December 1920, PCH 280 Barton, one year's service, fined 10/-.

138 LCCDR, 4 January 1934, PCC 249 Wearing, fined 10/- and transferred.

139 LCCDR, 6 October 1926, PCB 164 Roddan, cautioned.

140 LCCDR, 6 October 1926, PCB 119 Dodd, fined 15/-; LDRB, 25 January 1927, seven years' service, two defaults, 15/-.

141 BRB, 22 October 1914, PCB 67 Reginald Wright, joined December 1907, retired 1933, exemplary character.

142 MGO, 6 May 1915.

143 Allan Silver described a weakness of the Yeomanry since it enabled 'private persons sometimes to modify police missions to suit their own proclivities and convenience'. This was also true for policemen. Silver, 'The Demand for Order in Civil Society: A Review of Some Themes in the History of Urban Crime, Police, and Riot', in *The Police: Six Sociological Essays*, ed. David J. Bordua (New York: Wiley, 1967), p. 9.

with its artificial distinctions leaves unremedied.'[144] Most constables stayed within acceptable boundaries. But even normally dependable constables could cross the line when faced with a specific situation. A few constables could not differentiate between their lawful duties and their personal ideas of justice. Forces weeded these men out as fast as they could since they could undermine the standing of the entire police force.

One of the more common ways that constables interfered in law enforcement was by withholding information from the courts in order to generate what they considered to be the deserved result. Constables could know enough about the history of the accused to want him or her to gain a different sentence than the immediate charge warranted. PC Bond did not state 'in court all that he knew in favour of James Barret whom PC had in custody accused of larceny', and PC Andrews volunteered during a hearing that the accused had been previously convicted, 'a statement calculated to prejudice a fair trial'.[145] Juvenile Court Justices complained that constables were 'very reluctant to state anything which they may know in favour of the defendants'.[146] Magistrates had to remind constables that they could not withhold facts that might help or hinder the accused but had to tell the whole truth.[147] A Liverpool constable was evasive in his testimony during a licensing case although it is not clear if the constable was trying to help or hinder the licensee. Considering his seventeen years of service, the licensee could have been either a friend or foe from one of his beats.[148] Constables justified skewing their testimony by arguing that they wanted a fair result, but this practice could degenerate into constables using their power deceitfully or vindictively.

Despite the expectation that constables remain a professional distance from the public, men on a beat for any length of time could not help getting acquainted with its residents. If they believed someone was being mistreated or needed a friendly warning, they interpreted their job as giving them the responsibility to interfere regardless of the law. Like withholding information, this could be to the benefit or disadvantage of the people who gained their attention. Family life tended to cause the most problems on residential beats. While constables were only supposed to intervene in domestic affairs when the law required them to do so, they frequently gave out advice in the hopes of preventing minor problems from escalating. Constables often stepped in as marriage counsellors. PC Taylor found Mrs Ballard wandering the streets after her husband turned her out of the house. He took her home and tried to smooth things over with her husband who offered

---

144   LAR, 1909, p. 20.
145   BRB, 12 September 1903, PCA 21 Frank Samuel Bond, joined November 1902; BPO, 4 February 1905, p. 540.
146   BPO, 3 May 1905, p. 51.
147   BPO, 2 December 1902, p. 306.
148   LDRB, 16 January 1909, PCE 120 Smith.

the constable a cup of tea. However, after he left, Mr Ballard accused his wife of carrying on drinking with the constable and threw her out again.[149] No doubt similar conversations over cups of tea met with better results. Constables could feel compelled to give advice to parents. After James Crawford's step-daughter left the house with her baby carriage, PC Leff went to the door and told Crawford, "'If your daughter is not better controlled I will summons her the first time I see her in the street" and when asked what for said "She is encouraging the boys round this corner."' Leff denied making any threats, saying that 'he merely gave the parents of the girl some advice in a friendly way'.[150] Since people complained when the constable's interference was unwelcome, failed advice tended to be reported and only a few constructive examples made it into the records. In one case, PC Murphy was called to a house where a man was threatening to commit suicide by shooting himself. Instead of arresting the man for improper possession of a firearm and attempted suicide, he took the revolver, 'saying "I could arrest you. You have no licence" and returned the revolver to [the wife] ... to whom he said "Put it out of the way."' The constable did not report the occurrence. He denied that this was a neglect of duty, seeing his duty to protect the man as more important than his duty to arrest him.[151] Constables were never officially taught that dispensing advice was an effective way to keep the peace but experience showed them that a few careful words could ease potential problems. However, tactless or unsympathetic constables could create more problems than they solved, infuriating the public and undermining their good will.

Constables sometimes decided that the well-being of civilians had a higher priority than their duty to make arrests or issue summonses. Opportunities for bending the rules presented themselves whenever they encountered someone down on their luck. PC Hare found a man ill and destitute in the streets and took him to an infirmary for treatment rather than send him to a workhouse.[152] Young constables, however, could be hoodwinked by a good story. Twenty-four-year-old PC Banks got himself fined a half a crown for being too tender-hearted and not reporting a chimney fire. He explained,

I visited the dwelling house ... during the time the chimney was on fire 10.50 p.m. The occupier Andrew Prendergast, a night watchman employed by the Manchester Corporation, stated, that he [had] just thrown a piece of paper on the fire the flames from which ignited the soot in the chimney. He also informed me that he was only working a few nights each week and did not

149 LWCM, 2 February 1931, PCG 139 Taylor.
150 LCCDR, 8 June 1932, PCD 84 Leff.
151 LWCM, 26 February 1924, Murphy, admitted words, cautioned, p. 83.
152 Roberts, *The Classic Slum*, p. 81.

get much wages. I beleiving [sic] the man to be in poor circumstances, did not report him for summons. At that time I did not know the man had a grocers shop.[153]

The most common people to benefit from such generosity were local drunk and disorderlies. Constables were required to take any disorderly drunken persons to the station but they saw so many drunks that sending a few home in cabs was simpler than processing cases at the station, especially since many were familiar characters. PC Smethurst found a man half undressed sleeping in a culvert and so drunk that he thought that he was home in bed. Since the man was close to home, Smethurst simply made sure he got there safely.[154] To the distress of Chief Constable Rafter, one constable fetched a cab for a drunken man and woman standing in the doorway of the Old Royal and opened the cab door for them.[155] Looking after familiar characters and helping the unfortunate were part of constables' motivation but avoiding the bureaucracy required by cases was no doubt a factor as well.

Helping civilians could mean stepping in to right a wrong even when no law had been broken. These could be harmless acts of kindness such as when a shop assistant refused to change a toffee apple for a boy who used bad language. The boy appealed to PC Reeves. The constable walked the boy to the shop, and, 'to the delight of the crowd, offered to buy the boy another apple'.[156] However, exercising unofficial justice could shade into grey areas of inappropriate interference such as constables advising people in traffic accidents to take legal action even after being ordered never to express an opinion or give advice on such matters.[157] More seriously, constables resorted to menace. PC Tebbitt made a habit of hassling a man to let him know that he had his eye on him.[158] PC Croft confronted a homeowner after a servant was dismissed by her mistress, demanding a good character for the servant since he believed that the mistress had been unfair.[159] Constables did not even accept the verdict of the courts if they felt that the decision was wrong. When a case of cruelty to a horse was dismissed, PC Goodman took matters into his own hands and threatened the man with violence if it ever occurred again.[160]

---

[153] MPF, 27 October 1923, PCC 88 Richard Banks, joined May 1919.

[154] Smethurst, 'Reminiscences', pp. 75–7.

[155] BPO, 28 November 1907, p. 199.

[156] LCCDR, 18 September 1933, PCD 173 Reeves; admitted sending the boy back but denied buying the apple; shopkeeper accepted explanation.

[157] BPO, 11 May 1903, pp. 425–6.

[158] LDRB, 19 June 1914, PCE 141 Tebbitt, two years' service, fined 10/-.

[159] BRB, 4 January 1900, PCB 89 Herbert Henry Croft, joined December 1893, severely cautioned for improper use of authority.

[160] BPO, 2 February 1911, p. 440, BRB, 2 February 1911, PCC Thomas Fred Goodman, joined 1896, severely censured.

Men casting themselves as general arbiters of right and wrong rather than as law
enforcement officers eventually became useless as policemen.

Constables were under no circumstances either to aid or hinder cases involving
bailiffs or demands for payment as long as there was no disturbance. But constables
continued to do both, typically siding with the debtor rather than with the debt
collector. Birmingham policemen had to be reminded that, 'The collection of
debts, the service of civil process, ..., claims to property, and other matters of
civil right, ... are matters beyond the province of police inquiry.'[161] Most of these
cases involved tenants in trouble for not paying rent. When Miss Payne, employed
at the Tivoli Theatre, was unable to pay her rent, her landlord seized her luggage.
Feeling in need of support when finally able to pay her bill, she appealed to PC
Glisby. He accompanied her 'to a residence in Bath Row, to assist her in demanding
her luggage and to witness the tendering of a certain payment'.[162] Sometimes,
constables helped tenants recover their belongings even when they could not pay
the rent. After Patrick Maloney's landlady had retained his clothes for failure to
pay, PC Gale ordered her to produce the clothes and allowed Maloney to take them
away without paying his bill.[163] Constables often lived in lodgings themselves, so
perhaps it is not surprising that they sided with the tenants. However, this could
leave them open to charges of hindering the collection of just debts, which was
why forces tried to stop the practice.

Policemen persisted in getting mixed up in divorce cases in spite of frequent
warnings not to accept requests to accompany anyone as a witness. Why constables
responded to appeals to act as witnesses was never discussed but possibly they
received tips in return for their services. They also may have known the parties
involved and have sympathized with one of the spouses. In 1902, Rafter was
appalled when he learned that a constable had served as a body guard when a
person served a citation in a divorce case and was later summoned as a witness.
He desired 'to impress upon all constables that they should not in any way
interfere with private affairs, nor allow themselves to become mixed up with
matters which do not concern their Police duties'.[164] This caution had been
forgotten by 1916 when two constables went to a house with a man to be present
as witnesses in a divorce case. Rafter again reminded his men, 'It looks badly to
see police examined as witnesses in such cases.'[165] But constables continued to
get 'entrapped' in civil cases. In 1932, Rafter again warned men to be on their

---

[161]   BPO, 29 May 1913, pp. 473–4.

[162]   BPO, 15 August 1903, p. 551; BRB, 15 August 1903, PCA 146 Daniel Harry Glisbey,
joined May 1901, cautioned; nine awards, three defaults.

[163]   LCCDR, 17 October 1927, PCA 219 Gale, owing to landlady's poor eye-sight, charge not
proven.

[164]   BPO, 11 April 1902, pp. 63–4.

[165]   BPO, 8 February 1918, p. 372.

guard.[166] It is not clear if constables were helping husbands or wives more often since records typically referred to 'persons' or 'parties'. Either spouse apparently believed that a constable could be a useful friend in court and constables remained willing to oblige.

Serious corruption by constables rarely appeared in the record books, dishonest constables appearing to be no more or less common than dishonest employees in any occupation. While constables may have had more opportunity to commit wrongdoing, camouflaged by their uniforms, they also faced stiff penalties for breaching the public trust on top of breaking the law. Street betting was probably the most common source of police corruption, with policemen organizing networks of men accepting bribes from bookmakers to overlook the offence. Typically, only ringleaders were prosecuted even though other officers were involved. Another common form of corruption was accepting bribes to drop charges, usually small amounts offered to get a constable to 'forget about it'. In a few cases, constables took job perks too far and crossed the line into stealing though this tended to involve poor judgment rather than bad intent. Some constables got into trouble for using their authority for personal reasons. PC Wagstaff 'abused his authority as a Police Officer by arresting a man ... with whom he has had a personal quarrel'.[167] PC Harcourt was accused of using his position to threaten to report Mr Brennan to the Labour Exchange unless he gave a satisfactory explanation for not carrying out certain work.[168] The most unusual cases involved burglary and embezzlement but these examples of deliberately criminal constables remained isolated episodes.

Although an illegal sport, street betting was not considered to be criminal by the working class, including most policemen, and policemen did their best to ignore it. Even Parliament acknowledged that, 'The attempt to enforce obsolete laws, or laws manifestly out of harmony with public opinion, will always be liable to expose the Police to temptations and to react upon their morale and efficiency.'[169] Only if under pressure from the middle and upper classes to crack down on street betting did policemen act and then with mixed feelings. Policemen of all ranks recognized that street betting laws discriminated against the working class, outlawing off-course cash betting while allowing middle and upper-class credit betting. Liverpool PC Jervis protested against a law created 'to prevent the poor man from wasting his money' while allowing the rich the luxury of legal gambling. He concluded, 'it is hoped that the exaggerated conception of betting as a deadly sin will be succeeded by one which regards it as a diversion providing an outlet for the monotony of

---

166 BPO, 19 October 1932, p. 19,940.

167 BPO, 14 November 1903, p. 32, Wagstaff's leave stopped; PC Hillier's leave stopped for assisting him.

168 BDRB, 21 December 1925, PCA 114 Walter Harcourt, p. 31, charge not sustained.

169 'Report of the Royal Commission on Police Powers and Procedure', 1928–1929, Cmd. 3297, vol. IX, 127, p. 7.

everyday life'.[170] It was also impossible to halt the practice even if the police so desired. Fifty to seventy five per cent of working class men bet regularly, with bets amounting from sixpence to a shilling before the war and to half a crown afterwards. Short of arresting entire city blocks, policemen could not carry out their legal duty to suppress street betting.[171] Chief Constable Everett explained,

> It is a difficult task to enforce a law, which a large part of the community considers to be unequal. The police meet with opposition which would be otherwise absent, ill-feeling is created and re-acts on other aspects of duty, whilst a still more serious matter is the temptation held out to cloak offenses. The goodwill and ready co-operation of the public is essential for successful police action against all law breakers, and this attitude is seriously impaired under such circumstances.[172]

As long as betting activities did not disrupt the peace, constables turned a blind eye. Their senior officers, including chief constables, agreed with that particular neglect of duty.

But public pressures to suppress street betting could not always be ignored by police forces. In 1904 when a 'very influential Deputation' appeared before the Birmingham watch committee, Rafter had no choice but to insist that his men 'continuously and repeatedly prosecute every betting man'.[173] Constables disregarded his request and a year later he issued a similar order, this time warning that constables' arrest records would be monitored by their superintendents. This order increased the prosecutions for street betting but only because constables wanted to avoid getting into trouble and hoped to gain advancement through a long betting arrest record.[174] A year later, Rafter had to issue an order against this 'erroneous idea'.[175] Constables responded to orders to suppress street betting to improve chances for promotion, or to protect their jobs, but not to appeals that street betting was itself an evil.

---

170 PC Jervis, 'The Betting Dilemma', *Police Journal* 9:4 (1936): 473–8.

171 Ross McKibbin, 'Working-Class Gambling in Britain, 1880–1939', *Past and Present* 82 (1979): 155. See also Andrew Davies, 'The Police and the People: Gambling in Salford, 1900–1939', *Historical Journal* 34:1 (1991): 87–115, and David Dixon, *From Prohibition to Regulation: Bookmaking, Anti-Gambling and the Law* (Oxford: Clarendon Press, 1991).

172 LAR, 1926, p. 14. In 1929, a parliamentary committee recommended that the street betting law be rescinded, stating, 'We are satisfied that street betting presents an almost insoluble problem for the Police at the present time ... principally because a considerable section of public opinion regards the present law as class legislation' (PP, 'Report of the Royal Commission on Police Powers and Procedure', 1928–1929, Cmd. 3297, vol. IX, 127, p. 105).

173 BPO, 28 July 1904, p. 326.

174 BPO, 4 July, 3 August 1905, pp. 132, 158.

175 BPO, 30 May 1906, p. 390.

Not only did policemen not see any reason to enforce the law like other members of the working class, they bet themselves. Constables could be found studying sporting papers and arranged bets while taking breaks from their beats.[176] PS Howorth not only bet, his bookmaker was an ex-constable.[177] During a police raid of an illegal gaming house, a constable and a chief inspector were found playing cards for money but both escaped being taken into custody.[178] Such behaviour put constables in the awkward position of policing an activity in which they participated, one reason why police forces wanted the law rescinded. Not surprisingly, men protected their regular bookmakers by ignoring their activities and warning them of arrest. PC Thomson habitually made bets with Jacob Taylor and passed him information to avoid prosecution. Thomson had a clean seventeen-year record and ten rewards with the Manchester police, an unusually good police résumé, but he did not consider protecting his bookmaker to be a contradiction to good policing.[179] The betting of policemen was particularly embarrassing when men got into debt with bookmakers. Owing £26 to a betting commission agent, PC Jones was personally seen by the chief constable and given three months to clear his account.[180] Men were rarely punished as long as they paid their debts. Unless constables made the mistake of betting while on duty or could not repay debts, senior officers overlooked police betting. Since inspectors and superintendents bet themselves, they could hardly expect their men to refrain.

Senior officers rarely minded if constables ignored street betting. But protecting the lucrative business created the most common temptation for both individual corruption and widespread scandal. In one case, PC Jefcoate arranged a meeting between Joe Furnell, a bookmaker, and PC Evans to recruit Evans to 'wink at street betting'. After the meeting, Evans found a pound treasury note in his pocket.[181] Bookmakers in areas with heavy street betting routinely paid policemen to turn a blind eye. PC Thomas failed to report a betting business on his beat that was taking in £1000 in bets on good days even though the street 'was full of people waiting to be paid out'.[182] The arrest of substitutes for bookmakers was a common practice, satisfying demands for arrests without upsetting bookmakers' business.[183]

---

[176] LDRB, 27 April 1926, PCE 221 Tyson, six years' service, fined 15/-.

[177] LDRB, 9 October 1923, PSH 52 Howorth, twenty years' service, reduced.

[178] LDRB, 21 August 1916, PCA 278 Oliver, eight years' service, fined 20/-; Chief Inspector Robinson, twenty-six years' service, two defaults, reduced one class equalling a decrease in salary of £8 per annum.

[179] MWCM, 20 September 1906, vol. 32, no. 127, PCA 174 James Thomson, reduced.

[180] LCCDR, 20 August 1923, PCF 169 Jones, cautioned, no further action.

[181] BRB, 26 August 1919, PCB 177 Arthur Jefcoate, joined April 1899, dismissed, Evans complimented for turning Jefcoate in; BPO, 27 August 1919, p. 1068; BWCM, 26 August 1919, p. 118.

[182] LCCDR, 13 October 1921, PCC 168 Thomas, fined 20/-.

[183] See Davies, 'The Police and the People', pp. 91–3; 'Interview with Fancourt', pp. 7–8;

In some cases, constables passed on information regarding future arrests to warn bookmakers.[184] Street betting could create networks of officers working together with betting agents to protect their turf.[185] A largely working-class city, Liverpool was twice shaken by scandals involving policemen accepting payoffs for not enforcing street betting laws. In 1923, one superintendent, two inspectors, four sergeants, and eleven constables were disciplined for cooperating with a 'ready money betting business' for at least eighteen months. Only the superintendent was ordered to retire for not stopping the corruption. None of the officers under him were dismissed since disobeying their superintendent was recognized as difficult. Instead, the men were split up through transfers to other divisions.[186] At the Liverpool Assizes in 1927, nine constables were found guilty of bribery and corruption. All were dismissed for arranging fake arrests for street betting with local bookmakers. Four additional constables, while either not charged or found not guilty, were also dismissed. Their senior officers remained convinced that they had participated in the scheme and the constables had no senior officers to blame for their wrongdoing.[187] Overturning the law against street betting would have got rid of most police corruption with one action.

Street betting, while the most common, did not provide the only source of temptation for police corruption. The smaller the value of the temptation, the more likely constables were to consider something a 'perk' instead of dishonesty. The public handed them money and objects found in the streets, householders told them when they were gone on vacation, and shopkeepers neglected to secure their shutters. Some constables could not resist these enticements to pick up items or supplement their incomes. Constables were tempted by bribes, often from motor car drivers or from individuals caught in embarrassing circumstances, in return for not filing charges or not pursuing a case. In more serious cases, policemen threatened civilians to extort bribes. Crossing the line into clearly criminal behaviour, constables committed petty theft, burgled shops, and robbed householders. The most lucrative crime was embezzling funds from police societies. Such flagrant

---

Fancourt, 'The Police Service of George Frederic Fancourt', pp. 5–6; Fowler, 'From a Convict to a Parson', pp. 64–7.

[184] BPO, 15 November 1912, p. 308.

[185] The betting men's payments that Harry Daley described were part of a corrupt network rather than individual corruption *(This Small Cloud,* pp. 93–5).

[186] LCCDR, 18, 31 December 1923, supt ordered to retire, inspectors cautioned and transferred, sergeants cautioned, constables reprimanded and transferred.

[187] LCCDR, 23 November 1927, PCE 94 Thomas, PCE 296 Bird, PCE 109 Hyde, dismissed; PCH 411 Roberts, PCE 293 Harvey, PCE 134 Hodgson, PCD 226 Grounds, PCH 420 Stevens, PCE 299 Chaffell, PCE 96 Selby, PCE 281 Wilson, PCE 311 Harold, convicted and dismissed; PCE 165 Cranny, acquitted and dismissed; LDRB, 29 November 1927, PCE 109 Hyde, seven years, PCE 296 Bird, seven years, dismissed for fake arrests; also LCCO, 14 February 1928 for chief constable's statement on the case's 'severe blow at the integrity of the Service'.

offences were rare. This was not necessarily a sign of particular virtue but rather common sense. Constable might get away with holding onto stray umbrellas but not with breaking into shops on their beats.

A common form of dishonesty was keeping found property instead of turning it in at the station. Much of this could be put down to carelessness or absent-mindedness, at least initially. By the time constables explored their pockets, they might not want to bother with writing reports for minor incidents such as when PC Statter forgot to report that he had picked up money dropped by a tram conductor.[188] Often the constable's idea of a perk did not match that of his senior officers. PC Joad caught a ferret wandering loose and sold it for half a crown only to be fined twenty shillings when the owner inquired after the animal.[189] Owners inquired after items about half of the time, especially if valuable. Keeping found property handed in by a civilian was even riskier since both the owner and the finder might check on it. PC Alderman kept a half crown handed to him by a nine-year-old boy only to have the boy ask at the station about it.[190] Keeping more costly objects usually ended in dismissal or even prison because it was difficult to class these as perks. PC Bergin tried to hide that he had kept a £1 note handed to him by a boy by having a neighbour claim to have found it. Bergin was sentenced to two months in prison for this deceit.[191] But if the owner or finder of an item did not ask after it, constables could get away with keeping it. Unless an object was expensive, few men considered this to be stealing but rather good luck.

Unlike pocketing the odd half crown, bribery could not be disguised as unintentional though it typically involved equally small amounts. Like street betting, constables were usually tempted with bribes to overlook some offence. Petty thieves offered constables part of their loot to let them go, and disturbers of the peace tried to tip constables to convince them to look the other way. Constables sometimes claimed that bribery was common but this is nearly impossible to verify. Accepted bribes rarely made it into the records books since both parties had good reasons for keeping their transactions private. In one 1912 accusation, PC Scott, after his dismissal for adultery, wrote a letter begging for reinstatement. He wrote, 'I take the liberty of repeating what one of my officers said – When other officers sold & betrayed us, Scott was the only man who was true to his trust and refused bribes when he could have made pounds in money. Those men are still serving in the Force.'[192] He offered no details and he had his own reasons for inventing such a story. The few bribery cases recorded did not include how the bribe became known.

---

188   BWCM, 25 May 1914, cautioned, p. 102.

189   LDRB, 5 June 1916, PCF 216 Joad, five years' service.

190   BRB, 9 October 1935, PCD 262 William Alderman, joined June 1921, reduced for twelve months and transferred.

191   *Police Review*, 5 November 1915, p. 538.

192   MWCM, 28 October 1912, PCB 160 Henry Scott, five years' service, vol. 57, no. 4.

The civilian may have decided that the bargain had not been kept and that getting even with the constable was worth the exposure. A 1929 parliamentary committee remarked, 'The public must also bear its share and recognise that in this matter it has its own obligations to the Police, first and foremost in ceasing to regard the successful offering of a bribe to a Policeman as something of an achievement.'[193] So possibly civilians bragged of their bribes to someone who decided to report it. All but two of the bribery cases in the records were from Manchester. Either Manchester gave bribery special attention or the other forces handled it at the divisional level. It is unlikely that only Manchester had problems with this offence, nor that Liverpool, with its reputation for discipline problems, had none.

The most frequent charge linked to bribery was for indecency, worthy citizens not wanting publicity for even suspected actions. These bribes were almost always offered by men who had been harassing women, such as when two men 'annoying females' gave PCs Thomas and Taylor thirty shillings to take no action in the matter, an unusually large bribe.[194] A more modest bribe came from a man who gave PC Davis half a crown to let an indecency case slide.[195] Rarely, constables caught women as well; PC Kilburn took seven shillings from a couple in a compromising situation.[196] One vivid little episode took place at two a.m. one morning. Two 'gentlemen' had a cab take them to a house. A woman called from a window and refused to admit them but they kept banging at the door. Hearing the noise, PC Potts came up and ordered them to leave. The two men continued to drive around the neighbourhood in the cab. Potts came across them again and ordered the cab driver to move. When the driver refused, PC Potts took his name and address. One of the gentlemen then 'had a conversation with the officer' and gave him six shillings not to report the incident; what offence the gentlemen were committing was not mentioned. Potts pocketed the three two-shilling pieces and did not report these events.[197] In this case, possibly the cab driver reported the constable, annoyed at Potts for harassing him when he had a lucrative fare.

Accepting bribes from motorists was allegedly a common practice that chief constables did their best to discourage by threatening officers caught doing so with dismissal. However, only four cases appeared in the records of the three cities, one

---

[193] PP, 'Report of the Royal Commission on Police Powers and Procedure', 1928–1929, Cmd. 3297, vol. IX, 127, pp. 82, 106.

[194] MWCM, 11 May 1922, PCB 14 George H. Thomas, twenty-four years' service, three defaults, to resign, PCB 110 George Taylor, twenty-three years' service, seven defaults, reduced to lowest class, vol. 91, no. 60.

[195] BRB, 15 May 1911, PCC 96 George Ernest Davis, joined July 1905, reduced in class; BPO, 17 May 1911, p. 496; BWCM, 15 May 1911, p. 321.

[196] MGO, 2 July 1920, PCB 26 Arthur Kilburn, dismissed.

[197] MWCM, 12 September 1912, PCD 67 Arthur Potts, six years' service, one default, lost one week leave, vol. 56, no. 29.

each from Birmingham and Liverpool in the 1920s, and two from Manchester in
the later 1930s. In a typical scenario, Mr Agar insisted he had not been speeding
when a police car pulled him over. Telling PC Broad that he had been summoned
for speeding only two weeks before, Agar asked if the constable could 'forget it'.
Broad claimed that Agar then gave him £1 whereas Agar insisted that he did this
only after the constable had asked him, 'What is it worth?' A passenger in the car
admitted that Agar had been going five- to ten miles-per-hour over the speed limit
but conveniently did not hear the conversation about the bribe. The constable never
reported the speeding offence. Agar had a sudden attack of caution and reported the
incident to his solicitor who recommended that he report it to the police. Since no
one could agree on what had happened, PC Broad was not disciplined.[198] In a more
unusual case, PC Wishart accepted a loan of Mr Geldeard's car in return for not
reporting him for speeding. He got off with a reprimand, possibly because he had
not accepted money.[199] Another common accusation was that constables took bribes
to support motor drivers' cases in court, as PC Dyson did, receiving a florin and a
franc piece.[200] Traffic bribes account for few of the reported cases, the passing of
money through car windows possibly being easier to hide than other offences.

Not waiting for a bribe to be offered, a few constables demanded them,
taking advantage of situations that could lead to a summons or arrest. The
charges constables used to threaten people could be quite minor, such as when PC
Mattocks exacted two shillings from a man in return for not prosecuting a parking
violation.[201] PC Davies put a stellar career in Birmingham in peril, having earned
ten awards in four years on the force, by soliciting half a crown not to report a
chimney fire.[202] Another constable endangering a strong record was PC Thomas.
He had twenty-five awards in a fifteen-year career but then demanded five shillings
from Mr Barnes for not charging him with cruelty to his work horses.[203] Why these
men took such risks in return for small sums of money can only be guessed at.
Extorting money could backfire if the constable misjudged his victim. PC Clarke
caught Mr Hampson 'making water' in a side street in the company of a woman and
demanded seven shillings to refrain from charging him with indecency. Hampson
returned the next day and demanded the money back, threatening to report Clarke.

---

[198] MPF, 11 February 1936, PCA 278 George Edward Broad, appointed November 1924, case
not proven; MGO, 2 May 1930.
[199] MPF, 9 March 1939, PCF 123 Robert Wishart, appointed February 1936, reprimanded.
[200] BPO, 24 May 1923, PCC 139 Herbert Dyson, fined 10/- and to forfeit 3/- value of
gratuity, p. 6370. A florin equalled two shillings.
[201] MWCM, 1 May 1930, PCA 273 Thomas Mattocks, four and a half years' service, two
defaults, ordered to resign, vol. 139, no. 16.
[202] BRB, 28 April 1927, PCD 139 Ernest Davies, joined April 1923, ten awards; BDRB, 27
March 1927, fined 10/-, pp. 75–6.
[203] MWCM, 26 September 1912, PCB 14 George Henry Thomas, fifteen years' service, two
defaults, twenty-five rewards, reduced, vol. 56, no. 51.

Clarke paid but threatened to arrest him for bribery if anything was said about the matter. Hampson was so angry that he reported Clarke anyway and Clarke was dismissed.[204] Most of the constables who extorted bribes were caught before the war. They were fined or reduced in rank rather than fired. The two postwar examples were handled in opposite ways, reflecting the men's records. PC Davies was only fined ten shillings, his excellent career saving him from more serious consequences. Mattocks had a less impressive record of two defaults in four years and was ordered to resign. It is possible that higher postwar wages left constables with less incentive to risk their jobs over coerced bribes.

A few constables succumbed to the temptation to steal but most of the theft was petty, usually individual constables stealing portable objects that caught their attention. PC Spicer stole a cauliflower from a market cart,[205] PC Salsbury pocketed a postal order,[206] and PC Shipton could not give a satisfactory explanation for two fowls in his possession.[207] Ironically, constables sometimes stole items from householders who called them to investigate other crimes. PC Collins palmed a gold signet ring while visiting the premises of Mr Homer[208] and PC Rook stole a pearl-handled fruit knife from a house while taking a report about a burglary.[209] Perhaps they hoped that missing items would be blamed on the initial thieves. While taking small quantities of goods from the Liverpool docks was generally ignored, PC Edwards carried off two bottles of whisky and seventeen pounds of rice, hardly a trivial amount. He was fined £5 by the courts for theft.[210] Any policeman convicted of a crime was dismissed from the force. This could lead to dismissals for minor offences, but if a case ended in a conviction, a police force had little choice but to fire the officer.[211] Most of the theft was spontaneous, constables picking up small items in the course of their duties, and most of it took place before the implementation of better pay in 1919.

Isolated examples appeared of constables taking advantage of their special opportunities and knowledge to commit more serious criminal acts. Unlike petty thefts which were crimes of opportunity, these were planned and men were more likely to have accomplices, either other constables or family members. Unlike petty

---

204 MWCM, 12 December 1907, PCA 63 James Gladstone Clarke, three years' service, two defaults, dismissed; *Police Review*, 17 January 1908, p. 34. Mr. Hampson was not charged with bribery in order not to scare other informants from coming forward.

205 BPO, 23 June 1919, PCD 184 Alfred Spicer, p. 848.

206 BWCM, 1 July 1903, one month's imprisonment, p. 445.

207 BRB, 13 October 1913, PCB 156 Joseph Shipton, joined October 1897, cautioned.

208 BWCM, 4 December 1911, PC Charles Henry Collins, to resign, p. 342.

209 MWCM, 1 October 1914, PCD 158 John E. Rook, five years' service, vol. 64, no. 166.

210 LDRB, 27 February 1917, PCC 165 Edwards, twenty-one years' service, two defaults, dismissed. For more on the Liverpool docks, see Chapter 7.

211 The difficulty in distinguishing perks from theft is addressed in Chapter 7, including cases of men dismissed for trivial actions.

theft, these appeared in every decade, a sign that low pay was not the primary motivation. Constables tended to burgle businesses rather than homes since they could examine potential targets while carrying out their regular duties. If they were seen, civilians tended to assume that the constable had legitimate reasons to be there. Men staged robberies in every phase of their careers. After only a year on the force, two probationary constables broke into a lock-up shop and stole £2 worth of cigars, cigarettes, pipes, and cigarette holders. Suspicions were aroused when PC Chinar worked his beat in a 'very irregular manner'. Stolen items were found hidden at his fiancée's home. More items were found at the home of PC Shewan's father. The two constables were sentenced to three months' hard labour.[212] After eight years of service, PC Hargadon broke into a shop two nights in a row, stealing ten tins of preserved meat and eight bottles of beer, value twelve shillings, sixpence, and gave three tins and a bottle of beer to PC Gibbons with seventeen years' service. Both constables were sentenced to imprisonment, Hargadon to seventy days and Gibbins to fifty-six days.[213] Acting alone, five-year veteran PC Marston broke into a garage and stole a motorcycle and sidecar worth £120. Two months later, he broke into a shop and stole a safe and its contents valued at £468. Three additional charges were not investigated. He was sentenced to twenty-one months hard labour.[214] Stealing from homes was more unusual since riskier. Nevertheless, over a period of at least eighteen months, PC Martin used false keys to burgle houses on and near his beat, hiding property outside to be picked up later off duty or by his wife and fifteen-year-old daughter.[215] In the most serious and dangerous case, since it involved a witness, PC Eyres broke into a house, held up Mr Ede with 'an offensive weapon' and assaulted him 'with intent to rob him'. He was sentenced to four years of penal servitude.[216] Even though these cases created publicity, such serious crimes were exceptional.

The worst thieves in the force were constables who misappropriated funds from police societies. All of the embezzlement cases except one[217] took place after 1918 and all but one took place in Liverpool. After the war, police groups handled large enough sums to explain the attraction and postwar higher education requirements brought in constables better able to fake the books. One group that

---

[212] MWCM, 20 September 1906, PCB Albert Chinar, PCB Leslie Shewan, each one year's service, vol. 32, no. 126.

[213] LDRB, 23 August 1915, PCC 109 Hargadon, eight years' service, one default; PCC 211 Gibbons, seventeen years' service, three defaults.

[214] LDRB, 18 November 1924, PCB 203 Marston, five years' service, one default, three other charges not investigated but remained on file, dismissed.

[215] LHCWC, 31 August 1903, pp. 423–4, a large amount of stolen property was found at his house.

[216] BPO, 18 July 1929, PCB 175 William George Eyres, dismissed, p. 15595.

[217] LDRB, 6 August, 1910, PCD 130 Manning, ten years' service, one default, 'Improperly dealing with money handed to him for the benefit of the Police Athletics Society. Ordered to resign forthwith.'

managed substantial funds was the Liverpool Police Guild, an internal trading organization. While acting as division agent for the Guild, PC Barber collected £16 which he 'forgot' to pay into the account, about four months' pay.[218] Three years later, PC Goodman embezzled nearly £85 from the same fund, earning a month in prison. His sergeant only escaped dismissal for not reporting Goodman owing to the nearness of his retirement.[219] Police Federation funds were also prone to disappear. PC Moore resigned before he could be disciplined for 'misplacing' £140 from the account of the Joint Branch Board of the Police Federation[220] and PC Taylor of Manchester was dismissed for using the same fund for his personal use.[221] Ironically, even though these embezzlers stole more than almost all the other cases of theft, only one was listed as convicted of a crime. The others were dismissed or allowed to resign. White-collar crime seemed a safer course than stealing bottles of whisky, even for policemen.

Despite this long litany of disobedience, most constables made it through their careers with few or no disciplinary offences. Most minor problems were handled informally unless constables made a habit of breaking the rules after being advised to mend their ways. Constables learned to get around regulations when necessary and otherwise decided to put up with them to keep a decent job. Men who could not adapt to the discipline either left the force voluntarily or were dismissed when the number of their defaults became too high. Exceptions existed, especially before the war when men with five or even ten defaults might survive to take their pensions. The rapid turnover in the first few years of service, especially before 1919, suggests that many working-class men could not tolerate force discipline. The most important factors in the decline of police disciplinary problems were the drop in working-class drinking and the economic depression. Fewer drunken constables meant both better policemen and less time spent removing intoxicated officers from the streets. Fears of unemployment confined constables to breaking regulations less likely to lead to detection or dismissal. Constables could indulge in short breaks on their beats for months or years without their sergeants either discovering or reporting them, but they knew that they could not be found drunk or in possession of questionable items and survive in the force for long. But as long as personal discretion played a major role in policing methods, forces would never be free from men liable to corruption or who interpreted their duty in ways that did not conform to official expectations.

---

[218] LDRB, 24 August 1920, PCH 236 Barber, seven years' service, dismissed.

[219] LDRB, 25 September 1923, PCG 364 Goodman, four years' service, one default, dismissed; 9 October 1923, PSE 30 McDowall, twenty-six years' service, reduced to 6th class sergeant.

[220] LCCDR, 7 July 1930, PCH 188 Moore, cpt. C.S. Leslie. 'Con rendered his resignation on 8.7.30 & the CC accepted the same – the charge to remain on the file.'

[221] MGO, 4 September 1924, PCC 205 George Taylor, dismissed.

4

Factions and Friendships

All the men who left duty at 2 am used to sit and chat for half
an hour or more nearly every morning. The esprit-de-corps,
or comradeship at that time was very good, for we all used
to work pretty well together. But, before I retired from the
service, individualism was very rampant, the desire for power
being the dominant factor, as most of them were obsessed
with the idea to become superiors, before they had learned to
become good policemen.

Thomas Smethurst, 'Reminiscences', 1922[1]

POLICE UNIFORMS made the public susceptible to mistaking constables for
parts of a monolithic entity. In reality policemen acted out contradictory
patterns of internal hostilities and loyalties, both within ranks and up and down the
police hierarchy. Constables working street beats and traffic points united in their
resentment of policemen who worked as office staff and of the detective branch over
the distribution of privileges and recognition. Yet the same men belonged to rival
groups organized around patronage networks, regional backgrounds, and religion.
Both older and newer constables grumbled about the growing burden of duties but
quarrelled with each other over police practices and the importance of education,
particularly after the implementation of the Desborough recommendations in the
1919 Police Act. Men passed over for promotion or harshly punished resented men
perceived as unfairly gaining higher rank or being let off lightly for breaches of
regulations. Constables shared a common wariness of senior officers but also had
close friends promoted into the upper ranks who maintained their ties with their
less fortunate colleagues. Co-existing with a legion of disharmonies was a strong
sense of camaraderie. Mutual experiences and grievances provided common cause
for men from the same rank, division, or station, often in spite of other rifts.[2]

---

1   Smethurst, 'Reminiscences', p. 241.
2   Conflicts between the police and the public are addressed in Chapter 7.

This strange mixture of frictions and friendships resulted from the nature of the police force. It was a hierarchical organization of law and order made up of working-class men at all levels except possibly the office of assistant chief constable and chief constable.[3] No officer class existed to inspire awe in the ranks. Confrontations with senior officers were not a battle of one class against another but internal disputes between a working man who had made good and a man who might envy that success. Constables felt loyalty to their rank but also competed within it for promotion. They acted together against their senior officers to break police rules, and turned on each other to gain favour with those same officers. Sergeants, inspectors, and superintendents faced similar dilemmas over breaches of discipline by friends lower down the ranks, and over temptations to favour friends nominated for rewards and promotions. Any policeman could be vulnerable to abuse of authority by officers protecting men in their own group. Rivalry was structured into the force, not only through competition for promotion but through the existence of different departments. Each department had grievances against the others over priorities and interference, and over who was doing the most vital police work. All of this created a confusion of personal loyalties, rank loyalties, and competition for favours.

An understandable barrier existed between constables and everyone above them in the hierarchy. Constables needed favourable notice from their senior officers, as well as passing scores on examinations, to advance their careers. This left them vulnerable to senior officers who could order them to perform a variety of chores that might have little to do with policing. Constables and even sergeants with a useful pre-police occupation were expected to make their skills available at police stations and at officers' homes. Having plumbing experience, for instance, PS Stell was sent to a chief superintendent's house to repair a tap.[4] While such requests were outside their job description, it was foolish for a man to decline and it could be a useful way to be noticed by senior officers. However, constables resented being treated like servants, such as when they were 'asked' to do heavy duty cleaning at officer's homes or to wash their vehicles.[5] Constables were regularly assigned to clean the Liverpool chief constable's car, and PC Haynes, a mechanic, was expected

---

3   Up until the 1919 Police Act, Royal Irish Constabulary (RIC) officers, colonial police officers, and military officers typically became chief constables, including Birmingham's Charles Rafter and Cecil Moriarty, and Liverpool's John William Nott Bower and Leonard Dunning, all of the RIC. The Desborough Committee recommended that no one without previous police experience be appointed chief constable except in rare cases but exceptions continued to be made ('Report of the Committee on the Police Service of England, Wales, and Scotland', 1920, Cmd 574, vol. XXII, 709, p. 23).

4   LCI, 28 July 1920, PSH 17 Stell, hit in eye by valve he had to force out to fix the tap.

5   LCI, 17 December 1925, PCE 252 Byron's hand slipped and went through a window pane while cleaning a chief inspector's house; 11 October 1907, PCH 206 Poole jammed his hand between spokes and the back stop of a superintendent's phaeton while washing it.

to check the tyres and fit a sleeve on the engine.[6] Sometimes, senior officers abused their power to demand favours. Inspector Duncan forced a constable who did tailoring for the force to make private clothing for him on official time.[7] These favours united constables in a common grievance at being treated like cheap labour, though constables without a useful skill could envy those who got preferential treatment for being able to repair a superintendent's bad drains.

While their shared status at the bottom of the hierarchy did much to unify constables, internal dissension was chronic. Constables got on each other's nerves, often when they disagreed over the proper way to carry out their duties. Telling another constable how to do his job could quickly draw an angry reply. Irritated at PC Davies for reminding him that he needed to inform an occupant about an insecure shop door, PC Shearman shot back, 'I was not taking the trouble to do so – fuck them – they left the door open – let it be open.'[8] PCs Collier and Baker were caught 'wrangling together when preferring a charge against a Prisoner' over the appropriate way to proceed.[9] Constables particularly did not like having other constables expose their mistakes to senior officers, however unintentionally. After missing an open door later found by PC Sneyd, PC Dodd shouted at Sneyd, 'What are you trying to do finding bloody places open after me? What about 71 Oxford St? I tried it myself at 10/30 pm & it was quite alright then. Alright the first chance I get, I'll bloody well do you.'[10] Young constables still learning their duties could blow up at each other, such as when two probationers were fined for using 'improper language to a brother constable', presumably each other.[11] Distressed by 'Officers who were wrangling amongst themselves', Birmingham Chief Constable Rafter went so far as to remind his men that 'Constables must cultivate a kindly manner towards each other & live together in peace.'[12] Much of

---

[6]   LCI, 7 November 1926, PCH 146 Downes caught his head on the car's lamp, causing a flesh wound; 9 January 1927, PCH 127 Hughes did exactly the same thing on the same lamp; 17 January 1927, 21 March 1928, PCH 132 Haynes, jammed hand, hit hand with hammer.

[7]   LDRB, 18 December 1923, Insp. Charles J. Duncan; LCCDR, 24 December 1923, PCH 90 Duncan, resigned. PC Owen discovered that Inspector Duncan had falsified the tailor's time book to make it appear that a constable had been working full shifts when actually he had been spending half of his time making clothes for Duncan. Duncan compounded his offence by trying to get Owen to cover up the charge and then accusing Owen of being the guilty one when Owen refused. Duncan had to resign with the rank of constable.

[8]   LDRB, 13 December 1921, PCF 69 Shearman, one year's service, one default, fined 15/-, also fined 40/- for insubordination to his sergeant on the same occasion.

[9]   BPO, 18 October 1900, p. 283; BRB, 11 October 1900, 12 June 1902, PC Thomas Baker, joined April 1896, total six defaults, nine awards, retired 1921.

[10]   LCCDR, 10 January 1924, PCB 119 Dodd, given benefit of doubt.

[11]   LDRB, 29 November 1912, PCA 352 Sumner, seven months' service, PCA 269 Fitzsimmons, eight months' service.

[12]   BPO, 5 December 1903, p. 52.

this bickering was simply to relieve stress but it also resulted from disagreements over duties. Constables were accustomed to working alone and making their own decisions, so it is not surprising that they sometimes got on each other's nerves when required to work together.

Quarrels tended to be limited to insults but constables took the occasional swing at each other. Fights usually involved younger men, still short fused in reaction to perceived challenges to their competence; the 1920s saw more fights due to the youth of the forces. Older men with families became less likely to risk their jobs over an insult or slight. Fights could happen anywhere but reported ones mostly happened at stations and mess halls where constables were likely to run into each other for parade and meals. In a bad stretch for brawling in Manchester, two constables fought in a 'C' Division station parade room, and ten days later two constables fought in an 'A' Division mess room.[13] In a Birmingham mess room battle, PC Cullinane threw bread, and PC Thomas threw a bottle at PC Payne and then punched him in the mouth, later having to pay for Payne's two new teeth.[14] One suppertime fight broke out when national insults were hurled between Welsh and English constables. PCs Cooper, Davies, and Miller were sitting together when Davies said, 'Welshmen were better than any Englishman.' Cooper replied, 'There are bad and good on both sides.' PC Miller added something to which Cooper answered, 'One goat at a time.' At that, Davies jumped up and slapped Cooper in the face. According to Davies' account, Cooper had said 'that it was easy to see and know where I came from as soon as I opened my bloody trap and he further called me a bloody Welsh Goat'.[15] Fights sometimes broke out when constables met on their beats though this was less common or at least less reported. During one altercation, PC Jennings knocked down PC Smith with his bicycle.[16] Most fights were minor, rarely leaving more than red faces or bruised hands. More serious injuries resulted when men challenged each other to fight, making a contest out of it. After PC Cringle told PC Gleeson, 'If you want a fight, I'm your man anytime', they hurt each other so badly before being separated by a sergeant that they had to see the force doctor.[17] Habitual fighters were asked to leave. PC Wright sparred with PC Gardiner in the street during his first year on the force, and fought with PC Moran at the station two years later. After he hit a civilian the

[13]   MGO, 27 January 1928, PCC 30 Herman Holt, PCC 137 Albert Dewhirst, to resign; PCA 250 William Halstead, reduced to lowest class; PCA 200 Stanley Burfield, to resign.
[14]   BPO, 22 November 1901, both fined 20/- and transferred, p. 575.
[15]   MPF, 24 June 1925, PCA 36 Richard Davies, appointed May 1919, fined 10/-.
[16]   LCI, 13 August 1926, PCE 91 Jennings, PCG 156 Smith, both fined 40/-.
[17]   LCCDR, 7 May 1924, PCC 159 Cringle, PCC 279 Gleeson; LCI, 2 May 1924, Cringle, contused eye, cut eye and cheek, Gleeson, cut mouth.

next year, he wisely decided to go abroad.[18] In many ways, these altercations resemble insubordination, with sudden flashes of temper, often out of frustration or fatigue, that just as quickly fade away.[19]

Generational conflicts plagued all forces. New constables looked to veterans to learn their jobs but also could look down on older men with less education and rougher habits; in turn, experienced constables dismissed the newcomers until they had spent enough time on the streets to prove themselves to be real policemen. New men became old men, in competition with the next generation. New police acts that changed force conditions of service exacerbated these divisions. Men hired after the 1890 Police Act had better educations, drank less, and lasted longer than their pre-1890 colleagues. The starkest generational contrast existed between the pre- and post-First World War men. Ironically, efforts by the post-1890s men to improve the quality of policing and fairness of promotion created an often unpleasant breach between men recruited before and after the war. The demands of traffic duties and technologies, and the changes brought about by the police strikes and 1919 Police Act, modified policing dramatically.[20] Changes in police qualifications and methodology created hostility between prewar and postwar policemen. The 'old police' had survived harsh times together, including the disasters of the war and the police strikes in Liverpool and Birmingham, and resented the 'new men' who not only benefited from the 1919 Police Act without having paid for it yet often considered the old men to be inferior policemen. The 'youngsters' could be condescending towards men they saw as ill-educated and unrefined. This split continued throughout the interwar period with the two groups perceiving each other as different types of policemen.[21]

Generational conflicts tended to be argued in terms of experience versus education. Men hired under looser education standards could have perfectly successful police careers, and did not appreciate younger, better-educated men criticizing their lack of schooling. On the other hand, police duties kept expanding, such as the need to pass the St John Ambulance examination, and constables found themselves required to write reports with greater frequency. In the 1890s, a growing disparity became clear between the abilities of older and younger constables, with older constables too poorly educated to 'write, compose, and

---

[18]   Birmingham City Police Defaulters Books, 22 August 1902, 10 September 1904, PCE 52 Peter Paul Wright, joined July 1902, charged July 1905 with hitting a civilian, resigned to go abroad April 1906, p. 212.

[19]   For insubordination, see Chapter 3.

[20]   For more on the strikes, see Chapter 5.

[21]   This kind of rivalry also developed after the introduction of the Bramshill Police College special courses in 1948 between those qualifying under the old system and those with access to the courses. Experience again lost out to education. See Reiner, *The Blue-Coated Worker*, p. 195.

properly complete [their] own reports'.[22] Manchester Chief Constable Peacock insisted, 'If the older generation are to maintain their positions in the world they have to educate themselves, so as to be able, if not actually to compete with their contemporaries, to at least hold their own against them.'[23] The *Police Review* shared his concern and began a regular education column 'designed to aid Police anxious for Promotion or Self-Improvement', including spelling, shorthand, composition, arithmetic, and practical essays. They ran a law and practice column that answered readers' questions and explained new laws and amendments. Guide books such as Howard Vincent's *A Police Code and Manual of the Criminal Law* and Thomas Marriott's *A Constable's Duty and How to do it* went through multiple editions. Starting around 1900, police forces began offering classes for constables beyond the probationary period, funded by school board grants.[24] Peacock set up classes through the Manchester School Board in 1900 with 260 pupils. He even put together a booklet of lectures on police duties for the first course which was eventually printed and distributed to other forces. Also in 1900, Rafter set up a voluntary night school in Birmingham provided by the Education Committee, later known as the Police Institute. Subjects included reading, writing, dictation, composition, arithmetic, geography, and shorthand.[25] Liverpool had similar classes for its men. While attending these schools helped prepare constables for promotion examinations, their primary purpose was to improve the general education of constables.

In spite of initial high enrolments, both the Manchester and Birmingham schools were unable to keep more than a handful of students (see Table 1). Older men who had not attended school for many years were most likely to drop out. Birmingham's high attendance quickly faded away until by October 1900 only a third of those signed up attended class.[26] In December, Rafter responded by stopping the leave of one constable for neglecting to attend school after being ordered to do so.[27] He pointed out that the 'schools were placed at the disposal of the Police at the request of the men themselves, in the first instance, who complained that they had no educational opportunities in Birmingham'.[28] This warning had little effect. The reality of attending classes in their off-duty time had stifled educational aspirations.

---

22   Sir Robert Peacock, *Police Constables' Duties. Addresses by Robert Peacock, Chief Constable, City Of Manchester* (Manchester: Henry Blacklock and Co., 1900), pp. 6–7.

23   Peacock, *Police Constables' Duties*, p. 3.

24   Schools to improve policemen's education were also set up in Prussia at the turn of the century. See Herbert Reinke, '"Armed as if for a War": The State, the Military and the Professionalisation of the Prussian Police in Imperial Germany', in *Policing Western Europe: Politics, Professionalism, and Public Order 1850–1940*, ed. Clive Emsley and Barbara Weinberger (Westport, CT: Greenwood, 1991), pp. 55–73.

25   BPO, 17 January 1900, p. 116, 13 March 1900, p. 152; BWCM, 10 July 1900, p. 24.

26   BPO, 13 October 1900, pp. 281–2.

27   BPO, 20 December 1900, p. 328.

28   BPO, 11 February 1901, pp. 357–8. See also BPO, 3 September 1902. For a school-board

In typical Rafter fashion, he hectored his men to attend school, publishing their poor attendance records to shame them into getting to class.

Table 1. *Birmingham City Police School attendance,*
weeks ending 14 February, 28 February, 7 March, and 14 March 1901[29]

School	Number on books	Number present at all during week	Average number during week
Nelson Street	47, 46, 46, 46	13, 19, 15, 14	10, 14, 10, 11
Upper Highgate	90, 89, 89, 89	33, 40, 40, 31	19, 27, 27, 19
Camden Street	54, 54, 54, 52	30, 30, 28, 28	21, 23, 23, 31
Cromwell Street	53, 52, 52, 52	24, 29, 31, 24	16, 20, 23, 17
Totals	244, 241, 241, 241	100, 116, 114, 97	66, 84, 83, 68

Rafter's badgering began to have an impact and the school began to keep students. In April 1902, a teacher reported that, 'The discipline, attention and general conduct of the members have been excellent, and each one has shown not only a keen appreciation of the facilities for study placed at his disposal, but has utilised them to the best advantage.'[30] A 1904 *Birmingham Mail* article reported that classes were 'readily seized upon … by older members of the Force who recognised their deficiencies'.[31] By 1912, classes sizes were smaller, twenty to thirty students, but attendance was closer to perfect. Students who attended regularly did well on exams.[32] Peacock was less successful getting men to attend classes in Manchester. The initial good response to the courses flagged, and by 1911 Peacock had to have his superintendents warn absentees to attend.[33] In 1916, Peacock announced the next class session and 'earnestly requested [men] to endeavour to obtain the highest possible number of attendances'. A similar statement was made in 1918 after poor attendance in the first week of classes.[34] What seems clear from both cities is that a core group of dedicated constables with hopes for promotion attended classes but that many men preferred to stay at home, particularly older men who had given up their earlier expectations for promotion.

Despite hopes that older constables who needed basic skills would take

---

letter warning Rafter that if attendance did not improve, they would lose the grant funding the schools, see 20 February 1901, p. 362.

[29]   BPO, 17, 28 February 1901, pp. 360, 368; 7, 14 March 1901, pp. 376, 382.

[30]   BPO, 26 April 1902, p. 75.

[31]   *Police Review and Parade Gossip*, 23 September 1904, p. 459.

[32]   BPO, 20 December 1912, p. 353.

[33]   MGO 6 March 1911.

[34]   MGO, 7 January 1916; 11 January 1918.

advantage of classes, regular students were likely to be young men working to advance their careers. Joseph Fowler of the Manchester City Police left behind two notebooks that provide a glimpse of a constable dedicated to his education. He joined the force in 1909 and married Florence in 1910. In 1912, at age twenty-five, he kept a personal notebook that he used to practice his writing skills and to memorize bylaws and legal definitions. He gave it a whimsical title, 'From a Convict to a Parson', with a price of sixpence, perhaps spoofing the titles given to police memoirs. The notebook included cases written out as practice for giving testimony in court, and essays on miscellaneous subjects such as water shrews and the rivers of Lancashire. These appeared to be copied since the vocabulary and knowledge were unusual, but they were not exact copies since he made mistakes in his grammar and spelling. He probably was practising essay-writing for promotional exams. He wrote out spelling lists of medical terms, maths problems, and questions and answers about local byelaws. Interspersed among the essays and questions were a strange mix of beat directions, job expenses, details on his family life, and descriptions of his life on duty. The book includes two essays that appear to be his own compositions, one on a strike, expressing his distaste for protecting blacklegs, and one called, 'Give the Working Class a Chance'. His prose was caustic, his main criticism of 'gentlemen' in government not so much that they deliberately attacked working families but that they made no effort to find out the consequences of their actions on the poor. Fowler suggested that the 'gentlemen who are continually talking about putting parks in the towns' should instead 'open some soup kitchens in different towns and feed the hungry and help to clothe the naked'.[35] Clearly, his class loyalties remained strong. Besides working on his classroom education, he received permission to set up a 'physical culture course' with eight to fourteen members that included lifting dumbbells. His efforts brought him moderate success but not the hoped for promotion to higher rank. Nevertheless, he kept involved in education. A second notebook from late in his career, titled 'The Gentleman's Letter Writer', contained mostly sample letters and reports, as well as miscellaneous personal information. But it also included the script for his role as a district surveyor in a mock-trial being staged at Mill Street Station in 1931, the main station for his division, either to help train probationers or prepare men for promotion exams.[36] He also transcribed a speech by a Labour candidate in a general election, who argued that 'the Capitalists ... [have] a View of Robbing the working classes of this country of their rights and freedom'.[37] Even late in his career, Fowler

---

[35] Fowler, 'From a Convict to a Parson', p. 23.

[36] Joseph Fowler, 'The Gentleman's Letter Writer' (Greater Manchester Police Museum: unpublished notebook, 1931), p. 35.

[37] Fowler, 'Gentleman's Letter', p. 51. The candidate was 'Gorton'. It is unclear if the election was in 1931 or from an earlier year.

continued to be a strong advocate for working-class rights. He retired in 1933 after twenty-five years of service, well loved by local children for his duties at a school crossing but still a constable.[38] His success might have been greater if the 1919 Police Act had not introduced tougher standards for promotion examinations. He began as a post-1890 young man but after a dozen years in the force, he found himself one of the postwar 'old police'.

The education gap between the pre- and post-1890 men was clear enough to catch the attention of chief constables. However, it paled in comparison to the stark contrast of the pre- and post-1919 generation. This gap was highlighted by the struggles of prewar men to pass new promotion examinations while new men with little practical experience got promoted ahead of them. The Desborough Committee urged that promotion not be by examinations alone, 'because of the importance of initiative, tact, judgment, and other personal qualifications which cannot be gauged by means of an examination paper', but no system for measuring these qualities was defined, and the recommendation to have 'experience points' added into examinations scores was never implemented.[39] The lack of action on this added to the bitterness of many older men. Police forces did try to lessen the impact of these exams in their initial years. Sample examinations were made available for study and the *Police Review* regularly published examination papers and aids for studying.[40] Guides such as Ernest Booth's *Police Students' Manual* and H. Child's *Self-Education for the Police* published sample examination questions. In Birmingham, the first examinations were intentionally 'easy and simple so as not to place men at a disadvantage who had not been prepared for the examinations laid down by the new order'.[41] Yet eight sergeants and fifty-five constables, most having joined the force before 1910, failed the Birmingham promotional examinations in 1920. The most common subject failed was bylaws, closely followed by civics, evidence, and arithmetic. They did better in Acts of Parliament, criminal law, and police orders.[42] A year later, a sergeant was caught cheating but only reprimanded. The light punishment possibly reflected the chief constable's sympathies for the difficulties the sergeant faced.[43] However, efforts to soften the blow could not

---

38   MWCM, 27 October 1938, vol. 218, no. 62. His 1931 notebook includes the draft of a letter thanking his division for contributions toward a testimonial, apparently on his retirement but clearly written in mid-1931 based on later entries (Fowler, 'Gentleman's Letter', p. 41). He died in 1938 from cancer of the stomach at age fifty-one. He was survived by his wife, Florence, also age fifty-one.

39   'Report of the Committee on the Police Service of England, Wales, and Scotland', 1920, Cmd. 574, vol. XXII, 539, p. 10.

40   See *Police Review*, 4 May 1923, p. 238.

41   BPO, 21 July 1927, p. 13108.

42   BPO, 4 January 1921, p. 3083. Other subjects failed included English, general knowledge, and geography.

43   BRB, 15 July 1921, PSD 14 James Gledhill, joined 1904, sergeant April 1919, 4 awards,

remove the fact that policemen hired before the war suddenly found promotion more difficult to achieve. HMI Atcherley remarked, 'One feels very sorry for men who have been looking forward to promotion after steady application to duty and find themselves suddenly confronted with an examination which they cannot pass.'[44] That veterans floundered in the new examination system gave new men another reason to think less of them.

While older men faltered, young postwar men passed their examinations and gained promotion in record time, sometimes making sergeant within two or three years of joining the force, much to the annoyance of the prewar men. Cities faced desperate shortages of sergeants, having lost men to the war and to strikes, and the experienced men who normally would have been promoted could not pass the new exams. Throughout the 1920s, Birmingham remained twenty to thirty sergeants below their authorized strength until enough men hired after the war qualified for promotion.[45] The 1919 Liverpool police strike added an unhappy dimension to the problem of replacing sergeants. A Liverpool 'Old Slogger' reasoned that many older men had given up on promotion under the city's notoriously corrupt prewar system and had neglected their education. This left them at an even bigger disadvantage than for most men under the new system. Resentment was caused when constables with only a few years' service were promoted to sergeant over the heads of constables with twenty years' experience. 'Old Slogger' considered the promotion of two- and three-year men, just because they could pass the exams, to be totally unfair considering their lack of practical street experience.[46] HMI Dunning also worried that young men were being promoted on their paper qualifications, instead of their practical knowledge and experience.[47] The case of Liverpool PC O'Byrne illustrated this point. After only a year's service, O'Byrne was made acting sergeant. But instead of monitoring his men, Byrne was twice caught at a public house outside of licensing hours, not only drinking himself but in the company of seven of his constables who should have been on duty.[48] Not all young sergeants had such poor judgment but Birmingham Assistant Chief Constable Moriarty agreed that men lacking experience made poor officers. 'Mere theoretical knowledge derived from books or lectures will not make a policeman unless it is backed by practical training and experience.' He did add that police work in the

---

no defaults; BJSC, 15 July 1921; BPO, 16 July 1921, p. 3802.

[44] 'Inspectors of Constabulary report for year ended the 29th September 1921', PP 1922 (5) x, p. 6; also '… September 1923', PP 1924 (19) xii, 65, p. 16.

[45] BAR, 1919–1929.

[46] *Police Review*, 27 February 1920, p. 181.

[47] 'Inspectors of Constabulary report for year ended the 29th September 1924', PP 1924–1925 (2316) xv, 177, p. 6.

[48] LDRB, 24 May 1921, PCD 122 O'Byrne, one year's service, acting sergeant, dismissed.

1920s necessitated well-instructed and intelligent men.[49] The difficulties of older men taking the new examinations were never satisfactorily resolved.

Despite all the worries about young postwar men being promoted too quickly, in the rivalry between experience and education, experience ultimately lost ground when it came to promotion. Letters on both sides regularly appeared in the *Police Review* throughout the 1920s and into 1930s.[50] Older constables believed that young constables, with their fancy education, did not appreciate that much of policing could only be learned on the streets. 'J.A.P.' related how, when he was a young constable around 1900, a veteran constable had taught him in five minutes the names and 'professions' of a gang of thieves, valuable information that no training school could give him.[51] 'Chip off the Old Block' wrote,

> the 1929 Policeman does not drop quite so many 'h's' as did his forbear of twenty odd years ago. But an 'h' or two does not make a better Policeman, for without them the old-timer was no idiot ... Can the Policeman of to-day efficiently put into practice what he learns in theory, or was the 'old school' best?[52]

This was the central question. Although chief constables understood the dangers of theory without experience, and were themselves prewar men, they supported the new policies, knowing that policemen needed a thorough education to cope with more complicated policing methods and duties involving radios, automobiles, and other forms of technology. Older constables could only resent younger men being promoted above them and continued to cry favouritism if promotion seemed premature.[53]

On the other side of this conflict, for postwar constables, the pay was good, and the police force was transforming into 'the service' and a real career. The 'new men' had not experienced the pre-1919 injustices over pay and usage which had led to protests for a union and the right to confer, culminating in the 1918 and 1919 strikes. The stories of prewar adversity and wartime privations seemed like

---

[49]   Moriarty, 'The Police Recruit', p. 454.

[50]   For examples, see *Police Review*, 24 June 1921, p. 337, 5 August 1921, p.413, 24 August 1923, p. 452, 11 October 1929, p. 767, 1 June 1934, p. 407.

[51]   *Police Review*, 20 January 1928, p. 45.

[52]   *Police Review*, 27 September 1929, p. 719.

[53]   This rivalry was complicated by prewar pensioners left on their prewar, inadequate pensions under the 1919 Police Act. Their police friends saw this as indicative of their own value in the eyes of the 'new men'. The *Police Review* called the treatment of prewar pensioners and widows a 'disgrace to our legislature' but found it difficult to get Parliament to act (*Police Review*, 18 January 1935, p. 50). See also *Police Review*, 21 January 1921, p. 36; 4 March 1921, p. 122.

tales of frustrated old unionists to those who did not live through them. Instead, postwar men resented older men hanging on after retirement age and blocking promotion. Once an officer reached a certain level in the hierarchy, especially if he had an office job, it was difficult to remove him unless his health was poor. One 'Youngster' complained that promotion was being barred in his force by two officers over retirement age who refused to take their pensions.[54] Other letters to the *Police Review* expressed similar complaints. Yet just like the post-1890 men, the 1919 generation found itself at a disadvantage after the next war and found themselves suddenly the old men.

In addition to generational divisions, police forces were riddled with favouritism networks. Policemen not only helped each other survive, they helped each other get ahead. Networks could be small, organized around friendships and family, or larger groups tied to religious affiliations and membership in the freemasonry. Men with normally incompatible loyalties, such as street constables and office staff, could be united by their regional backgrounds or through having been through probationary training together. Once men from a group were promoted, favouritism networks could be set up within the hierarchy. Because forces did not have a separate officer class, these could extend from the bottom to the top of the police. Constables could brag that they took tea with superintendents; one caught working in his parents' public house told bar patrons that he could not get into trouble because of his friendship with the assistant chief constable.[55] Networks not only helped each other, they discriminated against outsiders, blocking them from promotion to save positions for themselves and imposing harsh discipline to discourage them from complaining. Such favouritism created acrimony. They were inherently corrupt, manipulating procedures for their own ends. They forced men into ethical dilemmas, having to decide whether or not to participate. Men without the right relatives or religion were united in their common grievances but some must have resented the integrity forced upon them through their lack of influential connections. Favouritism was particularly bad before 1919 when promotion was more arbitrary. But even after the introduction of new promotional exams and procedures, complaints continued of unfair practices. As long as officers were promoted from the ranks, constables would always have both friends and foes in high places.

The extent of favouritism varied from the city to city, often tied to the character of chief constables and the degree of open communication in a force. After surviving a corruption scandal in 1897,[56] Manchester became the city least beset by biased promotion and discipline, but this was more a matter of degree

---

54   *Police Review*, 1 April 1921, p. 179. See also *Police Review*, 9 January 1925, p. 20.

55   MPF, 28 November 1935, PCA 285 James Lowe Grisdale, appointed January 1929, reduced two classes and finally warned.

56   See *In the Matter of an Inquiry*.

than of overall fairness. The unusual presence of a chief constable who had started as a beat constable kept abuses from reaching epidemic levels. Peacock was more aware of how networks operated than a chief constable who came from outside the police. Not all the men liked him, but they generally believed that he was fair, in part because he had walked the streets and because he explained his decisions more than most chief constables. But favouritism could not be eliminated entirely. For years, Manchester continued to have problems with men too cosy with city officials, the root of the 1897 scandal. Peacock had to issue warnings against policemen canvassing members of the city council regarding promotions[57] and an 'Ex-P.C.' complained that there was too much sociability between watch committee members and 'certain members of the Force', causing feelings of unrest.[58] While less troubled by religious discrimination than other forces, 'Almost Despairing' warned that Mancunian 'men of religion' were using their influence to climb up the hierarchy,[59] and 'Junius' claimed that his father had been passed over for promotion since he attended chapel rather than the Anglican church. Junius also wrote, 'the higher appointments ... frequently fall to men whose chief claim may be that they are the sons of their fathers, or that they are good Masons'.[60] This was an unusual charge for Manchester; freemasonry was more commonly mentioned in connection to favouritism in Liverpool.

Favouritism in Birmingham was worse, caused in part by a lack of communication between the rank and file and the chief constable's office. Charles Rafter, an RIC man, was not easy to approach or to work under due to his obsession with detail and military precision. Hopes on his 1899 appointment that he would stop the role of 'influence' were quickly dashed.[61] According to bitter letters to the *Police Review*, favouritism in Birmingham was built on a foundation of nepotism. One superintendent was accused of assigning a constable who was courting his daughter to the detective staff after only three years' service.[62] As in Manchester, there were complaints of inappropriate socializing between senior officers and influential members of the public.[63] A common rumour claimed that game keepers could get their sons promotion if they gave superintendents a day's shooting. Men complained that the same constables were constantly picked for special duty in other cities which brought extra allowance money while the constables left in Birmingham had to do extra work to cover the beats left vacant without extra

---

[57] MGO, 12 October 1911.

[58] *Police Review*, 19 January 1900, p. 28.

[59] *Police Review*, 10 October 1902, p. 483. He did not specify which religion.

[60] *Police Review*, 16 July 1915, p.344.

[61] *Police Review*, 10 October 1902, p. 483.

[62] *Police Review*, 28 June 1912, p. 303.

[63] *Police Review*, 21 September 1906, p. 447.

pay.[64] Not only did men get favourable assignments, constables believed that men were given special immunity from disciplinary offences. Sergeants did not dare report certain constables because of their connections higher up the scale. In 1912 and 1913, constables began transferring to different police forces to get away from what they considered to be 'the curse of the service'.[65] During the war, accusations were made that some men were always being given 'cushy beats'.[66] While favouritism was less blatant after the war, letters to the *Review* complaining about Birmingham appeared regularly into the 1930s.

The favouritism in Liverpool was notorious throughout the country, founded on membership in the freemasonry and 'anti-Romish domination'. Each rank was suspicious of the others, and everyone hated the 'creepers' who stepped on those below them while flattering those above. A 'Senior Sergeant' noted that large numbers of sergeants were retiring immediately at reaching twenty-five years' service out of disgust at having young 'creepers' promoted to inspectorships over them.[67] Before 1919, superintendents gave the chief constable a list of names recommended for promotion which was simply accepted without investigation. This gave superintendents a great deal of power over their men. If a superintendent did not favour a man who had passed examinations, he could wait until the constable committed some minor default, such as gossiping, and bar him from promotion for not having a 'clean book'. On the other hand, a favoured man's misconduct was overlooked. Inspectors and sergeants also had ways of taking advantage of their positions since superintendents often based recommendations on their reports. In one case, having both a 'clean book' and a pass on the sergeants' examination, PC George Miles was passed over for promotion by those junior to him who had failed the exam. During the war he held sergeant's rank in the army but had to forfeit it on returning to the police. In an interview with his chief constable, Caldwell admitted that Miles' grievance in being overlooked was genuine. Miles finally received promotion when the National Union of Police and Prison Officers (NUPPO) put pressure on the force in 1919.[68] While blocking promotion became harder after 1919, Liverpool never shed its reputation for having entrenched patronage networks.

One of the nastier features of networks was the 'creepers' and snitches

---

64   *Police Review*, 28 February 1913, p. 99.

65   *Police Review*, 13 February 1914, p. 75.

66   *Police Review*, 5 October 1917, p. 315; see also *Police Review*, 22 March 1912, p. 135.

67   *Police Review*, 13 February 1903, p. 75.

68   DC, Evidence, questions 3792–9, pp. 1943–49. The career of Inspector John Syme of the London Metropolitan Police was ended by favouritism. He founded the National Union of Police and Prison Officers (NUPPO) behind the police strikes of 1918 and 1919. See Gerald Reynolds and Anthony Judge, *The Night the Police Went on Strike* (London: Weidenfeld and Nicolson, 1968), pp. 6–21.

who collected and even invented objectionable information on colleagues. The information could be used to keep men off promotion lists or to pressure men to keep quiet about abuses. These informers remained an affliction even after the 1919 Police Act. All cities had them but Liverpool continued to suffer more than most. Some men forwarded information to ingratiate themselves with their superiors. Liverpool PS Millington accused PC Stone of snitching, protesting, 'You are the fellow that is reporting the sergeants. You are a bright buffer to report anybody.'[69] 'Ultra Vires' described discontent caused by tale-bearing constables passing stories on to senior officers who saved them to use against men when they were brought up for disciplinary offences.[70] In one case, disciplinary charges against two constables were 'over-held' for five and three months after the default had occurred, an action forbidden by regulations. Apparently, someone decided that the two men should no longer have clean books.[71] Birmingham had to hold an official enquiry into the band, due to 'certain members of the Band ... in the habit of carrying mischievous tales reflecting on other members of the Band'.[72] Some informers operated to their personal advantage. A constable who wanted to be appointed to an assistant clerkship arranged for his landlady to send an anonymous letter to the chief constable accusing PC Mackay, the current assistant clerk, of having his meals taken to the station by two neighbour girls in return for money. This ploy was only partially successful. The charge was disproved but Mackay was transferred to another division. The constable did not get Mackay's clerkship, however, and was also transferred.[73] PC Price's plan also backfired. He falsely reported that PC Blackwell had had an affair with another constable's wife in order to lose him his position. Instead, Price was reduced in rank for oppressive conduct.[74] While these two men were caught, other tale-bearing constables continued to harm careers through passing on information, both true and false.

The networks most commonly complained of were organized around religion. Every city had problems with denominational conflicts, but religion was a particular problem in Liverpool due to the city's large Irish Catholic population and the prevalence of freemasonry among the Protestants. According to one estimate, in 1900 Liverpool had one Catholic superintendent out of eight, four inspectors out of

---

69   LCCDR, 28 December 1927, PSB 7 Millington. The charge was not proven but Stone eventually retired as a sergeant with thirty years' service.

70   *Police Review*, 13 March 1931, p. 224.

71   LDRB, 10 November 1925, PCC 133 Nixon, four years' service, accepted a free bottle of beer on 29 May 1925, fined 20/-; PCA 269 Stazicker, five years' service, one default, neglect of duty on 11 July 1925, fined 10/-.

72   BPO, 28 January 1931, p. 17648.

73   LHCWC, 2 February 1903, pp. 202–3.

74   LDRB, 15 November 1921, PCH 392 Price, two years' service, reduced for oppressive conduct.

forty-four, one sub-inspector out of fourteen, thirteen sergeants of 219, and eighty-four constables out of 1594,[75] a group that could easily be charged with forming a faction. Catholics were accused of helping Catholics but these numbers did not actually indicate disproportionate promotion rates. This did not prevent Protestants from harassing Catholics. In 1902, the *Catholic Herald* reported that a 'No Popery' epidemic existed among sergeants and inspectors who taunted Catholic constables with sneers at their religion and accusations of 'Fenianism'.[76] During the war, Irish constables complained that newspaper cuttings describing Irishmen running away to avoid army service kept appearing on station bulletin boards.[77] Feelings against Catholics escalated during the 1930s in reaction to an Irish trade war with Great Britain.[78] In 1930, a Catholic Police Guild was formed in self defence. The chief constable had to reassure Protestants that the guild did not have official standing and was purely a social society. The Protestants responded by forming their own guild. Neither group was allowed to attend meetings in uniform.[79] A year later a constable of unspecified denomination was disciplined for distributing sectarian pamphlets on police premises.[80] In 1932, an angry Liverpool police officer wrote to the *Police Review*, 'To-day, service, seniority, and experience do not appear to be considered at all, your religion or creed appear to be an important factor in regulating your progress in the Service.'[81] The *Review* deleted references to the denomination favoured.

In 1932, at least one Protestant network and possibly a Catholic one were operating in Liverpool. PC Roberts and PC Spenceley belonged to a Protestant group of unknown size, which used Spenceley's friendship with Assistant Chief Constable Winstanley to influence appointments. When Roberts wanted a position in the Criminal Investigation Department, Spenceley took tea with Winstanley and convinced him to recommend Roberts for the post. The evidence suggests that Winstanley was not a knowing part of the group, yet he still favoured a man on the recommendation of a friend. Inspector Hinchin was accused by Roberts of being part of a similar Catholic group that used its social and family connections to get ten Catholic constables and sergeants appointed and promoted. The existence of these networks was uncovered when Roberts accused Inspector Hinchin of charging him with a breach of discipline because he was Protestant while the inspector was Catholic. Not satisfied with this, Roberts also accused Winstanley of favouritism, using as evidence a letter from Spenceley telling of Robert's own appointment to

75   *Police Review*, 25 May 1900, p. 243.

76   *Police Review*, 14 March 1902, p. 125.

77   *Police Review*, 20 August 1915, p. 400.

78   *Police Review*, 17 January 1930, p. 36.

79   LCCO, 4 January 1930.

80   LCCO, 21 February 1931.

81   *Police Review*, 22 April 1932, p. 312.

the CID. It is possible that he was angry at Winstanley for not protecting him against Hinchin, or, since Winstanley had begun his career as a junior clerk and was one of the resented staff officers, Roberts let his prejudice against the office staff overwhelm his judgment.[82] The immediate result of his charges was his own dismissal and a caution for Spenceley.[83] The letter was evidence for the Protestant group's existence; the rest of the accusations were based solely on Roberts' testimony. Most likely, unofficial inquiries were made into Roberts' charges, and Winstanley, Hinchin, and other officers given advice on their conduct. For the rest of the 1930s, accusations of religious favouritism stopped appearing in the *Police Review*, suggesting that Liverpool cracked down on the problem.

Possibly the most serious acrimony existed between the street policemen and the office staff.[84] Policemen working the streets were united in their resentment of men who rarely had to work night shifts or Sundays even though they held the same ranks and often wore the same uniforms. The office staff began as clerks and moved up through the administration. Particularly galling was the fast promotion of junior staff within two or three years of joining, even though they often did not fulfil height requirements and had little or no street experience. In one case, the son of a chief constable did only three days at recruits' school and then went into the Aliens' office as a clerk. There he was immediately given the rank of constable and within four years would likely be serving in headquarters as an inspector.[85] In 1912, a deputation of Manchester inspectors, sergeants, and constables tried to stop this practice by requesting that constables serve eight years before being eligible for acting sergeant and sergeants serve three years before eligible for inspector, but the watch committee exempted the office staff from these restrictions.[86] The animosity was worst in Liverpool where constables with connections made it onto the staff, regardless of their clerical skills. The Liverpool records made this clear, written in sloppy, even illegible, handwriting unlike the copper plate found in Manchester and Birmingham. During the Desborough Committee hearings in 1919, when asked about the practice of improper promotion of office clerks, Inspector Dale of Newcastle-upon-Tyne City Police replied, 'I think Liverpool is the most prominent

---

82   Liverpool Watch Committee Orders to the Head Constable, 23 December 1901.

83   LDRB, 11 July 1932, PCD 114 Roberts, eleven years' service, dismissed; LCCDR, 30 August 1932, PCH 372 Spenceley, admitted, cautioned.

84   See Robert Reiner, *The Politics of the Police* (New York: St Martin's Press, 1985), p. 93, on rivalries between the street and management.

85   DC, Evidence, questions 3743, 3742, 3749–51, PC Smithwick, LCP, p. 191. See also DC, Evidence, question 2302, PC George Strangeways, LCP, p. 129.

86   MWCM, 8 October 1912, vol. 56, no. 80. They also exempted the detective branch and other special branches. With a similar lack of success, policemen requested that band members be made to work all shifts, including night shifts (BPO, 18 October 1919, p. 1296, 31 December 1920, p. 3056; MGO, 31 March 1921).

in the minds of the police generally.'[87] The favourable treatment of office staff was a major focus for 'seething discontent' since street constables did not consider clerks to be 'the real rank and file'.[88] A dangerous consequence of this split was a lack of communication between the street policemen and the men at headquarters. Busy with growing bureaucratic requirements, a separate band of clerk constables, sergeants, inspectors, and superintendents had little notion of conditions outside headquarters. In Liverpool, they even had a clerk chief constable, Francis Caldwell, from 1912 to 1925, an appointment bitterly resented by many as a blatant sign of favouritism. Street constables, disliking their paper-pushing colleagues, had few opportunities to spell out the differences between arrest statistics and their daily experiences of policing. This failure of police unity contributed to the unrest that culminated in 1919 police strikes in Liverpool and Birmingham.[89]

Street constables resented detectives as well, but not out of doubts of their policing credentials. This relationship combined envy and anger that detectives had challenging duties apprehending criminals which the men on the street rarely enjoyed. Detectives received plain-clothes allowances, had more flexible hours, and earned gratuities for successful cases. Street constables sometimes received gratuities for arrests and rescues but not as often and rarely as much. The public prestige detectives received for solving cases could be irritating to constables who discovered a case and had done the original footwork. The practice of using regular constables for special plain-clothes duty could raise false hopes for a transfer into the more esteemed CID. The injustice of being overlooked stung both because of the lack of recognition and jealousy of the detectives. Even popular culture was against the beat constable. While police detectives were initially portrayed as 'watsons' in popular fiction, police detective heroes became more common in the 1920s and 1930s, while street constables remained plodders if mentioned at all. When the public heard the word 'policemen', they usually thought of detectives rather than men on the beat. At the same time, detectives could become annoyed at constables who tampered with evidence through ignorance, or delayed turning it over through a desire to keep a little glory in a case. These mutual irritations caused problems over suspects and evidence. Beat constables considered detectives to be real policemen, unlike the office staff; they simply wished that they could enjoy similar benefits.

After the war, rivalries grew along with a growing complexity of departments. As detection becoming more technical, Criminal Investigation Departments expanded, requiring more specialists such as photographers, crime-scene experts,

---

[87]   DC, Evidence, question 2307, p. 129; also DC, Evidence, question 3806, PC Smithwick, LCP, p. 194.
[88]   *Police Review*, 31 July 1908, p. 363; 26 May 1916, p. 248.
[89]   The police strikes are addressed in Chapter 5.

and fingerprint men. Traffic departments needed men directing traffic, riding motorcycles, driving cars, and maintaining vehicles. Men had to run telephone exchanges and maintain the equipment. Telephones in police-box and pillar systems needed to be kept in good repair. All of this created more paperwork, increasing the size of the office staff. Constables had more options for promotion but felt more resentment if left on street beats. Men complained that new departments took all the exciting tasks and left 'the skimmed varieties for the consumption of the rest of the force'.[90] This proliferation of departments created new allegiances and rifts, adding to the already existing confusion.

In spite of these many quarrels and feuds, a day-to-day camaraderie persisted among the constables on the streets. The strict regulations and conditions created an atmosphere of cooperation to help each other ease the discipline and boredom of the beat. Being at the bottom of the police totem pole, constables naturally pulled together to enjoy a little mutual comfort and grumbling. Camaraderie involved little things that made a difference in easing some of the stringency of the job, such as getting around force bureaucracy. For instance, even though banned from 'calling up' men while on their beats, constables continued this favour for their comrades to help them get to parade on time.[91] This practice was so common that in 1937 the watch committee gave notice that it must cease, without having much impact.[92] In return, constables let men patrolling their neighbourhoods put their feet up in their kitchens, such as when PC Oakes invited PC Skinner into his home to take nearly an hour's break before dawn on 23 December 1912, and then lied to his inspector when challenged about it.[93] Constables took turns going to headquarters on pay days to pick up wage packets, rather than everyone going. They even signed each other's names though the strangely similar handwriting tended to give this practice away.[94] Though ordered to submit their own versions of events, men involved in the same occurrence wrote their reports together to check their consistency.[95] Constables wrote reports for each other, to 'oblige' one another, in spite of being forbidden to hand in reports not in their own handwriting.[96] Acting rather like a family that bickered with each other but resented outside criticism, constables lied and prevaricated to cover up the misdemeanours of their colleagues. When disciplined for such offences, constables replied that they were

---

[90]   Tarry, 'Mechanization as an Aid to Police Duties', p. 212; *Police Review*, 19 January 1934, p. 36.

[91]   BPO, 24 November 1908, p. 485.

[92]   BPO, 24 February 1937, p. 27932.

[93]   BPO, 11 January 1913, p. 365.

[94]   BPO, 18 April 1902, p. 68.

[95]   BPO, 2 July 1908, pp. 389–91.

[96]   BPO, 15 May 1913, p. 463.

common practices regardless of the regulations. Even constables who were part of favouritism networks normally practiced the rituals of camaraderie both for their own comfort and for the practical reason that alienating too many colleagues could lead to problems later. Regardless of connections upwards, daily life still had to be lived at the lowest level.

While many police friendships began between men from the same group of recruits or from the same network, men from the same stations and on adjacent beats could put aside any differences in their common goal of getting through their shifts with a minimum of annoyance. Despite all their training that they patrol constantly and by themselves, men never stopped seeking each other out to take unauthorized breaks. During a dull stretch of election duty, PC Preston and PC Dunleavy passed the time playing cards,[97] and PCs Thornley and Taylor passed a cold night in front of the furnace fire in a church cellar playing checkers.[98] Another pair of constables enjoyed shared cigarettes and beer in the chauffeurs' room of a garage.[99] PC Binning took a break during his annual leave to oblige a colleague. While relaxing at the Church Tavern, he fetched a pint of beer for PC Sullivan, who was directing traffic nearby.[100] Men of all ages committed these offences together, the 'youngsters' having discovered what the older men already knew, that promotion did not come to everyone in spite of their education, and that friendships made the job a little easier. Only a year before his retirement, PS Dodd shared a spot of whisky with PC Moran, with five years' service. Dodd even covered up the fact that Moran had to be sent home drunk in a taxi cab to save Moran from discipline charges.[101] Another pair of senior and junior men shared a few too many drinks together one June afternoon while on neighbouring beats.[102] Regardless of any frictions, the man on the next beat was a constable's best friend during tedious stretches of duty. Even with connections, only so many constables could be promoted to sergeant; most figured out that being on friendly terms with each other was to everyone's advantage.

Helping each other out included lying to cover up each other's misbehaviour, especially when defaults seemed trivial or were a 'one time' occurrence. Chief

---

97   BOR, 4 December 1930, PCE 92 Alfred Preston, PCE 203 Victor John Dunleavy.

98   MGO, 26 February 1930; MPF, 17 February 1930, PCD 128 Edward Thornley, appointed April 1924. They were caught when the sergeant noticed their bicycles outside the church and went to investigate. Thornley replied to the charge, 'Very good Sergt, we have been caught, that's all.'

99   BPO, 22 September 1938, p. 29973.

100   Birmingham City Police Disciplinary Book 'D'Division, 7 April 1924, PCD 40 Robert James Binning, PCD 91 Edward Sullivan, p. 56.

101   LDRB, 10 March 1925, PSH 28 Dodd, twenty-four years' service, one default (1908), PCH 135 Moran, five years' service.

102   MWCM, 17 June 1920, vol. 82, no. 114, PCE 27 Gilbert Firth, fifteen years' service, one default, PCE 2 Samuel Elkin, six years' service, one default.

Constable Peacock lamented 'that very often when reports of misconduct are being investigated false statements are made by Police Officers'.[103] Serious actions could get a man reported by his fellow constables but generally loyalties to each other outweighed their loyalties to the 'reputation of the force'. In one instance, PC Roberts reported that his roommate, PC Widdars, was ill when in fact he was suffering from a hangover.[104] Lies were often a matter of silence. PCs Caldwell and Jones did not report that the Queen Adelaide public house was insecure because they also knew that PC Harrington was drinking inside.[105] Constables would cover for each other when a colleague was not where he was supposed to be. When PC Graham failed to 'ring on' from his police box, PC Chapman 'rang on' for him even though Graham had not actually paraded for duty. Chapman explained, 'I thought I was doing him a good turn.'[106] When Inspector Dyer asked PC Gillbanks the whereabouts of PC Rogers, he replied that Rogers had gone to the lavatory when he was actually loitering in the mess room.[107] PC Brown, while acting sergeant, 'well-knowing at that time that Con "C" Wilson was absent', drunk and unfit for duty, reported that his section had been properly dismissed, hoping that no one would notice Wilson's absence.[108] Constables did favours for their sergeants both as friends and in hopes of getting a good report. When PS Griffiths was unfit for duty through drink, two constables 'overheld' reports of his condition for eighteen hours until he was sober, making proving the offence more difficult.[109] When PS Brierley neglected a case of illness in the streets, PCs Morris and Frankland made 'a false and misleading statement' when his case came before the chief constable.[110] PC Jordan went so far as to hide the fact that a fellow constable who had deserted from the army had been to his house.[111] Part of the fabrications and prevarications was a genuine protective reflex against the upper ranks but constables no doubt hoped that their colleagues would return the favour, particularly if later promoted.

The daily camaraderie of policemen hopefully lessened the rivalries and antagonisms, allowing constables to carry out their duties without too much aggravation. For many men, being on good terms with each other paid off better

---

103   MGO, 13 July 1900.

104   LDRB, 3 October 1908, PCE 100 Widdars, one year's service; PCE 195 Roberts, four years' service.

105   MGO, 12 July 1900, both dismissed.

106   MPF, 3 January 1937, PCC 226 Charles William Chapman, appointed July 1930.

107   LDRB, 11 June 1929, PCE 92 Gillbanks, three years' service, PCE 234 Rogers, five years' service.

108   LDRB, 26 January 1926, PCC 221 Brown, five years' service.

109   MGO, 1 August 1929.

110   MGO 24 October 1930.

111   LDRB, 8 May 1916, PCA 273 Jordan, eleven years' service, one default, allowed to resign. Also threatened to take legal proceedings against the inspector who had found out about the deserter.

than too blatant an alliance with a faction. Constables could help each other out and still reserve special favours for their particular friends if they exercised a moderate amount of tact. Preventing divisions from becoming blatant often depended on the leadership of chief constables willing to crack down on abuses. Peacock was able to restore some equilibrium in Manchester after its scandal but Rafter failed to silence accusations of nepotism and favouritism. Since the staff at headquarters was often cut off from rumblings among the street ranks, perhaps a scandal could be required to make headquarters aware of problems in their own forces. Forces unable to rein in factionalism could be undermined by critical breakdowns, with men from different groups unable to trust each other. There is no question that rampant corruption in the Liverpool force was a major cause of its collapse in 1919, with nearly 1000 men fired for striking. Despite this disaster, religious favouritism continued to plague the force into the 1930s when Chief Constable Kennedy finally seemed able to quieten many complaints. No force was free of factionalism but most avoided the extremes of Liverpool. Yet even there, constables realized that promotions could be slow if they came at all, even for the best connected, so it made sense to be on good terms with the men on the next beats. A colleague might be a different age or religion but he could still be handy in a crisis and an agreeable companion during long hours of duty.

5

Police Unions and Federations

There is no comparison between what is expected from the policeman of to-day and the policeman of old ... [But] because we have evolved from the 'Bobby of old' to what we are to-day, you are not paying us as much as the lowest paid labourer.

PS George Miles, Liverpool City Police

We believe that policemen have for years suffered in silence; they have had no medium through which they could voice their grievances excepting through a few friends in Parliament.

PC William Sinclair, Birmingham City Police

[I]t was considered by the authorities that we had means of representation. We put forward that it was not so and that up to the present we have many grievances but have no means of airing those grievances.

PS Matthew Seaman, Manchester City Police[1]

DURING THE NINETEENTH CENTURY, policing had been ranked as an unskilled working-class job, comparable to unskilled agricultural labourers. Three-quarters of constables left with under five years' service, and only fifteen per cent made it to retirement age.[2] Few of the men patrolling the streets qualified as experienced policemen. With the 1890 Police Act and growing police responsibilities, this began to change. In Manchester, of the men joining between 1900 and 1914, only a third left with under four years' service, and nearly a quarter put in at least twenty-six years of service.[3] The numbers remaining in the force might have been higher if the First World War had not drawn away so many men. Fewer

---

1   DC, Evidence, pp. 184, 297, 173.
2   Steedman, *Policing the Victorian Community*, p. 93.
3   Manchester City Police roster cards, 1900–1914. For more complete length of service figures, see Chapter 10.

men treated the police as a casual job, and policemen began to see their work as a career requiring special skills, rather than simply a regular wage. However, watch committees continued to treat policemen as unskilled labour. Part of this was their desire to save ratepayers' money, but part was a failure to recognize that policing was evolving into a more complex and demanding occupation. Conditions of service, training, and pay continued to reflect the police force's nineteenth-century origins. To economize, watch committees also resisted appeals to increase wages to keep up with inflation. In the years leading up to the war, not only was police pay not improving along with their responsibilities, their real pay was declining.

Beginning around 1900, at the same time that unionism was spreading through many working-class occupations, policemen struggled to find a voice within the police force.[4] Ideally, they wanted to change their conditions and pay to match the skilled status that policing now deserved. More urgently, they needed pay increases to stop inflation from eating away their wages. Initially, few considered unionizing. All but the most aggrieved men recognized the paradox of joining a union while policing strikes. Instead, their attempts to influence watch committees and chief constables took place within the accepted boundaries of police conduct, relying on petitions and delegations. But these measures largely failed. Watch committees did not want to spend the money, and chief constables did not comprehend the financial pressures on their men. Frustrated at being ignored, policemen wrote increasingly angry letters to the *Police Review and Parade Gossip*. By 1910, they toyed with setting up a union or some other formal organization. Few supported the idea of policemen 'downing tools' but a union could provide them with the clout they needed to be taken seriously. In the years immediately preceding the First World War, tiny police unions appeared in some forces. Under the stresses of wartime inflation, the union movement came to life, culminating in the London Police Strikes of 1918, and the Liverpool, London, and Birmingham Police Strikes of 1919.[5]

The police strikes resulted in pay scales that recognized policemen's skilled status but had less success in gaining policemen representation within the force. The

---

4   For more on police efforts to organize, see Joanne Klein, 'Blue-Collar Job, Blue-Collar Career: English Policemen's Perplexing Struggle for a Voice in the Early Twentieth Century', *Crime, Histoire & Sociétés/Crime, History & Societies* 6:1 (2002): 5–29. Portions of this chapter are drawn from the article.

5   Many works exist on the union activities of the working class in the prewar period. Henry Pelling's *A History of British Trade Unionism* (London: Macmillan, 1987) provides a more traditional view. John Benson's *The Working Class in Britain 1850–1939* (New York: Longman, 1989) addresses unionism from a more social context. Also C.J. Wrigley, ed., *A History of British Industrial Relations 1875–1914* (New York: Harvester, 1982) and H.A. Clegg, et al., *A History of British Trade Unions since 1889*, vols I and II (New York: Clarendon Press, 1964, 1985). On police forces and strikes, see Roger Geary, *Policing Industrial Disputes: 1893–1985* (Cambridge: Cambridge University Press, 1985), and Jane Morgan, *Conflict and Order: The Police and Labour Disputes in England and Wales, 1900–1939* (New York: Clarendon Press, 1987).

1918 London strikes resulted in better pay scales and the creation of the Committee on the Police Service of England, Wales, and Scotland, known as the Desborough Committee. The 1919 strikes forced the committee not only to focus on pay but to take seriously rank-and-file concerns with training, promotion, corruption, and favouritism. Both strikes uncovered a disturbing lack of awareness in the upper ranks. Chief constables had to admit surprise at their own men's difficulties living on their wages and at the deep resentment caused by corrupt promotion practices. The 1919 Police Act, with its better pay scale and new promotion requirements, reflected efforts to respond to these problems. How to give policemen a voice within the force proved more difficult to resolve. Membership in unions was banned. Instead, the committee created the Police Federation to act as an advocate for the men. However, it remained weak and relatively ineffectual throughout the interwar period since it had no power to back up its proposals. Men were hesitant to join an organization that felt like a counterfeit union. It was no coincidence that Manchester, which did not experience the strike, had the most active federation, and Liverpool, shattered by the strike, had a federation in name only. Mancunians had no fired police strikers or 'black legs' to make them feel uncomfortable participating in the Federation. Ironically, the Federation was also weakened by the standardization of pay, pensions, and promotion. Before 1919, policemen had used better conditions in other forces as leverage for change in their own. While this still held true for some matters such as uniforms and shift details, major changes now had to be addressed nationally rather than locally.[6]

Policemen had worked to improve their work conditions before the 1900s but their unskilled status left them in a weak position with local and national governments. In 1853 Manchester staged a protest 'strike' through mass resignations but the men were simply replaced. In London, they held two short strikes, one in 1872 against poor pay and conditions and one in 1890 calling for a union, but these accomplished nothing beyond the firing of the strike leaders. Policemen petitioned Parliament, but the government took its time studying requests. A 1870s and 1880s campaign for pension rights only succeeded after the 1889 Great London Dock Strike convinced Parliament that they needed reliable policemen to control tumultuous unions. Policemen had better success in 1885 with a national petition requesting the police franchise, receiving the vote for Parliamentary elections in 1887 and municipal elections in 1893.[7] Policemen noted that national campaigns,

---

[6]   For a long-term perspective on police pay and conditions from 1829 to 1965, see J.P. Martin and Gail Wilson, *The Police: A Study in Manpower*, (London: Heinemann, 1969).

[7]   Steedman, *Policing the Victorian Community*, pp. 124–30, 132–6; Emsley, *The English Police*, pp. 95–8; V.L. Allen, 'The National Union of Police and Prison Officers', *Economic History Review*, 2nd ser., 11:1 (1958): 133; Reynolds and Judge, *The Night the Police Went on Strike*, pp. 202–25. The entire Liverpool City Police signed the franchise petition and sent it on to Manchester (MWCM, 9 July 1885, p. 51, 18 November, 1 December 1886, pp. 240, 248).

while slow, worked better than local ones, and that petitioning could produce results. At the same time that this became clear, they gained a way to communicate with each other across force lines.

In 1893, John Kempster founded the *Police Review and Parade Gossip*, a national newspaper targeted specifically at the lower ranks, where policemen could air their grievances and compare local conditions.[8] For the first time, policemen could read about what was going on in other forces with training, conditions of service, promotion, personnel, and a variety of other issues, and see how their local force measured up. They could voice their opinions in letters to the editor and find out what other policemen had on their minds. Common issues soon became obvious. Policemen wanted better pay and regular days off, and an end to corruption and favouritism. They wanted recognition for the change of policing from an unskilled to a skilled occupation. They wanted the right to confer with the legal authorities over them. The *Review* became a national forum for coordinating pressures on local and national government. Kempster was a strong advocate of government action and used the *Review* to mount campaigns on pay, a weekly rest day, pension rights, and other conditions of service. He supplied detailed information on different forces so that policemen could see their local conditions in national context and use that information in their petitions for improvements at home. He also worked to pressure Parliament to adopt national policies to end sometimes enormous discrepancies in force conditions. While most early campaigns inspired by the *Review* were local, policemen could now compare strategies and results with each other nationally. Knowing that they were part of a nationwide movement for change gave them a new confidence and sense of direction. Through the *Review*, policemen found common cause with each other.

The most immediate issue was pay and the criteria used to set it, the one issue that could unite policemen in spite of any other antagonisms. Before the First World War, wages matched those of agricultural workers, and rare increases in pay meant that policemen were underpaid even according to that standard. Inflation accelerated the deterioration of pay until by 1914 many policemen found it difficult to make ends meet. As the economic distress grew, so did calls for some mechanism for the rank and file to have their concerns both heard and acted upon. No system existed for policemen to bring complaints before watch committees and chief constables beyond petitions and delegations which were typically ignored. The usual arguments against raising pay included boot and rent allowances, uniforms, and free medical attendance given policemen. The lack of response to carefully researched and detailed requests for better pay led

---

8   The Chief Constables Association, also founded in 1893, provided similar opportunities for the heads of borough forces to compare local conditions in a national forum (Emsley, *English Police*, pp. 100–1).

to growing agitation for some kind of police association and the right to confer. The frantic need for better pay due to wartime inflation, downplayed by oblivious authorities, culminated in the creation of the National Union of Police and Prison Officers (NUPPO) and the police strikes of 1918 and 1919. Poor communication between police headquarters and the streets left authorities unaware of the severity of rank-and-file discontent until it was too late.

In January 1900, in response to urgent requests from readers, the *Review* launched a national campaign to pressure governments to improve police pay scales, most of which had not been adjusted since the 1890 Police Act (see Table 2). Policemen hoped that surging union activity would convince governments to take their petitions seriously. To help men make their cases, the *Review* published a list of 122 English borough rates of pay for constables, including the strength of each force and pension requirements. Manchester and Birmingham constables began at twenty-four shillings a week, and Liverpool at twenty-five shillings. This was typical of borough forces regardless of size.[9] In their demands for better pay, policemen often used the ideal police image from their instruction books to bolster their case. They argued that they had to have special physical, moral, and educational qualifications, that, unlike soldiers, they had to 'campaign' every day of the year and that, overall, 'our duties are more "responsible, onerous, and difficult" than those which have to be faced by any other body of public servants'.[10] But the campaign had limited success. In the next few years, some forces did get two or three shilling increases in pay but many did not. Nowhere did pay increases reflect a shift of policing from unskilled to skilled status.[11]

As part of this national campaign, policemen in Manchester and Liverpool immediately began petitioning their watch committees for better pay. In March 1900, a delegation of Manchester inspectors, sergeants, and constables told the watch committee that policemen were paid less than 'all classes of workmen' and 'all Corporation workmen'. They argued that 'if we are to maintain an independent and respectable station in life, it is absolutely necessary that our wages should be increased to enable us to do so'. In spite of these arguments, the

---

9   *Police Review and Parade Gossip*, 12 January 1900, pp.15–16. Forty-six forces began at 24/-; twenty-two at 23/-; twenty-one at 25/-; fourteen at 22/-; eleven at 21/-. A handful of forces made 26/- or 27/- a week and a couple made 20/- or 19/-. Very small forces paid both high and low wages so size was not the deciding factor. Larger than most forces, Birmingham had a strength of 700 men; Liverpool had 1460; Manchester 1031.

10   *Police Review*, 3 May 1901, p. 207.

11   According to Robert Roberts, the average adult male industrial worker earned £75 a year in 1910, the average middle-class man £340. Average police wages would be about the same as those of the industrial worker. He also stated that from 1896 to 1912, the purchasing power of the pound had dropped from 20/- to 16/3d. His claim that Manchester police were given a pay rise in 1912 to prevent sympathy with strikers is not borne out by internal police records (Roberts, *The Classic Slum*, pp. 18, 84, 99).

Table 2. *Starting pay for constables, 1900–1939, in shillings/pence per week*

	Birmingham	*Liverpool*	*Manchester*
1900	24/-	25/-, increased to 25/7	24/-
1901			26/-
1903	26/-		
1914	29/-		28/-
1915	War bonus 2/6 (September)	War bonus 1/6 (July)	
1917	War bonus 4/6 (December)	War bonus: married 6/-; single 3/- (December)	War bonus 6/- (April)
1918	War bonus 13/6 (May); increased to 20/- (July)	War bonus 10/8 (January); increased to 13/4 (May)	Pay 35/- (March); war bonus 16/- (April); increased to 20/- (August)
1918	Met Scale 43/-; war bonus 12/- (September), adopted after the 1918 London Police Strikes	Met Scale 43/-; war bonus 12/- (September), adopted after the 1918 London Police Strikes	Met Scale 43/-; war bonus 12/- (September), adopted after the 1918 London Police Strikes
1919	Desborough Scale 70/- (July); part of 1919 Police Act	Desborough Scale 70/- (July); part of 1919 Police Act	Desborough Scale 70/- (July); part of 1919 Police Act
1931	Ten per cent pay cut on recommendation of Committee on National Expenditure; abolished 1933	Ten per cent pay cut on recommendation of Committee on National Expenditure; abolished 1933	Ten per cent pay cut on recommendation of Committee on National Expenditure; abolished 1933
1933	New entrants 62/-; after three years' service 70/-	New entrants 62/-; after three years' service 70/-	New entrants 62/-; after three years' service 70/-

Sources: *Police Review*, 12 January 1900, p. 15; BPO, 1 September 1915, p. 36; 12 August 1919, pp. 1003–4; BWCM, 15 July 1903, pp. 447–52; 19 December 1916, p. 5; 16 June 1917, p. 103, 8 October 1917, p. 159; 1 May 1918, p. 301; 22 July 1918, p. 345; 9 October 1918, p. 391; Birmingham City Police Revised Scale of Pay 2 September 1918; LCCO, 15 October 1918, p. 42; Liverpool Watch Committee to the Head Constable, 26 November 1900; LWCM, 25 July 1916, p. 574; 12 December 1916, p. 98; 29 November 1917, p. 28; 29 January 1918, pp. 152–3; 28 May 1918, p. 342; 25 September 1918, p. 513; MGO, 6 February, 1901; 8 January 1914; 21 November 1917; 21 March 1918; 29 August 1918; 2 October 1918; 10 October 1918; 30 July 1919; MWCM, 3 April 1916, no. 54, vol. 70; 4 January 1917, no. 19, vol. 73; 'Report of the Committee on Police Pay (New Entrants)', 1932–1933, Cmd. 4274, vol. XV, 379.

watch committee postponed consideration of the request for a year for economic reasons.[12] At the same time, however, Chief Constable Peacock's salary was increased from £800 to £1000.[13] A Manchester inspector wrote in response to this news, 'it seems hard that their request for increased pay should have to be put back because the authorities have been too lavish in their expenditures'.[14] Manchester eventually received a rise of two shillings a week in February 1901 but this kept them within the 1900 national average.[15] Liverpool sergeants and constables acted in July 1900, submitting a petition more detailed and thoughtful than most. They quoted rent increases from sixpence to a shilling over the last five years and noted that artisan wages were now ten to fifteen shillings in excess of police wages. Yet, they were 'expected to keep up a position equal to them and to clothe our children respectably'. They pointed out that they and their families were entirely dependent on the constable's wages. Their wives could not work and their children had a difficult time finding jobs, unlike manufacturing areas such as Manchester and Birmingham. They requested a rise of two shillings a week, but in November the watch committee increased the pay for probationers by only sevenpence a week, and otherwise the scale remained unchanged.[16] That the Liverpool petition did not include inspectors probably would not have made a difference in the result but the cooperation of constables, sergeants, and inspectors in Manchester indicated the better cross-rank communication there than in most forces.

Birmingham policemen under the watchful eye of Rafter were slower to act. Rumours of a similar petition existed early in 1901 but nothing came of them. Letters in the *Review* belittled the Birmingham motto of 'Forward' since they were one of the last forces to receive a pay rise but the men themselves did little to forward their cause.[17] In October 1901, superintendents and inspectors successfully petitioned for better pay but the constables and sergeants lacked the initiative to get a petition off the ground.[18] Finally, in November 1901, 'A' division solicited permission from Rafter to meet and put forward a delegation regarding pay, duty, and leave.[19] That same day, Rafter wrote a letter to a superintendent expressing his distaste for 'subversive activity'. He considered 'furtively signing a round-robbin, circulating anonymous circulars among members of the

12   MWCM, 22 March 1900, vol. 10, no. 7, 13 June 1900, vol. 10, no. 138; *Police Review*, 30 March 1900, p. 154.

13   *Police Review*, 30 March 1900, p. 153.

14   *Police Review*, 22 June 1900, p. 291.

15   MGO, 6 February 1900.

16   LWCM, 23 July 1900, pp. 172–6; *Police Review*, 21 September 1900, p. 448; Liverpool Watch Committee Orders to the Head Constable, 26 November 1900.

17   *Police Review*, 28 June 1901, p. 303.

18   *Police Review*, 18 October 1901, p. 496; 25 October 1901, p. 508.

19   BPO, 23 November 1901, p. 574.

Force, unauthorised or secret meetings, anonymous letters to the press putting forward alleged grievances ... derogatory to the character and discipline of the Birmingham City Police Force ... highly insubordinate and reflects discredit ... upon those ... taking part in such proceedings'.[20] He was particularly annoyed by paragraphs showing up in local newspapers. While he gave permission for 'A' division to meet, their petition was shelved by the watch committee during the Lloyd George riots in December 1901 and was then lost.[21] Only in July 1903 did constables and sergeants present a successful petition to the watch committee. Even that was a mixed blessing. It gave one and two shilling rises to some men but others got no rise at all.[22] Birmingham had such a bad reputation that, after this new pay scale appeared, the *Review* called its watch committee 'the most indifferent and the meanest towards its Police of all the great corporations in the country'.[23]

Despite mostly poor results from petitions, policemen persisted in them as their pay continued to erode, not having obvious alternatives. Still lacking even the modest pay increases gained by Manchester and Birmingham, a 1907 Liverpool delegation of constables presented an elaborate petition signed 'on behalf of the elected delegates from each Division representing 1605 Constables'. It included the weekly budget of a married man with under fifteen years' service and two children, receiving £1/13/3d. a week. Expenses for rent, coal and light, groceries, vegetables, butcher, fish, milk, friendly societies, flour and yeast, and the Tontine society came to £1/10/9d. This left only half a crown for education, repairs, clothing, newspapers, amusements, the doctor, tobacco, holidays, tram fares, fruit, sweets, and church. They pointed out that rent allowances were only given for 'approved' neighbourhoods where they could ill afford to live. They detailed how inflation undermined their wages, making it impossible 'to keep up a respectable appearance required of him and his family'. Finally, they compared their pay to the better pay in Leeds and Blackburn forces. The petition ended with the insistent demand that 'we are entitled to have justice meted out to us'. The watch committee responded curtly that it was 'unable to accede to the constables' request'.[24] Manchester's police kept petitioning as well. In 1911, a request for a shilling rise failed and in 1912 they tried again, pointing out that it had been ten years since their last pay rise. The watch committee rejected the request.[25] In 1913, Birmingham policemen tried a more creative tactic. Protesting against

---

20   BPO, 23 November 1901, p. 574.

21   *Police Review*, 28 June 1901, p. 303; 25 July 1902, p. 351; 13 February 1903, pp. 75–6.

22   BWCM, 15 July 1903, pp. 448–52.

23   *Police Review*, 7 August 1903, p. 381.

24   LWCM, 14 May 1907, pp. 350–4. This budget is similar to those submitted to the *Police Review* by police wives (see p. 258).

25   MGO, 7 April 1911; MWCM, 20 February 1912, vol. 53, no. 183.

inadequate compensation for extra duty during a railway strike, they refused to sign their pay sheets for the extra pay. The watch committee considered one day's extra pay sufficient to cover any extra duty. The men protested that the extra pay did not recognize men who had worked up to four extra days or men who had not performed any strike duty at all. The watch committee told local papers that they had not heard of any serious dissatisfaction about the pay and discounted reports that between 300 and 400 men, about a third of constables, had refused to accept the extra pay. The ranks' efforts to change the pay award were ignored as the actions of a 'few grumblers'.[26] Because watch committees persistently failed to listen to their concerns, support for a police union began to spread among the rank and file.

Policemen had even less success changing pension standards than in improving pay. For many, one consolation for poor pay and conditions was looking forward to their pensions. This made pensions almost more controversial than pay, since many policemen believed that watch committees did everything they could to avoid paying them and then tried to pay as little as possible. After decades of petitioning Parliament, policemen had been granted pensions in the 1890 Police Act, which allowed a policeman to retire after twenty-five years' service, or after fifteen years on medical grounds. But despite the national legislation, watch committees constantly fiddled with pensions. To keep pension rates low, they granted non-pensionable allowances for boots, rent, and so on, instead of paying men higher pensionable wages that would cover the same expenses. They set age minimums, usually age fifty-five which was the maximum age allowed under the Act, that required men to stay in the force for as much as eight or nine years past the twenty-five years set out in 1890. Committees argued that men retiring on pension before age fifty-five became a long-term drain on the rates. Most forces had a twenty-six-year service minimum to receive the full pension in addition to the age minimum. Liverpool's minimum was increased to thirty years in 1903 to save money on pensions though allowed half pensions after twenty-six years.[27] Manchester required thirty years for any pension.[28] Policemen everywhere wanted the 1890 Act to be the standard. They argued that they felt worn out by age fifty, and keeping them on broke their health.[29] More importantly, particularly in forces such as Liverpool with favouritism problems, they feared losing their pensions altogether if they committed a default after they should have been allowed to retire. However, policemen made even less headway with pensions than with pay.

---

[26]   *Police Review*, 24 October 1913, p. 508.

[27]   LHCWC, 10 July 1905, p. 213.

[28]   DC, Evidence, question 5542, p. 268. Beginning in 1903, Liverpool constables could retire on half-pay pensions after twenty-six years, and two-thirds-pay pensions after thirty years (LHCWC, 10 July 1905, p. 213).

[29]   See *Police Review*, 28 February 1902, p. 99; 4 March 1904, p. 117; 27 May 1904, p. 255.

Only the 1919 Police Act stopped watch committees from side-stepping national pension standards.[30]

The lack of response from watch committees was not merely frustrating; by 1910 the real value of police pay and pensions had dropped below 1900 levels. Manchester was losing men to the city tram service which paid their drivers thirty-five shillings a week after four years' service, instead of after fifteen years in the police. In Birmingham, it took twenty years to reach thirty-six shillings a week and they were as much as four to six shillings a week behind other forces at certain levels. The city was losing men at an alarming rate.[31] Liverpool had received no pay increases at all, except for the trifling sevenpence given new recruits in 1900. Grievances over compensation grew louder and more belligerent. One Manchester constable asked his colleagues, 'Are you going to let the authorities "economise" for ever, at your expense?'[32] In 1914, watch committees finally granted pay increases in Manchester and Birmingham, with Manchester recruits now beginning at twenty-eight shillings and Birmingham at twenty-nine shillings a week.[33] But these increases were not enough to cover the growing cost of living. Liverpool remained at their 1900 pay. By this time, police unionism was taking hold in the rank and file.

Policemen began connecting the persistent lack of response from watch committees with regulations against their right to organize. Not long after the *Review*'s 1900 pay campaign yielded mixed results, letters began debating the option of unionizing. Other workers were unionizing successfully, and letter-writers challenged their colleagues to think of a better way to get authorities to listen to them. As petitions kept failing and pay kept eroding, letters to the editor became

---

30   Complicating the pension debate were reserve systems, allowed under the 1890 Police Act but seen by many as a way that watch committees reneged on paying pensions. The system allowed men eligible for pensions to retire, securing their pensions, and then be rehired. They received their pensions and about two-thirds of their old rate of pay, and agreed that their pension could not be retabulated at the higher rate of pay. The system was adopted in Liverpool in 1898 and in Birmingham in 1902. For men fearful of serving after twenty-five years for fear of losing pensions, the system gave them security. Others saw it as a manoeuvre by watch committees to get men to accept lower pensions in exchange for safety. Most men chose not to join reserves. The reserve system ended with the 1919 Police Act.

31   *Police Review*, 26 September 1913, p. 459; 22 March 1912, p. 139; 11 July 1913, p. 327.

32   *Police Review*, 8 March 1912, p. 111.

33   MGO, 8 January 1914; BWCM, 8 October 1917, p. 159, copy of August 1914 Scale of Pay. The Manchester pay rise was impeded by removing the age limit for maximum pensions which hurt about 300 older police officers who had joined under the system allowing them maximum pension at age fifty-five (*Police Review*, 16 January 1914, p. 31). Delegations representing inspectors, sergeants, and constables met with the watch committee to remedy the anomaly but the committee could not recommend any alteration in the new pay scale (MGO, 31 January, 3 February, 14 March 1914). The issue was still alive and unresolved in a *Police Review* article of 5 February 1915, p. 67.

more heated, comparing police conditions with Russian autocracy and Saxon slavery, where masters could grant requests and be seen as benevolent but slaves could not make those same requests without being labelled disloyal.[34] 'One and All' insisted that if postmen and street sweepers could organize into federations to protect their interests, then so should the police.[35] A Manchester constable wondered why, 'when the whole industrial community is at war with the powers that be, the Police forces of this country ... are apparently the weakest set of men in the whole community'. He suggested that policemen use the industrial 'war' to their advantage.[36] By 1910, police unionism was 'in the air'. In 1911, rumours of a Birmingham union reached Rafter but nothing could be confirmed.[37] In 1912, the same year that Francis Caldwell was promoted chief constable from the despised 'office clerk track', the Liverpool watch committee denied a request from constables for permission to form a union.[38] News that a Paris police union had received official recognition in 1913 encouraged English police unionists.[39] In September 1913, the *Review* ran an advertisement informing London policemen that they could secretly join a union.[40] In October 1913, a week after the failed Birmingham pay protest, a tiny police union appeared there. It aimed to ensure fair promotions, give legal representation in discipline cases, fully implement the weekly rest day, and achieve better pay and allowances. Its secretary insisted that the union was not a breach of force rules but Rafter begged to differ. In a police order, he stated that any private meetings of policemen were contrary to regulations unless of a 'legitimate purpose' cleared with him.[41] Rafter, like most chief constables, believed that the majority of his men was opposed to a union. But in the pages of the *Review*, letters debated between having a full trade union with a right to strike or having an association with only the right to confer. They debated whether their organization should also have a political lobby group. The men were no longer debating whether or not they needed their own organization.[42]

Even while letters to the *Review* debated the issue of police unionism, the *Review*'s editor tried to divert attention to a new campaign in the hopes of demonstrating that policemen did not need a union to be heard. Kempster was one of policemen's strongest advocates but he was alarmed at the growing militancy of

---

34   *Police Review*, 1 June 1906, p. 261; 17 January 1908, p. 34.
35   *Police Review*, 11 March 1904, p. 124. Both he and 'Brum' believed that at least policemen should support the Police and Citizens Friendly Association, a lobby group supported by voluntary subscriptions (*Police Review*, 12 January 1906, p. 20).
36   *Police Review*, 8 March 1912, p. 111.
37   Emsley, *The English Police*, p. 133.
38   LWCM, 12 February 1912.
39   Allen, 'The National Union of Police and Prison Officers', p. 133.
40   Emsley, *The English Police*, p. 99.
41   BPO, 30 October 1913, p. 587.
42   *Police Review*, 31 October 1913, pp. 523–4.

the support for a union. In January 1906, the *Review* began a national campaign to lobby local and national governments to grant policemen a weekly rest day. Before 1910, policemen had no guarantee of any regular time off. In 1900, they typically had one free day a month. Watch committees resisted adding more days since this required hiring men to cover every beat. The *Review*'s campaign focused on fairness. Other workers enjoyed one day off a week so this should not be denied to constables who were expected to act as moral examples and upholders of the constitution. Reasons giving by a 'Manchurian' in favour of 'one rest day in seven' included:

> (1) It is a Divine command; therefore a human duty. (2) It is a human need. We suffer if we do not attend to it. We need a more regular cessation, which we believe would improve our health ... (5) Having only one Sunday off clear in every three months, it kills all desire for attending to the spiritual side of our nature, thereby causing a weakening of character; and unfits us for doing Police duty as it should be done.[43]

Any comments by the public in favour of the rest day made their way into the *Review*'s columns. During Manchester's Church Parade, Councillor Howell, a watch committee member, argued in favour of 'One-Day' as part of the committee's duty to the men. An inner-city missionary wrote an approving letter to the *Manchester Courier*, contending that the police officer 'is a man whom we should all try our best to keep fit: fit to discharge his manifold duties both by keeping our streets clean from all crime and in discharging often-called-on ambulance duties'.[44] Missionaries and ministers campaigned for the 'One-Day' from Sabbatarian motives. Policemen themselves recognized that they had to work on most Sundays, but asserted that one rest day a week was a common right of man and beast.

But watch committees did not fulfil Kempster's hopes for a successful campaign. Letters to the *Review* showed that the weekly rest day had only added another grievance between policemen and the legal authorities over them. Mixed results mirrored the problems with the pay campaign, reinforcing the inadequacies of petitions. In 1907 the Birmingham watch committee begrudgingly approved an increase to two free days per month for sergeants and constables, pointing out that this required hiring twenty-six more men.[45] In 1908, Manchester was slightly more generous, allowing men one day a fortnight. But the next year when sergeants petitioned to have their pay match sergeants in other forces, the watch committee rejected their request since they had received the additional day off the year before.[46]

---

[43] *Police Review*, 10 September 1909, p. 442.
[44] *Police Review*, 11 February 1910, p. 70.
[45] BWCM, 1 August 1907, p. 116.
[46] MWCM, January 1909, vol. 42, no, 77.

In 1909, the Metropolitan and City of London Police forces were granted a weekly rest day, but watch committees resisted following suit. Birmingham postponed consideration 'pending a definite expression of opinion from the rate payers as to whether that expense should be incurred'.[47] Manchester told a delegation of policemen that 'they must be able to give a reason for spending an extra £10,000 a year'.[48] A Liverpool constable warned of dangerously low morale while policemen elsewhere got their day.[49] A constable outside of London complained, 'Why the Metropolitan should be singled out for this boon we fail to see, except that they happen to be constantly under the eye of Parliament.'[50] Finally, the high level of national strike activity convinced Parliament to enact the Police (Weekly Rest Day) Act in 1910 as a way to prevent police unrest. But Kempster could not celebrate this victory. Watch committees were slow in implementing it, finding 'emergencies' to excuse setting it aside. Letters soon complained that the Act was being ignored in the name of economizing. The foot-dragging of watch committees simply reinforced the need for a union.

Calls for a police union were momentarily silenced with the outbreak of war on August 4, 1914, but the economic strains of wartime soon made arguments in favour of a union even more compelling. Police pay quickly became inadequate to cope with wartime prices and within a year, forces began to grant non-pensionable war bonuses in an attempt to match inflation. Watch committees considered these bonuses to be temporary, since after the war prices were expected to return to prewar levels. Bonuses soon became a divisive issue since each force had its own policies, with some men receiving a great deal more than others. In July 1915, Liverpool awarded a bonus of one shilling sixpence, followed in September in Birmingham which awarded half a crown.[51] While better than nothing, these sums did little to help police budgets. In October 1915, Manchester men complained that they were not receiving a bonus but were being disciplined for not paying their debts.[52] In March 1916 three divisions finally petitioned the watch committee, declaring that they had 'loyally refrained from petitioning for more pay until we cannot now obtain bare necessities and view with alarm the continued rise in the cost of all commodities'.[53] Ten days later, an editorial in the *Review* expressed concern that Manchester policemen were losing confidence in their city to treat them honourably, tempting them to join a police union active in London.[54] In April, they received a bonus of

47   *Birmingham Evening Dispatch* as quoted in *Police Review*, 11 February 1910, p. 70.
48   *Police Review*, 10 September 1909, p. 442.
49   *Police Review*, 22 October 1909, p. 507.
50   *Police Review*, 10 September 1909, p. 442.
51   LWCM, 12 December 1916, p. 98; BPO, 1 September 1915, p. 36.
52   *Police Review*, 22 October 1915, p. 507.
53   MWCM, 21 March 1916, vol. 70, no. 32.
54   *Police Review*, 31 March 1916, p. 151.

six shillings.[55] By the end of 1916, bonuses had to be increased again. By 1918, bonuses had slowly climbed to twenty shillings in Birmingham and Manchester, and to thirteen shillings fourpence in Liverpool. Allowances for dependents of policemen serving in the armed forces (see Table 3) were also a source of strain.[56] In 1914, Birmingham wives complained that they received only twelve shillings while Manchester and Liverpool wives received fifteen. In June 1917, Liverpool wives petitioned the watch committee for larger allowances. The city increased the wives' allowance to twenty shillings, followed in August by Manchester, and only in October in Birmingham.[57] This inconsistency between cities, each following its own schedule for bonuses and allowances, caused resentment in every force making less than another. Prewar frustrations with watch committees became intensely focused under the pressures of war. Resentment escalated when policemen were told that demands for more pay were disloyal and unpatriotic.

Table 3. *Family allowances for policemen called up for military service 1914–1918, in shillings/pence per week*

	Birmingham	Liverpool	Manchester
1914	Wives 12/-; children under age fifteen 2/-; parents dependent on unmarried son 8/- (August)	Wives 15/-; children under age fifteen 2/6 (August)	Wives 15/-; children under age fifteen 2/-; parents dependent on unmarried son 8/- (August)
1917	Wives 20/-; children 3/- (October)	Wives 20/-; children 3/6 (June)	Wives 20/- (August)

Sources: BWCM, 7 August 1914, pp. 114–15; 3 October 1917, p. 309; LWCM, 12 June 1917, p. 476; 12 June 1917, p. 476; MGO, 20 August 1914, 16 August 1917.

By the end of 1917, policemen had had three years of non-pensionable bonuses on top of inadequate pensionable wages. Men argued that watch committees were economizing at their expense by denying them pensionable pay for so long. Police pay was so bad that men were violating the condition against outside work to stay out of debt and jeopardized their health in pursuit of economies. Men grew produce in their gardens and sold it, or bicycled out to farms to work as

---

55   MWCM, 3 April 1916, no. 54, vol. 70.

56   In December 1916, Birmingham had nearly 300 men in the army and navy; six months later Manchester had nearly 700 men in the services (BWCM, 19 December 1916, p. 2; MWCM, 7 June 1917, vol. 74, no. 20).

57   BWCM, 7 August 1914, pp. 114–15; 3 October 1917, p. 309; LWCM, 12 June 1917, p. 476; 12 June 1917, p. 476; MGO, 20 August 1914, 16 August 1917.

labourers. Wives were sneaking out to work.[58] All forces were losing men to high-paying war occupations. Some men thought this attrition was yet another plot by watch committees to get out of pension obligations.[59] Constables pointed out that they were being scoffed at by their neighbours whose wages had doubled while their wages stayed the same.[60] Forces finally began adopting new scales of pay. In October 1917, Birmingham increased pay to thirty-one shillings a week;[61] in November, Liverpool adopted a scale starting at thirty-five shillings, its first pay rise since 1900.[62] But Manchester was late, just as it had been with bonuses. In January 1918, a Manchester constable complained that if local authorities did not 'wake up' and pay the men a just wage that they 'will be wanting Policemen after the war'.[63] Finally, in March 1918, Manchester adopted a scale starting at thirty-five shillings, and increased their bonus to sixteen shillings.[64] But the new scales were not enough to survive on without bonuses, the cost of living having increased by anywhere from eighty to 130 per cent since 1914.[65] Watch committees still hoped that bonuses were only a temporary expediency of wartime.

On top of anxieties over pay, policemen lost their newly won weekly rest day, wartime shortages of policemen making it impossible to maintain. The day after war was declared, orders went out that 'Leave to all members of the Force will be stopped at once', an action necessary due to the emergency.[66] Men understood the need for this but the inconsistent handling of rest days piled onto frustrations already fuelled by anger over pay and allowances. Some men received wages for working extra days, others did not, and none had the same arrangements for rest days. In Manchester, by the end of November, men were allowed one day in fourteen. In January 1915, one day in seven was restored only to be changed back to one day in fourteen in June as the number of policemen leaving for the front lines increased.[67] In Birmingham, all leave was stopped from August to October, changed to two days a month and then to a weekly rest day from November 1914 to November 1915, then changed back to two days a month for the remainder of

---

[58]   Letter from Manchester 'Sufferer', *Police Review*, 18 February 1916, p. 75; 31 March 1916, p. 151; 24 November 1916, p. 466.

[59]   *Police Review*, 22 October 1915, p. 507.

[60]   *Police Review*, 3 August 1917, p. 243.

[61]   BWCM, 8 October 1917, p. 159.

[62]   LWCM, 29 November 1917, p. 28.

[63]   *Police Review*, 18 January 1918, p. 19.

[64]   MGO, 21 March 1918; MWCM, 10 April 1918, vol. 76, no. 99; 7 August 1918, vol. 77, no. 65; 22 August 1918, vol. 77, no. 72.

[65]   DC, Evidence, question 2157, p. 122. According to Ministry of Labour figures, building labourers' wages had increased 115%, engineering labourers' 152%, railway labourers' 83% to 165%, and carters' 86% to 120%.

[66]   MGO, 5 August 1914.

[67]   MGO, 27 November 1914, 22 June 1915.

the war. In Manchester, the men were paid for the extra days they worked, but in Liverpool and Birmingham, pay was delayed. In Liverpool, 'seething discontent' forced the watch committee to allow one day in ten in December 1914, a Liverpool policeman arguing that suspending the rest day for a reasonable period was acceptable, but doing so for an indefinite period was not. The watch committee accused the men of being unpatriotic. Policemen responded by boycotting their weekly War Fund contributions.[68] Soon afterwards, Liverpool went to one day in fourteen. They were finally paid for working on their lost rest days in 1917.[69] Birmingham police did not receive pay for their lost days until January 1919.[70] Weary of being 'economised' by watch committees and overwhelmed by duties for a war that never ended, policemen lost patience with the authorities over them. Years of having their requests belittled made it clear that they needed to take stronger action to ensure fair treatment.

In 1914, while many policemen talked about unionizing, actual union activity had been slight in most forces except for London. But as wartime conditions degenerated and authorities persisted in saying that everything was fine, interest in a union grew. Men continued to pressure authorities to match their pay to inflation, and watch committees and many chief constables kept insisting that pay scales were adequate, especially since policemen had pensions to look forward to and did not need to save. Liverpool Chief Constable Caldwell was later forced to admit that he had no knowledge of family budgets for constables and was surprised to learn that they were stretched to the limit.[71] This breakdown in communication was not new but the war gave it urgency. Disillusioned policemen began listening to representatives from the NUPPO, the union from the London Metropolitan area. NUPPO branches began to spread, especially after the union adopted a 'no strike' policy in 1917 in response to police discomfort with the strike option. Manchester men, angry at receiving bonuses and pay increases later than other forces, had a branch by April 1917. A delegation of five union members appeared before their watch committee, which expressed surprise that the branch existed. Even faced with a union, the committee insisted that 'every facility is given … to members of the Force who desire to bring any grievances they may have before the Chief Constable or the Watch Committee', and that they could think of no cause for dissatisfaction among the men. Peacock issued a general order against supporting the union but the persistent belief that conditions for policemen were fine, despite evidence to the contrary, gave weight to the NUPPO's arguments that policemen needed one.[72]

---

68   *Police Review*, 11 December 1914, p. 596.
69   LWCM, 29 November 1917, p. 28.
70   BPO, 8 January 1919, p. 403.
71   DC, Evidence, p. 277.
72   MWCM, 25 April 1918, vol. 76, no. 106.

In August 1918, sensing that the war would soon be over and wanting to use the war to pressure the government, the London NUPPO suddenly took action without consulting its other branches. On 22 August, Peacock complained to the Home Office that PC Thiel of London was agitating for the NUPPO in Manchester. Sensing trouble, that same day Peacock convinced the watch committee to reinstate the weekly rest day, to begin 1 September, and to increase the war bonus to twenty shillings. The existence of the local NUPPO branch convinced the watch committee to take Peacock seriously.[73] Three days later, Thiel was dismissed by the Metropolitan Police. On 29 August 1918 Peacock announced the new bonus and weekly rest day to his men,[74] the same day that the Metropolitan and City of London police forces struck for better pay, recognition of the union, and reinstatement of Thiel.[75] Catching many policemen by surprise, the NUPPO had abandoned the 'no strike' policy.[76] The constant denial of problems from authorities had finally reached a snapping point. The frustrations of wartime convinced a majority of London policemen to risk their jobs in order to gain a voice and provide for their families. Even then, peer pressure and intimidation were necessary to convince many to strike. Strike organizers rationalized that it was necessary for an overwhelming majority of policemen to strike if demands were to be taken seriously.

The strike embarrassed the government since the NUPPO's demands for better wages were publicly perceived as just. Even *The Times*, which called the strike a mutiny, believed that the policemen had a legitimate case.[77] In spite of a general conviction, even among policemen, that policemen should not 'down tools', the question remained why it took a strike for the government to listen to police grievances. That the London Commissioners could insist that no serious unrest existed days before the strike showed how serious the lack of communication

---

[73]   MWCM, 22 August 1918, vol. 77, no. 72.

[74]   MGO, 29 August 1918.

[75]   Joseph F. King, 'The United Kingdom Police Strikes of 1918–1919', *Police Studies* 11:3 (1988): 133.

[76]   Short accounts of the 1918 and 1919 strikes from the official point of view are given in Sir Arthur L. Dixon, *The Home Office and the Police between the Two World Wars* (London: Home Office, 1966), pp. 5–20, and Sir William Nott-Bower, *Fifty-Two Years a Policeman* (London: Edward Arnold & Co., 1926), pp. 283–302. The police point of view is given in Reynolds and Judge, *The Night the Police Went on Strike*. On the NUPPO, see Allen, 'The National Union of Police and Prison Officers'; on Birmingham, Richard Shackleton, 'The 1919 Police Strike in Birmingham', in *Worlds of Labour: Essays in Birmingham Labour History*, ed. Anthony Wright and Richard Shackleton (Birmingham: University of Birmingham, 1983), pp. 63–87; on Liverpool, Ron Bean, 'Police Unrest, Unionization and the 1919 Strike in Liverpool', *Journal of Contemporary History* 15:4 (1980): 633–53; see also A.V. Sellwood, *Police Strike – 1919* (London: W.H. Allen, 1978), King, 'The United Kingdom Police Strikes of 1918–1919', and Klein, 'Blue-Collar Job'.

[77]   *Police Review*, 13 September 1918, p. 292.

between headquarters and the men on the streets had become.[78] In hindsight the Home Office realized that 'the absence of any regular machinery for the submitting of local or collective representations left grievances in too many instances without any satisfactory outlet, and this led to increasing agitation for the "right to confer" and to the appearance of [the NUPPO]'.[79] It had been too easy for authorities to believe what they wanted to believe, and to discount conflicting evidence as coming from malcontents. The knowledge of the part played by disaffected policemen in the Russian Revolution was on the government's mind. With the country still at war, Prime Minister Lloyd George had few options but to resolve the strike quickly. None of the strikers was dismissed since it would be impossible to replace them in wartime. Thiel was reinstated. The new 'Met scale', starting at forty-three shillings with a twelve shilling war bonus, was issued. Lloyd George promised to investigate grievances, setting up the Desborough Committee. He made a garbled statement about the union, giving policemen the impression that the NUPPO would be officially recognized after the war.[80]

Instead of quieting police unrest, the quick success of the strike brought to the surface years of discontent in other police forces. Policemen suddenly found that they had an organization that was being taken seriously by authorities. Having experienced the strike from a distance and not seeing policemen menaced by colleagues into leaving their posts, policemen elsewhere only saw that acting together could bring about tremendous results. Forces suddenly had active NUPPO branches affiliated with Trade and Labour Councils, much to the horror of chief constables. Even more disturbing, the ranks often elected NUPPO members to give testimony to the Desborough Committee, set to begin in spring 1919. The union focused debate not only on pay but on systemic problems of corruption, favouritism, promotion, assignments, and discipline. The NUPPO claimed 50,000 members in November 1918.[81]

In Manchester, to counteract NUPPO influence, Peacock quickly set up meetings with his men. On 5 September 1918, he gave permission to a committee of sergeants to institute 'a scheme for providing representative committees to deal with matters relating to the Police Service'.[82] But the Manchester branch of the NUPPO remained vocal. In October 1918, they sent a delegation to

---

78   *Police Review*, 6 September 1918, pp. 283–6; included press comments.

79   Dixon, *The Home Office*, p. 6.

80   King, 'The United Kingdom Police Strikes of 1918–1919', p. 134.

81   *Police Review*, 6 September 1918, p. 286; Shackleton, 'The 1919 Police Strike', p. 65; Birmingham City Police Superintendents' Reports and Confidential Letters, 2 November 1918, pp. 500–1. Sir Edward Henry, commissioner of the Metropolitan Police, 'was quite convinced that the Trade Unions had set themselves to get control of the Police through the Police Union' (Dixon, *The Home Office*, pp. 6, 8).

82   MGO, 5 September 1918.

Peacock requesting that the union be recognized, that pay be increased 100 per cent, and that a non-contributory widows' pension be created. He replied that their current pay and bonus matched the Met scale and remained sceptical that NUPPO represented the force. The Manchester union threatened to strike but decided to give the watch committee time to consider their demands.[83] Peacock issued a general order reminding policemen of regulations against a union but also announced that he was 'desirous of speaking to the members of the Manchester City Police on the question of Pay and Conditions of Service'. He arranged to meet with all ranks at Central Hall on 9 October 1918.[84] He allowed the men to vote on whether they should keep their current pay, which matched the Met scale but included a twenty-shilling non-pensionable bonus, or whether they preferred to adopt the Met scale. Favouring pensionable pay, the men voted for the Met scale.[85] Peacock's willingness to meet with his men helped prevent disputes from getting out of control. But his men could not fail to notice that it had taken the London strike to gain this consideration.

Liverpool Chief Constable Caldwell's reaction was similar to Peacock's, immediately allowing his divisions to meet to discuss pay and conditions. However, unlike Peacock, he did not attend any meetings. In September, even though Caldwell had advised them to limit meetings to delegates from each division, the men held mass meetings that involved all ranks. On 25 September 1918, based on their decision, the city adopted the Met scale.[86] On 7 October 1918, Caldwell announced that his men could vote on whether to adopt a flat sixteen-shilling war bonus or to keep the twelve-shilling Met bonus that added two and a half shillings per child, stating that he was 'desirous of ascertaining the opinion of the majority of the members of the force'.[87] However, unlike Manchester, where the main issue was pay, Liverpool men were concerned with entrenched favouritism and corruption. That same month, rumours estimated that ninety per cent of the Liverpool force had joined the NUPPO because, as PC Smithwick remarked, 'more promotions were made by the back door than the front'.[88] Caldwell himself

---

[83]   *Police Review*, 13 September 1918, p. 293; 6 September 1918, p. 286; MGO, 2 October 1918; *Police Review*, 11 October 1918, p. 324, reprinted letter and reply in full under title, 'The Manchester Ultimatum'; *Police Review*, 18 October 1918, p. 334. Ironically, the 1919 Police Act increased their pay scale by 100 per cent.

[84]   MGO, 2, 8 October 1918.

[85]   MGO, 10 October 1918; MWCM, 17 October 1918, vol. 77, no. 117.

[86]   LCCO, 3–7 September 1918, pp. 21–3.

[87]   LCCO, 7 October 1918, p. 39. The vote was 568 for keeping children's allowance, 556 for adopting a flat rate, with ninety-eight ballets blank (LCCO, 15 October 1918, p. 42). Only 1222 men out of approximately 2200 voted.

[88]   *Police Review*, 18 October 1918, p. 334. Smithwick later became the constables' representative to the Desborough Committee and PS George Miles, another active member of NUPPO, the sergeants' representative.

symbolized promotion based on connections rather than street experience. While visiting Liverpool in October, Birmingham Chief Constable Rafter learned that London PC Thiel was there organizing the local branch of the NUPPO.[89]

In Birmingham, Chief Constable Rafter was less accommodating than Peacock or Caldwell. On 7 October 1918, when Peacock and Caldwell were allowing votes and meetings, Rafter issued a statement allowing for a permanent elective representative committee to study grievances and handle requests for meetings. This was as far as he was prepared to go. At the same time, he reminded the men that both he and the watch committee looked after their interests. He saw no need for an organization, regarding the union as the work of outside agitators and internal traitors.[90] On 9 October, the watch committee adopted the Met scale.[91] His men understood the futility of sending NUPPO delegations to talk to him or the watch committee. However, his sharp condemnation of the union did not stop his men from organizing a branch. Rafter was infuriated to read in a local newspaper that the Trades and Labour Council had received an application for affiliation from the newly formed NUPPO branch in Birmingham.[92] He considered the union as a sign of 'Bolshevism in England' and he refused to allow an officer to attend a London NUPPO conference.[93] Soon, men were complaining of victimization since union members were passed over in the latest round of promotions.[94]

At the same time that chief constables responded to the strike locally, the national government recommended that representative boards be created as an alternative to the NUPPO. But the boards were not a success. Watch committees did not take them any more seriously than prewar delegations, and policemen saw them as a tool to undermine the union. In Manchester, when their representatives tried to present grievances, watch committee members 'were drawing different figures and different animals, etc., on the papers, taking no notice; others were

---

[89]   Birmingham City Police Superintendents' Reports and Confidential Letters, 2 November 1918, p. 502.

[90]   BPO, 7 October 1918, pp. 257–9; *Police Review*, 18 October 1918, p. 334.

[91]   'Birmingham City Police Revised Scale of Pay (To date from 2nd September, 1918)'; BWCM, 9 October 1918, p. 401.

[92]   Birmingham City Police Superintendents' Reports and Confidential Letters, 2 November 1918, pp. 499–502. This branch probably grew out of the 1913 union. It is difficult to accept Shackleton's assertion that the Birmingham NUPPO branch was initiated by the local Trade Council and not by the policemen themselves. He primarily used Trade Council records and local newspapers, not police records. A combination of both taking action is more probable (Shackleton, 'The 1919 Police Strike', p. 65).

[93]   Birmingham City Police Superintendents' Reports and Confidential Letters, 7 November 1918, pp. 503–4.

[94]   Birmingham City Police Superintendents' Reports and Confidential Letters, 2 November 1918, pp. 500–1, 26 November 1918, p. 505; BJSC, 3 March 1919, p. 4; *Police Review*, 2 May 1919, p. 150.

going in and out of the room'.[95] In February 1919, Manchester policemen declared the boards disbanded and that further business should be given to the NUPPO branch.[96] Birmingham policemen disliked the board since they had to present their case and retire; the watch committee made decisions behind closed doors.[97] In spite of this arrangement, the board did eventually get leave restored and have pay given for lost leave days during the war.[98] Knowing that Rafter would never tolerate the NUPPO, supporters of the board decided to be realistic and use what representation they could. But others hoped for more by sticking to the union, creating dissension within the ranks. Caldwell allowed Liverpool policemen to vote on whether or not to set up representative boards. The vote was 449 in favour of the boards and 738 against, with nearly 1000 not voting at all.[99] In light of the vote, Caldwell decided not to create boards but failed to respond to the danger signals the vote indicated. Less than a quarter of the men considered it worthwhile to try the boards. Many believe that the boards would come under the control of some faction; many thought official representation was pointless given the entrenched networks in the force; many preferred the union. The boards were too obviously meant as a government alternative to the union.

In spring 1919, the Desborough Committee began holding hearings, and city officials, chief constables, and policemen of all ranks arrived in large numbers to testify. Given the press coverage of NUPPO activity as well as the testimony of their own men, chief constables and other authorities could not pretend that everything was fine now that the London strike was over and the Met scale in place. Many of the policemen elected by their colleagues to testify were NUPPO members or from representative boards. Many had served in the war. While few of them supported a strike policy, they were committed to changing the way policemen were treated by authorities. Questioning was detailed and relentless. Committee members pressed hard at witnesses giving vague or inaccurate answers, forcing high-ranking officials to admit their ignorance. They became impatient with authorities insisting that police pay was basically adequate but then qualifying this when pressed for details. They also challenged policemen making broad claims regarding pay and representation, but their exaggerations out of a desire for better treatment created a better impression than officials ignorant of conditions in their own forces.

---

[95]   MGO, 5 September, 26 November 1918, 11 January 1919; DC, Evidence, Insp. S. Latham, MCP, p. 169; PS Matthew Seaman, MCP, p. 174.

[96]   MGO, 13 February 1919; *Police Review*, 21 February 1919, p. 60.

[97]   DC, Evidence, PC William Sinclair, BCP, p. 299. PS William Clowes, BCP, representative committee secretary, also testified.

[98]   BPO, 5 April 1919, p. 658.

[99]   LCCO, 18 November 1918. Reynolds and Judge (*The Night the Police Went on Strike*) and Sellwood (*Police Strike – 1919*) state that police authorities in Liverpool forbade formation of the boards but this vote result contradicts that conclusion.

The central question behind both setting a new pay scale and giving policemen representation was the status of policing as an occupation. To the men, policemen had evolved from unskilled workers into skilled professionals deserving to be taken seriously but the Desborough Committee had to be convinced. Witnesses gave strong statements insisting that policemen were not ordinary workers. Manchester Inspector Latham explained that 'the duties of a police officer [were] such as demand a keener intelligence, better physique, sounder judgment, fearless courage, and a higher moral character than are considered necessary in many other callings'.[100] Birmingham PS Clowes agreed and ranked policemen with the professions or highly skilled trades, adding that they have to 'undertake continuous hours of study in order to make themselves proficient in their duties as constables owing to the increasing and complex nature of the legislation which is continually being introduced'.[101] Liverpool PS Miles argued that if the police force had been created as a new institution in 1919, Parliament would offer £800 a year to obtain the paragons of virtue and wisdom needed for the job.[102] Some authorities persisted in categorizing policemen as unskilled 'because the skilled workman is required to be a man of considerable intelligence'.[103] But HMI Leonard Dunning supported the ranks, pointing out that the lowest ranking constable 'is clothed by law with powers of individual action, which … must be exercised with great discretion, upon his individual judgment'. The exercise of discretion put policemen in a different class from other public servants.[104] The Desborough Committee was convinced that policemen were skilled workers, though not professionals. While not quite what policemen hoped for, this was one of the most important achievements of the strikes.

The Desborough Committee soon realized that the Met scale was already insufficient to support a police family at a respectable level, let alone high enough to rank policemen with skilled workers. Less than a year after calling the Met scale perfectly adequate, chief constables suddenly recommended substantial increases. Hearing the testimony of their men convinced many to update their views, if only not to appear ignorant of their own occupation in public. Caldwell and Peacock advocated a base pay for constables of sixty-four shillings per week, compared to seventy-two shillings per week for dock labourers, calculating that benefits added twenty per cent to the value of the wage.[105] Policemen recommended a scale beginning at eighty or ninety shillings a week.[106] Men argued that their pay

---

100 DC, Evidence, question 1982, p. 110.
101 DC, Evidence, question 3144, p. 166.
102 DC, Evidence, question 3563, p. 184.
103 DC, Evidence, question 9403, p. 433.
104 DC, Evidence, question 1422, p. 78.
105 DC, Evidence, question 1980, p. 110; questions 5714, 5720–7, 5742–53, pp. 276–7.
106 DC, Evidence, Insp. Samuel Latham, MCP, p. 166; P.S George Miles, LCP, p. 186;

should be higher since 'the public generally value a thing according to the price they pay for it' and 'it is necessary for the public safety that he should be placed beyond such influences' as corruption and bribes.[107] On 1 July 1919, the committee recommended a new pay scale beginning at seventy shillings a week, more than double prewar scales, and recommended that free housing be provided through allowances or police housing. They rejected the traditional idea that police should be paid at similar rates as agricultural or unskilled labourers, stating that police work had changed so materially over the last twenty years that the new responsibilities of the force should be better rewarded.[108] They agreed that policemen's special relationship with the community required that they maintain a respectable standard of living, free from the temptations of bribes and tips.[109] In response to testimony on pensions, they recommended a half-pay pension at twenty-five years' service with increments up to a two-thirds pension at thirty years, and they got rid of the hated retirement age minimums.[110] Later, young policemen complaining about pay and pensions were reminded that at least they did not have to serve under the old system.[111] The one sore spot for many policemen were recommendations against a union and for a new Police Federation. Policemen feared that an official federation would be used to punish anyone who opened 'his mouth for the ventilation of any just grievance'.[112] But at least the committee recognized the need for some organization to represent the interests of the lower ranks.

While the Desborough Committee was meeting, the NUPPO remained active, claiming that ninety per cent of most forces had joined the union.[113] While real numbers were much lower than this, that so many police witnesses before the committee were NUPPO members added to its prestige. The quick success of 1918 and the proliferation of union branches went to the heads of its leaders. NUPPO made excessive demands regarding recognition of the union, pensions,

Sergeant William Clowes, BCP, p. 295. Weekly earnings of other occupations included corporation street sweepers, fifty-five shillings; tram drivers, sixty-five shillings; cotton porters at Liverpool docks, sixty-eight shillings sixpence; and London unskilled labourers, sixty-eight shillings ('Report of the Committee on the Police Service of England, Wales, and Scotland', Part I, 1919, Cmd. 253, vol. XXVII, 709, p. 9).

[107] DC, Evidence, pp. 184, 188, 303.

[108] 'Report of the Committee on the Police Service of England, Wales, and Scotland', Part I, 1919, pp. 5, 7, 9, 13.

[109] 'Report of the Committee on the Police Service of England, Wales, and Scotland', Part I, 1919, p. 8.

[110] Full details of the 1919 Police Act pension in Chapter 10. See also 'Report of the Committee on the Police Service of England, Wales, and Scotland', Part II, 1920, Cmd. 574, vol. XXII, 539, pp. 13, 24.

[111] *Police Review*, 10 February 1922, p. 68.

[112] *Police Review*, 15 August 1919, p. 328.

[113] *Police Review*, 2 May 1919, p. 150.

overtime pay, and victimization of union members. But with the committee hearing testimony, the union could no longer argue that striking was the only way to get authorities to listen to them. Rumours spread that the committee was recommending a substantial pay increase. In May 1919, hoping to gain momentum back from the committee, NUPPO leadership sent out a misleading national ballot, a yes vote comprehending a demand for better pay, reinstatement of PC Spackman dismissed for union activities, and the right to strike. Chief constables quickly warned their men that anyone participating in a strike would be dismissed without pension rights. The Liverpool statement added that 'fear of intimidation will not be accepted as an excuse for failing to parade for duty'. [114] With the war over, authorities could take a firm stand. Most policemen preferred to wait and see what the committee recommended. On 1 June 1919, the NUPPO claimed that nearly 45,000 ballots were in favour of the right to strike and that under 5000 were against it.[115] But on 13 June the *Review* reported that the Manchester branch of the NUPPO had voted against a strike and that many were resigning from the union now that pay demands had been satisfied.[116] As a final move, the national government promised policemen a £10 advance on their new wages to be given out on 31 July 1919, the day set for the strike to begin. This effectively took the wind out of the NUPPO's sails.[117]

The NUPPO had miscalculated, forgetting that many London policemen had only gone on strike in 1918 under the pressures of wartime and when intimidated by union members. Most policemen continued to question the legitimacy of a police strike and remained annoyed that the NUPPO had abandoned the 1917 'no strike' policy without a vote of the membership. Even if they supported a strike, striking was too risky now that the war was over, especially with the pay issue resolved. Typical for many forces, Manchester policemen believed that most of their demands had been satisfied by the committee. Despite rumours that ninety-five per cent of Manchester men had struck, a meeting of their union branch voted unanimously to remain loyal to their oath. They could not see how a police union could be associated with other unions and effectively police strikes at the same time. PC Houlden told the meeting that 'There was ... a force somewhere in this country trying to lead the National Union of the Police to become the thin end of the wedge for a social revolution. (Cheers) ... He hoped they in that room would say unanimously, "This must not be in Manchester." (Cheers).' They did, however, send a statement to the government requesting that certain clauses in the 1919 Police Act be deleted or altered. These included the requirement that policemen

---

114 BPO, 30 May 1919, pp. 798–9; MGO, 31 May 1919; LCCO, 31 May 1919.
115 *Police Review*, 8 August 1919, p. 318.
116 *Police Review*, 13 June 1919, p. 226.
117 BWCM, 23 June 1919, p. 63; 23 July 1919, p. 88; BPO 31 July 1919, p. 968; 12 August 1919, pp. 1003–4; MGO, 30 July 1919; Allen, pp. 136, 138–9.

resign from organizations and penalties on anyone 'causing disaffection'. They also requested that the new Police Federation be allowed to address individual cases of discipline and promotion.[118] Changing from having one of the more active NUPPO branches, Manchester stepped away from the union when the issue changed from pay to the right to strike.

Since their main grievance had been pay, it was easier for Manchester men to take these positions than for men in Birmingham and Liverpool. They did not have the serious problems with lack of communication and favouritism entrenched in the other two cities. For Birmingham and Liverpool, the pay issue may have been settled but they also wanted genuine access to the right to confer rather than an official organization such as the Federation. The difference in the response to the strike in each city reflected that Birmingham's problems were smaller than Liverpool's. Rafter may have been autocratic and paternalistic but Birmingham did not suffer the degree of entrenched manipulation of promotion and discipline found in Liverpool. Nationally, policemen in other forces would not risk losing their jobs and the new pay scale to gain recognition for the NUPPO and for a right to strike that few supported. Only around 1000 Metropolitan and City of London men struck. Nationally, only Birmingham, Liverpool, and its neighbouring towns, Birkenhead and Bootle, struck.

The call to strike was answered in Birmingham by at least 119 men, including three sergeants, nine per cent of the official strength of 1,340.[119] More went on strike but snuck back on duty. Others were not reported by their senior officers immediately, allowing them to change their minds when the strike's failure became obvious. The overwhelming majority of strikers had good service records, and two-thirds had from five to fourteen years of service.[120] It is possible that they hoped

---

[118]   *Police Review*, 15 August 1919, p. 328; MGO, 5 August 1919. Because of the prohibition of policemen belonging to any association discussing issues of pay, pension, or conditions of service, the Chief Constables' Association changed their byelaws to conform with the Police Act, 1919. The chief constables vehemently denied that their association was in any way a union (Chief Constables' Association Annual Report, 4 June 1920, p. 9).

[119]   'A' division lost forty-two men, 'C' lost thirty-eight, and 'E' lost thirty-nine. 'B' division only lost one man. One hundred and eighteen were regular police, one a police reservist. Two had twenty years' experience or more, twenty-two had fifteen to nineteen years, thirty from ten to fourteen years, forty-nine from five to nine years, sixteen had less than five years. A complete list of the men dismissed is in BPO, 2–3 August 1919, pp. 972–5, and BWCM, 5 May 1920, pp. 13–22. One hundred and twelve of the men were married (*Police Review*, 11 March 1927, p. 182).

[120]   Shackleton, 'The 1919 Police Strike', pp. 71–3, 78; BPO, 2, 3, 4 August 1919, pp. 972–5, 978–9; 3 August 1919, pp. 976–7; 15 August 1919, p. 1016. To reward men who stayed on duty, all disciplinary reductions in class were cancelled in calculating the new scale of pay and, initially, dismissed strikers received no arrears in pay. This was changed in January 1920 since it was not legal (BPO, 5 August 1919, p. 980).

that this strike would free promotion from favouritism the same way that the 1918 London strike had improved pay. They may even have hoped to be rid of Rafter The leader, PS Edward Taylor, one of the officers who had rescued Lloyd George from rioters in 1901, was quickly dismissed 'for inciting men to leave their duty ... and going out on a Police Strike'.[121] All strikers were fired. By 3 August 1919, Rafter congratulated men who remained 'staunch and true to their honourable undertakings'. He blamed the strike on prison warders, rather than on policemen, refusing to admit that his men might have grounds for discontent.[122] Policemen who had remained on duty urged him to hold an enquiry 'for the purpose of punishing the real offenders and the exculpation and rehabilitation of those who are found deserving'. Rafter declined. Not surprisingly, a delegation from 'A' division failed to convince him to consider reinstating strikers.[123] He did not even allow a voluntary collection on behalf of strikers in 1920.[124] The Birmingham strike failed and the strikers were never rehired.

Nationally, Liverpool was the only force where enough men answered the call to strike to cripple the city.[125] There, pay was only part of the problem. Its rampant favouritism exacerbated already poor communications between constables and senior officers. Grievances were structural and cultural, against unfair promotions, unjust disciplinary practices, neglect of outlying divisions, and preferences given to clerical staff. Networks blocking the promotion of outsiders and skewing discipline cases to favour members had survived wartime, and men returning from the trenches in 1918 and 1919 found themselves out of touch with old networks and left out of new ones. New pay scales did not address these problems, and the 1919 Police Act excluded the new Police Federation from decisions on promotion and discipline, prime concerns of the Liverpool rank and file. If other forces were satisfied with their pay, at least half of the Liverpool force disagreed. But they had a difficult case to make. Fights over pay and pensions were at least tangible; ending corruption needed not just government intervention but changes in Liverpool's police culture. Men benefiting from the current system would not easily let it go.[126]

---

121 BRB, 2 August 1919, PSC Edward Taylor, joined September 1896; Shackleton, 'The 1919 Police Strike', p. 63.

122 BPO, 3 August 1919, pp. 976–7.

123 BWCM, 15 August 1919, pp. 108–9, 1 September 1919, p. 120.

124 BJSC, 5 July 1920, p. 163.

125 At 11:20 pm on 31 July 1919, the following phone conversation between Essex Street and Hatton Garden stations occurred: 'Sergt Collins Speaking. who is PC 316 a. Answer Smithwick he says the men have no right to be on duty there is a strike on. Inspr Ford infd. Message sent to Chief Supt.' Hatton Garden was headquarters (Liverpool City Police Strike Book, 31 July 1919).

126 For an excellent study of how police forces develop their own local cultures, see Marilynn S. Johnson, *Street Justice: A History of Police Violence in New York City* (Boston, MA: Beacon Press, 2003).

On 31 July 1919, at least 1000 Liverpool constables and sergeants went on strike out of an official strength of 2200. Similar to Birmingham, some men changed their minds before officially noticed. The first count of strikers was a low 300, probably a result of officers trying to protect men whom they hoped would return to duty.[127] Due to the critical shortage of men, the watch committee agreed to reinstate strikers who paraded for duty before 8:00 pm on 1 August 1919, hoping to encourage any men striking through intimidation to return.[128] But PS George Miles urged strikers to remain firm since 'they had fought for liberty in France but now they were fighting for themselves'.[129] Two sergeants and fifty-two constables returned to duty. As in London the year before, strikers intimidated colleagues to ensure success. Pickets threatened PC Summersall with 'personal violence' if he did not return home. When he reported for duty the next day, he had been dismissed.[130] PC Dolan had gone off duty on 1 August feeling ill and was told to consult the doctor. However, strikers wrote messages on the pavement in front of his house and he was too frightened to go out. He, too, was dismissed for striking.[131] While regulating traffic, PC Swift was intimidated by a crowd of strikers. He went to the station, dropping off an application for his pension, and went home. He stayed there for a week saying, 'I never refused duty until I was terrorised.'[132] The official number of men finally dismissed for striking included forty-eight sergeants and 907 constables, although watch committee minutes listed 910 constables dismissed and the 1919 Annual Report noted 903 constables dismissed.[133] Similar to Birmingham, half of strikers had from five to

---

127   Liverpool Strike Book, 1 August 1919.

128   LCCO, 1 August 1919.

129   Liverpool Strike Book, 1 August 1919, report of John Leathom Flood, a Lever Brothers clerk present at the meeting; report of Birkenhead Insp. Birch.

130   LWCM, 11 January 1921, pp. 442–5. Due to Summersall's eye injury while on duty in 1918 which was progressing towards blindness, the chief constable agreed to 'see what can be done in the matter' in spite of Summersall's striker status.

131   LWCM, 6 January 1920, pp. 319–21.

132   LWCM, 17 February 1920, pp. 486–7. Dismissed as a striker, he finally got his pension since he had applied for it while still on duty.

133   LWCM, 19 August 1919, pp. 453–5; LAR, 1919, p. 4. The average length of service for sergeants was eighteen years. Eighty constables had twenty years or more, seventy-eight had fifteen to nineteen years, 171 had ten to fourteen years, 331 five to nine, ninety-one one to four, and 159 under a year's service, for a total of 910. In a log kept of strikers in 'A' division, the division rumoured to be the fast track to promotion, eleven out of fifty sergeants struck, three later asking for readmission. One hundred and eighty-six out of 234 constables struck, eighty per cent, forty-seven asking for readmission. None of the strikers was readmitted. The official count was twelve sergeants and 184 constables (Anon., *Short History of Members of A Div. during first ten days of Police Strike August 1st to 10th 1919*, anon., n.d.). The discrepancies in numbers could be the result of changing criteria in determining who was a striker, or could, ironically, be clerical errors.

fourteen years of service, with similar hopes that the strike could end corruption in the force.

The strike threw the city into confusion. The shortage of constables led to two days of rioting, destroying whole streets of shops. Looters seriously injured nine policemen, and more suffered bruises and sprains. To restore order, 1400 troops were scattered throughout the city, and the battleship, HMS *Valiant*, and two destroyers were sent to protect the docks. The striking PC Morley was so appalled at the rioting that he arrested two men for breaking and entering shops during looting on 3 August 1919.[134] To make up for the severe shortage of men, pensioners were reactivated and not released from duty until May 1920.[135] New recruits were rushed onto the streets without the normal two-month training.[136] In the chaos of getting new policemen into uniform, a striker from the Bootle force managed to join the Liverpool force on 25 August 1919, and served for eight years before his previous record was discovered.[137] Policemen who stayed on duty were rewarded. Those who worked continuously were granted four weeks' pay, those recalled from leave or illness who worked extra hours, three weeks' pay, those who remained loyal but did not work long hours, two weeks', and those who returned to duty after striking and remained loyal one week.[138] The NUPPO denounced the rioting as 'conduct calculated to discredit the strike which will form a pretext for the purpose of calling upon the use of the Military interference' but never freed itself from blame for causing it.[139] Instead, the public now supported the policemen who refused to go out and were left to police the riots. The violence reinforced the belief of most policemen that, whatever other pressures a union might bring to bear, striking was not an option.

Almost before the strike was over, both dismissed and serving policemen

---

134 Liverpool Strike Book, 2 August 1919, report of the Chief Supt of A Division on three strikers asking to be taken back; 4 August 1919, report of Insp. Ford; 16, 22 August 1919, two reports of PS Mybroie.

135 LCCO, 5 March 1920.

136 LCCO, 7, 10 August 1919 and following; *Police Review*, 18 March 1921, p. 150; LWCM, 19 August 1919, pp. 453–5; LCCO, 20 August 1919; LWCM, 30 September 1919, p. 670.

137 LDRB, 7 February 1928, PCC 201 Barrett. He was immediately dismissed.

138 Liverpool Strike Book, 22 December 1919, chief constable's order. Only two months after the strike did the watch committee pay strikers arrears in pay, which strikers did not receive until Christmas Eve, 1919.

139 Liverpool Strike Book, 2 August 1919, report of the chief constable on disposition of troops and magistrates; LCI, 3–4 August 1919; Reynolds and Judge, *The Night the Police Went on Strike*, pp. 168–9; Dixon, *The Home Office*, p. 18; Liverpool Strike Book, 3 August 1919, report of Chief Supt A Division. Looting and rioting during the 1919 Boston police strike also lost public support for a police union and dismissed men were never reinstated. Cyril D. Robinson, 'The Deradicalization of the Policeman: A Historical Analysis', *Crime and Delinquency* 24:2 (1978): 143.

appealed to governments and watch committees to reinstate all strikers except for ringleaders, using the 1918 strike as a precedent for clemency. They argued that most strikers had been 'tricked', 'coerced', or 'seduced' into walking out in the turmoil of the moment.[140] Sir Watson Rutherford, representing Liverpool strikers who had quit the union and begged to be reinstated, claimed that the strike was engineered from outside the force 'by a conspiracy of misrepresentation and lying on the part of some irresponsible wirepullers'.[141] The Liverpool watch committee also received a number of letters from private citizens asking that strikers be reinstated if they were not leaders of the strike.[142] Nine strikers who had been prevented from taking their pensions due to the war were awarded their pensions when the war officially ended in August 1921 but calculated on the pre-Desborough pay scale.[143] Because of the violence of the strike, no strikers were reinstated.

The fate of most strikers from Liverpool or Birmingham was hard to follow. By the end of November 1919, six striking sergeants and fifty-one constables in Liverpool's 'A' Division were employed, but many men had left the city so it was impossible to know who found work.[144] Once tempers cooled in Birmingham, the force unofficially assisted strikers and helped them to find employment.[145] In a 1927 report, of fourteen strikers who gave their current wages, only four earned seventy shillings a week or more and nine earned sixty shillings or less.[146] Under the 1924 Labour government, proposals were made to reinstate strikers without success. Because of the rioting, Liverpool was especially against the return of strikers who had 'let the city down'.[147] A 1924 Parliamentary committee concluded that strikers had a case for reinstatement since none of the 1918 strikers had been dismissed. However, even if strikers were only 'weak and foolish rather than designedly disloyal', to reinstate them would appear to condone the 1919 strike and make another strike possible, besides insulting men who remained loyal under trying conditions. The committee recommended that rateable deductions be returned to strikers on behalf of their families which was done in most places. Birmingham only returned rateable deductions on an individual basis after the passing of the

---

140   *Police Review*, 15 August 1919, p. 328.
141   LWCM, 20 August 1919, pp. 482–4.
142   LWCM, 26 August 1919, p. 486.
143   LWCM, 17 February, 11 May 1920, pp. 484–7, 689; Liverpool City Police Pensioners Register, 31 August 1921.
144   Brogden, *On the Mersey Beat*, p. 21; Liverpool Strike Book, 26 November 1919, letter from Chief Supt.
145   BWCM, 8 May 1925, report no. 5, p. 4.
146   BWCM, 5 October 1927, report no. 9, pp. 2–5. Six of the men, including three with the highest wages, worked at the local Cadbury Bros plant. Two Cadbury employees refused to state their wages, one only saying it was less than a constable's wages and one refusing outright. The other Cadbury employee earned sixty shillings.
147   *Police Review*, 4 April 1924, p. 183.

1926 Police Pensions Act.[148] While policemen who had served with strikers got on with their careers, bitterness remained that the 1919 strikers did not receive the same consideration as the 1918 London strikers.

Yet, even though the 1919 strike failed, it took place while the Desborough Committee was still meeting. That another strike could happen so soon and could again take authorities by surprise made committee members wonder if police leadership was simply incompetent. The strike sent a clear message that police discontent was not simply a matter of pay. The committee focused on testimony regarding representation, favouritism and corruption in making their 1920 report. To improve leadership, no one without police experience could be appointed as chief constable unless in exceptional cases. Pay, pensions, medical care, and allowances were carefully outlined and the weekly rest day and annual leave were regularized to prevent watch committees from meddling to save money. Recognizing the growing complexity of policing, training, education, and instruction books were improved. To minimize favouritism, promotion was based on standard national examinations as well as chief constable's recommendations. Disciplinary authority was given to chief constables with the right of men to appeal dismissal to a tribunal appointed by the Secretary of State. To ensure that forces were following these recommendations, more inspectors of constabulary were added.[149] While the committee outlined an ideal situation, policemen could now point to their report if authorities tried to diverge from it.

The 1919 defeat of the NUPPO ended any serious demands for a police union, already banned in the new police act. The Desborough Committee, however, did see the necessity for policemen to have an organization that gave them the right to confer and so created the Police Federation. Each force had separate branches for constables, sergeants, and inspectors which could also hold joint branch meetings. Most forces had branches that met jointly more often than separately. The main purpose of the Federation became rather reactive, hanging onto the gains made in the Desborough Report. Its mottoes included 'What we have we hold'[150] and 'the Desborough Report, upon which we take our stand'.[151] Feelings towards the Federation were mixed. Some were enthusiastic, some feared compromising promotion by seeming too involved, some felt it was a tool of the state, and some

---

[148] 'Report of the Committee on the Claims of the Men Dismissed from the Police and Prison Services on account of the Strike of 1919', PP, 1924–1925, Cmd. 2297, xv, 265, pp. 28, 34; *Police Review*, 9 January 1925, p. 23, 11 March 1927, p. 182; BWCM, 27 July 1927, report no. 3, p. 5.

[149] 'Report of the Committee on the Police Service of England, Wales, and Scotland', Part II, 1920, pp. 23–5.

[150] *Police Review*, 10 August 1923, p. 427; 28 July 1922, p. 360.

[151] Statement of the Joint Central Committee of the Police Federation to the Geddes Committee, quoted in Dixon, *The Home Office*, p. 288.

were indifferent. Apathy was the major problem. The *Police Review*'s optimistic articles on the work of the Federation always ended with an appeal to men to take an active role, suggesting that the active remained a minority. Convincing policemen that the Federation represented their interests was not helped when leaders of local branches let their authority skew their judgment. In a revealing incident, when the national Federation branch sent out a questionnaire regarding 'temporary' pay cuts in 1925, the Birmingham branch sent it out to their men with detailed instructions on how to vote. Men were told to vote against pressing for abolition of the cuts regardless of the result, and to vote in favour of the Federation negotiating for the best bargain possible. These instructions were hardly likely to result in a true measure of the views of the men.[152] By the 1930s, men feared that the Federation threatened to turn into a '"grumbling club" or the like of a third-rate trade union' instead of using its position to present ideas on 'fundamental matters of efficiency'.[153] The Federation was not allowed to interfere in individual cases of promotion or discipline, a prime concern for policemen, though boards did make statements to watch committees about individual cases anyway if only to register their opinion. In 1939, the Federation still did not have its bearings and had not established itself enough to effect major changes or to prevent revisions to the Desborough scale.[154]

The Manchester Federation joint boards were particularly active, not surprising in a force that seldom hesitated in voicing its opinions and had united behind its union branch in rejecting the strike. With their better history of communication across ranks and fewer problems with favouritism, cooperation had a better chance of success. Holding office in their Federation did not impair promotion, one constable representative in 1925–1926 reaching the rank of superintendent by 1934. The Federation regularly brought matters before the chief constable, generally on leave, overtime, pensions, retirement, the equal distribution of duties, and problems with uniforms. While not always successful, the chief constable at least knew which issues were troubling his men. Yet even though the Federation was active, their

---

152 BPO, 2 May 1925, p. 9845 interleaf.

153 *Police Review*, 30 October 1936, p. 402.

154 In 1924, a Parliamentary committee considered adjusting the Desborough scale downwards, but decided that the scale should be left alone given the unsettled economic conditions ('Report of the Committee appointed to consider possible readjustments in the Standard Conditions of Service of the Police Force in Great Britain', 1924, Cmd. 2086, xii, 61). The government lowered pay for recruits to sixty-two shillings in 1933, arguing that it took five years for a constable to be fully trained so he should not receive full pay until he is truly a policeman ('Report of the Committee on Police Pay (New Entrants)', 1932–33, cmd. 4274, xv, 379, pp. 6, 11–12). For a description of the boards, see Constable J.M. Branthwaite, 'The Genesis, Aims and Scope of the Police Federation System of England and Wales', *Police Journal* 1:1 (1928): 19–30, and Anthony Judge, *The First Fifty Years: The Story of the Police Federation* (London: Police Federation, 1968).

accomplishments were mostly on minor issues. In one of their early actions, in 1921 they requested permission to smoke when retiring from duty, as was allowed in the Metropolitan Police Force. They were given permission to smoke but only on the upper level of tram cars.[155] In 1922 constables protested that the facilities given for the *Police Chronicle* were not allowed to the *Police Review*, which was officially frowned upon, and their request was granted.[156] In 1923, the Federation requested that classes offered in 1921 and 1922 be re-established, and in 1926 asked that the lectures given by experienced police officers on police law and procedure in 1921 be revived.[157] Uniforms received a great deal of attention. After asking if their collar numerals could be affixed on the epaulets since the metal backings were chafing their necks, the next set of collars was lined to prevent that problem.[158] They asked to stop wearing helmet chin straps in the summer since it gave them odd tan lines and this was allowed except for processional occasions.[159] Men disliked wearing gloves, but when the Federation asked that gloves be optional in wet weather, this time the chief constable could not agree.[160] In a more significant success, in 1926 the Federation protested an attempt by the watch committee to re-establish a fifty-five-year age minimum before retirement, compelling men to stay in the force beyond 25 years. The policy was not adopted.[161] Peacock and Maxwell published the resolutions and their responses in the General Orders so the men knew what was being discussed. Often requests dealing with pay, pensions, retirement, and allowances were listed as 'under consideration by the Home Office'. Requests were rarely granted outright.

The Manchester Federation did have one major victory, but it took ten years to achieve it. In 1924, they sent a request to the chief constable asking that officers below the rank of superintendent with twenty-six years of service and drawing the top pay within their rank should take their turn on street duty. This request included clerical officers, the group much resented by street officers. They wanted station officers back on the streets in the hopes of reminding them of the realities of life on patrol. They also hoped that a dose of patrolling in one of England's rainiest cities would convince them to retire and stop blocking promotion. Peacock gave the equivocal reply that this action would be taken where feasible. In 1927, a similar request that men with twenty-six years service be placed on street duty met with a similar response from Chief Constable Maxwell. Finally in 1934, retirement in Manchester was made mandatory for all ranks above constable, except in special

---

155 MGO, 31 March 1921.
156 MGO, 16 February 1922.
157 MGO, 15 June 1923; MGO, 17 December 1926.
158 MGO, 20 December 1927.
159 MGO, 29 August 1930.
160 MGO, 19 November 1924.
161 MGO, 2 September 1926.

cases, when qualified for the full pension at thirty years of service.[162] Senior officers could no longer sit in the higher ranks indefinitely, barring junior officers from promotion.

The Liverpool Federation was less successful. Liverpool men refused to believe that the Federation would make a dent in entrenched networks or could resist coming under the control of some faction. In 1923, PC Barton provided a rare sign that a local Federation even existed when he threatened to 'put it before the Federation' after he was accused of malingering on the sick list, the only example of using the Federation as a threat in the records.[163] One of its few reported accomplishments came in 1922 when the Federation requested permission to smoke when going off duty a year after the Manchester Federation's request, arguing that not only the Metropolitan Police but also the army and navy allowed it. The additional argument led to the request being granted. But in 1932 smoking in uniform was once again prohibited after public criticism of the habit.[164] In 1935, Chief Constable Wilson had to issue a special order begging men to take an active role in the Federation. Five out of twenty-one positions on the boards were vacant with no one nominated to fill them. He believed that the lack of support came from the failure to avert 1933 cuts in recruit pay, leading to the feeling that the Federation was useless.[165] Local Federation officers believed that without his encouragement the boards may have ceased to function.

The difficulties the Federation faced in challenging accepted policies was clear in Birmingham policemen's long struggle to adopt a standard shift system. Most police forces had three shifts: 6 am to 2 pm, 2 to 10 pm and 10 pm to 6 am.[166] Birmingham's day beats ran in split shifts, not continuous eight-hour duty, the first from 6 to 10 am and 2 to 6 pm, and the second from 10 am to 2 pm and 6 to 10 pm. Working the split shifts forced constables to spend twice as much time and double tram fares every day travelling to and from work or else spending the four-hour intermediate period wasting time in the city. Continuous duty had been terminated in 1882 on the argument that split shifts caused less strain on policemen's health. In 1903, constables had requested a return to the eight-hour shift but the watch

---

[162]   MGO, 29 May 1924; 20 December 1927; 19 January 1934.

[163]   LDRB, 13 February 1923, PCA 196 Barton, three years' service.

[164]   LWCM, 21 February 1922, pp. 360–1; 28 June 1932, p. 667.

[165]   LCCO, 24 July 1935. The *Police Review* believed his appeal to the force was unique in Federation history and reprinted it in full (*Police Review*, 22 November 1935, p. 494). In 1933, the Manchester Federation thanked Chief Constable Maxwell and the watch committee for their public support of the abolition of the temporary ten per cent deductions in police pay begun in 1931 on the recommendation of the Committee of National Expenditure (MGO, 3 November 1933; The Police Federation of England & Wales, *Annual Report of the Manchester City Police Joint Branch Board: for the Year 1933–34*, p. 3).

[166]   LSO no. 2, 1914, 1919, p. 1. Men typically served four weeks on nights, two on mornings and two on afternoons.

committee denied it as 'inconvenient and unworkable'.[167] The issue was left on hold during the fights over pay and rent days but was revived in 1928 by the Birmingham Federation. The watch committee replied,

> the eight hours continous [sic] tour of duty on the streets, with only a short interval for meals, would involve heavy strain upon a man's physique and a continous lowering of the vitality, with a resultant increase in liability to sickness. With regard to the point raised … that the present system gives the members inadequate time to enjoy the Sports Ground, the Committee do not feel that the men would be more likely to indulge in physical exercises after a continous tour of eight hours on the street.[168]

They added that living far from police stations was a personal choice and so travel time would not be considered in their decision. This answer annoyed men whose housing options were limited to approved lists. In 1932, another request received a similar answer, adding that continuous shifts would require the added expense of hiring relief men for meal times, who were not necessary with a split shift. The fear of added expense remained the core of the matter for the watch committee.[169] Rafter, with his emphatic monitoring of everything from proper cleaning to correct vocabulary, had probably convinced himself that split shifts were healthier for the men and would not be budged. Birmingham's shifts remained an anomaly, with Manchester, Liverpool, and nearly every other force in the country having continuous shifts without adverse effects. Finally, after the death of Rafter in 1935, the committee agreed to try eight-hour shifts on a trial basis for one year in 1937. In April 1938 Chief Constable Moriarty informed the committee that no difficulties had been experienced and the health of the men was sound.[170] After ten years and with the support of a new chief constable, the Federation won its point.

The dilemma of giving policemen the right to confer was never satisfactorily resolved in the interwar period. Until the Police Federation was given real negotiation and arbitration powers in the late 1940s, its recommendations, requests, and protests could be ignored.[171] The Desborough Committee had regarded 'the maintenance of a sound *esprit de corps* and relations of mutual confidence between

---

167   BWCM, 15 July 1903, pp. 448–52.
168   BPO, 30 January 1928, p. 13779.
169   BWCM, 6 April 1932, report no. 1, p. 3.
170   BWCM, 7 April 1938, report no. 5, p. 4.
171   Robert Reiner, in *The Blue-Coated Worker*, describes how the Federation was restructured into a real negotiating body of the rank and file in the late 1940s in response to heavy attrition rates, before which no proper negotiating or arbitration machinery existed (p. 30). In the 1970s, the Federation was still prohibited from involvement in promotion and discipline cases though it did help give advice and assistance in such cases (pp. 54, 88–93).

the various ranks as one of the principal tests of the efficient management of a police force'.[172] This required a dramatic shift away from pre-1919 watch committees and chief constables ignoring the petitions of police delegations in favour of tradition and economy. Policemen were no longer the casual workers of the nineteenth century. Police work now required a constantly increasing knowledge of law, first aid, motors cars, radios, Morse code, and other technologies, and working with a public armed with telephones and demanding attention. In 1919, the Desborough Committee established that policing was now skilled labour, and policemen immediately began pushing to be recognized as a profession. To maintain a viable police force, authorities had to bring policemen into partnership rather than treat them as employees without a voice. Chief constables and watch committees began listening more carefully than they had before the strikes, if only out of anxiety. But the lower ranks remained sceptical that their forces could pass the test of mutual confidence.

---

[172] 'Report of the Committee on the Police Service of England, Wales, and Scotland', Part II, 1920, p. 9.

6

The Police and the Public: Animosity

It is most aggravating to a police officer to be severely assaulted when in the execution of his duty, especially when there may possibly be a big crowd watching his ill-treatment, not one of whom will lend him a helping hand, but many of whom are in all probability encouraging his assailant. Nevertheless, when you have once secured your prisoner and handcuffed him, it is very cowardly on your part, and very reprehensible indeed, to strike or otherwise assault your prisoner.

Sir Robert Peacock, 1900[1]

MUCH OF THE ANIMOSITY between policemen and the public displayed itself in 'incivility', hurling insults back and forth, but also regularly crossed the line into physical conflicts. Disputes often began in different perceptions of appropriate behaviour. Constables exercised discretion in deciding which laws to enforce, whether to make arrests or issue summonses, and what force was merited. Civilians tended to think that constables were overreacting to minor offences when stopping them, charging them, or arresting them. Conflicts rarely had obvious guilty or innocent parties. Both sides typically made some provocative gesture, and both sides believed that their own actions had been entirely justified in the circumstances. In the final analysis, however, constables were expected to prevent conflicts, not take part in them. The character of these run-ins tended to reflect the class of the people involved. Clashes between policemen and the working-class public resembled the insubordination and fighting among policemen; they yelled at each other and threw punches, usually in sudden outbursts that just as quickly died down, with the worst brawls involving groups of men.[2] Confrontations across

---

1   Peacock, *Police Constables' Duties*, p. 8.
2   For more on working-class insults and fights, including men, women, and children, see

classes, usually a working-class constable and a middle-class civilian, often involved social superiors finding themselves at a disadvantage with their social inferiors and reacting with scathing remarks. Class differences were reflected in the insults. Working-class civilians and policemen told each other to mind their own business and challenged each other's manhood. Middle- and upper-class civilians tended to be patronizing, telling constables how to do their jobs, and they easily took offence at orders from policemen. No one, including the policemen, reacted well to having their respectability and status questioned.[3]

Physical violence was mostly limited to police encounters within the working class, varying from shoves, bites, and kicks to more serious blows from weapons. Major injuries were rare. By the early 1900s, working-class resistance to policing tended to take the form of routine but irritating harassment of constables, often during arrests.[4] A prisoner's struggles could draw the sympathy of bystanders, and constables could hardly let prisoners go, resulting in skirmishes. If prisoners resisted, constables preferred using enough force to minimize injuries and escapes, but prisoners and witnesses measured appropriate force more narrowly. Younger constables were more inclined to violence than older ones, being more likely to take challenges personally and less willing to back off once confrontations began. Older men had more experience at diffusing tensions, but they, too, could be drawn into fights. Physical conflicts became more likely when people had been drinking, when more than one person was involved on either side, and when combatants were young. The worst violence included all three, often arrests for disorderly conduct outside of public houses. Even though forces recruited better-educated constables after the 1919 Police Act, the reported physical encounters with civilians remained fairly constant. According to Liverpool records, injuries to constables caused by prisoners or crowds stayed at about forty per cent of total injuries, with spikes during 1911 transport strikes, after the 1919 police strike when most constables were young, and during the 1926 General Strike.[5]

Chapter 9. See also Joanne Klein, '"Moving On", Men and the Changing Character of Interwar Working-Class Neighborhoods: From the Files of the Manchester and Liverpool City Police', *Journal of Social History* (2004): 407–21.

3   By the twentieth century, the working class had its own standards of respectability based on independence, community, and self respect. See F.M.L. Thompson, *The Rise of Respectable Society: A Social History of Victorian Britain 1830–1900* (London: Fontana Press, 1988) and Richard Hoggart, *The Uses of Literacy* (New York: Penguin, 1958).

4   For mid-nineteenth-century patterns, see Robert Storch, 'The Plague of the Blue Locusts: Police Reform and Popular Resistance in Northern England, 1840–57', *International Review of Social History* 20 (1975): 61–90; 'The Policeman as Domestic Missionary: Urban Discipline and Popular Culture in Northern England, 1850–1880', *Journal of Social History* 9:4 (1976): 481–509.

5   LCI, 1907–1929; 1937–1939. The one exception was during the war, with twenty-five per cent. In April 1906, the Liverpool injury count dropped suddenly from anywhere from

But while injuries remained common, as working-class drinking declined, they became less severe. This consistent proportion of civilian caused injuries suggests that the relationship between policemen and working-class civilians did not change dramatically during the early twentieth century. Yet even though the injuries continued, one sign of shifting attitudes was a postwar increase in working-class civilians rescuing constables and assisting constables in making arrests. This was probably a combination of the working class becoming less tolerant of public drunkenness, and more willing to help now that policemen were giving attention to middle- and upper-classes traffic lawbreakers.

The middle and upper classes readily got into verbal disputes with constables, but rarely struck out at them. Instead, they sent letters of complaint to chief constables, the press, and influential friends. These cross-class arguments became more frequent as traffic increased in volume. The working classes had adjusted to policing in the nineteenth century and now the higher classes had to adjust in the twentieth century.[6] They discovered that it was easier to champion the police when their regard was directed elsewhere. Policemen quickly learned that traffic lawbreakers resented being caught just as much as petty thieves did, and could be just as noisy in their protests. Incivility became a dominant concern for chief constables in the 1920s and 1930s, as more higher-class civilians found themselves on the receiving end of police attention for the first time. Instructed to 'shame the public by being polite' in response to their rudeness, constables nevertheless got tired of receiving abuse for enforcing laws for which civilians held them personally responsible.[7] Telephones added more opportunities for incivility. Civilians came to expect immediate responses to their demands for police attention at the same time that policemen were being stretched thin by traffic duties. Impatient civilians and constables annoyed at being called for minor problems could quickly irritate each other. Some members of the working classes also owned motor cars and telephones, and had similar run-ins with constables. But the higher classes were still learning how to cope with police attention, with the added complication that policemen were 'beneath them' on the social ladder.

Most encounters that constables had with the public were with the working class, if only because this class made up the majority of the local population. All three cities were heavily working class, with Liverpool at roughly ninety per cent of

---

fifty to 150 assaults a month to single digits. It is difficult to believe that assaults on police dropped so precipitously and permanently in one month. It is more likely that the criteria used for classifying and recording assault injuries changed. Totals after the war crept into the teens at the same time that the number of policemen grew. Higher numbers only occurred during strikes and riots (LCI, 1904–1929, 1937–1939).

6   For the sake of brevity, the middle and upper classes will be referred to as the higher classes.

7   *Police Review and Parade Gossip*, 5 April 1929, 'Turn the Other Cheek', p. 256.

its inhabitants. Conflicts generally limited themselves to verbal exchanges. Civilians annoyed at being told to move along or questioned about their dog licences lashed back with rude comments. Women could be just as confrontational as men, calling constables 'bloody sods' and 'dirty bastards'. While advised to ignore such remarks, constables gave as good as they got, telling civilians to 'shut their traps' and 'bloody do what you're told'. Mistaken assumptions about a situation or confrontational attitudes often created problems, provoking an angry reaction. Hostility could flare up through misunderstandings both ways. PC Findlay found a couple in a shed and imagined that they were there for some amorous purpose. He ordered them out 'in an improper manner' when in fact they had taken shelter there from the rain.[8] Similarly, a man complained that a constable was spying on him and his fiancée while they were sitting by a hedge while in actuality the constable had gone into the field 'for a natural purpose'.[9] Few working-class complaints of verbal abuse appear in police records since few bothered to report it, preferring to settle the matter on the spot. In one case, a middle-class civilian complained on behalf of a worker, an unusual example perhaps motivated by the worker being black. During an Orange parade, PC Jones saw a black man mount an entrance to St George Hall to take pictures and said, 'I wouldn't allow a white man up there so I'm certainly not allowing you.' Jones admitted the remark but explained that 'a wrong construction had been put on what Con meant'. Chief Constable Wilson concluded that Jones had been 'indiscreet in his choice of words' and was advised on 'how to address people'.[10] Constant reminders from chief constables that constables should refrain from 'improper language' and from getting into arguments with civilians make it clear that incivility was a chronic problem.

One of the few cases involving a working-class verbal exchange, and possibly a physical blow, portrayed a characteristic situation of opposite interpretations of the same events. It involved groups of young men on both sides, one of the more volatile kinds of meetings. PCs Ellison and Harris encountered a group of six young men while on the way to a disturbance, with the result that PC Ellison and Jack Malone exchanged words. Their statements were a typical example of contradictory perceptions. Malone, a twenty-year-old baker, stated that he and five friends had been walking along a road in pairs when two constables had come up behind them. In passing them, one of the constables caught his arm. Malone said 'sorry' but the constable struck him in the face. When Malone asked why Ellison had struck him, the constable threatened to arrest them if they did not 'get along'. PC Harris, on the other hand, stated that he and Ellison had passed six youths walking

---

8   LDRB, 5 May 1905, PCG 98 Findlay, seven years' service, one default, reprimanded.
9   LDRB, 5 May 1927, PCG 138. The man admitted he had been annoyed at the interruption but accepted the constable's explanation.
10   LCCDR, 18 July 1934, PCA 117 Jones. For racial problems in Liverpool see Brogden, *On the Mersey Beat*, ch. 6.

abreast. As they walked past, one of the men mimicked the constables, and the rest began to clap their hands. PC Ellison turned around, caught one of them by the shoulder, and asked, 'Is that all the respect you have for a Policeman[?]' The youths replied that 'You could do nothing if you had that uniform off' and 'Don't forget their [sic] is six of us to you two.' The constables ignored them and went on their way to the disturbance. Ellison agreed with this account, adding that 'if my hand did brush against any part of him it was entirely due to him turning to run away'. Malone felt strongly enough about Ellison's actions to report him. Both Malone and the constables portrayed their own actions as reasonable, and left out details that might reflect badly on them. While it was likely that the young men had mocked the constables, Chief Constable Maxwell decided that Ellison should have restrained his impulse to react and fined him twenty shillings for unlawful exercise of authority.[11]

In addition to insulting constables immediately, the public could strike back by making complaints against them. These were often exaggerated or even false. Civilians might hope to get out of an arrest or summons, or at least cause the constable some grief. For instance, after being arrested for prostitution, Rose Wright accused PC Richardson of stealing three shillings from her.[12] Generally, police forces were thorough in investigating complaints but a civilian with a convincing story could get a constable into trouble. False charges could be made in retaliation for minor incidents. Soon after PC Royston called at a house in response to a complaint against it, an anonymous letter accused him of habitually visiting the place. Officers kept observation at the address but Royston never called on or entered the house so no action was taken against him.[13] Sometimes, in their initial anger at attracting police attention, civilians lodged complaints but then failed to follow them up once their tempers cooled. Mrs Marion Jones charged PC Breeze with 'trumping up charges against boys in the neighbourhood' after he threatened her son with a summons for trespassing on a railways right of way, but she did not appear at the hearing regarding her complaint.[14] Quite a few complainants failed to come to hearings for any number of reasons. They might not have been able to away from work, they may have feared getting fair treatment at a police hearing, or they may have changed their minds about pursuing the complaint. Simply making the complaint may have provided them the satisfaction of annoying the police.

A practice that commonly led to public hostility was constables making

---

11   MPF, 23 August 1931, PCC 150 John Ellison, appointed February 1925, MGO, 28 August 1931.

12   LCCDR, 21 October 1920, PCA 244 Richardson, complainant Rose Wright, 17 Wilton Street, allegations unfounded.

13   LCCDR, 5 July 1939, PCB 114 Royston, no charge framed.

14   BRB, 30 September 1918, PCE 88 Charles Henry Breeze, joined April 1893, no appearance of complainant.

arrests when issuing a summons was more appropriate. Regulations stated that if individuals desisted from minor violations that did not disturb the peace, and if their identity and address were known, constables should issue a summons rather than make an arrest. But constables regularly decided against summonses. Some of this was a desire to avoid the paperwork and hassle of issuing a summons. Constables also hoped that making arrests would reflect well on their diligence. But they might choose to make an arrest to teach the offender a lesson, either due to personal animosity or distaste for the offence. Police forces had steady problems with constables arresting 'respectable' citizens for offences which constables decided should be treated as 'unrespectable', particularly public drunkenness. In one case, a 'respectable citizen' was arrested at his own shop door and charged with being drunk and pushing a constable.[15] Compounding the problem, once offenders learned that they were to be arrested rather than summoned, they might resist or run. Constables even chased individuals into private homes for insignificant offences. These arrests could lead to constables being assaulted, making it even more desirable that summonses be issued instead. Warnings against unnecessary arrests had short-term results but had to be repeated regularly. In 1901, Rafter advised his men of 'the necessity of using more discrimination in arresting persons, as he notices numbers of persons are arrested for very trivial offences, and who would certainly appear if they had been summoned'.[16] He had to repeat this in stronger terms in 1902 and 1903, remarking that he 'cannot but think that very often Officers pursue this course of following persons into houses to arrest them simply to avoid the subsequent trouble of serving a summons'.[17] The warnings had to be repeated again in 1925 and 1934.[18] But solving a problem immediately with an arrest had appeal and constables persisted in avoiding the more bureaucratic option.

While many disputes limited themselves to 'words' and complaints, physical assaults between constables and working-class civilians remained a continual problem from 1900 to 1939. The most serious attacks occurred in the early 1900s, a result of heavier working-class drinking and light sentences for assaults. Rafter feared that constables who felt unprotected by the bench were using their truncheons more frequently in order to gain some immediate justice, exacerbating police–civilian violence.[19] In a 1901 study, the Birmingham watch committee found that every constable was assaulted at least once a year, yet magistrates handed down only small fines or short sentences to their attackers. The city took

---

15   BPO, 12 December 1903, pp. 55–6. The watch committee decided that the constable had exceeded his duty in making the arrest rather than giving the man a summons.

16   BPO, 28 June 1901, p. 480.

17   BPO, 22 April 1902, p. 10407; 28 January 1903, pp. 343–5.

18   BPO, 8 October 1925, p. 10405; 27 March 1934, p. 21957.

19   BWCM, 23 September 1901, pp. 179–83.

action after PC Gunter was killed in July 1901. Gunter had gone to investigate a disturbance and, after he told a crowd to desist, eight men beat him to death with brick ends.[20] After this, in cases of assault on policemen, Rafter employed counsel in order to get heavier penalties. The cases that he forced to go to trial ended in five-year rather than one-month sentences.[21] Nevertheless, only six months later, PC Blinko nearly had the top of his skull cut off when two brothers attacked him with a hatchet.[22] Liverpool and Manchester also had problems with assaults, with 1324 reported assaults on Liverpool police in 1898 and 1383 in 1899, and Manchester with 234 and 300 assaults in the same years.[23] But by the end of 1902, HMI Eden commented hopefully that although there were 'a great many assaults on the police [in Manchester] ... the majority of the cases were not of a very serious character'.[24] Liverpool records had a preponderance of trivial injuries after 1903. With the working class becoming more sober, including the constables themselves, and with fewer constables treating policing as a casual job, serious police and civilian assaults decreased. Civilians and constables continued to inflict minor injuries but few seemed determined to kill each other.[25] The worst violence persisted in encounters involving groups of civilians, constables, or both, with allies egging each other on, leaping to each other's defence, and not wanting to look weak in front of witnesses.

Unlike the injuries caused by civilians, police violence rarely made it into the records unless someone complained or the assault was severe enough to result in charges. When a prisoner got 'coshed', policemen were unlikely to report it themselves. In 1902, a year after the death of PC Gunter, a Birmingham justice protested to Rafter that prisoners were regularly complaining to station sergeants of being assaulted by arresting constables but that sergeants failed to report the complaints. The chief constable told his men that it reflected poorly on the force when these charges came out in court, but the majority of assaults remained unreported.[26] Police assaults of civilians could be severe if only because constables

---

20   BWCM, 23 September, 13 November 1901, pp. 179–83, 209. Three men got fifteen years each for manslaughter.

21   BWCM, 23 September 1901, pp. 179–183.

22   BWCM, 12 February, 24 September 1902, 14 January 1903, 10 April 1905, pp. 263, 338, 376, 94. The assailants were brothers, ages twenty-eight and nineteen, of no fixed abode. Blinko lived but took three years off on medical pension to recover. The reason for the attack was not given.

23   'Inspectors of Constabulary report for year ended the 29th September 1900', PP 1901 (200) xxxii, 1, p. 75.

24   'Inspectors of Constabulary report for year ended the 29th September 1902', PP 1903 (122) xxviii, 275, p. 103.

25   Martin and Wilson note a drop in assaults on policemen from the 1890s to the period after the First World War (*The Police*, p. 23).

26   BPO, 1 May 1902, pp. 79–80.

had heavy boots and dense truncheons. Regular reminders that truncheons only be used in self defence and never against a prisoner's head suggested that constables were violating these limitations fairly often. In 1905, Rafter lamented that 'another case has occurred in which a Police Officer has improperly used his staff in pursuing a man who was running away from him'.[27] In 1916, he had to warn explicitly that staffs 'must not be used to beat prisoners'.[28] In 1931, PC Trafford, perhaps showing off police ruthlessness to patrons at a public house, told the licensee and customers that he had been kicked by a prisoner and had 'split open the head of that person' in retaliation, that police officers 'treat prisoners revengefully and brutally', that a superintendent had 'taken two recruits to a prisoner in a cell and told them that he was a man who kicks policemen and that they knew what to do with him', and that 'recruits were incited … to ill-treat a prisoner'. He was charged with making false statements but the force would hardly admit that he was correct.[29] Into the late 1930s, a Manchester constable remembered how illegal rubber truncheons were commonly used to pacify prisoners. PC Robert Mark admitted to breaking a man's leg while loading him into a police van but was never reported for it.[30] Few complaints of constables abusing prisoners led to charges. The majority were dropped and the constables given advice by their superintendents. Fifty-year-old Mr Willasey went so far as to turn in a petition from neighbours who had seen him kicked in the stomach by PC Corlett, but the charge was withdrawn.[31] Unless the evidence of assault was clear, accusations rarely led to disciplinary action beyond a lecture on proper conduct, since investigations tended to find that the force necessary to prevent prisoners from assaulting constables or from escaping. Many accusations of police violence made by civilians were considered 'explained'.[32] Similar to constables not feeling supported by magistrates, civilians feeling ignored by police authorities could be tempted to assault constables and at least gain immediate satisfaction.

Constables used violence against civilians for a variety of reasons. Men at the end of their shifts might take direct action to punish petty offenders rather than

---

[27]   BPO, 29 July 1905, p. 155. PCD 55 James Grady had to resign after 'unnecessarily striking' a civilian with his staff (MGO, 19 December 1913).

[28]   BPO, 22 January 1916, p. 169.

[29]   BPO, 11 February 1931, PCE 36 Sydney Arthur Trafford, reduced in class and finally cautioned, p. 17701.

[30]   Mark, *In the Office of Constable*, p. 28.

[31]   LCCDR, 3 October 1938, PCG 130 Corlett, charge denied. Frederick Styles complained that PCD 101 William Sale had intentionally tripped him, causing him to be thrown to the ground. The charge was dropped when Styles did not appear to testify (BRB, 29 September 1919, joined 1912).

[32]   In one example, PCA 77 Albert John Clewes was accused of pushing Al Briscoe in the back of the neck while he and three friends were singing on a footpath. The matter was considered explained (BRB, 5 July 1911, joined October 1905, one default, eight awards).

go to the trouble of arresting them and doing paperwork. Constables used force as rough justice. They could find it easier to mete out a blow on the spot than bother with a charge or if not sure that a charge would stick. They could be frustrated at the release of a prisoner who they felt was guilty and hand out their own punishment. Drunk constables were prone to violence, such as the 'practically mad drunk' PC Brennan who, seeing the Salvation Army singing Christmas hymns, 'took off his belt and cape, rushed amongst the singers, and commenced to strike right and left'.[33] Violence commonly occurred during arrests. Constables assaulted prisoners resisting arrest, and they assaulted civilians attempting to rescue prisoners. In spite of Peacock's advice, it was difficult not to respond to abuse from a crowd, especially when bystanders attacked them. All sides tended to declare that their actions were taken purely in self-defence. The violence increased with every individual added to the crowd. Constables were more likely to use excessive force to protect a colleague, and civilians in defending some unfortunate individual. In a few cases, constables were simply bad policemen. They let their authority go to their heads, or had violent temperaments. Some were too prone to assume that all prisoners were violent and habitually resorted to violence. PC Davenport combined a number of problems; he was drunk, he arrested a man on a false charge, and he inflicted a severe scalp wound with his truncheon.[34] These men rarely lasted long unless they had good connections, a possibility more common before the war than afterwards.

Before the war, a common form of rough justice involved constables disciplining boys as a way to discourage future offenders. Constables regularly struck small boys on the ear and hit them on the head with their gloves;[35] PC Edwards went so far as to drench a boy with water from a hose.[36] Since unruly boys could not be arrested, threatening them or boxing their ears seemed like an appropriate way to teach boys a lesson.[37] Many constables believed that they were treating boys the same way that they treated their own sons or that they themselves were treated by their fathers. Police authorities discouraged this unofficial parenting since it created a bad impression with the public. Witnesses complained if they thought constables were

---

[33]   MWCM, 7 January 1904, PCB 197 William Brennan, five years' service, one default, reduced to the lowest class and finally warned, vol 194, no. 22. Three young women and a man were knocked down, and Brennan had to be forcibly restrained. He admitted going to a private house and becoming drunk but had no recollection of attacking anyone. He was initially dismissed but the Salvation Army asked that he be reinstated. Later he personally apologized to each of them.

[34]   BPO, 19 April 1900, PCD 34 Harry Davenport, dismissed, p. 172.

[35]   BPO, 19 March 1904, p. 130.

[36]   LDRB, 1 June 1905, PCF 170 Edwards, nine years' service, reprimanded. A number of constables 'exceeded' their duty by assaulting a boy (BWCM, 28 January 1903, pp. 387–8).

[37]   For an excellent study on this relationship, see David Wolcott, *Cops and Kids: Policing Juvenile Delinquency in Urban America, 1890–1940* (Columbus: Ohio State University Press, 2005).

being too harsh or if their own children were targeted. Annie Beech complained when PC March struck her twelve-year-old son on the face in her beer house. When she remonstrated with him, he beat her off with a blow to the arm and chest.[38] Sometimes the boys defended themselves. A boy stopped by PC Marshall for kicking a piece of paper responded by kicking the constable.[39] Most constables limited themselves to a quick blow meant to sting rather than injure the boys but a few more extreme cases occurred. In one, PC Brook beat a twelve-year-old boy with a cane and extorted a confession by threatening to birch him and put salt on the wounds. The boy had apparently committed some offence at a local school and the police were called in.[40] No reports of constables striking boys appeared after the war, in part because changes in school attendance laws took more boys off the streets. Constables continued to discipline boys, similar to the advice they commonly handed out to adults, but seemed less likely to hit them.

Another prewar problem involved men bringing their private quarrels to work, mostly spontaneous scenes but occasionally premeditated revenge. These included getting into fights with friends and acquaintances while on duty. In a typical case, while visiting a cabman's hut to take an unsanctioned break, PC Foxcroft quarrelled with the cabby and hit him three times.[41] More seriously, constables used their uniforms to disguise revenge as official business. PC Woodings convinced PC Smith that two brothers were guilty of an unspecified crime and got him to accompany him to their house. Once there, Woodings broke into the house and violently assaulted the two men. The matter was serious enough that Woodings was sentenced to six weeks' hard labour and Smith was fined twenty shillings and costs by the Birmingham Police Court.[42] As with other assaults, the violence escalated and events became more complicated with each person drawn in. While in plain clothes at a refreshment house for unknown undercover duty, PC Keating and PC Finneran made the acquaintance of two men. The four men began arguing with each other, and the constables left, threatening that they would be waiting outside. When the two men left, the constables knocked them down. Mrs Shaw, the elderly proprietor, ran out to stop the fight and was struck in the face. PC McArthur heard the disturbance and came to investigate. Mrs Shaw complained of being assaulted but McArthur refused to arrest Keating and Finneran when he recognized them as

---

38   BRB, 20 June 1910, PCC Joseph Turner March, joined December 1905, reduced and transferred, three defaults, three awards, dismissed for striking in 1919.
39   LCI, 18 April 1905, PCA 65 Marshall.
40   BPO, 13 November 1909, PCC 237 Brook, six years' service, one default, dismissed.
41   MWCM, 19 July 1900, PCD 158 William Foxcroft, reduced two classes, vol. 16, no. 4.
42   BPO, 10, 22 May 1900, pp. 183, 192; BWCM, 22 May 1900, PCE 39 James Woodings, PC John Thomas Smith, p. 4. The watch committee dismissed Woodings, but decided that Smith had 'acted indiscreetly, but that he was misled by the erroneous statements and conduct of Woodings' and, because of his excellent record, only severely cautioned him.

constables. McArthur may have thought that the fight resulted from the constables trying to make an arrest, not realizing that it was a private fight.[43] The tendency of these quarrels to drag in unsuspecting colleagues, as well as the damage these fights did to the reputation of the force, motivated police authorities to treat these cases with severity, usually dismissing the men. Only one case appeared after the war. In 1929, in retaliation for a grudge, PC Perrins made an unlawful and violent arrest of Ernest Uebersax, 'arousing him from his bed regarding a light in his house, [and] demanding to see his Dog Licence'. He convinced PC Closs to assist him in taking the man to the station where they accused him of being drunk and disorderly and of kicking Perrins while on the way to the station. The station sergeant refused the charge and Perrins was dismissed.[44] The disappearance of these cases may be linked to a decline in working-class violence in general and to fewer constables treating their jobs as casual employment.

Immediately after the war, forces experienced a brief outbreak of serious assaults. In 1919, one officer speculated that an increase in resistance to arrest 'may be the effect of the time, or the war spirit or … a decline of public respect for the police since the [1918] strike'.[45] In addition to general economic and political unrest, in Birmingham and especially in Liverpool, constables faced more hostility due to working-class resentment of police 'scabs' hired after the 1919 strikes. Police assaults on civilians similarly increased. Unlike most examples of severe injuries, these assaults involved individual constables taking out frustrations on single individuals. While some cases could be blamed on young men rushed into uniform, others involved experienced men who seemed to lose all sense of reasonable behaviour. In one case, PC Morgan threw away a clean twelve-year record and seven awards, an usually good career. Something provoked him to beat up Mr Hurley, striking him in the face, kicking him between the legs, kicking him on the back after he fell, and then searching him without just cause. Morgan was ordered to resign.[46] In another example, PC Maddams struck Claude Grattridge in face with such severity during an arrest that he appeared before the stipendiary magistrate and was fined £5 or twenty-one days' imprisonment.[47] By around 1922,

43   MWCM, 19 July 1900, PCD 187 Keating and PCD 86 Finneran dismissed; PCD 131 Robert Graham McArthur, ten years' service, five drinking defaults, four neglects of duty, six defaults for being in public houses, reduced to lowest rank, vol. 16, no. 4. Finneran dropped his handcuffs at the scene, which were used to connect him to the brawl.

44   BOR, 22 August 1929, PCC 58 Ernest Edward Perrins, dismissed, PCC 132 John Anthony Class, reduced to lowest class; BPO, 26 September 1929, p. 15809; BRB, 26 September 1929, PCC 132 John Anthony Class, joined August 1920.

45   DC, Evidence, question 506, Basil Thomson, Assistant Commissioner, CID, Metropolitan Police, p. 30.

46   BRB, 29 December 1919, PCC 105 Edward Sidney Morgan, joined February 1908, seven awards, to resign.

47   BDRB, 17 August 1921, PCE 192 George Maddams, dismissed, pp. 45–6.

this upsurge in violence ended. Enough time had passed since the war and the police strikes for hostilities to fade and for probationary constables to settle into their new careers. After this, serious violence restricted itself to riots and strikes, rarely occurring during typical duties.

The most common clashes took place during arrests, confrontations that could be dangerous for both prisoners and constables. Prisoners feared constables making free use of their truncheons, and feared police boots, such as when PC Forster viciously kicked a prisoner on the leg.[48] Constables had cause to be wary of prisoners. Uncooperative prisoners could cause an assortment of injuries, not necessarily on purpose. One prisoner grabbed hold of an iron railing and PC Houghton struggled to free him. The prisoner suddenly let go and fell on top of Houghton.[49] Escape attempts could lead to injuries, such as when PC Callister and a female prisoner were dragged several yards after she caught hold of a passing tram car.[50] Since many arrests had witnesses, some prisoners felt that they had to put up at least token resistance to look good for the crowd. In turn, constables could not simply release a struggling prisoner without losing the respect of the crowd and making their job impossible. Some force to restrain a prisoner was unavoidable. While policemen could be too rough, prisoners also provoked that response. Prisoners who kicked constables on the legs or butted them in the stomach were not in a position to complain when constables replied with a whack from their truncheons. At the same time, constables had to avoid provoking prisoners into resisting, either through derogatory remarks or inappropriate aggression.

Most injuries inflicted on constables were relatively minor, caused by prisoners of both genders kicking, butting, and biting to get free. Liverpool records show a relatively steady rate of minor injuries caused by prisoners or crowds with two or three incidents a week which was not unduly high, considering overall numbers of arrests. Riots and strikes led to larger numbers of injuries caused by bricks and other missiles, but even then few of the injuries were more than cuts and bruises.[51] Rowdy but rarely vicious behaviour was a normal part of business. Biting was a favourite tactic, and constables sometimes had to be treated for septic poisoning as well as for the bite.[52] Biting could be combined with other attacks, such as when PC Blair was bitten on the finger by a woman who also kicked him and hit him in the face.[53] Butting and knocking down constables was another

---

[48]   MGO, 2 April 1914, PCB 98 John Forster, to resign.

[49]   LCI, 20 January 1912, PCG 158 Houghton.

[50]   LCI, 11 April 1905, PCA 94 Callister.

[51]   LCI, 1903–1930, 1936–1939. Nineteen eleven and 1925–1927 saw the highest numbers of injuries, a result of strikes.

[52]   PCB 153 Hodgkinson and PCG 224 Giles both suffered septic poisoning after prisoners bit them (LCI, 13 January 1912, 3 June 1914).

[53]   LCI, 3 October 1903, PCD 104 Blair.

common manoeuvre. One agitated man made his escape after knocking down PC Cross,[54] and PC Preston suffered severe shock after a prisoner knocked him down and jumped on him.[55] Constables were kicked and hit, the watch committee having to buy PC Reid artificial teeth after a prisoner kicked out a few real ones.[56] Some prisoners managed to escape, making assaulting constables seem worthwhile, but others remained in custody even after spirited fights. PC Connolly managed to arrest a man he caught posting indecent bills in a public urinal even though the man hit Connolly in the face, butted him on the chest, and knocked his head against a metal partition.[57] One prisoner thought he had evaded the police after striking PC Kelly in the face and hitting him with a brick. He jumped through a window to escape, but had the misfortune of landing on PC Matthews.[58] Not all attacks on constables were undeserved even from the police point of view. PC Rogers had been ordered not to arrest a woman but did so anyway. He was assaulted and rendered unfit for duty but the police authorities gave him no sympathy, stopping his leave and sick pay.[59]

Prisoners rarely used weapons. When they did, weapons tended to be improvised items such as loose bricks. Sometimes, constables had their truncheons used against them. A violent prisoner grabbed PC Power's truncheon and severely beat him, including fracturing his elbow,[60] and another kicked PC Preston in the legs and stomach and wrenched away his truncheon, hitting him violently on the back of the head.[61] During the war, a few constables were attacked by American soldiers. In what may have been constables trying to restrain disorderly soldiers, PC Shimmin and PC Smith suffered severe cuts on their heads and hands when three American soldiers struck them with batons.[62] Constables began encountering guns after the war, mainly service revolvers and war souvenirs. Most appeared during robberies. PC Corlett found three men who had robbed a post office hiding behind some trucks and moved towards them with his truncheon drawn. One shot him, the bullet going through his arm into his body and lodging under his shoulder blade.[63] Luckily for the constables, the robbers missed more often than not. Two constables chasing a fugitive were shot at six times when only ten to fifteen yards

---

54   LCI, 10 September 1903, PCF 202 Cross, injury to forehead and cut on back of head, severely shaken, went off duty.

55   LHCWC, 21 October 1911, PCF 140 Preston.

56   LHCWC, 19 June 1905, PCB 138 Robert Reid, p. 181.

57   LCI, 17 November 1903, PCA 324 Connolly.

58   LCI, 1 October 1903, PCA 219 Kelly, PCA 188 Matthews.

59   BPO, 4 September 1902, PCD 114 William Rogers, p. 207.

60   LCI, 26 May 1922, PCD 251 Power.

61   LCI, 4 September 1905, PCG 73 Preston.

62   LCI, 1 November 1918, PCG 90 Shimmin, PCG 189 Smith. An American soldier hit PCA 158 Neary on the head with his baton (LCI, 24 May 1918).

63   MWCM, 13 June 1918, vol. 77, no. 6; *Police Review*, 7 January 1927, p. 7. The men were

from the man but escaped injury.[64] Knife injuries appeared less often than guns. In one case, a woman convicted for improper conduct stabbed PC Anderson in the back with a jack-knife while he was on traffic duty in revenge for testifying in her trial.[65] No other knife wounds were in the surviving Manchester, Birmingham, or Liverpool records even though constables had people draw knives on them. PC Hayes was struck several times with a sword but not actually stabbed with it.[66] It is possible that the constables' thick uniforms prevented most knife injuries. More typically, prisoners used whatever was handy, such as the prisoner who threw chipped potatoes at PC Coleman,[67] one who hit PC Cummins with a saucepan,[68] and one who struck PC Kinrade with a tin of corned beef.[69] Constables sometimes had things dropped on them from windows, including flower pots and boots. PC Hewlitt was talking to the keeper of a lodging house when a man dropped a stool onto his head from a first-floor window.[70] But the most common weapons remained hands, feet, and heads.

Coping with drunken prisoners could be particularly troublesome for constables who often just wanted them to move along or who tried to take them home, not arrest them.[71] But individuals confused or belligerent from drink only saw a constable trying to take them into custody and ruining their night out. Continual problems were caused by intoxicated women who had a difficult time walking, tended to beat at the constables, and attracted sympathetic witnesses with their cries. One bystander told PC Brookfield to let a drunken woman go. When the constable refused, the man struck him on the back of the neck and kicked him.[72] Mary Kelly 'remonstrated' with PC Fripp for his rough handling of a drunk women. He allegedly replied, 'You mind your own business you bloody

---

later found by detectives. PCD 120 Clarke was shot by a bank robber. The bullet went through Clark's shoulder; the robber was arrested (LCI, 13 October 1926).

64   MWCM, 29 November 1922, vol. 94, no. 52. Injuries from firearms were rare and usually accidental. Most gun wounds resulted from careless behaviour by the constables. While on special duty, PC Delderfield accidentally fired his gun 'by tampering with it'. He was not entrusted with a revolver again (BPO, 29 April 1915, p. 528). While examining a revolver on duty parade, PC Whalley accidentally discharged it (MGO, 27 May 1921). A man digging in his garden unearthed a loaded pistol and turned it in at a police box. Trying to move it to get at a report, PCB 79 Ernest Brown shot himself in the hand (MPF, 27 August 1933, appointed February).

65   LCI, 28 December 1926, PCE 197 Anderson; Brogden, *On the Mersey Beat*, p. 146.

66   LCI, 26 July 1904, PCD 101 Hayes.

67   LCI, 10 February 1905, PCD 110 Coleman.

68   LCI, 17 April 1908, PCB 122 Cummins.

69   LCI, 8 February 1918, PCE 166 Kinrade.

70   LCI, 30 September 1905, PCA 305 Hewlitt.

71   For example, see Brogden, *On the Mersey Beat*, pp. 92–3.

72   LCI, 10 May 1914, PCG 143 Brookfield.

sod.' He was cautioned to be 'tolerant with prisoners & not to heed bystanders remarks'.[73] PC Anderton had a drunk female kick him, strike him in the face, and spit on him. While taking her to the station, a sympathetic crowd knock him down.[74] Drunken groups were especially dangerous. PC Mulligan 'asked five or six men who were shouting & singing in Boundary Lane to desist & go along quietly'. Instead, he sustained a kick 'about the body, blow on the face & cut lip, skin peeled off legs &c'.[75] Similar to other assaults, weapons were rare. PS Stevens was shot in the leg while disarming a drunken army sentry with a rifle but this was unusual and possibly accidental.[76] As working-class drunkenness decreased, these confrontations became less common but intoxicated prisoners never ceased to be a challenge.

Assaults and injuries involved not only the constable and prisoner but often sympathetic bystanders. The sight of a drunken woman or man, of a friend, or of anyone however guilty who looked pathetic in police custody frequently led witnesses to throw things at constables, to kick them from behind, or to try to rescue the prisoner. It was almost standard procedure for someone in the crowd to chuck something handy at a constable with a prisoner. While struggling with prisoners, PC Vallance had a bucket of ashes thrown over him[77] and PC Gill was hit with a boot-black's block.[78] PC Hood was not even arresting a group of youths, but simply taking their addresses, when a bystander struck him on the mouth.[79] Rescues were generally not successful since constables could summon aid with their whistles, but people kept trying.[80] One determined effort was thwarted by the timely arrival of more constables. After Richard Smith was arrested for drunkenness, Mr Gillam led the crowd in rescuing Smith and attacking PC Waldron. In the confusion, Smith got away but PC Waldron managed to arrest

---

[73]   LCCDR, 3 November 1926, PCA 226 Fripp, complainant Mary Kelly, 30 Osmond Street, Rock Ferry.

[74]   LCI, 19 September 1903, PCB 252 Anderton. In spite of all this, he only suffered a slight injury to a finger.

[75]   LCI, 30 August 1908, PCB 181 Mulligan.

[76]   LCI, 10 October 1914, PSE 4 Stevens.

[77]   LCI, 10 June 1904, PCC 145 Vallance.

[78]   LCI, 19 September 1903, PCB 66 Gill.

[79]   LCI, 24 April 1904, PCD 168 Hood. In an unusually grave case, two constables escorting a prisoner were attacked by a man with a cut-throat razor. PC Rimmer was cut across the face and saved from having his throat cut when his coat button deflected the blade. The other constable let go of the prisoner, attacked the man, and got the razor away from him. Rimmer lost so much blood that a magistrate was sent to the hospital to take his statement. Why the man attacked the constables so ferociously was not explained (*Police Review*, 11 October 1907, 'Savage Attack on Liverpool Constables', p. 485).

[80]   While drunk off duty, PCF 224 Kearns, two years' service, tried to rescue a prisoner in police custody (LDRB, 13 March 1914, dismissed).

Gillam. Smith, meanwhile, was arrested by newly arrived PC Kimberly. Smith's brother made a determined effort to rescue him again, leaving PC Kimberly with a black eye and bloody nose and PC Bushell, who had arrived to help handcuff Smith, with a dislocated thumb. Smith, his brother, and Gillam all ended up in jail.[81] Participants did not necessarily take the violence personally. PC Smethurst's only observation after a brawl between a crowd and about eight constables was, 'I felt the effect of my struggle for many a day, but I suppose that such things are all in the game.'[82] At court the morning after a similar brawl in 1938, an enormous navvy saw one of the constables who had arrested him the evening before. Robert Mark remembered, 'Far from there being any hard feelings he greeted me cheerfully and we went off for a drink together.'[83]

Cases of assault often involved complicating factors where it was difficult to assign blame clearly to one party or the other. Deciding who had crossed the line into an assault or who had had the last opportunity to defuse a situation was rarely straightforward. Just deciding whether or not an assault had happened could be difficult. In June 1915 at around 11:00 pm, an encounter took place between PC Bollington and Jane Stokes, whose husband was missing in action in Europe. Afterwards, he was convicted of assaulting her and sentenced to a month's hard labour. The evidence against him stated that he had pushed Mrs Stokes from behind while she was waiting for a friend, asked what she was doing there, and ordered her to go home before he kicked her there. Mrs Stainsbee testified that the constable kicked Mrs Stokes three times, causing her to fall, including once inside her own house. He appealed the conviction, arguing that he had ordered a group of six women to 'move on' but that Mrs Stokes had refused. She 'was very excited, and shouted that he ought to be at the front'. PC Bollington said that after she tripped on a kerb, he helped her up and took her home, ordering her to stay there. She immediately left the house and he put her back inside again. The court decided that Bollington had not assaulted Mrs Stokes, and implied that her charge against him had been vindictive. In this instance, both Stokes and Bollington believed that they had legitimate grievances, and from their own point of view, they did. No reason was given why the women had to 'move on' and Stokes believed that she had a right to wait for a friend. PC Bollington, on the other hand, was expected to keep public order and move on loiterers blocking walkways. What Bollington considered to be reasonable force was believed to be excessive by the women. Stokes could easily blame the constable for her fall even if he did not actually kick her. Taunting him for not being at the front probably agitated Bollington into rougher behaviour

---

[81]   *Police Review*, 23 August 1907, p. 400. The landlord of a public house kept Gillam in custody while Waldron went for assistance.

[82]   Smethurst, 'Mems.', p. 118; also Mark, *In the Office of Constable*, p. 28, for similar statement by a civilian.

[83]   Mark, *In the Office of Constable*, p. 28.

than necessary. Neither party was free from blame though it was the constable's responsibility not to let a minor situation get out of hand. Regardless of the court's final decision, whether or not Bollington used inappropriate force against Stokes remained unclear.[84]

Demonstrations, riots and strikes were in a different category from conflicts arising out of normal duties.[85] Situations involving crowds of excited people and large numbers of policemen almost inevitably ended in some form of violence, and rarely was either side entirely innocent of provocation or retaliation. It was easy for an embattled 'us versus them' mentality to take hold on all sides. In some instances, the police first crossed the line into violence; in others, civilians did. The 1901 Lloyd George riot in Birmingham, for example, began with an angry mob attacking a public hall with bricks and battering rams but ended with a civilian being killed by a blow from a police truncheon. Official investigations normally acquitted the police of unnecessary force. After Liverpool sectarian riots in 1909, set off by a Catholic Procession, an investigation withdrew or disproved all charges of excessive force against the police.[86] Nevertheless, the testimony made it clear that policemen, faced with a riot threatening to get worse, had responded aggressively, pushing and striking civilians indiscriminately to disperse the crowd. Unfortunately, the results of such investigations meant that police forces did not look for better ways to control disturbances. Throwing large numbers of constables at crowds was often their only strategy. While this might be necessary to restore order, it could provoke more violence. It encouraged the police to rely on force to resolve the crisis and created an atmosphere of fear.[87] Bringing in outside support was nearly always a bad idea, 'foreign' police seeming like an occupying army. The 1911 Liverpool transport strike had been reasonably calm until the arrival of Birmingham constables sparked violence.[88] During the 1911 Manchester strikes, the use of 500 policemen from other towns as well as hundreds of troops resulted in police brutality. During a

---

84   *Police Review*, 3 December 1915, 'Charge against a Birmingham Constable', p. 585.

85   Jane Morgan goes too far in suggesting that policemen were working-class while off duty but were anti-union while on duty although she acknowledges that constables could be resisting protests or strikes against their will. She grants that 'Apart from their use in labour disputes, the police seem to have remained broadly popular with the local community' (*Conflict and Order*, p. 280).

86   *Police (Liverpool Inquiry) Act, 1909, Commissioner's Report; Liverpool Police Inquiry Before Mr. Arthur J. Ashton, K.C., Commissioner.*, vol. 4–5. Thirty-one constables and sergeants were injured in the riots, seven seriously, including a fractured jaw, a scalp wound and various cuts and bruises (LCI, 20 June 1909).

87   For a series of case studies on police actions during disturbances, see Richard Bessel and Clive Emsley, eds, *Patterns of Provocation: Police and Public Disorder* (New York: Berghahn, 2000).

88   Mike Brogden, *The Police: Autonomy and Consent* (London: Academic Press, 1982), pp. 186–7.

railway strike the following year, requests for outside policemen were turned down by chief constables without men to spare, and no conflicts occurred.[89] By 1930, chief constables were learning that, 'If strange Police come into a place during times of disturbances it is always fatal.'[90] With local policemen, crowds remained volatile but injuries tended to be minor cuts and bruises.

Chief constables advised their men to remain calm when faced with hostile crowds, but even calm men had to quell the chaos somehow. Rows of policemen pushing back crowds and ordering them to disperse were pushed back by civilians caught up in their cause and holding their ground. Stand-offs could quickly degenerate into territorial battles. The day before the Lloyd George riot, Rafter warned constables against 'losing their temper in any way, or from retaliating if they are struck ... they must put up, with a good humour, with a great deal of buffeting about'.[91] A few days afterwards, PC Baldwick bragged to a hairdresser that he had struck several people with his truncheon and helped disperse the crowds.[92] Regardless of orders to use truncheons only in self-defence, the line between self-defence and aggression blurred during riots. Testimony afterwards inevitably included blows from truncheons and even inspectors wielding their sticks against civilians.[93] During disturbances where crowds targeted Germans, blacks, or equivalent groups, constables felt justified in taking whatever measures necessary to defend innocent people from mobs. Civilians in turn attacked constables with anything handy. During a 1911 newsboy strike, PC Morrison arrested the strike leader for molesting newspaper vendors. The prisoner and the crowd responded by butting him on the face, cutting his mouth and kicking him on the legs.[94] During the 1915 anti-German riots in Liverpool, crowds hurled stones and bricks at constables,[95] and during a 1904

---

89   Roberts, *The Classic Slum*, pp. 93–4, 98n. While Roberts condemned police violence during the 1911 strikes, in one of his stories he uses the character of a former policeman invalided out of the force after being beaten with his own truncheon during the 1899 dockers' strike, treating the attack as simply a passing misfortune since the man found another job with the help of a connection (p. 245).

90   Chief Constable James Wilson of the City of Cardiff, 'Report from the Select Committee on the Amalgamation of Police Forces', 1931–1932 (106), vol. 123, p. 62. During the 1984 miners' strike, picketers and policemen had fewer problems with violence if their accents were similar.

91   BPO, 17 December 1901, p. 1.

92   BRB, 24 February 1902, PCC Thomas Baldwick, joined December 1891. He was reduced in class, 'such statement being false'.

93   LCI, 4 July 1923. PCB 178 Thomas was struck on the head by Inspector Marshall's stick during a disturbance at an Orange procession.

94   LCI, 29 August 1911, PCG Morrison.

95   LCI, 9–10 May 1915, nine constables and sergeants injured.

disturbance, someone dropped a brick on PC Reilly from a third-storey window.[96] Liverpool race riots in June 1919 injured a dozen police officers, including one constable who was shot in the head and another who was kicked 'by an infuriated mob … whilst rescuing a nigger'.[97] During the 1919 police strike, looters injured nine officers, including a sergeant attacked by a brick while investigating rifle fire.[98] A year later, PC Garstang got hit on the head with his own truncheon during a demonstration.[99] It is perhaps not surprising that constables with little to guide them, besides admonitions to remain calm, interpreted self-defence broadly during riots.

In addition to their fear of injury, constables did not like demonstrations, strikes and riots since they demanded behaviour that was not typical to their daily routines. During their usual work lives, constables exercised considerable discretion in enforcing the law. But this freedom was nearly impossible during strikes and disturbances. They were under the eyes of senior officers and feared losing their jobs if they did not follow orders. This created frustration since they normally had more autonomy to enforce or ignore orders as they saw fit. Constables' lack of independence, combined with their dislike and fear of rioting, tended to create a more military disposition during disturbances. They obeyed orders, did not ask questions, and protected each other. Adding to the stress, no matter how much constables might agree with the cause of a demonstrator or striker, most could not allow violence, however justified the provocation. Finally, strikes produced resentment against policemen which made policing away from picket lines harder for constables.

Policing strikes could be particularly difficult for constables since they might sympathize with the strikers even while condemning strike violence.[100] Two constables left behind descriptions of strikes showing their ambivalence towards being called in. Stalybridge PC Thomas Smethurst and Manchester PC Joseph Fowler both did their duty but had serious misgivings about their orders. Smethurst described policing strikes as a source of 'very much anxiety'.[101] He

---

96   LCI, 31 January 1904, PCA 110 Reilly.
97   LCI, 5–11 June 1919, PCC 245 Brown, PCC 154 Corkhill.
98   LCI, August 1919.
99   LCI, 1 September 1920, PCD 279 Garstang.
100   For police and striking see Geary, *Policing Industrial Disputes*; Morgan, *Conflict and Order*; and Barbara Weinberger, *Keeping the Peace? Policing Strikes in Britain 1906–1926* (Oxford: Berg, 1991), 'Police Forces and Public Order in England and France during the Interwar Years' in *Policing Western Europe: Politics, Professionalism, and Public Order 1850–1940*, ed. Clive Emsley and Barbara Weinberger (Westport, CT: Greenwood, 1991) and 'Police Perceptions of Labour in the Inter-war Period: the Case of the Unemployed and of Miners on Strike', in *Labour, Law and Crime: an Historical Perspective*, ed. Francis Snyder and Douglas Hay (New York: Tavistock Publications, 1987).
101   Smethurst, 'Reminiscences', p. 28.

was particularly thoughtful in his analysis. In a 1914 description of an 1888 mill strike, he wrote:

> When a strike or lockout occurs in any trade, it nearly always involves the police, and entails a lot of extra duty for them. It also causes friction between the strikers and police, for they seem to forget that although the police as men, may sympathise with them, and know that they are only asking for what is right and just; yet, as public servants the police have a duty to perform in keeping order, and protection of life and property; therefore, if they think fit to use force, they can only reasonably expect to be resisted by the police in the maintaining of those things in the execution of their duty.[102]

Recalling a 1895 printers' strike in 1922, he called the boss a 'Union Smasher' who had made 'much unpleasantness', and who, after making the district too hot to hold him, 'went away, but not in the bold autocratic style in which he had come, but like a thief who lurks and slinks in the shadows of the buildings and disappears under cover of the night, unknown, unhonoured and unsung'.[103] He described industrial disputes as involving the police 'in their meshes', and wished that employers could settle their problems with workers without resorting to blacklegs. During the printers' strike, he described the job of protecting blacklegs as 'very distasteful' to policemen, but that it had to be done.[104] PC Fowler agreed. He wrote a detailed description of escorting blacklegs during the 'Brooks & Doxeys Strike' in Manchester in November 1912. He was ordered by his sergeant to meet blacklegs coming off their shifts and see them safely onto tram cars home. Along with other constables, he rode the tram with the blacklegs after seeing around twenty-five pickets get onto the next car. Fowler reported that he 'took charge of those Blacklegs & prevented them from being assaulted by the Picketts who had followed', even walking one man to his door. Even though Fowler detested the use of blacklegs, his training could not allow him to stand aside while men were assaulted by a mob.[105] Constables learned to compartmentalize their sympathies with strikers from their duty to preserve order. During the 1926 General Strike in Liverpool, one constable had no philosophical problem with policing the strike while sending money home to his striking miner family.[106] Constables understood

---

[102] Smethurst, 'Mems.', pp. 38–9.

[103] Smethurst, 'Reminiscences', p.146.

[104] Smethurst, 'Reminiscences', p. 133.

[105] Fowler, 'From a Convict to a Parson', pp. 56–7. For more on Fowler's views on the working class and authorities, see pp. 117–18.

[106] Brogden, *On the Mersey Beat*, p. 157. On the General Strike see D.E. Baines and R. Bean, 'The General Strike on Merseyside, 1926', in J.R. Harris, *Liverpool and Merseyside* (London: Frank Cass & Co., 1969), pp. 239–76, also *Police Review*, 28 May 1926, p. 286. Robert Reiner

their duty to prevent violence during strikes but few enjoyed strike duty. Most were glad to get back to their normal rounds.

Even though rowdy arrests and missile-throwing demonstrators remained routine, a significant increase in civilians coming to the rescue of constables added a new dimension to police and working-class conflicts after the war. This happened occasionally before the war, but afterwards over twenty-five men and women were rewarded for rescuing constables from crowds in Manchester, Birmingham and Liverpool, and more went unrecognized. Civilians put themselves at risk while helping constables but did so nonetheless. James Whittle, for instance, heard that three men were attacking a constable nearby, left his house, and tried to rescue the constable. He was himself wounded, requiring stitches for a head wound, and had to be rescued by constables who later arrived on the scene.[107] Two factors contributed to this shift in attitudes. Working-class drinking and violence was decreasing, making civilians more willing to help constables trying to keep the peace. The other change was traffic. Increasing numbers of lawbreakers with motor cars had attracted popular hostility due to reckless driving even before the war. After the war, this anger grew along with rising traffic injuries and fatalities.[108] The working class saw constables giving more attention to drivers, contributing to a stronger identification with constables as their protectors against higher-class lawbreakers. Most of these rescues involved saving constables from other members of the working class, but more civilians after 1918 were siding with the constables and helping them to 'set the law in motion'.[109]

As tolerance for public drunkenness declined, civilians came to the assistance of constables struggling with drunken prisoners, even joining in against violent prisoners and determined rescuers of prisoners. In a typical case, seeing PC Rooks

---

cites a case of an inspector who both supported the CND, including joining their marches, and policed their rallies, which involved taking them into custody. 'O.K., maybe with reluctance, but nevertheless if it is required that I do it as a policeman, it is done, full-stop.' He also found that the average constable in the 1960s and 1970s sympathized with unions except when they had too much power (Reiner, *The Blue-Coated Worker*, pp. 126, 235). The 1984 miners' strike caused ambivalent feelings for chief constables who, as working-class men, identified with the plight of the strikers regardless of other duties (Reiner, *Chief Constables*, pp. 183–5).

[107]   BWCM, 5 February, 1936, report no. 1, p. 3. The three men were arrested and Whittle was awarded five guineas. Gerald Collier Forty was thanked for helping PCB 114 Peck after a man had drawn a knife and assaulted the constable (BWCM, 3 March 1926, p. 9).

[108]   See Clive Emsley, '"Mother, What *Did* Policemen Do When There Weren't Any Motors?" The Law, the Police and the Regulation of Motor Traffic in England, 1900–1939', *Historical Journal* 36:2 (1993): 357–81.

[109]   'Inspectors of Constabulary report for year ended the 29th of September 1924', PP 1924–1925 (2316) xv, 177, p. 10. One common theme in all of these examples was that no one seemed to use telephones to summon help. Instead, civilians relied on police whistles and going to the nearest station for reinforcements.

being kicked by a drunken man, Neville Roberts came to his assistance and helped restrain the man in spite of being kicked and struck himself.[110] Sometimes, rather than a crowd uniting to rescue a drunken prisoner, the crowd split into factions siding with the constable or with the prisoner. After arresting Mr Reed for being drunk and disorderly, PC Hawley was attacked by men trying to rescue Reed. Two women and a man came to Hawley's assistance. One woman grabbed Hawley's whistle and sounded the alarm before a member of the crowd grabbed it from her, and the other woman sent a boy to the nearest station for help. The man suffered a broken foot while helping Hawley hold the prisoner until police reinforcements arrived.[111] Another case finally took three constables, three civilians and a taxi cab to subdue three violent prisoners. It began when PCs Sedgwick and Leech saw three drunken men 'importuning' pedestrians. The constables asked them to stop bothering people and then followed the men at a distance to ensure that they did so. The men stopped outside a music shop, started arguing with each other, and one of them threw a wine bottle through the shop's window. The constables arrested them but the three men acted 'like enraged lunatics', throwing the constables to the ground and kicking them. A taxi driver driving by came to assist and restrained one of the men. Another constable arrived and helped PC Leech escort a second man to the local station. PC Sedgwick was left with the third man who nearly overpowered him until two more civilians helped Sedgwick get handcuffs on him. The taxi driver volunteered his cab to take the prisoner he had caught and the third man to the station.[112] None of these civilians had anything to gain from helping the constables and often suffered injuries themselves. While most were rewarded and given medical assistance, what motivated them seemed to be more a dislike for an unfair fight even when it was a constable on the losing side.

About a quarter of civilian rescues were carried out by women, most commonly by sounding the alarm with the constable's whistle, often at considerable risk to themselves. Seeing PC Merry on the ground being kicked by a crowd in front of a hotel, Alice Clarkson pushed her way in, grabbed the constable's whistle, jumped on the running board of a passing motor car, and blew the whistle until she arrived at the nearest station. Meanwhile, two men went to Merry's assistance and all three sustained injuries from the crowd. Officers summoned by Clarkson rushed to the scene and arrested the men involved.[113] PC Macaulay had a run

---

[110] BJSC, 15 June 1932, PCE 274 George Rooks, pp. 202–1.

[111] MWCM, 14, 28 July 1927, vol. 117, no. 85, vol. 118, no. 19. The men of Hawley's division took up a subscription to reward the three and help the man's wife while he was in the hospital.

[112] MWCM, 21 October 1938, vol. 218, no. 95. All three constables ended up on the sick list with facial cuts, bruises on their legs and bodies, and one injury to the stomach.

[113] MWCM, 1 September 1932, given £5 each, no mention was made of the driver of the motor car, vol. 162, no. 27.

of particularly bad luck, having been rescued by women twice in two weeks. Seeing a hostile crowd attack Macaulay, who had arrested a man for assaulting him, Elizabeth Mahon sounded the alarm with Macaulay's whistle while her son helped him hold his prisoner. During the struggle, she broke a finger and had her purse stolen. They were each awarded £4 and she had her loss made good. Another woman rescued Macaulay from another hostile crowd, again using his whistle to sound the alarm and then running to the nearest station to get help. She was awarded £2.[114] The women who helped constables did not always limit themselves to going for assistance; they actively involved themselves in rescues. When Thomas Kelly pulled a knife on PC Gordon, Margaret Hayes pulled Kelly off the constable, grabbed the knife and threw it down a sewer grid. Kelly ran away but Hayes told Gordon where he had gone. With Kelly arrested, the crowd began throwing things at the constable but Hayes threw a shawl over his head to protect him and sent a girl for assistance. She personally restrained the prisoner until help arrived.[115] What all the women had in common was that they either went for assistance personally or sent someone to get it. While men sometimes sent for help as well, they were equally likely simply to throw themselves into the fray.

In addition to helping constables coping with public disorder, civilians became more likely to help policemen make arrests or inform them of crimes in progress. For instance, after seeing two men breaking into premises, sixty-three-year-old Thomas James told the nearest constable who arrested the men in possession of a skeleton key.[116] Some civilians took a more active role in foiling criminals. After detectives saw housebreakers enter a home, William Gill volunteered to ride his motorcycle to the nearest station to get help. He returned and helped restrain one of the criminals.[117] Leslie Roberts was thanked for helping two constables arrest three housebreakers.[118] Constables sometimes asked civilians for help, especially if they needed a car. PC Bean flagged down John Evans' car and came aboard. They gave chase to a stolen car and compelled the driver to stop.[119] Civilians followed suspected criminals on their own initiative. After seeing a robbery committed, John Eccles gave chase on foot while Frank Hayes, a motor van driver, went to

---

114   MWCM, 5 January 1933, vol. 165, no. 59. For a case of a working-class woman who habitually came to the rescue of constables in the Liverpool Chinatown, see Brogden, *On the Mersey Beat*, p. 103.

115   LWCM, 23 June 1913, awarded with a gold watch worth £5; Hayes ran a general shop with her husband; pp. 490–1; Liverpool Watch Committee Orders to the Head Constable, 28 July 1913, also given a silver medal and certificate from the Liverpool Shipwreck and Humane Society.

116   BWCM, 30 October 1935, rewarded two guineas, report no. 3, p. 3.

117   BWCM, 4 January 1933, p. 12.

118   BWCM, 5 June 1929, p. 17.

119   BWCM, 1 March 1933, p. 29.

inform PC Jones. Hayes drove PC Jones after the fugitive who had stolen £35 from a gown manufacturer.[120] George Hutt saw two men coming from the back of a billiard hall early one morning and followed them on a bus until he found a policeman. The men were found with stolen cash and cigarettes.[121] What sets these examples apart from the typical 'hue and cry' was that none of these men were victims of the crimes. Catching a criminal had an air of excitement for them; they were playing a real game of 'cops and robbers' and siding with the cops.

At the same time that the working class was assisting and rescuing constables, the middle and upper classes were charging constables with incivility. Because of driving, they were finding themselves receiving professional attention from the police for the first time. Before motor traffic, many in the higher classes could ignore constables altogether unless asking for directions. Constables enforced law and order primarily in the working-class world, not in theirs. When they did encounter constables, they treated them like they treated their servants. But as more people became drivers and therefore possible lawbreakers, the relationship between the higher classes and policemen shifted, with few free from professional police attention.[122] The higher classes discovered that having their behaviour monitored was uncomfortable, a lesson that the working class had already learned. Much to their annoyance, policemen seemed to treat them like any lawbreaker. They could not know that constables viewed their excuses and arguments as little different from anyone unhappy at being caught or that constables had heard it all before. Many were offended by constables' working-class style of speaking and mannerisms, and many charges of incivility had their roots in cross-class misunderstandings. The higher classes were ill prepared to cope with this serious disconnect between their image of policemen as social inferiors and the legal authority that policemen now wielded over them.

The higher classes persisted in letting their class attitudes dominate how they interacted with constables. They saw constables as beneath them, confusing 'public servant' with personal servant. When constables refused to defer to them, the result was often incivility. For instance, while working at a polling booth, a solicitor ordered a constable to get him a taxi. Uncertain what to do, the constable reported to his sergeant who replied that his job did not include ordering taxis. The solicitor, on hearing this, became 'overbearing and rude'.[123] When constables persisted in doing their duty, the higher classes tried to take control by mentioning

---

[120] BWCM, 3 April 1935, awarded two guineas each, p. 39.

[121] BWCM, 4 January 1933, p. 13.

[122] 'Whereas before 1919 the constable had seldom to exercise authority over persons of a different social order from his own, that is now a common incident of his daily life' ('Report of the Committee on Police Pay [New Entrants]', 1932–1933, Cmd. 4274, vol. XV, 379, p. 8).

[123] LCCDR, 24 April 1929, PSB 32 Gray, complainant P. Kelly, Esq., solicitor, 15 Lord Street, chief constable accepted sergeant's version of the affair.

influential friends. When PC Martin questioned Mr Finn about a driving offence, Mrs Holden kept interrupting with remarks about her friends at court and the police officials she knew and that she would get them to stop the summons.[124] They could be annoyed when lowly constables made inquiries rather than senior officers. When PC Ashcroft inquired after an unlicensed dog belonging to Mrs Dawes, her husband threatened to report him to an inspector who was his 'personal friend' for daring to question his wife.[125] These efforts to put policemen in their place rarely worked, an even more infuriating outcome. They wrote letters of complaint insisting that constables had been rude and overbearing, and viewed constables as arrogant. Constables always insisted that they had behaved with courtesy, and saw higher-class resistance to their authority as disrespectful. It was not surprising that 'words' were often exchanged.

For constables, just as annoying as the higher classes treating them as servants was their telling constables how to do their jobs. This usually included getting in the constables' way. Harry Waterhouse made such a nuisance of himself at a police station that the station sergeant finally ordered him to leave for wasting police time.[126] After one exasperated constable told a civilian, 'I know my job', Rafter reminded his men against comments that may not be serious but were unnecessary, since civilian complaints 'lead to a tremendous amount of correspondence and trouble, and a great deal of time is lost in investigating them'.[127] Constables busy with their duties could quickly become impatient with unsolicited and often faulty advice. While directing passengers at a landing stage at the docks, PC Nevin had a man advise him to divert the passengers to another route. Nevin replied that he only took orders from senior officers. The man then found PS Brockbank and ordered him to make Nevin apologize. Brockbank refused and remarked that the man 'might be a gentleman but he did not speak like one'.[128] Higher-class civilians sometimes insisted that police orders did not apply to them. One 'gentleman' tried to pass through a police barrier, only to be stopped by PC Kelly. When he could not convince Kelly to let him across, the gentleman told Kelly that he would take his number. Kelly, trying to inject some humour into the situation, replied that 'he could not take his number, but he could have a look at it'. In most such cases, chief constables considered the matter 'explained' and offered constables advice on

---

124 MPF, 18, 24, 25 February 1938, PCD 206 James Cameron Martin, appointed April 1937, given advice on dealing with the public. Finn was fined ten shillings for traffic violations in spite of Mrs Holden's friends at court.
125 MPF, 6 April 1926, PCD 125 Frederick Ashcroft, appointed January 1922, the episode was considered explained.
126 BRB, 20 November 1905, PSA Oliver Harvey, joined March 1893, made sergeant February 1904, matter considered explained.
127 BPO, 26 September 1932, p. 19842.
128 LCCDR, 21 September 1923, PCA 146 Nevin, PSA 3 Brockbank, explained.

speaking to the public. Unfortunately for Kelly, Rafter was not amused, remarking that it was 'by ungracious actions of this sort that the name of the Birmingham Police Force is dragged in the mud'. He ordered that Kelly be reported on 'as to his manner of dealing with the general public and of his fitness to remain in the Police Force'.[129] Most chief constables and senior officers were more tolerant of the occasional blunder. As more encounters produced more complaining letters, chief constables kept issuing orders to avoid incivility but constables were rarely punished for hasty or misinterpreted words.

One detailed case encapsulates how higher-class attitudes could overwhelm all other considerations, showing a refusal to treat policemen seriously as human beings. It began when Manchester PC Thorpe attended a church dance in his home town. One of his friends asked him to help deal with a drunken man who was trying to enter the hall. Learning that the man had paid the entrance fee, Thorpe commented that it hardly seemed fair to charge the man and then throw him out immediately. He did, however, escort the man outside and advised the man's friends to take him home. The Rev. Thorburn, who only witnessed this last event, concluded that the man was a friend of Thorpe's and that Thorpe had insisted that the man be allowed to enter the hall. The next day, Thorburn went to the local sergeant to complain and ordered the sergeant to warn PC Thorpe not to return to the dance hall. The sergeant advised Thorpe to stay away for a few weeks until Thorburn calmed down. Two months later, Thorpe returned to the dance hall but Thorburn refused to let him in. Thorburn refused to listen to Thorpe's explanation of what had happened, and refused to admit Thorpe when he made a visit to the vicarage to explain. Instead, Thorburn wrote to Chief Constable Maxwell. Investigations found that Thorpe's version of events was supported by numerous witnesses, and the investigating superintendent concluded that it was both 'a very trivial complaint' and 'a very vindictive complaint'. The Reverend Thorburn refused to give up his belief in PC Thorpe's misconduct. Thorpe finally promised to stay away from the hall and the matter was dropped. Perhaps Thorpe could have explained himself to Thorburn sooner but he could not have anticipated the Reverend's stubborn denial that he could be mistaken.[130]

From the 1920s onwards, the bulk of complaints for police incivility involved traffic encounters, when the higher classes were most likely to be on the receiving end of police attention.[131] 'Road manners and customs' were still being learned and

---

[129] BPO, 20 November 1902, PCA 36 Patrick Kelly, pp. 290–1.

[130] MPF, 5, 12, 14, 15, 17, 18, 19, 22, 25, 29, 31 January 1938, PCB 145 Jack Thorpe, appointed January 1937. In the evidence, his superintendent commented that Thorpe was a competent cricketer and a promising officer.

[131] For a detailed account of the problems of class and cars, see Emsley, '"Mother, What *Did* Policemen Do"', pp. 357–81.

standardized, leading to many misunderstandings and altercations.[132] Motorists and constables argued over driving errors and confusing traffic direction signals, both convinced that they had made no mistakes. After a series of complaints in 1924, Rafter informed his men that he was

> quite aware ... of the attitude assumed by a large number of Motorists who seem to be indignant of any restraint. A large number of them either say they did not see the signal, or that they did not understand it, or they did not think it was intended for them; and a very considerable number of them write to complain of the conduct of the Constables towards them ... The complaints of incivility are often put forward by Motorists caught in a breach of the Byelaws as a kind of counter-stroke and a means of trying to evade being summoned.

He went on to advise that the best way to ensure that a summons 'stuck' was to avoid any grounds for complaint.[133] A similar statement appeared in 1929, with a warning that constables too frequently were forgetting themselves and getting into verbal wrangles with motorists.[134] In 1930 and 1935, Rafter lamented the 'very frequent complaints' about altercations between constables and motorists.[135] Liverpool records had numerous complaints from motorists of rude treatment, often from motorists guilty of licence or light offences. The constables were generally advised to be more courteous and civil but rarely charged.[136] In 1935, Chief Constable Wilson told his men that he was 'well aware that some motorists are inconsiderate and difficult and as unpleasant as possible, but that provides no warrant for a policeman to act in similar fashion'.[137] What constables found particularly annoying was that 'the public were increasingly coming to expect the Police to keep the roads safe for them and yet objecting to police action against themselves when they were at fault'.[138] This dichotomy, praising policemen when they were useful and damning them when they were enforcing traffic laws, caused much police heart-burning.

Motorists going 'just a bit' over a speed limit or taking a corner a bit wide, and constables who had given first aid to crash victims or had been hit while directing traffic were bound to consider each other to be overreacting to trivial issues. Each side tended to exaggerate the sins of the other. Mr Lake swore that

132   Stenson Cooke, 'Road Manners and Customs', Chief Constables' Association Annual Report, 3 July 1925, pp. 13–24.
133   BPO, 19 March 1924, p. 8150.
134   BPO, 4 February 1929, pp. 15052–3.
135   BPO, 2 July 1930, p. 16823; also 1 May 1935, p. 23656.
136   LCCDR, 1920s, 1930s.
137   LCCDR, 10 January 1935.
138   Dixon, *The Home Office*, p. 259.

he had mistaken a hand signal, rather than ignoring it, but when he apologized the constable retorted, 'The greatest sorrow of my life is that you were ever granted a driving licence.'[139] Mr Carew was similarly confused by or ignoring a hand signal, provoking PC Davies to shout, 'Keep to the right you balmy little blighter.'[140] Complaints could be the result of misunderstandings. Mr Davies complained that PC Millington had been uncivil to his wife and blamed her for a motor accident. Millington was able to explain to Mr Davies' satisfaction that he had been shouting at Mrs Davies to get her out of the way of a runaway lorry.[141] Much of this verbal warfare came about because the higher classes were not accustomed to taking orders from constables and easily took offence when their behaviour was challenged. The constables in turn became impatient with resistance to their authority and the often patronizing attitude of drivers.

Policemen were at their least courteous in the aftermath of traffic collisions. Constables busy attending to the injured had little patience for interfering civilians, however well-meaning. PC Somerville finally told William Cassidy to shut up and mind his own business after Cassidy got in the way of his first-aid efforts for an injured girl,[142] and PC Pagan pushed away Miss Halsall, a health visitor, who was underfoot while he was attending to a street pileup.[143] Unskilled, inattentive and aggressive drivers put pedestrians, constables and other drivers at risk, and policemen had no tolerance for their excuses or regrets. After retrieving a fatally injured twelve-year-old girl from in front of a lorry, PS Griffiths 'brandished his stick in a threatening manner and said ... that it was through [the driver's] carelessness & excessive speed that the girl was killed'.[144] As early as 1912, PC Fowler complained of 'Motor Drivers ... driving to the common danger of the public'. He wrote,

> If the Justices we have sitting in the Courts in Manchester today would put heavy fines on these so called Motor Drivers there would not be one half of the Death's [sic] in Manchester which are regularly occuring [sic] day after day and week after week by the way the Motor Drivers are allowed to travel in the streets of the City and its outskirts.[145]

---

[139]   LCCDR, 8 November 1938, PCE 63 Moran.

[140]   BOR, 17 July 1930, PCD 102 Kenrick Davies, denied, Mr Carew withdrew the complaint.

[141]   LCCDR, 27 May 1927, PCC 72 Millington, complainant W.J. Davis, 79a Berkeley Street, no charge framed.

[142]   LCCDR, 19 December 1921, PCB 97 Somerville, complainant William Andrew Cassidy, 33 West Derby Street, case dismissed.

[143]   LCCDR, 12 July 1926, PCD 90 Pagan, cautioned, also 14 July 1926, PCD 304 Prince for not reporting witnessing same.

[144]   LCCDR, 16 October 1923, PSF 3 Griffiths, cautioned for incivility.

[145]   Fowler, 1912, p. 34.

Constables came to see drivers as a public menace, contributing to the general unpopularity of traffic duty and doing little for their relationship with the higher classes.

In 1935, Chief Constable Wilson advised that 'Police must ... be careful not to behave as if they regarded all motorists as offenders at heart', but some constables could not resist the temptation to treat traffic as a kind of battle with drivers.[146] When PC Birken found an illegally parked car on his beat, instead of issuing a ticket, he turned on the car's lights and ran down the battery. He left a box on the steering wheel with the message, 'This is *not* a car park and proceedings will be taken if you leave this car here again. P.C. on Beat.' Mr Etheridge returned fifteen minutes later to find his battery dead.[147] PC Francis caught hold of the collar of Mr Lucas, a motor driver, and gave him a good shaking for an unspecified offence.[148] Constables could let the power of directing traffic go to their heads. PC Schee seemed to be having a bad day and decided to hold up a funeral procession, causing it to miss a boat arranged to take it over to Birkenhead.[149] In a case that brought out the worst in PC Paice, he obstructed the journey of a car hired for Sir Ofori Alta, Paramount Chief of the Gold Coast Colony in Africa, in Manchester on an official visit. The driver of the car asked Paice for directions to the Ship Canal offices but Paice refused to answer unless the man got out of the car. He then delayed the car from crossing the intersection for five minutes out of spite or out of racist disapproval of the chief. A detective inspector witnessing this was about to speak to Paice about the unnecessary delay when he let the car through. The English secretary for the chief remarked, 'That appears to be a pig of a fellow', a decided understatement.[150] While Paice's actions were unusually harsh, many constables were tempted to mistreat drivers in return for the lack of respect that they often received from drivers.

Police incivility became a chronic problem in the 1920s and 1930s, a direct result of more contact with the higher classes. Liverpool Chief Constable Everett reminded men that 'his fellow citizen is entitled to just, courteous, considerate, and sympathetic treatment, which strengthens the upholding of the law in far greater degree than oppressive action could ever achieve'.[151] Articles kept appearing in the *Police Review* on the advisability of the 'soft answer', and chief constables

---

[146] LCCDR, 10 January 1935.

[147] MPF, 20 October 1929, PCB 244 Arthur Birkin, appointed October 1926, admitted offence, fined 5/-.

[148] BDRB, 15 January 1921, PCA 94 Charles Francis, p. 13; BJSC, 28 January 1921, p. 255. Francis was called upon to resign in July 1921 for assaulting two men and unlawfully arresting a man (BDRB, 27 July 1921, p. 38).

[149] LCCDR, 19 August 1916, PCA 122 Schee. He was 'spoken to' for this offence.

[150] MPF, 13 July 1928, PCA 22 William Paice, appointed March 1919, admonished.

[151] LCCO, 12 December 1927.

repeatedly warned their men to avoid 'a high handed attitude'. Young constables were advised not to be 'too conscious of [their] official authority'.[152] Constables took the position that it was the higher classes that was becoming more antagonistic. A New Scotland Yard official remarked, 'Ardently anxious that his neighbour, and the nation at large, be made to toe the line, the average Englishman is indignant to the point of fury when his own individual toe is affected.'[153] Faced with this irate public, constables argued that they were only responding in kind, increasing the mutual incivility.

By the 1900s, constables and the working class had settled into a pattern of frequent but usually minor conflicts. Violence continued to be a problem but at the same time, more civilians were willing to assist constables in their duties. Constables and the middle and upper classes were still figuring out their new relationship. Their conflicts rarely became physical because drivers were rarely arrested, and because the higher classes tended to view constables as inferior opponents. But the animosity could be just as strong as between constables and prisoners. The higher classes jumped to the conclusion that constables were acting inappropriately just as often as did members of the working class, and for similar reasons. No one liked to believe that his or her behaviour was inappropriate or illegal, and everyone connected attention from a policeman with loss of status. The combination of less working-class violence and more police contact with the higher classes made the 1920s and 1930s decades of incivility.

---

[152] BPO, 4 August 1933, p. 20989, 20 December 1937, p. 29382; *Police Review*, 5 April 1929, 'Turn the Other Cheek', p. 256, 10 September 1937, 'The 'Soft Answer' & Its Implication', p. 234.

[153] H. Alker Tripp, Assistant Secretary, New Scotland Yard, 'Police and Public: A New Test of Police Quality', *Police Journal* 1:4 (1928): p. 531. In the 1970s, a constable stated, 'A person likes the police until such time as he gets reported for a parking offence. Then straight away ... you're bastards, that's the end of it' (Reiner, *The Blue-Coated Worker*, pp. 73–4).

7

The Police and the Public: Fraternizing

> The average policeman in the streets gets into conversation
> with the average man in the street.
>
> PC Herbert Waight, 1919[1]

IN THE COURSE of their daily lives, constables came into contact with many
levels of society, and, as shown in the previous chapter, these meetings could be
antagonistic and violent. More often, outside of traffic infractions, encounters were
prosaic and civil. Members of the middle and upper classes usually only approached
policemen to ask for directions or for minor assistance. Small businessmen were an
important exception, tending to exchange greetings with the constables patrolling
their streets. Most police contact was with the more numerous working class.
Living in crowded cities, they were more likely to be victims of theft and violence,
and they often used public spaces for work and leisure.[2] Becoming friendly with
local constables made practical sense, both to engage their help and to persuade
them to look the other way. These interactions tended to be familiar simply because
constables were working-class themselves, sharing their interests and habits.
Civilians and constables shared drinks on and off the job, they practiced perks
customary to their occupations, and they played against each other on company
sports teams. Constables used their status to help civilians, both through a myriad
of small courtesies and more formally through charities. The working class was
not blind to the benefits of having working-class constables and they used this

---

1   DC, Evidence, question 71345, London Metropolitan Police, p. 75.

2   'It is not the rich who suffer most from crimes against property, the poor man who has
to make good the pennies stolen from his penny-in-the-slot gas-meter is a greater sufferer than
the merchant whose safe is robbed, and the poor women who comes home to find her little
household treasures gone is a greater loser than the rich one who loses her diamond necklace'
(LAR, 1907, Leonard Dunning, p. 28). See also 'Inspectors of Constabulary report for year
ended the 29th of September 1923', PP 1924 (19) xii, 65, p. 9.

connection to their advantage whenever they could. Animosities and conflicts were part of internal class ups and downs; individuals might agree in many ways but have different views on specific situations. But overall, working-class contact with policemen was reasonably neighbourly.

The men who joined the police force had working-class social and work habits that they rarely lost.[3] If they ever thought about it, they argued that their class made them better policemen, connecting them to the regular patterns and networks of the communities they policed. Constables walking their beats could hardly avoid getting to know people, and they knew that familiarity with routines helped them do their jobs. The tedium of an eight-hour shift could be broken by passing the time with a shopkeeper, cab driver, or night watchman, and they might pick up useful information. Despite all orders against it, constables rarely escaped being caught gossiping at least once in their careers, though most sergeants did not report minor infractions. Civilians similarly welcomed a break in their day, and recognized that constables could be an excellent source of news. These encounters could lead to friendships, sometimes crossing the line from gossiping to more prolonged fraternizing in comfortable spots and to sharing a drink in public houses or private kitchens. Other working-class habits they shared were perks and pilfering. Every occupation had extras that were not included in regular earnings but were seen as normal bonuses. Perks could be as basic as taking home office pencils or extra lumber or bricks, or eating food at a restaurant or bakery. Most workers kept these extras to a manageable amount that was accepted by employers as part of normal costs. Policemen had regular perks, such as gifts of cigarettes, food and drinks from people on their beats, and were included in dock pilfering networks in Liverpool. Like other workers, a few policemen interpreted perks so liberally to shade into pilfering until even their fellow workers believed that they were not only stealing but endangering the perk system for others. But most workers developed a good sense of what perks were tolerated, and were satisfied with reasonable extras.[4]

Policemen met civilians through more formal activities as well, notably through company-sponsored sports teams and charity work. Particularly after the war, many companies set up teams, and police teams played tram workers, postal workers and other occupational teams in both regular matches and charity

---

[3]   Robert Reiner's research showed that policemen were not insulated from the general population, having work experience outside of the police. See *The Blue-Coated Worker*, p. 152.

[4]   See Clive Emsley, 'Fiddles, Perks and Pilferage', in his *Crime and Society in England, 1750–1900* (New York: Longman, 1987), for an excellent study of unofficial occupational extras which were generally seen as customary rights. See also Emsley, *The English Police*, pp. 241–7, Jennifer Davis, *Law Breaking and Law Enforcement: the Creation of a Criminal Class in Mid-Victorian London* (Ann Arbor, MI: University Microfilms, 1986) and Philips, *Crime and Authority in Victorian England*, pp. 180–95.

matches.[5] The most common was football, but sports included cricket, swimming, boxing, rugby and even water polo. Sports gave the men a chance to earn respect from colleagues and peers, often playing against men they met on the job or where they lived; however, poor play could leave constables at a disadvantage. The other major formal activity was police charities, with policemen regularly holding events and raising money for community projects such as hospitals, missions, prisoners' aid and the RSPCA. The largest were Police-Aided Clothing Associations. Each city's group had its own criteria for aid, but everywhere policemen nominated children they encountered on their beats for decent clothing, including shoes and coats. This allowed children to attend school and older children to find work. Contributions to charities were common within the working class. While employers, including police forces, sometimes expected their employees to contribute, about half of working-class families regularly subscribed to charities without outside pressure.[6] These formal and informal practices show that constables remained linked to working-class culture, interacting with members of the working class on a daily basis in familiar ways.[7]

The most basic encounters between constables and civilians were their conversations, anything from casual greetings to close relationships. Constables regularly gossiped and fraternized with civilians. On day beats, they exchanged greetings with newsagents, grocers, barbers, shoe-shiners and shopkeepers who stood in their doors and said 'good morning'. In residential areas, they chatted with housewives and servants running errands and scrubbing doorsteps. At night, constables met watchmen, prostitutes, late-night drinkers, early morning delivery men and the destitute. During a long patrol, it was only natural for constables to stop for a few minutes to rest and share a little conversation, often with people equally inclined to welcome a break. Senior officers overlooked this familiarity with civilians more than any other banned activity. Every policeman who had worked a beat understood that it made sense to be acquainted with its people, who reciprocated both out of friendship and for the advantages of knowing the local constable. For a constable to be reported, he must have been caught in a particularly flagrant offence, ignored advice on exercising more discretion in his conversations, or been caught by a superior on a bad day. In one obvious infraction, PC Williams joked with patrons he knew during an official visit to a public house, exclaiming, 'Holy Jesus! You are all caught' and 'Oh! My bold Killoran. How are you doing

---

5   For a 1933 commentary on and spoof of company sports, see Dorothy L. Sayers, *Murder Must Advertise*, chapter 18, opening pages, numerous editions.
6   Frank Prochaska, 'Philanthropy', *The Cambridge Social History of Britain 1750–1950*, vol. III (Cambridge: Cambridge University Press, 1990), pp. 359–370. Also Frank Prochaska, *The Voluntary Impulse: Philanthropy in Modern Britain* (London: Faber and Faber, 1988), pp. 27–31.
7   For police domestic life, which also followed typical working-class patterns, see Chapter 9.

Pat?'[8] While such blatant familiarity might be punished, official witnesses to the usual bantering and greetings were rare. On average, Manchester, Birmingham and Liverpool senior officers only reported gossiping three or four times a month and the more serious fraternizing two or three times a month in each city. Younger officers still learning how to disguise their socializing tended to reported more for gossiping, while more established men with close ties on their beats tended to be the ones caught lounging in back kitchens with the neighbours. But the overwhelming majority of instances went unnoticed or unreported.

Policemen themselves rarely had a problem with gossiping, but middle- and upper-class civilians thought that it looked unprofessional and casual. Their complaints, rather than concerns of senior officers, triggered regular police orders against gossiping. Chief constables tried to maintain a basic standard of police professionalism, but despite efforts to impose the ideal of the aloof policeman, the reality of the gossiping policeman prevailed. Police orders from Birmingham Chief Constable Rafter show his long and futile battle to stop 'this most objectionable practice'.[9] In 1902, he told the force 'that he has had numerous complaints, (and which he himself has personally noticed) of Constables gossiping on duty'.[10] He followed this up with a memorandum to superintendents, ordering them to enforce regulations against gossiping, complaining that 'No improvement whatever has taken place notwithstanding repeated orders on the subject ... It is observed that whilst the abuse of gossiping continues as bad as ever, no Constables are brought before the Orderly room on account of it.'[11] That same day, he sent an order to the entire force, calling gossip 'the worst fault that a Police Force can be capable of'.[12] Despite all of this, two months later, Rafter complained that 'the supervision of Sergeants and possibly Inspectors has been extremely lax' regarding gossiping.[13] No matter how often Rafter warned against it, he was being ignored by policemen at all levels. In April and July 1903, after the Lord Mayor complained to Rafter and the Watch Committee about constables gossiping on duty, Rafter lamented that 'All the orders on the subject seem to have been of no effect.' He issued yet another order and demanded that all policemen of all ranks

---

[8]   LDRB, 24 March 1936, PCK 257 Williams, twenty-three years' service, fined 15/-, successfully appealed.

[9]   BPO, 11 August 1902, p. 182. Birmingham was not the only city with these problems though Rafter's style of leadership left behind the most evidence. In 1927, Liverpool Chief Constable Everett sent out a general order that, 'Complaints continue to reach the Chief Constable of the prevalence of the habit of gossiping by uniformed Constables when on duty' (LCCO, 17 November 1927).

[10]   BPO, 11 August 1902, p. 182.

[11]   BPO, 15 August 1902, p. 183.

[12]   BPO, 16 August 1902, pp. 186–7. He followed this up with another memorandum to superintendents, insisting that the order be enforced (BPO, 18 August 1902, pp. 187–8).

[13]   BPO, 22 October 1902, p. 257.

sign it.[14] This tactic failed, and in March 1904, he issued another order against gossiping.[15] If the entire force wished to speak to civilians, he could do nothing to stop it. The problem remained intractable. In 1920, Rafter complained about 'the great amount of Gossiping that is going on by Police Constables in uniform on duty, which has become notorious, and is a matter of much comment'. He had witnessed constables gossiping with civilians, with tram inspectors at the tram termini, and with each other.[16] As an indication of how badly his campaign against gossiping had failed, in 1926 he had to issue orders against gossiping by the door of his own office.

> Every Constable, Chauffeur, &c. who arrives seems to ask, 'What is the latest?' The entrance porch is becoming a kind of 'gossip club'. This must be stopped and the man in charge of the door will see that no loose talking takes place. Members of the Force who come to the Chief's Constable's Office for duty must not enter into conversation; the Chauffeurs must stand by their cars ready to move; they are there to work and not to talk.[17]

As Rafter's constant orders make clear, the police force failed to be convinced that gossiping was a problem.[18] The idea that policemen should perform their jobs with a minimum of conversation was not only disagreeable, most men considered it to be bad policing. Effective policing required more than a uniformed presence, it depended on information. Policemen could gather this more quickly and easily if they had a good relationship with each other and with the people on their beats.

While much of the concern with gossiping was that it looked unprofessional, chief constables worried that constables could be sharing confidential information. Most constables exercised common sense, but talk became a problem when men forgot themselves enough to share sensitive information or when their complaining about work became indiscreet. They faced regular temptations to divulge private details, especially when people knew their occupations and hoped for juicy details and inside information. Rafter was legitimately annoyed that 'Matters which should have remained confidential only, are becoming public through the careless talk of Policemen'.[19] Constables could get carried away by their ability to share

---

14   BPO, 22 July 1903, pp. 536–7.
15   BPO, 23 March 1904, p. 137.
16   BPO, 18 March 1920, p. 1942.
17   BPO, 8 May 1926, p. 11271.
18   Rafter issued additional orders against gossiping on 11 June 1931 (BPO, p. 18180) and 7 April 1933 (BPO, p. 20542).
19   BPO, 8 May 1926, p. 11271. See also BPO, 3 November 1930, p. 17289. Rafter instructed recruits 'that what they hear and see in the course of their duties or during their police service is not their own property to do what they like with' (BPO, 2 August 1927, p. 13137).

privileged information, such as when PC Bull told a waiter at a fish shop that two men were constables, not realizing that they were in plain clothes to collect evidence.[20] Some young constables were so disarmed by Edward Bailey's interest in their routines that he was able to impersonate them and commit robberies.[21] While most indiscretions were harmless, constables talked when they knew that they should not, such as PC Bonds who was found 'expressing opinions' with a witness in a case, bringing into doubt their integrity as witnesses.[22] Another problem was policemen getting too friendly with reporters, giving them information prematurely or disclosing confidential material. Policemen were warned against the press, reminded 'to be on their guard against insidious persons trying to worm out information'.[23] Manchester Chief Constable Maxwell issued an order against divulging confidential information after news articles appeared where 'It was quite evident that such articles have been written up from information obtained from Police sources.'[24] In one case, a reporter was present when a suicide was brought to a mortuary and published details of the case, including the suicide note, before the coroner even knew the suicide had occurred.[25] Policemen sympathized with temptations to talk, but were less tolerant of men talking with civilians about fellow policemen. Taking personal complaints outside the force created bad feelings, and it could undermine the force's reputation. Men caught doing it were heavily penalized. PC Chinn was reduced in class for conversing with a painter and a decorator about a retired superintendent;[26] PC Young 'obscenely vilified' an inspector and sergeant to a civilian at five in the morning, perhaps in frustration after a bad shift, and was also reduced in class.[27] Yet despite concerns, most constables did not readily share confidential material. Equally, chief constables could not prevent constables from spreading less vital information. Talking about work was too normal for policemen to refrain from it.

Conversations easily led to longer visits and evolved into regular stops. Police records repeatedly noted instances of constables taking unauthorized breaks with civilians. Men were found chatting in watchmen's huts, food shops, blacksmith's forges and private homes. In typical cases, PC Irving shared a drink with a lamp

---

20   BDRB, 26 April 1925, PCA 135 Harold George Bull, not proven, p. 15.

21   BPO, 22 October 1902, p. 257.

22   BPO, 14 September 1903, PCA 21 Frank Bonds, leave stopped, p. 567.

23   BPO, 11 June 1931, p. 18180.

24   MGO, 29 December 1933. Rafter also complained about confidential matters making it into the press and warned against gossiping generally (BPO, 7 April 1933, p. 20542).

25   BPO, 23 March 1904, pp. 137–8.

26   Birmingham City Police Defaulters Books, 30 April 1904, PCE Joseph Thomas Chinn, joined October 1891, reduced, p. 245.

27   BRB, 26 September 1929, PCA 236 Reginald Grisold Young, joined May 1927, reduced in class, one default, twelve awards; BPO, 26 September 1929, p. 15810.

lighter, PC Roberts played checkers in a railway clerk's office and PC Cocker idled in a confectionery shop.[28] Constables stretched out errands into impromptu visits, such as when PC Bullman stopped at a tobacconist to buy cigarettes, leaned against the counter, and talked to the assistant instead of getting back to work.[29] After making official calls at private homes, constables were invited in for cups of tea,[30] and constables investigating insecure premises found themselves invited to private parties.[31] Many men were reported at least once for this type of offence. After a while, they got better at not getting caught. Visits could become a regular part of a beat schedule. If found, the constable's friends insisted that he had only just arrived, that he had been there on official business and, if necessary, denied that he had shared any alcohol. In a typical case, a superintendent saw PS Starkie enter a fish shop and disappear into the back. He watched the owner get a jug of beer from a public house but was himself seen from a window. He heard 'consternation' and saw Starkie climb over the back fence into the next yard. The superintendent asked the wife if he could speak to the policeman but she denied that any policeman was there. When the superintendent found the chair that Starkie used to scale the wall, the wife begged him not to get the sergeant into trouble.[32] In return for civilians protecting them, policemen protected their friends, such as when PC Patrick Slattery hindered a meat inspector in his duty to give a friend time to hide any diseased meat.[33] Many such cases make it clear that friendships between civilians and policemen were a normal part of life.

One of the more common places for unauthorized visits were public houses, a mostly male working-class social centre. Regulations banned policemen from entering public houses in uniform except on official business, and the law forbade

---

[28]   LDRB, 4 March 1913, PCC 190 Irving, five years' service, fined 20/-; BPO, 7 July 1920, PCE 266 James Harold Roberts, fined 10/- and censured, p. 2357; BRB, 5 October 1934, PCC 153 Thomas Ganeth Huws Cocker, joined June 1932, fined 20/-.

[29]   MPF, 3 February 1923, PC 74 Arthur Bullman, appointed July 1919, fined 5/-.

[30]   MPF, 17 October 1924, PCE 41 Charles Pickford, appointed April 1919, fined 5/-. Other examples include constables invited in to check chimney fires or while making enquiries. (See Chapters 4 and 5.)

[31]   MPF, 28 December 1928, PCC 192 Frank Lord, appointed November 1924, not proven.

[32]   MWCM, 10 October 1912, PSC Starkie, twenty years' service, five rewards, five defaults, reduced to constable, vol. 56, no. 74.

[33]   'In this case the Police Officer acted in a most extraordinary way. The shopkeeper shouted at him to go into the shop, and told him that the Meat Inspector was a "wrong one" and that although the latter produced his authority signed by the Lord Mayor, appointing him Meat Inspector, the Constable took him from the shop, and brought him to the Markets to be identified as a Meat Inspector before he would assist him, thus giving the shop-keeper an opportunity of removing any diseased meat which might have been the object of the Inspector's visit' (BPO, 24 September 1908, severely censured, pp. 424–5).

licensees from serving a policeman in uniform.[34] But the public house was too much a part of life to be removed from constables' routines. A constable coming off duty often stopped for a pint on the way home rather than change first, such as when the still uniformed PC Pettit stopped at The Dolphin for a supper of bread, cheese, and pickles.[35] Constables ignored the ban on visiting public houses authorities considered to be unsavoury even when off duty and out of uniform. PC Jones was found with another constable in a public house with an undesirable reputation. On being advised of the place's reputation, he replied, 'I don't think so.'[36] Not content with breaking police regulations, constables regularly broke the law against drinking during prohibited hours, both on and off duty, along with the rest of the working class.[37] Knowledge of friendly havens was passed on from one generation of constable to the next. PC Taylor introduced two probationers to a provisions shop that backed onto a public house. When caught there by their superintendent, they claimed to have been visiting the water closet and four civilians backed them up.[38] Constables caught in public houses had the ready excuse of using the lavatory or official business, such as PC Bennett's response that he had been telling a licensee that a door was insecure.[39] Constables denied drinking and justified their visits by arguing that the best place to get news was at a public house. As the level of working-class drinking dropped, particularly after the war, the loitering continued without as much alcohol.[40]

Sharing an illicit drink with civilians was mostly harmless, but some constables

---

[34]   A police order warned against drinking while on duty since it often led to the prosecution of the publican and the discredit of the constable (BPO, 29 March 1913, p. 414, also LSO 6 March 1914, pp. 3–4; MGO, 18 April 1935).

[35]   BDRB, 4 December 1926, PCA 196 Charles William Pettit, cautioned, p. 64.

[36]   BPO, 2 December 1913, p. 13; LCCDR, 20 July 1927, PCA 198 Jones, charged with insubordination, withdrawn.

[37]   PCC 39 William Collins, nine years' service, two defaults, was found while off duty in a beer house kitchen during prohibited hours with eight men, one woman and a gallon of freshly drawn beer (MWCM, 17 April 1902, vol. 17, no. 14). PCD 204 Shirley, twenty-four years' service, six defaults, was caught in plain clothes while off duty at a public house on his beat gossiping with a number of men, a severe breach of regulations (LDRB, 12 June 1916, transferred, reduced). While keeping observation on a hotel suspected of breaking prohibited hours, an inspector and sergeant saw PCA 158 Edwin Parrott, seven years' service, four defaults, leave with other patrons while off duty in plain clothes. The licensee admitted that she knew he was a constable (MWCM, 11 October 1928, reduced and finally warned, vol. 126, no. 48).

[38]   MWCM, 28 November 1900, PC Saycell, PC Sprague, probationers, to resign, PC Taylor, ten years' service, dismissed, vol. 12, no. 76. Saycell and Sprague later admitted drinking rum but only because they had colds. The civilians insisted only they had drunk the rum.

[39]   MPF, 22 December 1922, PCA 54 Leonard Bennett, appointed September 1914, cautioned.

[40]   See Dingle, 'Drink and Working-Class Living Standards'.

had looser standards of appropriate company than even many of their colleagues could accept. It was one thing to joke with prisoners at the station but quite another to join prisoners for a drink, such as when PC Shaw visited a public house with a man he had just arrested for street betting,[41] and when PC Jenks shared a bottle of beer with a man he had arrested for stealing fowl.[42] Constables could be sympathetic towards deserting soldiers and sailors, allowing them to stop for a drink before returning them to their units.[43] They skirted police regulations regarding 'consorting with undesirable people'.[44] Police authorities defined what made a person objectionable but standards could be vague. PC Jones was asked to resign for 'associating with thieves, prostitutes, and a betting man', but charges generally were not that specific, such as when PC Delderfield was censured for 'associating with persons of loose and questionable character'.[45] Constables were advised to keep respectable company with people 'at least their own equals' but who qualified was open to interpretation. PC Rose was accused of keeping bad company but was given the benefit of the doubt over whether he knew the characters of the people involved.[46] Other constables clearly knew that individuals were unsuitable. Three Liverpool constables observing a public house suspected of being a haunt of disreputable characters and of serving liquor during prohibited hours were themselves caught drinking at the pub with five men and women running a ready-money betting scheme.[47] Even such blatant cases typically only involved drinking, rarely more serious offences. Nevertheless, a constable habitually caught 'keeping bad company' risked being let go for not having a good police character. Similar to other offences, successful constables learned how far they could push their fraternizing without jeopardizing their positions.

Along with continuing their working-class social habits, constables remained part of workplace perk practices. These included collecting tips, gifts and favours,

---

41   BRB, 10 December 1906, PCC 66 Lewis Shaw, joined September 1904, reprimanded; dismissed for striking 1919.

42   BRB, 7 May 1906, PCD 72 James Jenks, joined 1899, man found not guilty, cautioned and leave stopped; BWCM, 7 May 1906, p. 139; BPO, 8 May 1906, p. 373;

43   PCD 78 Edward Carroll allowed a naval deserter to get drunk while escorting him to his ship (BPO, 1 February 1906, p. 309; BRB, joined May 1904, leave stopped, severely cautioned). PCD 67 A. Potts was fined 2/6d. for allowing a soldier in his custody to enter a beer house and obtain intoxicating liquor (MGO, 3 March 1916).

44   PCF 124 Grace, two years' service, one default, was reduced on this charge (LDRB, 2 May 1909). PCD 107 was dismissed for 'improperly entering a Cricket Club pavilion; also associating with persons of undesirable character' (MGO, 19 September 1931).

45   MGO, 29 June 1911, PCA 54 Henry Jones; BPO, 2 December 1913, PCE 40 Fred Delderfield, p. 13. PCE 163 Albert Harding, joined July 1910, was reduced and cautioned for associating with a convicted thief (BRB, 8 April 1918).

46   LCCDR, 22 November 1920, PCB 212 Rose.

47   LCCDR, 8 January 1924, PCG 201 Howe, PCE 314 Rees, PCB 151 Doolin, all transferred and reprimanded.

as well as occasional small-scale pilfering. Police authorities frequently lamented that accepting tips and gifts from the public was demeaning to constables. Rewards in return for some service, like returning a dog, was treating constables like servants. But most constables viewed such extras as a normal part of working life. Tipping declined after the war when pay improved and police recruits became better-educated men, but never disappeared entirely. Instead, money tips tended to be replaced by small gifts and favours. As one interwar constable remarked, 'Bottle of beer's not a bribe. It was the custom – a given thing.'[48] Most occupations had at least a few unofficial extras, including pocketing the odd object, so constables accepted these as normal additions to their wages. This made it impossible for authorities to eradicate the practice.

Accepting unofficial tips mirrored the official practice of awarding gratuities to constables in recognition of special cases of first aid, rescues and detection. Constables were supposed to direct civilians to give gratuities to police authorities where they could be declined or distributed officially depending on circumstances. Not surprisingly, constables evaded this uncertain process, especially when many tips did not meet police standards. Since rewards were acceptable in officially sanctioned circumstances, constables felt free to accept them unofficially, even distributing tips meant for a group of officers.[49] Unsanctioned tips were given for specific actions as well as for a general reward for doing their jobs satisfactorily. Holidays such as Christmas, birthdays and anniversaries were a common occasion for giving tips, and if a householder had a reason to celebrate, the local constable often benefited. Authorities tried to discourage tipping, and men caught accepting tips were heavily fined and even forced to resign. But a shilling or two came in handy and everyone from probationers to twenty-year veterans continued to accept tips throughout their careers, both before and after the war.

One reason why constables did not report tips was that they were given for services that constables were offering the public unofficially. Police forces sometimes provided policemen to private companies such as theatres or industrial sites in return for private payment.[50] Individual constables were simply copying this on an individual scale. The most common practice was giving special attention to an empty premise or house. Authorities ordered constables emphatically and repeatedly not to make such arrangements, but constables continued to see them as a legitimate and rewarding extra. In a typical case, PC Foley agreed to watch a

---

48   Brogden, *On the Mersey Beat*, p. 110. Leonard Dunning, for instance, was particularly against tipping constables. See 'Inspectors of Constabulary report for year ended the 29th September 1926', PP 1927 (2) xi, 979, pp. 3–4; '…September 1927', PP 1927 (130) xi, 1015, pp. 5–6; also *Police Review and Parade Gossip*, 19 July 1929, pp. 554, 561.

49   BPO, 6 October 1931, p. 18627.

50   Chris Williams, 'Constables for Hire: The History of Private "Public" Policing in the UK', *Policing and Society* 18:2 (2008): 190–205.

private dwelling while the occupant was on vacation and received a shilling tip.[51] Another common problem was constables being hired for private functions, such as when PC Chilton was paid five shillings to do special duty at a wedding, even though outside employment was banned.[52] A few enterprising constables took the idea of extras too far. A garage paid PC Kidd for every car that he directed to them for repairs after being in crashes. This practice was discovered when he asked for a similar payoff from another garage, which refused and reported him.[53] In 1936, Rafter was so distressed by 'irregular payments' that he warned his men to stop rendering services to 'outside firms, inside football grounds, &c ... [and to decline] money ... received ... in consequence of police services such as restoration of property, finding of motor cars ... [and] attention to vacant premises'.[54] But similar to gossiping and fraternizing, the practice continued despite numerous orders against it. Constables viewed earning an extra shilling or two to be a normal bonus of wearing the uniform, and considered these unofficial services to be part of the regular neighbourly interactions of their beats.

In addition to tips, policemen accepted small gifts as perks. A regular perk could evolve out of a constable's duties. He might do a shopkeeper a good deed and be rewarded with free cigarettes or a few sausages. The constable then took a special interest in the shop and the cycle continued. A shopkeeper could also begin the relationship by giving a constable a present to assure extra attention.[55] Once a practice was established, it could continue indefinitely. In one arrangement, workmen at the Royal Small Arms factory gave money and drinks to PCs Burrows and Priddey, and in return, the constables recommended that people lodge at the homes of factory workers.[56] Both householders and professional drivers often gave constables rides in return for a little friendly attention. Newspaper van drivers not only gave constables rides but also free newspapers.[57] Constables habitually

---

51   BPO, 9 January 1903, PCB 87 Cornelius Foley, leave stopped, order to pay 1/- to 'B' division recreation fund, p. 329.

52   BRB, 6 February 1904, PCC 161 George Chilton, joined May 1897, leave stopped, 5/- to be paid to 'B' division recreation fund.

53   MPF, 24 May 1938, PCA 296 John Kidd, appointed January 1929, fined 10/-.

54   BPO, 20 March 1936, p. 25147.

55   A van man gave PCH Glover a free pork pie (BWCM, 20 February 1917, reduced, p. 257). PCD 203 Monaghan was cautioned for accepting gifts of cigarettes from the daughter of a shopkeeper (LCCDR, 15 June 1923). PCF 169 Jones and PSF 33 Barlow were given threepenny loaves of bread by a bread and flour dealer (LCCDR, 10 March 1924, adjourned for three months pending future behaviour).

56   BPO, 10 October 1903, PCR 212 William J. Burrows, PCR 45 Charles Priddey, pp. 1–2.

57   LCCO, 29 May 1928, constables ordered to stop accepting rides from civilians for fear of later compromising situations. PCB 128 Hilton Oliver Raine was fined 10/- and had his leave stopped for accepting a present of newspapers from a van driver (BRB, 1 May 1902, joined October 1901; BPO, 1 May 1902, p. 79).

rode the platforms of tram cars and omnibuses without paying, despite continual orders against it. The men appreciated the rides, conductors and drivers enjoyed the company, and passengers approved of the security.[58] Such mutual arrangements were common in working life, with the grocer putting aside the best tomatoes for the baker in return for the best loaf of bread. Constables simply added their particular services to the existing practices.

The line between an acceptable perk and one shading into coercion or illegality was difficult to draw. A free meal might be considered acceptable, but going in search of free food might be questionable. Accepting free food or drink implied a service in return so some constables were careful about how often they accepted perks from a single source while others were less sensitive. Since policemen inspected places of entertainment, some constables had no problem with using this duty to watch movies and live performances for free.[59] A few used their jobs to get perks for friends and relatives. PCs McConnell and Jones both got friends into theatres by passing them off as policemen,[60] and while on duty at the Pageant Ground, PC Wright got his son in without a ticket.[61] At the extreme were those who sought perks as a mandatory part of the job, taking gifts but not necessarily reciprocating the service. Licensees were particularly vulnerable to such abuses since they feared having their licences revoked and needed to be on good terms with policemen if disorder broke out.[62] Local perk patterns could vary and constables needed to fit their expectations to local expectations. Perks that provoked public complaints or attracted official attention could endanger the practice for everyone. But as long as perks kept within reasonable limits, both constables and civilians benefited.

The most common reported police perk was receiving free beer and sometimes other alcohol from businesses and private citizens. For licensees, this was an easy way to be on good terms with local policemen. Often, bottles of beer were left in doorways for the constable to pick up as a regular arrangement.[63] PC Henshaw stopped by a public house for a regular glass of beer, once tickling Ellen

---

[58]   Orders against this: BPO, 28 March 1916, p. 259, 4 January 1917, p. 521; MGO, 1 September 1921, 20 September 1929.

[59]   BPO, 30 October 1922, p. 5604; Clive Emsley, *Policing and Its Context 1750–1870* (New York: Schocken, 1983), preface.

[60]   BPO, 2 November 1901, PCB 78 Denis McConnell, leave stopped, p. 562; LDRB, 13 February 1923, PCD 146 Jones, three years' service, one default, reduced.

[61]   LDRB, 18 August 1907, PCF 53 Wright, fifteen years' service, ordered to pay for ticket, reprimanded.

[62]   PCB 68 Mackay, twelve years' service, four defaults, asked a licensee of a beer house to supply him with beer whilst on duty and to take the beer to him on his beat in what appears to be a coerced perk (LDRB, 15 June 1906, successfully appealed).

[63]   PCC 103 William Bell was reduced for 'receiving a bottle of beer from underneath the yard door of the beer house' (MGO, 6 December 1900). PCB 161 Graham Deeley received a

Wheeler under the chin and saying, 'I will see you tomorrow night.'[64] In 1900, Manchester's government inspection approval was delayed until the force could show that they were taking steps to stop constables from receiving gifts of beer at public houses, often during prohibited hours.[65] But the practice was difficult to stop since even high-ranking officers accepted free bottles of beer and liquor.[66] Like any perk, constables might coerce drinks and businessmen might use drinks as bribes. When visiting a wine and spirit merchants while off duty, PC Campbell was given a gift of liquor, though records leave it unclear whether Campbell demanded or was offered the gift.[67] In addition to businesses, civilians repeatedly treated constables to drinks, such as when a man slipped a bottle of stout into a constable's pocket and when 'a gentleman' gave a constable on traffic point duty two bottles of whisky.[68] Such drinks tended to be gestures of good will made to constables out in bad weather and to constables directing traffic, both to keep them warm and to alleviate the boredom. The practice of offering free drinks became less common in the 1930s with the decline in working-class drinking but it never disappeared.[69]

Perks included not only gifts but also the more uncertain area of picking up items on the job. Most people sensed the subtle difference between perks and stealing, and items were generally of low value. Like tips and gifts, police authorities condemned the practice for giving the force a bad image, and constables taking items risked being prosecuted for theft. While items could be found anywhere, the Liverpool docks were a particular problem. Discarded materials, such as grain and fruit that spilled from ships and broken containers, were routinely given to

---

bottle of beer from an employee of Messrs Davenports while on duty (BJSC, 28 January 1921, reduced, p. 255).

[64] LDRB, 11 October 1921, PCB 177 Henshaw one year's service, one default, to resign.

[65] *Police Review*, 2 February 1900, p. 53. In 1914, constables were reminded that 'they are strictly prohibited from receiving gratuities from licensed persons no matter whether the licences are for the sale of liquor or for places of public entertainment' (BPO, 8 July 1914, p. 196). While working on the docks, PCA 227 Evans, nineteen years' service, six defaults, was given a free sample bottle of rum by a customs official (LDRB, 23 February 1908, reduced to probationary class).

[66] MGO, 4 June 1915, Superintendent Walker, reduced to chief inspector, took his pension.

[67] LDRB, 27 September 1927, PCA 260 Campbell, seven years' service, one default, also that he 'proceeded through the streets after having divested himself of his jacket, vest, & hat' and assaulting a civilian, required to resign.

[68] LDRB, 13 March 1916, PCE 67 Whittamore, sixteen years' service, fined 20/-; MWCM, 13 June 1907, PCA 66 Thomas Sillitoe, fourteen years' service, six defaults, to resign for drunken behaviour, vol. 36, no. 68.

[69] In 1990, a senior police officer told me of being on night duty as a probationer in the 1960s with a veteran constable who had a regular pattern of beer pickups on his beat. Typically, a bottle was left for him in a doorway. The officer thought the veteran must have consumed about six pints over the course of the night with apparently no ill effect.

dock workers. Odds and ends of timber were picked up for home improvement projects.[70] Dock workers regularly handed things on to constables or allowed constables to pick up stray items themselves. In some cases, constables received perks in return for favours, such as when PC Rogers posted a parcel for a dock worker and was given 'a quantity of fish'.[71] Constables assigned to dock gates were supposed to challenge workers carrying suspicious material but often neglected to do so since they were taking home items themselves. Constables had to exercise care not to abuse dock perks since different companies had their own views on perks. PC Thom picked up four oranges that he found in a dock gutter, usually an accepted practice, but unfortunately the shipping company had strict rules on found items. They charged him with stealing fruit worth three pennies from a broken case and he was sentenced to two months' imprisonment.[72] But such extreme examples were unusual. A few dock workers and constables did cross from scavenging into illegitimate dealings. One foreman sold timber on the side for a quarter of its cost, and PC Edom not only bought the timber but allowed it off the docks knowing that it was not salvage.[73] But most workers condemned such practices since they jeopardized abundant legitimate dock perks. More than enough free material was available without stealing more.

The Liverpool City Police struggled to stop dock perks if only because the regular sight of constables going off duty carrying salvage contradicted the image of police neutrality. Firing constables caught with dock materials tended to be counter-productive since most senior officers did not agree with such a harsh

---

[70] PCE 77 Armstrong, joined June 1881, was reduced for receiving timber on the docks and not reporting it. PCE 60 Harper, joined September 1898, was fined 10/- for allowing the timber out of the dock without demanding a pass for it (LDRB, 23 October 1900). PCD 244 Branton, four years' service, allowed a man to take timber off the docks without a permit from the owners (LDRB, 12 April 1912, fined 10/-). PCC 162 arranged for his father to remove a gift of timber from the docks (LCCDR, 6 July 1922, resigned). PCE 271 Herbert Clifford Ridsdale, joined April 1921, was ordered to resign after being found with timber taken from Woolworths without proper authority (BDB, 28 November 1934; BPO, 28 November 1934, p. 22989).

[71] LDRB, 24 June 1930, PCA 225 Rogers, ten years' service, resigned.

[72] LDRB, 23 July 1929, PCE 130 Thom, three years' service, dismissed; Brogden, *On the Mersey Beat*, pp. 68–9. The sentence was appealed and changed to Thom being bound over for a year. PCD 253 Husgrove found a 'bunch of raisins' in a dock shed and kept them, thinking they had been discarded. A charge of stealing was dismissed, but he was forced to resign from the force (LDRB, 22 November 1912, eight years' service). PCC 123 Carrier, two years' service, was discharged with a caution by a magistrate for stealing eighteen ounces of grain, value 3d., but dismissed from the force (LDRB, 1 November 1915). PCE 187 Walker was ordered to resign after being fined £5 for receiving two bottle of pickles and a half pound of tea from the second officer of a ship (LDRB, 27 November 1917).

[73] LCCDR, 3 July 1922, PCC 284 Edom, resigned.

punishment and often benefited from dock perks themselves.[74] Even a major 1902 scandal involving dock perks, a sergeant and three senior officers, did not halt the practice.[75] Only two years later, an attempt to make an example of constables found 'petty pilfering' backfired. PCs Ferrington and Allen were employed on the dock of a company that made patent manure, and they took some from a broken bag home to their gardens. They were dismissed but appealed. The company sent a letter stating that foremen had permission to give friends samples of goods, one foreman testified that he had allowed the constables to take some manure, and two petitions bearing 739 signatures supported the constables. In response to this barrage, the watch committee decided to reinstate the constables and simply reprimand them.[76] The perk was too well established for the chief constable to treat it as an illegitimate act. Twenty-five years later, Liverpool Chief Constable Everett was still reminding his men, 'It cannot be too strongly emphasized that, in whatever circumstances property anywhere may be, whether protected or unprotected in the sense of being properly packed, or on insecure premises, or in broken cases, or whatever its value, the stealing of it calls for the most drastic action.'[77] But similar to gossiping and fraternizing, police regulations could not overcome such an entrenched practice.

---

[74] PSA 53 Brockbank was accused of taking stolen straw and of smuggling sausages and corn off the docks in his helmet. Neither charge could be confirmed (LCCDR, 27 September 1923).

[75] In 1902, PS Welsh of Liverpool successfully charged the force with false imprisonment after being declared mentally unfit for service and pensioned. He unsuccessfully charged three officers with conspiracy. The case accused Chief Supt Sperrin, Chief Insp. Strettell and Insp. Duckworth of having Welsh committed for lunacy after he made accusations that they had used him to obtain illegal merchandise from the docks. He had letters showing that Sperrin had accepted dock 'corn sweepings' to feed his poultry and cigars for Christmas. Dock masters and porters commonly gave 'sweepings' to anyone who asked and Welsh regularly supplied superior officers with the grain. The cigars were presents to the non-smoking Welsh from a sailor cousin which he offered to Sperrin. Welsh had letters showing that Strettell had solicited free tram tickets for his daughter from Welsh, as well as presents of tobacco, butter and eggs. Sperrin and Strettell were reprimanded for soliciting and accepting presents from a subordinate without the consent of the chief constable. Duckworth was accused of assisting Sperrin and Strettell in getting rid of Welsh once he threatened to make the letters public. Welsh was called 'a thief and a receiver of stolen goods' by the chief constable but Sperrin and Strettell were not held accountable for receiving the same goods. It was never decided whether or not this practice was legal although the Corn Trade Association and Dock Board claimed it was not. Sperrin had learned about the corn in 1892 from Supt Irvine who also got corn and cigars from Welsh. Welsh also claimed he did not get fair treatment since he was Irish Catholic (LWCM, 31 October 1901, pp. 309–21; 15 November 1901, pp. 339–40; 24 March 1902, pp. 583–4; 2 June 1902, pp. 683–5; 30 June 1902, pp. 3–22; *Police Review*, 4 July 1902, pp. 315–17; 25 July 1902, p. 351).

[76] LHCWC, 14 November 1904, pp. 412–14; Liverpool Watch Committee Orders to the Head Constable, 14 November 1904.

[77] LCCO, 9 July 1929.

Most constables treated perks carefully to protect their positions but a few could not resist the allure of free merchandise. PC Maudesley planted a hammer he fancied where he could take it home after duty. He made the mistake of telling this to a constable less liberal-minded about his idea of a perk.[78] Showing a similar lack of judgment, PC Little drove into a garage and filled his car with petrol without paying.[79] A few constables got into trouble for accepting as perks items stolen by someone else. Since companies often let employees take home samples or damaged goods, PC Hullett did not question a gift of onions from a night watchman. Unfortunately, the watchman had stolen them from the company and Hullett could not convince his chief constable that he did not know.[80] In what was clearly a case of stealing, PC Ashcroft asked a boy working at a motor dealer if he could buy motor oil cheaply without the owner's knowledge, figuring that the owner would not miss a few gallons. He did not realize that the boy reported this conversation to his senior officers. When he visited again, the boy agreed to cooperate after being coached by an inspector and sergeant who were hiding in the next room. When Ashcroft returned to pick up the oil, he was confronted by the inspector. Luckily for him, the coaching of the boy confused the case so he was fined rather than fired.[81] Constables with such a poor sense of the line between perks and stealing more often did not last long in the force.

One area of police and public interaction encouraged by police authorities was participation in recreational and athletic events. Sports were important 'not only to the happiness and health of the men, but also to the furtherance of mutual good feeling between the citizens and the Force'.[82] Before the war, police football games, boxing matches, and other sports were common. In 1905, the Birmingham police played a football match against the Birmingham postman at the YMCA annual sports day, and the Liverpool police had a cricket team and a football team.[83] Manchester had a City Police Athletic Club that held an annual sports day and had recreation rooms open to the force.[84] Most of these teams were fairly small and few forces had proper facilities for practices and matches. After the war,

---

[78]   LCCDR, 18 February 1922, PCC 287 Maudesley, ordered to resign.

[79]   Birmingham City Police Defaulters Books, 12 May 1939, PCC 44 Wilfred George Little, joined March 1930, dismissed.

[80]   LDRB, 27 April 1906, PCE 283 Hullett, seven years' service, one default, dismissed.

[81]   MPF, 20 March 1928, PCD 125 Fred Ashcroft, fined 20/-.

[82]   LAR, 1925, p. 13. 'It is now an accepted fact that sport and recreation play an essential part in the majority of people's lives ... Apart from the obvious physical advantages accruing, sport promotes not only healthy inter-force rivalry and esprit de corps, but also fosters the good relationship between the police and the public which is essential nowadays to both' ('Inspectors of Constabulary report for year ended the 29th September 1938, PP 1938–39 (83) xiv, 317, pp. 16–17).

[83]   BPO, 25 August 1905, p. 173.

[84]   MGO, 29 June 1900; February 1912.

working-class sports teams became widespread, and most business and towns added amateur teams. Police forces joined this trend, providing both sports and a variety of entertainments for the many young postwar recruits.[85] The *Police Review* began printing 'Exercises for Health' and listing scores from police sporting events and Association Football.[86] By 1921, policemen injured during official police sports events were considered to be injured on duty, including the continuation of wages while off work.[87] Liverpool divisional committees organized whist drives, dances, concerts, minstrel shows and boxing competitions with other forces. Their football team played in a city league against teams from other occupations.[88] Birmingham police set up a social club with a billiards room, darts room, concerts and other events, and a sports club when the force acquired its own sports facilities in 1922. This included a cricket pitch, football field, lawn tennis, badminton, quoits ground, bowling green, club house and pavilion.[89] In 1923, Manchester added a swimming club to its athletic club.[90] In the 1930s, most forces could field teams in the principal sports, leading HMI Atcherly to conclude that 'this more or less modern development of police life has largely contributed to improving the general state of efficiency and has done wonders in bringing out the proper Service spirit'.[91] Injuries sustained in sports events led some police authorities to worry about losing men to the sick list but most forces agreed that the benefits of better police fitness and increased force morale outweighed the risks of injury.[92]

Forces began developing reputations based on their sports teams which did not necessarily match the positive benefits that authorities hoped for. After a poor showing at a 1921 sports tournament, Chief Constable Peacock suggested

---

85 'With so large a number of young men in the Force it has been found necessary not only to provide for their education and training, but also to cater for their amusement and recreation during their "off duty" hours. The Committee of the Police Athletic Society is to be congratulated upon their efforts in this respect' (LAR, 1922, p. 3).

86 For example, *Police Review*, 18 March 1921, p. 150.

87 BJCS, 28 January 1921, p. 253.

88 LCCO, 29 January 1922.

89 BPO, 21 March 1927, p. 12612. This was replaced in 1927 with the thirteen-acre Tally Ho Sports Ground which is still used as a training and sports centre by the West Midlands Police force.

90 MWCM, 13 December 1923, vol. 100, no. 85.

91 'Inspectors of Constabulary report for year ended the 29th September 1934', PP 1934–35 (41) x, 943, p. 9.

92 *Police Review*, 7 September 1928, 'Police and Football', p. 695. LCI, 16 August 1913, PCB 145 Jewkes and PCB 185 Hodgson collided with each other in a cricket match, cutting their foreheads; 17 October 1919, PCG 78 Jones broke his arm playing football when he collided with a player from the other team; 26 October 1921, PCF 185 Connell went to heads the ball in a football match and collided with another player, loosening a tooth; 18 October 1924, PCF 185 Connell was kicked on the thigh during a football match at Bromborough; 24 April 1925, PCF 203 Tandy was kicked on the knee in a football match against the Wallasey Tramways.

not holding another one unless 'Manchester Police will make a credible display against other Forces, as it is not very desirable to promote a Tournament for the purpose of advertising other Police Forces'.[93] Liverpool did so poorly in police competitions in the early 1930s that they stopped supporting the Police Athletic Society until urged to do so by their chief constable.[94] Birmingham, however, became one of the most competitive forces. They set up internal sports leagues with each division fielding teams in a variety of sports.[95] Divisions developed their own specialities. For instance, 'R' division won at billiards but was bad at football while 'E' division won at football but lost at billiards.[96] Competition could be quite fierce. In a 1936 match between 'D' and 'E' divisions playing for the Brown Cup, a fight broke out and the local Country Football Association had to issue cautions against two constables for unsportsmanlike conduct.[97] Such altercations probably earned Birmingham police respect from many working-class peers, especially since the Birmingham police teams tended to win. It was not, however, the upright play expected by police authorities.

The police and civilian interactions most supported by police authorities were the growing areas of general public assistance and social welfare.[98] Policemen were expected to answer every conceivable question of the public who expected them to be knowledgeable on local information as well as serve as a kind of approachable legal aid. They were on the spot in many situations that demanded attention, even if events did not fit their job description except in the broadest sense of public order.[99] More formally, they raised money for a variety of charities, ranging from prisoners aid to outings for children. The most extensive assistance involved the vague area of social welfare. This could include anything from delivering informal words of advice to participating in Police-Aided Clothing Associations. In his 1923 description of policing as a vocation, Sir Robert Peacock reminded constables

---

[93]   MGO, 4 November 1921.

[94]   LCCO, 25 July 1935. The force began to issue a weekly pamphlet outlining the society's activities to try and increase participation (LCCO, 13 January 1936).

[95]   BPO, 4 January 1922, p. 4508; 3 August 1922, pp. 5285–7.

[96]   BPO, 3 April 1925, p. 9724.

[97]   BPO, 12 March 1936, p. 25107. PCD 252 Alexander Proud sustained a concussion and PCE 113 Reginald Williams was kicked.

[98]   See Chapter 2 for the expansion of police service duties, especially after the First World War.

[99]   See Punch and Naylor, 'The Police: A Social Service'. Monitoring phone calls to three Essex towns for a fortnight, they found that 59 per cent of calls were service requests and 41 per cent were law enforcement requests. They also found that even during regular office hours, people turned to the police and not to professional social services because it was both quicker and easier to call the police, and because policemen seemed more reliable than social workers. This suggested that the working class had integrated policemen into their culture and that social workers had yet to reach that level of acceptance.

that the welfare side of their work was as important as the more obvious duties of preventing crime.[100] Commenting on changes in the police force in 1937, the Manchester Lord Mayor described policemen as welfare workers.[101] Policemen often ended up acting as welfare workers simply because they were there, the basic reason why they became convenient for all types of assistance.

The willingness of civilians to appeal to policemen showed that they saw constables as an obvious avenue for help. These deeds were rarely reported but the few that were show a variety of neighbourly actions, such as helping shopkeepers put up shutters,[102] and helping people locked out of their houses. In one case, two policemen used a knife to force open a kitchen window for a woman who forgot her keys.[103] Sometimes, constables interpreted neighbourly assistance a little too generously for authorities, such as when PC Cox left his beat to get a man a cab.[104] While examining an insecure tobacconist shop, PC Hill even sold cigarettes to a customer who came in thinking the shop was open.[105] In a more serious call for help, a group of German boy scouts became separated from their leader while en route from Scotland to London. No lodgings could be found by scouting officials for the boys since they had little money, so the boys were left at the Manchester Town Hall. A police superintendent took the matter in hand, housed the boys in the living quarters of a police station overnight, fed them dinner and breakfast, and sent them on their way in the morning.[106] This action hardly fit police duties in any obvious way and yet it seemed appropriate for the police to step in when no clear alternative presented itself. In all cases, someone needed help, small or large, and a policeman was a visible option even if the help required had little to do with policing.

Policemen often met people requiring assistance that they could not provide directly. In response, the police gave contributions to existing charity institutions, set up their own organizations, and raised money for special causes. Some police charities began at the instigation of police authorities, others at the request of

---

100   City of Manchester, *Police Instruction Book*, pp. 15–16. Leonard Dunning found it difficult to draw a line between police and social welfare work since preventing crime was a part of social work ('Inspectors of Constabulary report for year ended the 29th of September 1928', PP 1928–1929 (50) ix, 43, p. 6). He also lamented that better use was not made of 'the experience which the police are gaining every day upon subjects closely affecting the welfare of the public' (LAR, 1907, p. 20).

101   MAR, 1937, p. 3.

102   LCI, 22 March 1924, PSE 18 Davis, crushed little finger when it was caught between shutter and brickwork.

103   LCI, 21 April 1916, PSG 17 Saul, cut right hand, finger.

104   BPO, 28 November 1907, PCA 58 Leonard Cox, leave stopped, p. 200.

105   BDRB, 22 July 1928, PCE 284 Joseph Edward Hill, cautioned, p. 105; BPO, 17 October 1928, p. 14667.

106   MWCM, 30 August 1934, vol. 186, no. 29. Expenses were covered by 'C' division.

the policemen themselves. Charities included medical attention for the poor, helping the unemployed and released prisoners, buying poor children Christmas treats, and clothing children so they could go to school or earn money. The Manchester Police Force's annual charity ball raised money for the Police-Aided Clothing Association, the Northern Police Convalescent Centre, Seven Springs Camp, the Discharged Prisoners' Aid Society, the NSPCA, the Police Court and Prison Gate Mission, and a wide variety of hospitals.[107] The Birmingham Police Charity Sports Day gave money to a similar list, and from 1901 to 1929 raised nearly £15,000.[108] Funds were often raised at special events, such as when a 1935 football match between Manchester police and the unemployed raised £275 for King George's Jubilee Trust Fund.[109] Civilians reciprocated when policemen faced similar crises, since such charities were a standard part of working-class culture. For instance, after PC Lewis Jones was killed attempting to stop a runaway horse, a Liverpool newspaper set up a public collection, raising £120 for his widow and seven children, three under the age of fifteen.[110] The groups that appeared most frequently were the unemployed, workers affected by workplace disasters, and children.

Of all police charity activity, by far the most important group requiring their assistance were children, and the most well known police charities were the Police-Aided Clothing Associations. Manchester's PACA was founded in 1902, Liverpool's in 1885, and Birmingham's in 1884, making it possibly the oldest in England.[111] Birmingham and Liverpool solicited contributions from the public while the Manchester PACA was funded by the policemen. Associations were run by influential members of the cities, but constables reported the children requiring the aid. Only children seen by constables were recommended so children needing clothing were instructed to speak to the constable on the beat where they lived. Constables were told to question the child, 'being careful to do so kindly, so as not to let the child think it has got into trouble'.[112] The family was investigated by volunteers and policemen, and approved children, especially

---

[107] MAR, 1928, p. viii; 1929, p. viii; 1930, p. viii; 1931, p. xx; 1932, p. xxi; 1933, p. xxiv; 1934, p. xxviii; 1935, p. v; 1936, p. 5; 1937, p. 8; 1938, p. 50.

[108] BPO, 7 October 1905, pp. 212–13; 17 October 1906, p. 502; 9 October 1907, p. 165; 3 July 1912, p. 216; 29 July 1916, p. 374; 13 August 1918, p. 143; 26 June 1919, p. 869; 20 July 1921, p. 3815; 21 August 1922, p. 5343; 25 October 1923, p. 6974; 26 September 1924, p. 8903; 2 December 1926, p. 12156; 24 November 1927, p. 13566;19 December 1929, p. 16158.

[109] MGO, 17 May 1935; MAR, 1935, p. 11.

[110] LHCWC, 13 June 1904, PC Lewis Jones, aged forty-eight, twenty-three years' service, pp. 233–4; *Police Review*, 17 June 1904, p. 298. Jones died from a fractured skull. During his funeral procession, neighbourhoods lowered their blinds as a sign of mourning. The City Mineral Water Company, whose horse had bolted, sent a wreath to the funeral.

[111] BPO, 21 August 1919, p. 1033.

[112] LSO 13, March 1912, p. 1.

those approaching wage-earning age, were provided with clothing.[113] Parents were warned that 'unless the children are taken thoroughly clean, no clothing will be issued to them' but this was more a concern with spreading lice than a moral issue.[114] Constables trying to help specific children occasionally made exaggerated reports to try to ensure approval.[115] Constables nominated so many children that associations were periodically forced to request that no further applications be made.

Finding clothes for children received more attention than all other police charities combined. A police station generally served as the clothing depot. To raise money for the PACA, the Manchester police held an annual dance and the Birmingham police held a police sports day. Further collections were made when the association needed extra funds and special football matches, concerts and matinee shows were held to raise money.[116] Liverpool's PACA staged special one-day street collections every year, bringing in £4502 in 1928, £3825 in 1929, £3771 in 1930 and £3202 in 1932.[117] With the exception of Birmingham, which was efficient at fundraising and not hit as hard by the economic depression, the 1930s saw a drop in contributions. Manchester's dance, for instance, dropped from its usual £300 contribution in the 1920s to only £150 in 1933.[118] In Liverpool, funds were so low only children in absolute necessity could be helped in 1933.[119] Funds picked up again by 1938 and helping children remained a top priority.

---

[113]   The clothes were marked so that they could not be pawned. Pawnbrokers and clothing shops were informed to look for the markings. Technically, the clothing was lent, not given, so buying PACA clothing would be receiving stolen goods. Liverpool constables were ordered to 'keep a look-out for the child; if he notices that the child is not wearing the clothes ... he will enquire, and should he find that the clothes have been dealt with illegally, will report the case' (LSO 13, March 1912, p. 2). Also Brogden, *On the Mersey Beat*, pp. 101–2.

[114]   BPO, 5 November 1901, p. 567.

[115]   LDRB, 16 January 1909, PCH 130 Pratt, thirteen years' service, 'Making a false statement in a report upon the application of a boy for clothing ... Reprimanded'.

[116]   BPO, 24 March 1900, police matinee, p. 157; 11 April 1900, football match between police and Smallheath football club to raise money for PACA, p. 168; 3 February 1902, police concert, p. 20; 2 September 1902, invited to play a football match against the Diocesan Police Court Mission in North Stafford to raise money for the mission, previous year Liverpool had played the match, p. 521; 15 May 1907, £9 earned at football match between 'C' division and 'a team supplied by Wm Light, Esq.', p. 65; 20 June 1908, £22 raised in football match between 'C' division and Birmingham postmen, p. 374; 24 February 1926, £147/4/9d. raised at football match between police and Tramway Dept, p. 10990; 26 March 1926, £30/1/6d. raised at match between 'C' and 'D' divisions, p. 11051. In 1930, a Manchester Charity Matinee raised £200 (MAR, 1930, p. viii).

[117]   LCCO, 21 November 1928, 26 October 1929, 28 October 1930; *Police Review*, 24 June 1932, p. 489.

[118]   Manchester PACA Annual Report for 1932–1933 and 1933–1934, p. 2.

[119]   LCCO, 30 September 1933.

Associations in different cities were not identical. The object of the Manchester PACA was specifically to clothe children licensed to trade in the streets so that they could work; only when that was accomplished did it clothe 'others, being the children of necessitous parents'.[120] Manchester would not help children under age nine since they could not work, and rejected cases where the parents were 'rough'.[121] Liverpool, on the other hand, had a policy of clothing 'ALL insufficiently clothed children … irrespective of any questions as to why their clothing is insufficient, or whether the parents are drunkards or bad characters, able or unable to provide clothing'.[122] The basic reason for this more generous attitude was that Liverpool's association was more under the control of its policemen rather than of middle-class volunteers as in Manchester. Policemen tended to be less moralistic and more realistic about the conditions in which children often had to live. Even though PC Smethurst was scornful of the irresponsible habits of some parents, he did everything he could to help their children, including reporting extreme cases to inspectors of cruelty to children.[123]

Besides supplying clothing, policemen participated in a variety of activities to improve the quality of life for children. Police officers acted as volunteers in city Boys' Clubs and provided recreation rooms at police stations. They gave free swimming and life-saving instruction, boxing training, first-aid classes, music lessons, and wireless construction and telegraphy classes. Constables coached local football teams.[124] Every year, Birmingham policemen donated to the Daily Mail Christmas Tree Fund, which provided toys and treats for needy children.[125] For King George's Jubilee, the children of the Northern Police Orphanage were given

---

120   The Manchester Police-Aided Clothing Association (For Needy Children). Annual Report for 1926–1927 (Manchester: Chas. Sever Ltd.) p. 13. The 1927–1928 report observed that 'the approaching winter is going to be one of the most trying for all charities, as the amount of unemployment is increasing' (p. 4).

121   Manchester PACA Annual Report, 1904–1905, p. 12.

122   LSO 13, March 1912, p. 2.

123   Smethurst, 'Mems.', pp. 127–31. He later described parents of neglected children as being 'selfish and ungrateful creatures, who only worked at intervals, ate and drank like gluttons, wallowed in their filth, and slept like hogs. The gratification of their appetites and passions seemed to be their dominant traits, all other matters being to them secondary considerations. They brought children into the world, caring very little how they grew up, so that they did not interfere too much in their own liberty' ('Reminiscences', p. 109).

124   MAR, 1937, pp. 8–9.

125   BPO, 14 December 1907, £10/18/1d., p. 215; 1 January 1910, £20, p. 176; 21 December 1912, £21/11/6d., p. 356; 20 December 1913, £21/3/8d., p. 51; 24 December 1914, £24, p. 415; 24 December 1915, £15/0/4d., p. 137; 19 December 1916, £13/3/6d., p. 504; 15 December 1917, £13/4/0d., p. 288; 23 December 1918, £10/8/0d., p. 375; 24 December 1919, £2/10/0d., p. 1538; 30 December 1920, £23/5/8d., p. 3052; 24 December 1921, £45/13/0d., p. 4464; 30 December 1922, £23/2/7d., p. 5881; 7 January 1924, £25/18/9d., p. 7573; 24 December 1928, £31/14/9d., p. 14910; 19 January 1929, £3/13/0d., p. 14999.

a day trip to the Belle Vue gardens and the Manchester zoo, and a substantial lunch with entertainments afterwards.[126] Part of this generosity was simply a desire to help children, especially at holidays. However, their motives were also practical, hoping that positive attention and activities would encourage children to become law-abiding citizens. In particular, policemen were meant to provide good role models for boys.

While not as high a priority as children, charity for adults received constant attention, tending to be for workers faced with economic hardship and funding for free beds in hospitals. Birmingham policemen contributed regularly to the Lord Mayor's Unemployment Distress Fund, and in 1908 initiated a collection for the City of Birmingham Aid Society to help 400 distressed families.[127] Collections were made in response to workplace disasters, often linked to coal mining. In 1911, relatives of persons killed in the Hulton Colliery explosion received £50 from the Manchester police force, in 1929 Birmingham police donated £100 to the Lord Mayor's Coalfield Distress Fund, and in 1934 Liverpool police raised £105 for the Gresford Colliery Disaster fund.[128] War also prompted charity, with Liverpool police donated £2662 to fund aid for wives of men fighting at the front, prisoners of war and men who returned wounded.[129] All of these charities were meant to help families in distress, often with hardships that policemen had experienced themselves, had seen experienced by their friends and family, or had witnessed on their beats. With the exception of prison missions, none targeted improving anyone but rather had straightforward economic goals meant to help families get medical attention or get back on their feet financially.

Charities targeting civilian adults were mirrored in charities and insurance schemes benefiting policemen, reflecting shared fears of financial and employment disaster. Some charities were official, such as the Hospital Saturday Funds. Forces donated quarterly sums to these funds and in returned received priority to hospital beds and convalescent homes such as the Northern Police Convalescent Centre.[130]

---

126 MAR, 1935, p. ii.
127 BPO, 3 December 1904, £32/5/9d., p. 444; 14 October 1908, pp. 450–2; 23 June 1921, £47/17/0d., p. 3704; 19 January 1923, £52, p. 5954; 5 April 1924, £59/11/8d., p. 8211.
128 MGO, 5 January 1911; BPO, 8 May 1929, p. 15341; LCCO, 4 October 1934. Numerous and regular examples of charity giving appear in police records in all three cities.
129 LCCO, 3 December 1918.
130 In Birmingham, policemen contributed 1d. per week before the war, rising to 2d. per week by 1928. The rate was raised to 3d. a week in 1932. For examples see BPO, 6 June 1901, pp. 465–6; 21 June 1911, p. 527; 30 June 1920, p. 2332; 6 October 1928, p. 14631. Liverpool had mandatory subscriptions to the Harrogate Convalescent Fund, established in 1906, to fund a bed every year. Constables paid 1/6d. per annum, sergeants 2/-, raising around £170 a year, and in return they had free access to Harrogate when recommended by the medical officer (LCCO, 9 October 1919, 11 October 1926, 23 October 1930, 13 December 1934). Liverpool raised £90 in 1919 and £210 in 1922 for Hospital Saturday Fund (LCCO, 20 May 1919, 12 May

Policemen contributed to the Police Mutual Assurance Association, founded in the 1880s for the benefit of police pensioners and their wives, and then to the Police Mutual Assurance Society, founded in 1921 when the PMAA developed financial problems.[131] In 1926, Birmingham set up a Police Pensioner's Benevolent Fund to help prewar pensioners who lost benefits in the reorganization of the PMAA into the PMAS.[132] In 1927, Liverpool created a special Recognition Fund that helped policemen in financial difficulties due to accidents, sickness and family troubles with small loans.[133] The focus again was on medical needs and economic hardships. Even with their police benefits, policemen and their families could suffer from financial crises and require special assistance just like other working-class families.

In addition to more formal giving, policemen helped colleagues in emergency situations. This charity was part of more general charity networks within the working class where anyone could be faced with an unexpected crisis beyond their financial abilities to cope. In a typical example, when PC Martin's apartment burned down, his division collected £45 to help him replace furniture and effects.[134] Men commonly took collections for constables forced to retire early due to injury or illness. PC McIvor's division collected £15 to help him when he was forced by severe illness to retire,[135] and £66 was raised to set up PC Hubball in a business after he went blind.[136] In 1936, Liverpool constables set up a Police Benevolent Association to regularize such contributions.[137] The higher ranks helped out not only with money but with their particular services. During the war, senior officers found positions for men returning injured from the army. PC Tilley was given a job as a civil clerk at his old scale of pay when found too ill to be a constable, and PC Jones lost an arm but was reinstated and attached to the division training

---

1922). Harrogate was under the management of the International Christian Police Association, founded 1883 (*Police Review*, 4 May 1906, p. 207).

[131] BPO, 16 August 1921, p. 3905; Captain S.A. Wood, 'The Police Mutual Assurance Society, a Notable Achievement', *Police Journal* 3:2 (1931): 242–9.

[132] BPO, 30 July 1926, pp. 11538–40. Men contributed 1d. a week and donated money from dances to buy an insurance policy to cover eighty-five hardship cases. The Retired Officers Association responded, 'We realise that Birmingham is the only Police Force to show in a concrete form their deep sympathy with the old P.M.A.A. members for which we are sincerely grateful.'

[133] The fund was created in 1927 from a subscription of £1256 given to the police in recognition of their services during the 1926 General Strike (LCCO, 20 January 1927).

[134] LCCO, 7, 28 December 1921, 10 January 1922. PCs Russell and Cullon received £32 each after medical retirements (LCCO, 29 June, 28 October 1927).

[135] BPO, 27 March 1908, pp. 283–4.

[136] BPO, 19 January 1923, p. 5954.

[137] LCCO, 15 June 1936. When a member died or retired on medical grounds, other members donated 1d. from their pay, with a minimum of thirteen weeks' membership to benefit.

special constables.[138] Even less patriotic injuries were accommodated. PC Hull, who lost a leg in a rabbiting accident, was given a position in the Fire Brigade telephone and alarm room.[139] Chief constables helped police pensioners find jobs as night watchmen, day time-keepers or security men.[140] These customs of 'passing the hat' and helping each other out through connections were normal working-class mechanisms to cope with unexpected emergencies, and people participated knowing the favour would be returned if necessary.[141]

The extensive documentation of positive civilian and police interaction shows that policemen remained part of the working-class community. Joining the police force did not separate the men from civilian life. Policemen and civilians continually gossiped and fraternized, they participated together in perk and pilfering practices, and they assisted each other in financial crises. They did each other favours, they shared news and information, and they played each other on sports teams. Having a police friend was a reality for many civilians, sometimes a reciprocal relationship or sometimes simply a friendship. The working class created a niche for constables, adapting to the presence of the police force and turning it to their benefit whenever possible. The policemen themselves retained their working-class habits even after years in the force and despite concerted efforts to reform them of their gossipy, pilfering ways.

---

138 BPO, 25 January 1915, p. 440; 16 July 1915, p. 8; 26 July 1918, pp. 92–4; 15 January 1917, p. 529.
139 LWCM, 7 February, 25 April 1933, pp. 30, 94. The watch committee also bought him an artificial limb, price £29.
140 BPO, 8, 10 March 1900, pp. 148–50.
141 See Prochaska, 'Philanthropy', pp. 360–70.

8

The Police and the Public: Women

Complaints having been received from the public of Police
in uniform gossiping and walking with girls and women, it is
pointed out that such conduct is neither seemly nor creditable
to the Force, and offenders will be dealt with on disciplinary
charges. Officers and Sergeants are requested to check all
such conduct and in addition warn females of the result to the
Constable of their action.

Liverpool Chief Constable's Orders, 1919[1]

AS SEEN IN PREVIOUS CHAPTERS, constables had both friendly and acrimonious relationships with civilians, including women, that fit into the larger working-class culture. Police efforts to maintain police neutrality had limited success, and nowhere was discipline more aggravating than when it disrupted men's contacts with women. Women created a particular strain between the strong male culture fostered in police forces which reinforced working-class male chauvinism and force expectations that men behave with the utmost civility. This culture created a tendency to treat women as subordinate at the same time that it created indignation when senior officers meddled in courtships and other consensual relationships. Forces tried to restrict contact with women as much as possible, realizing that the police image was particularly vulnerable when it came to how policemen treated women. Already banned from fraternizing with civilians, constables were discouraged from talking to women to avoid the unfortunate image of men flirting on the job. While any violence towards the public was punished, even minor verbal and physical offences against women, such as asking for or giving unwelcome kisses, met with stiff penalties. Despite police authority concerns, constables were rarely reported for problems involving women. Defaults involving both willing and coerced relationships with women made up only about three per cent of all discipline cases in Manchester, Birmingham and Liverpool, suggesting

---

1   LCCO, 24 October 1919, p. 305.

a combination of forces being reasonably successful in encouraging good behaviour towards women and male police culture being willing to overlook these types of offences. Probably, as well, senior officers remembering their own courting days handled many minor instances informally and simply advised constables to limit their flirtation to off-duty hours.

Constables walking beats certainly had opportunities to meet women unusual for many men. That they worked alone no doubt contributed to the many concerns, real and imagined, regarding constables and women. During the day, they met women working at shops, doing errands and at home doing chores. After dark, they met women out socializing but also runaway girls, prostitutes and drunks. They helped women cross intersections, gave directions and answered questions about trams. Constables had legitimate reasons to talk with women, such as reporting smoking chimneys, lost children and missing property, which could easily stretch into conversations and cups of tea. Like any other police and civilian contact, constables and women enjoyed breaks from their daily routines, sharing information, and making friends. These interactions could lead to friendships and courtships but constables learned to be careful in their behaviour. Indiscreet constables were caught embracing women in doorways, kissing women in sheds, and having intercourse with women in alleys, sometimes ending in pregnancy and bastardy cases. Constables encountered cooperative women, including wives willingly committing adultery, teenage girls sneaking out at night looking for men, and bored domestic servants, but also forced their attentions on women, making improper suggestions, hurling insults and committing assaults. They consorted with prostitutes, often met on their beats and without the prostitute's consent. Some behaviour was banned by police forces worried about the reputation of the force, but was not necessarily condemned by working-class society, similar to other police and civilian interactions. But though constables may have had more possibilities of female company than most men, they risked more for succumbing to temptation. Voluntary relationships carried out during work hours or that created adverse comment were punished. Constables assaulting women, verbally or physically, quickly lost their jobs. Police forces never deviated from their belief that a policeman who could victimize a woman, even a prostitute, was not worthy of the uniform.

Between 1900 and 1939, around 250 cases of sexual misconduct appear in Manchester, Birmingham and Liverpool police records, and many more went unreported. Punishable activities included gossiping and idling with women, verbal harassment, willing and unwilling physical contact, consensual sex, bastardy cases, rape and liaisons with prostitutes. Men could be disciplined for their actions both on and off duty. Not all cases were proven and some spurious charges had vindictive origins. These cases reveal male attitudes towards women that were to some extent shared both by the men reported for misconduct and by the men investigating the charges. A common assumption was that women out after dark without male company could not be entirely respectable. Even women with men were suspect if they were found in questionable circumstances. Another prevalent attitude, particularly in the bastardy cases, was the double standard that men could be in sexual relationships before or outside of marriage and still be good husbands, but women who did so were not as desirable as wives. However, in spite of any perceived lack of respectability of individual women, policemen were expected to defend them as they would any other citizen. Most constables protected women from being victimized, regardless of their respectability, and even prostitutes sent for policemen if they had problems with customers. A significant minority of constables took advantage of women but if caught, they were not likely to remain in the force.

About half of sexual misconduct cases were voluntary relationships that came to the attention of police forces as a result of gossip, misbehaviour on the job, or unwanted pregnancy. A third of these cases involved constables gossiping or idling with women on duty. These resembled similar cases involving men, but forces particularly disliked them for the jokes they provoked at police expense. Physical contact between unmarried couples, such as kissing and embracing, made up another third. Pregnancy and bastardy cases made up the final third. It is difficult to judge how typical these cases were since voluntary relationships only appeared in the records when a constable refused to marry his pregnant girlfriend, got caught with her at work, or was reported by disapproving civilians. Considering that engaged working-class couples would anticipate the wedding night, a great deal of sexual activity most likely was never reported.[2] Some cases, particularly the bastardy cases, were difficult to classify. At least some bastardy cases may have involved the rape of the woman. Some relationships were instigated, often aggressively, by women who followed constables around their beats, and could almost be classified as involuntary on the constable's part.

The other half of the sexual misconduct cases involved constables coercing sex from women or sexually assaulting them in some way. As with any sexual assaults, many women hesitated before telling anyone so no doubt many never made it into police records. These cases almost always took place after dark. A third of these

---

2   See Elizabeth Roberts, *A Woman's Place: An Oral History of Working Class Women 1890–1940* (Oxford: Basil Blackwell, 1984), pp. 16–17, 72–80; Lucinda McCray Beier, '"We Were Green as Grass": Learning about Sex and Reproduction in Three Working-Class Lancashire Communities, 1900–1970', *Social History of Medicine* 16:3 (2003): 461–80; Lucinda McCray Beier, *For Their Own Good: The Transformation of English Working-Class Health Culture, 1880–1970* (Columbus: Ohio State University Press, 2008), pp. 208–63; Steve Humphries, *A Secret World of Sex: Forbidden Fruit: The British Experience 1900–1950* (London: Sidgwick and Jackson, 1988), pp. 18, 26, 46, 67ff, 97ff; and John R. Gillis, *For Better, For Worse: British Marriages, 1600 to the Present* (Oxford: Oxford University Press, 1985), pp. 277–8.

cases involved sexually explicit verbal abuse of women. Another third include unwilling physical contact, such as constables trying to embrace women against their will, and threatening to arrest women unless they cooperated in having sex. A final third of this subset of cases involved prostitutes. While some of these encounters could be categorized as normal business, they repeatedly described constables either coercing prostitutes into having sex in order to avoid arrest or using their authority to obtain favours and bribes. While only a minority of constables used their powers to assault women, they were enough to give policemen a bad name. It was bad enough for a civilian to threaten a woman, it was far worse for a constable paid to protect women to abuse that position. For this reason, any circumstance in which a woman was sexually assaulted in even the smallest way, including verbal remarks, usually lost the constable his job.

Patterns of involuntary and voluntary cases reflect both relaxing attitudes towards sexuality and the link between sexual behaviour and the age of constables. Before the war, involuntary cases outnumbered the voluntary roughly two to one. They were about even during the war and the early 1920s. In the late 1920s and 1930s, the relationship reversed, with voluntary cases occurring twice as often as involuntary cases. The number of involuntary cases before and after the war remained roughly the same, but the voluntary cases doubled as social attitudes relaxed and when a large per centage of constables were young. During the war, few cases made it into the record books because many younger constables were absent at the front and supervision relaxed. The highest periods of all reported sexual activity were just before the war and in the 1920s, both times when the majority of police officers were young men. With the exception of verbal harassment, which occurred at the same level throughout the period, the number of involuntary cases increased immediately after the war, remained high in the early 1920s and declined thereafter. The number of voluntary cases increased rapidly just before the war, and remained high throughout the 1920s before declining in the 1930s. The general decline in the 1930s mirrored the decline in defaults overall as a result of better discipline and decreased drinking. For defaults involving women, the decline also reflected the ageing of constables, many of whom were married and had families by the 1930s.

Before the war, police forces viewed any sexual misconduct, verbal or physical, voluntary or involuntary, as incompatible with police work. A sexual innuendo could end a constable's career. During the war, however, the attitude towards the voluntary cases relaxed slightly. Some policemen entering the army had dependent illegitimate children and forces agreed to pay these children allowances. Wartime brought a more open and active atmosphere of sexuality with poorly supervised young people amassed around army camps and in big cities. After the war, while police forces still reacted strongly against voluntary sexual misconduct, they were more willing to wait and see if any public repercussions occurred before punishing men.[3] Bastardy cases stopped leading to automatic dismissal and misconduct was more likely to lead to fines or reductions than to forced resignations. Nevertheless, a policeman involved in even minor sexual activity on his beat risked losing his job. Involuntary cases continued to lead to dismissal or severe reductions. Policemen were expected to protect women, not take advantage of them, or even appear to take advantage of them.

While for any disciplinary charge, police forces had to be careful that actual infractions were punished and no innocent men were penalized, sexual misconduct charges were especially difficult since most situations had no witnesses. The few investigations for which extensive documentation exists rarely provide a clear picture of what occurred. Statements from the alleged victims and from the constables often seem equally convincing or equally suspect. About ten per cent of all cases were left as 'not proven' or 'not framed' (insufficient evidence to proceed) if no clear evidence pointed one way or the other. Even so, senior officers closely supervised the constables from these cases to make sure that no further situations took place. In only about three per cent of cases were constables found innocent. Some resulted from women getting a constable's collar number wrong, accusing men with clear alibis. In a few cases, women clearly made vindictive false charges against constables. But overall, because of the sexual nature of cases, watch committees and chief constables tended to assume that women only lodged complaints if their stories were genuine. They preferred to err on the side of strictness rather than let a sexual offender go unpunished. This may have encouraged some women to report constables, knowing that the men were likely to be punished, but many women remained hesitant to report such cases to police forces.[4]

In most sexual misconduct cases, the confidential disciplinary reports included more or less unambiguous details but the more public daily orders simply read 'discreditable conduct'. PC Court, for example, was charged with 'indecently assaulting complainant by placing his hand upon her private parts', and Gertrude Rowell accused PC Banning of remaining in her house against her wishes and 'taking hold of her hand & placing same near his private parts'.[5] In both cases,

---

3   Robert Roberts, calling the 1920s the 'high days', described the shock caused by knee-length skirts showing female legs, the 'new permissiveness' and dance halls, as well as the changes in behaviour caused by the knowledge of rubber sheaths acquired by young men during the war and passed on to younger generations. The shortage of young men caused by wartime casualties may also have encouraged women trying to find husbands to be less careful about preventing pregnancy (*The Classic Slum*, pp. 222–4, 229–35).

4   The evidence for the above paragraphs comes from approximately 250 cases from a variety of police records for each city, including police orders, disciplinary report books, personnel files, rosters and daily report books.

5   BDRB, 6 July 1921, PCB 190 Arthur Court, pp. 35–6; BJSC, 15 July 1921, p. 337; BPO, 16 July 1921, p. 3802; part of charge read, 'neglect of duty in not giving safe custody

the phrase 'private parts' was absent from the daily police orders. Since both men were dismissed, rephrasing the charges could not have been to protect their future in the force. As part of this watering down of the public orders, actual or attempted rapes were rarely reported as such, though at least some of the undefined assaults were probably rapes. PC Horner was allowed to resign for 'assaulting a woman', and PC Kinnish was dismissed for 'improperly interfering' with two young women, which could mean anything from embracing them to ravishing them.[6] In one instance that was most likely a rape case, the particulars were so shocking that the chief constable put nothing in writing and only stated the facts verbally.[7] This editing of details did not exist for any other type of charge. Forces may have left the daily orders vague in order to drive home that any unwelcome attention towards women would end a man's career. Possibly, explicit charges were toned down to prevent any sympathy towards guilty constables for getting caught for what might be considered a manly offence.[8] Considering the sexual nature of many of these cases, forces may have decided to keep events quiet to protect those involved and to prevent events from becoming too public.

Roughly half of the reported sexual misconduct cases were voluntary relationships varying from gossiping with women to 'quick ones' in passageways to affairs with married women while their husbands were away. Constables tended to be physically fit, made steady wages and had promotion prospects, so women considered them to be eligible partners both as husbands and lovers. Since working-class couples had difficulties finding privacy, a constable boyfriend had the bonus of knowing about safe places to meet. Policemen could get into trouble for being caught with girlfriends while on the job, often for neglect of duty, but not usually while off duty in plain clothes. Exceptions to this included when a minor was involved or the parents complained. Not surprisingly, constables resented intrusions into their off-duty relationships and some quit rather than accept this level of supervision. If the girlfriend got pregnant, the constable could also get into trouble if he failed to marry her and she complained, or if he failed to keep up with payments in bastardy cases. In all of the voluntary cases, police forces tended to make image their primary consideration in deciding on charges and punishments.

---

to a female'. Birmingham City Police Disciplinary Book 'D' Division, 19 July 1923, PCD 213 William Thomas Banning, dismissed, p. 48; BPO, 27 July 1923, p. 6686.

6   BPO, 3 July 1902, p. 142; LDRB, 24 November 1905, PCB Kinnish, two years' service.

7   PC Cartwright 'disgrac[ed] himself as a Police Constable' by indecently assaulting Harriett Booth, and PC Leivers both acted indecently towards Booth and 'neglect[ed] to protect a respectable woman and conceal[ed] gross misconduct committed by P.C. Cartwright'. Both men were ordered to resign (MWCM, 1 October 1914, PCB 47 George Cartwright, five years' service, one default, four awards; PCB 108 Thomas Leivers, sixteen months' service, vol. 64, no. 166).

8   See Emsley, *The English Police*, pp. 217–23, for evidence of a strong male police culture, and boasts of sexual conquests.

Even talking to a woman while in uniform was considered a serious matter since forces wanted to avoid the stereotype of constables spending their time chatting with domestic servants over the area railings. Gossiping was neglect of duty, but to be caught gossiping with a woman was also 'neither seemly nor creditable to the Force'.[9] Similar to other gossiping, members of the public tended to make complaints after seeing 'members of the Force, especially young Constables, gossiping with women in the streets'.[10] Even constables on traffic point duty managed to pass the time talking with women.[11] Forces saw all this gossiping as a particular problem since, unlike most misconduct with women, it occurred during the day time just as often as at night. In one case, while waiting to give testimony in court, PC Brooks sat talking with a woman and, when challenged by his sergeant, replied that he saw no harm in it.[12] Constables often knew the women as neighbours or friends. When PC Press's sister-in-law saw him while he was observing a brothel in plain clothes, he had her accompany him on part of the road so he would not be suspected of being a constable. While let off with a small fine, the chief constable made it clear that talking to women while on duty was not acceptable in any circumstances.[13] Police forces were not being narrow-minded but rather trying to maintain a professional image of police constables, similar to the broader condemnations of gossiping and fraternizing.

While gossiping and idling tended to be daytime activities, plenty of what the records called 'carnal connection' took place after dark. Constables found plenty of women willing to engage in sexual activity with them, particularly after the war. The status of the majority of these women was difficult to determine since little information was given on them in the records. Women were referred to as 'a girl', 'a young woman', 'a woman' or 'a female', the inference being that 'a female' was lower in class than the girls and women. Any woman aged eighteen or younger was considered to be a girl. Only a tiny portion of cases involved 'females' so most of these women must have been considered to be from respectable families. Women thought to be prostitutes were labelled as such so presumably the women were not simply prostitutes hired or coerced by constables. None of the women was considered to be 'a lady' but it is impossible to know if none was middle or upper class or simply that no woman caught in this situation could be called a lady. Most

---

9   LCCO, 24 October 1919.

10   MGO, 17 September 1925.

11   PCE 202 Charles Henry Taylor managed to regulate traffic and gossip with a woman at the same time and got a caution on his record (BDRB, 29 December 1922, p. 127). PCE 251 William Dayman was reduced in class for gossiping with a female while on traffic duty (Birmingham City Police Defaulters Books, 24 September 1926).

12   MPF, 19 November 1934, PCE 83 Eli Frederick Brooks, appointed January 1922, fined 5/-.

13   MPF, 25 November 1924, PCC 201 Thomas Press, appointed February 1921, fined 5/-.

encounters occurred in doorways, alleys or sheds, similar to any other working-class amorous adventures [14] In one case of particularly poor timing, PC Gildroy was busy with a woman in a doorway and failed to notice that a tobacconist's shop on his beat was on fire.[15] When PC Wright was discovered having intercourse with 'a woman Marion Swindells ... in a passage ... at 11.45 pm ... whilst on duty in uniform', he tried unsuccessfully to explain why Swindells had her arms around him, stating, 'I was only talking to the above woman ... as she said to me you have some white at the back of your coat'.[16] Liverpool policemen assigned to the docks had the option of allowing women into the police dock huts. Some women made a regular habit of hanging out around constables, one girl having affairs with at least three young constables assigned to dock duty.[17] Senior officers tended to assume that any constable alone with a woman could be up to no good. One superintendent thought that PC Tandy had stopped a woman in a car for an immoral purpose. Luckily, Tandy was able to explain that the woman's lights had gone out when she drove over some tram lines and he pulled her over to turn them back on.[18] Given the heavy penalties for being caught in compromising situations with women, constables had to exercise care in their interactions with women, more so than gossiping or fraternizing with men.

Police relationships with women that took place away from work made it into the records if something went wrong or if someone informed the force. Consensual sex that became public tended to receive stiff penalties, such as when PC Taylor and Miss Phyllis Parsons were caught making love in a field by the Worcestershire County Police one Friday afternoon and Taylor was asked to resign.[19] Typically, working-class couples refrained from sex until an engagement existed. If the woman got pregnant, they assumed that they had to move forward their wedding

---

14   Humphries, *A Secret World of Sex*, pp. 29–30. PC Pearson found PCA 123 Ewen in a doorway with a woman 'with his person exposed'. Ewen first ran away and then tried to bribe Pearson (LCCDR, 19 September 1927, denied, charges withdrawn). PC Jump lost his position when he was caught 'acting in an indecent manner towards Mrs Ivy Holliday, (25) ... when in an entry ... on duty in uniform' (BPO, 3 December 1936, PCE 271 Percival Taylor Jump, probationary, p. 26566).

15   BRB, 25 March 1920, PCA 64 Ambrose Gildroy, joined April 1919, to resign; BPO, 25 March 1920, p. 1968.

16   MPF, 14 March 1922, PCB 38 Albert Wright, appointed April 1914, fined 10/-; in 1927 he was reduced two classes for assaulting a neighbour (see p. 279).

17   Over a two-year period, PC Griffiths 'had immoral relations with a girl under 18 years of age' while on duty on the docks and PCs McMain and Mawdesley had relations with the same girl over a fifteen-month period (LDRB, 16 March 1906, PCC 327 Griffiths, ten years' service, to resign; PCC 147 McMain, six years' service, PCC 106 Mawdesley, three years' service, dismissed, they also refused to participate in an identification parade).

18   LCCDR, 9 July 1937, PCG 121 Tandy, explained.

19   BPO, 9 May 1934, p. 22132.

date. In most instances, that was the only consequence of the pregnancy. Police cases involved times when the constable refused to marry the woman either because he did not want to marry her or he believed that he was not the father of the child. Women tended to anticipate the wedding night only if they believed that they were engaged, though exceptions existed. Men, however, were more likely to have sexual relations with women they had no intention of marrying, sometimes misleading the women to get what they wanted. Ironically, a pregnant girlfriend could be discarded for being unrespectable, reflecting common double-standards regarding the toleration of premarital sex for men versus for women.[20] Police evidence does suggest that more premarital sex was taking place in this period than John Gillis or Elizabeth Roberts discovered from oral evidence. Two-thirds of the voluntary cases involved physical contact between unmarried couples; and yet oral evidence suggests that premarital sex was fairly uncommon. Considering that voluntary relationships only made it into the records in unusual circumstances, these cases can be only a small portion of the activity taking place between unmarried couples. Apparently, members of the working class later insisted that premarital sex was rare at the same time that many of them engaged in it. Considering the links between sexuality and respectability, especially for women, this reticence is not surprising. Since couples generally married, premarital sex may later have been remembered as part of the marriage so not really counting as inappropriate.[21]

One well-documented case, though unusual in the extent of the charges, illustrates a number of typical situations that made it into the records, including different expectations where the woman assumed pregnancy would lead to marriage but the man did not. PC Bamford got at least three women pregnant over seven years and tried to convince two of them to terminate the pregnancy using illegal abortifacients. He had known each of the women for years, either from his beat or as friends of the family. What is clear is that Bamford had no intention of marrying any of them even though they were from eligible backgrounds. In one case, he had known thirty-year-old Florence Cheetham for three years since his beat included a hotel where she was a domestic servant. In 1937, they had gone to a public house together and later had sex in a passage way. As he left, he said, 'Name it after me kid.' He did not see her until a month later when she told him she was pregnant. He answered, 'Fancy you having a baby. Come on and I'll see what I can do.' He took her into another passage, had sex with her again, and told her to go to a woman who could start her periods again. He added that he had got another woman pregnant

20   Beier, "'We Were Green as Grass'", pp. 474–5; Gillis, *For Better*, pp. 277–8; Roberts, *A Woman's Place*, pp. 15–16, 72–80; Humphries, *A Secret World of Sex*, pp. 67ff, 95ff; Jeffrey Weeks, *Sex, Politics and Society: the Regulation of Sexuality since 1800* (New York: Longman, 1989), pp. 60–3.

21   See Beier, "'We Were Green as Grass'", for analysis of how oral accounts and actual events could diverge in the case of premarital sexual activity to protect reputations.

and this treatment had worked within a fortnight. When she tried to get him to help pay for the treatment, he laughed it off. She later wrote to Bamford, asking why he had not answered her letters after she had done as he had asked, 'going to that so called lady doctor taking stuff to move what nature put there, throwing away hard earned money every week without results'. She hoped that they were 'destined to face the world' together, clearly wishing that he would marry her. When she finally contacted the police force in desperation, he claimed that Cheetham had followed him around his beat and made such a nuisance of herself that he requested her to leave him alone while on duty. He denied having sex with her. Two months later she died from complications from the abortifacient drugs but no solid evidence could connect Bamford to her death.[22] In 1939, Bamford got his sister-in-law's sister, Lily Neill, pregnant. Neill wrote to the chief constable asking if Bamford planned on paying maintenance. Bamford again denied the accusation. In 1943, he got Anne Scally pregnant, tried to get her to use illegal abortifacients, and again denied that the baby was his. No promise of marriage was mentioned by the women, but both Cheetham and Scally assumed that he would marry them after they got pregnant. Since Bamford denied everything, the chief constable could do little unless the women took Bamford to court for maintenance. Cheetham had died and neither Neill or Scally went to court. However, the information was kept in Bamford's personnel file and his superintendents informed of the cases. No further cases appeared and he may have married a nurse he had been courting. Perhaps he settled down after marriage and after his senior officers made it clear that his conduct was under scrutiny and that no more accusations would be tolerated. He remained a constable and no commendations appeared in his file so this may have hindered possible advancement.[23] While no other case on this scale was documented, it is significant for showing the extent of Bamford's sexual encounters, the willingness of women from respectable families to go along with him, and his knowledge of acquiring abortifacients. At least some members of the working class had embraced the more permissive atmosphere.

Not only men could be aggressive in looking for willing company. Women,

---

22   A policewoman was sent to the shop with a cover story to get the pills and potion which were then analysed. The pills contained aloes, a cathartic, and the potion penny-royal, an aromatic oil containing benzene. The use of abortifacients was not uncommon and often was disguised as medicine to help a woman's regularity. See Humphries, *A Secret World of Sex*, pp. 76–7; Jane Lewis, *Women in England, 1870–1950: Sexual Divisions and Social Change* (Bloomington: Indiana University Press, 1984), pp. 17–18; Roberts, *The Classic Slum*, pp. 127–8; Beier, *For Their Own Good*, pp. 246–52. Humphries mentioned savin, rye, lead, gunpowder, iron filings and rusty water as traditional remedies, and Roberts mentioned penny-royal syrup, aloes, turpentine and 'the controlled fall downstairs'. Lewis discussed abortions as a 'female initiative' which here was obviously not the case.

23   MPF, 9, 11 December 1937; 20, 24, 25 July; 18, 22 September 1939; 9, 10, 11 March 1943; PCC 30 James Gamble Bamford, appointed March 1931.

even young teenagers, who found a uniform with a steady income attractive went so far as to follow constables around on their beats night after night. More than one instance showed women pursuing constables, sometimes looking for marriage but other times only looking for male company. In a detailed Manchester case, sixteen-year-old Mary Kemp routinely approached constables on their beats in the central 'A' Division. Her parents had died when she was fourteen, and since then she had been working as a domestic servant. Clearly, she made a practice of sneaking out at night to meet men. Her story came out when she was picked up by a sergeant after fainting in the street and she was found to be 'destitute and orphaned'. Kemp had no qualms about giving detailed statements about her sexual conduct. Accusations against PC Butcher were serious enough to lead to his dismissal. In Kemp's statement, she had been waiting for a tram car around 11:30 pm when Butcher offered to walk her home when he came off duty at midnight. When they met, he instead asked her to go home with him and she consented. He then took her to his lodging house, where they sat together on a sofa. She stated, 'I turned my back to him he then struggled and pulled me back. I told him if he didn't stop it I would scream.' Eventually, they had intercourse and fell asleep, and he took her back into town early the next morning. She looked for him the next night and she went with him again. This time, they had sex in a passageway. She came to his beat once more the next week and they went back to his lodgings and had sex again. She visited his beat one final time only to learn that he was talking to another girl. She refused to speak to him after this. According to her statement, she was not a prostitute because she wanted nothing from him. It is impossible to know how much of Kemp's statement was accurate. She could easily have drawn on other experiences to make her statement since it is apparent that she wandered the streets at night on a regular basis, and her jealousy gave her a motive for getting Butcher into trouble. Even though she provided explicit details on her sexual encounters, her tone remained utterly detached. Her initial resistance to Butcher seemed more for the benefit of the interviewer, and she did not seem particularly upset about it. Except for her jealousy of the other girl, Kemp did not appear to have had any particular feelings about Butcher nor did she bring up any thoughts of marrying him.[24] What is clear from this case, the Bamford case, and similar instances in the records is that men and women looking for sexual encounters outside of steady relationships or promises of marriage could find them.

Women who got pregnant and expected the men to marry them sometimes turned to police forces to force the constables to cooperate. But this needed to be used as a last resort since constables often lost their jobs in consequence. When

---

24   MWCM, 22 September 1931, PCA 108 Ernest Butcher, eighteen months' service, dismissed, unsuccessful appeal, vol. 153, no. 34; also MPF, PCA 82 James Wilfred Percy, appointed September 1930, case not proven.

she became pregnant, Miss Hafferty gave PC Hardy 'the chance to marry her & he has refused'. After she complained to the police, the chief constable decided that he 'was not satisfied with Cons Conduct & advised him to resign' which he did.[25] The lack of commitment to a serious relationship of some men was apparent. PC Cropper resigned from the force at his own request when he found out that his girlfriend was pregnant, thinking it would hurt his career. When it turned out to be a false alarm, he asked to be reinstated, adding that he was 'willing either to marry the girl or have nothing further to do with her'. His readmission was declined.[26] Men often resigned before investigations could be carried out, preferring to avoid embarrassing revelations or being compelled into marriage. They may also have hoped that resigning rather than being dismissed might improve their future employment prospects. In a typical example, after getting his landlady's daughter pregnant, PC Thompson promised to marry her but then refused to 'assist her in any way'. He denied the charges but resigned before the case proceeded.[27] In all of the pregnancy cases, the men without exception denied being the fathers even though they often admitted having sex with the women. The women often admitted having had 'connection' with the man only once, trying to protect their own reputations. Since constables in these cases tended to be young with only a few years' experience, this was often their first experience with this level of police intrusion into their private lives. This was another reason at least to consider resigning.

Sometimes other family members reported constables for getting women pregnant, hoping that a marriage could restore the family's respectability. The step-father of Irene Casson, aged eighteen, reported PC Smythe for getting Casson pregnant. Smythe admitted to 'misconduct' with Casson and promised to marry her, but he still denied that he was the father of her baby. Smythe insisted that 'the girl's parents are trying to force the marriage to save her character'. The chief constable decided that Smythe's 'behaviour reveals him to be unfitted for the service' and he was discharged.[28] Relatives of constables were not immune from involvement in these loves gone wrong and showed that constables were often refusing to marry women from their own class who were eligible as wives. PC Pendleton lodged with the parents of PC Lonsdale and their daughter. Pendleton and Miss Lonsdale 'misconducted' themselves and she became pregnant. When PC Lonsdale reported Pendleton for getting his sister pregnant, Pendleton made

25   LCCDR, 6 September 1927, PCB 136 Hardy, complainant Miss M. Hafferty, 40 Newtown Street, Duns, Berwickshire.
26   LWCM, 19 January 1914, p. 202.
27   LCCDR, 13 November 1930, PCD 121 Thompson, complainant Miss Florence Smith, c/o Nurse Smith, Chalbury, Charlington, Oxford, denied, resigned, no charge was framed.
28   LCCDR, 3 April 1929, PCD 133 Smythe, complainant H. Salisbury, 4 Holland Street, stepfather of Irene.

'a false accusation against Con 389 G Lonsdale'. The accusation was not specified but may have been getting his sister into bad company or possibly incest. Pendleton resigned before the case proceeded.[29] Even though their daughters and sisters became pregnant outside of marriage, these male relatives did not disown the women but rather took action either to protect the woman though a marriage or to punish the man for his bad conduct. However, while they spared the women from having to complain themselves, some women no doubt would have preferred to keep their situations private.

In some cases, the constables' denials of being the fathers of children were found to be correct on investigation. These false accusations resulted from women looking to blame any convenient man for their condition, genuinely uncertain of who the father might be, or making malicious charges against constables. When Marjory Roome, aged twenty-one, gave birth to a child at her parents' home, she told them that PC Hill was the father. Hill denied the charge and investigations proved that it was 'a mere concoxtion [sic]'. Possibly she gave his name to protect the real father or because she did not know for certain herself when her parents insisted that she give a name.[30] In another case where the woman may have had more than one lover, Nellie May Blissitt accused PC Jackson of being the father of her child. She filed a bastardy case but this proved that Jackson was not the father of the baby since it had been conceived a month before he met Blissitt. Jackson's superintendent 'gave Con some good advice & put him on his guard against circumstances of this kind arising in future'.[31] The constables facing these accusations were fortunate that their lack of responsibility could be proven. It is quite possible that other constables could not prove their innocence and were disciplined or lost their jobs as a consequence.

While police forces could not compel constables to marry women, they could make constables pay if women went to court and got a maintenance agreement. In some of the bastardy cases, the constable had no intention of marrying the woman due to her lower status or, ironically, due to her character. But in most cases,

---

29   LCCDR, 28 March 1923, PCH 316 Pendleton, complainant PCH 389 Lonsdale. In another case involving a constable's family, while the family of PC Pepper was on holiday, PCE 94 Galloway visited their house without their consent to see Edith Rice, seventeen years old, and 'there had carnal connections' with her. Rice was the sister-in-law of PC Pepper, with whom she was lodging. Three months later he was found in a doorway 'having carnal connections with Edith Rice'. Galloway denied the charges but resigned before the case could proceed (LCCDR, 16 October 1933).
30   MPF, 1 September 1928, PCB 139 Victor Edward Hill, appointed February 1920; Roome's parents had no idea she was pregnant until the baby was born. She claimed to have had connection with Hill once along a road.
31   LCCDR, 13 July 1928, PCF 149 Jackson. Mary Harkin had a bastardy summons served against PCA 255 Irving but the case was dismissed when it came to trial (LCCDR, 13 April 1924).

the woman was obviously from the same class as the constable and sometimes a friend of the family or a neighbour. For personal reasons, sometimes involving an engagement to another woman, the constable did not want to marry the woman or had changed his mind about the relationship. Before the war, successful bastardy cases generally led to dismissal of the constable since such public misconduct was considered to bring discredit on the reputation of the force. This was hardly to the benefit of the woman and child since it took away their source of support. Since constables knew that bastardy cases would lose them their jobs, police forces usually did not learn of maintenance orders unless the constable got into arrears on his payments. Constables sometimes lied to protect their jobs. After being served with a bastardy summons, PC Davis told his superiors that the case against him had been withdrawn and he denied any involvement with the woman. He was called upon to resign when an inquiry proved that he had actually settled the matter out of court to save his position.[32] During the war this strict attitude changed. It was now thought to be better for the reputation of the force that constables fulfil their responsibilities. Dependents of policemen in the armed forces were paid the standard weekly stipend even if they were illegitimate children.[33] This policy continued after the war, and the number of bastardy cases more than doubled. This gave the women an advantage not shared by most women since they could appeal to the chief constable if child support payments became delinquent without risking constables losing their jobs. When PC Jones twice got behind in his payments, each time arrangements were made to ensure proper payments. On the second occasion, he was warned that he would be dismissed if it happened again.[34] As long as the men supported their children, no disciplinary charges were made against them and their jobs were not affected.[35]

One interwar bastardy case was reported in detail due to extenuating circumstances that required extra action from the police. While more complex than typical cases, it shows a variety of issues that commonly arose when men got women pregnant, refused to marry them, and made child support agreements. In April 1926, PC James Hunter began 'keeping company' with Ellen McBride, a letter-press feeder employed by one of the city councillors. She understood that this relationship was being conducted 'with a view to marriage'. At the same time,

---

32   BPO, 13 September 1912, p. 255.

33   A weekly payment of 5/- was continued to the illegitimate child of PC Holbrook when he joined the army (LWCM, 28 September 1914, p. 109).

34   LCCDR, 18 March, 25 July 1921, PCB 69 Jones, complainant Chief Inspector Walsh, warrant department.

35   PCD 119 Dodd was summoned in a bastardy case, the matter was adjourned as long as he made his payments (LCCDR, 17 June 1922). When PCG 144 Kilduff got Hilda Davies pregnant, the matter was adjourned as long as no public scandal resulted and he paid for the maintenance of the child (LCCDR, 8 August 1929, p. 136).

however, PC Hunter was courting a schoolteacher from Newcastle. '[C]ertain things have happened between J. Hunter' and McBride and she became pregnant. In July, when she told him, he told her that he was engaged to the teacher but that he would do the right thing and marry her instead. She feared, correctly, that he was lying to her, and he married the schoolteacher that weekend. She wrote to the Manchester chief constable for help and in November 1926, a legal agreement was drawn up between McBride and Hunter, arranging for him to pay her £20 when she was confined and a further £50 if the child lived for three weeks. These payments discharged any further obligations from Hunter for the support of the child, and McBride promised not to divulge the child's parenthood or apply for an affiliation order against him. Possibly McBride did not pursue a normal maintenance order against Hunter since she preferred getting the lump sums rather than weekly payments.

PC Hunter's tidy plan to put his premarital adventures behind him came apart almost immediately when his lover and wife did not behave as he anticipated. For obscure reasons, McBride was befriended by Hunter's wife during the pregnancy. This friendship could have resulted from Mrs Hunter's jealousy, generosity or curiosity about her husband's former lover and child. In April 1927 the child was born and Hunter paid £20 towards McBride's stay in a nursing home. McBride then began making demands for money not in the original agreement, including asking for £20 so that she could have the child adopted. A week later, McBride showed up with the baby while only Mrs Hunter was home, told her that she had to leave for a few days because her mother was dying, and left the baby with Mrs Hunter. Eleven days later, the Hunters still had the baby since the children's home that set up adoptions could not take it until arrangements were made for its care. Leaving the baby with the Hunters may have been McBride's way of punishing Hunter for his treatment of her. When the baby was three weeks old, Hunter did not pay McBride the £50, wanting to wait until the baby was placed in a home. He feared that McBride would take the money and disappear, leaving him with the child. McBride proceeded to apply for an affiliation order, still leaving the baby with the Hunters and not going to see it. In response, Mrs Hunter paid McBride the £50 on her own initiative, and McBride dropped the maintenance order. The baby was presumably placed in a home, for nothing else appeared on the matter in the files.[36]

This case shows a man trying to minimize the consequences of getting a woman pregnant and her efforts to get as much restitution as she could and to punish him for abandoning her. It is unlikely that Mrs Hunter knew of her husband's involvement with Ellen McBride until after she married him. It could not have been an encouraging start for a marriage to know that her husband had got another

---

[36]   MPF, 23 July, 15, 27 November 1926, 25 April, 5 May 1927, PCA 83 James Scott Hunter, appointed July 1925.

woman pregnant while he was courting her and then to have the mother leave the baby on her hands. McBride believed that it was her right to have Hunter pay for the baby's care since he was responsible for it and had refused to do the right thing by marrying her. A man engaged to two women did occur now and then, though not usually with such dramatic results. Hunter may have hoped that the woman who got pregnant first would be the one he wanted to marry though no evidence suggests that he had sex with his wife before the marriage. He may have used the excuse of an engagement to get McBride to have sex with him without any intention of marrying her, a common enough tactic. While this story was unusual, the case shows both typical patterns and the willingness of McBride to use whatever power she had to get satisfaction from Hunter.

About fifteen per cent of the consensual relationships involved single constables having affairs with married women. Most of these women had absent husbands, either because they worked away from home or because the couple was separated. When a husband was absent for extended periods, some groups within the working class did not necessarily view adultery as wrong. In the case of sailors' wives, it was reasonably normal for the wife to find someone else to support her while her husband was at sea into the early decades of the twentieth century.[37] In Liverpool, constables could easily meet wives of sailors on their beats and some of these friendships became love affairs. Wives of commercial travellers also had affairs with constables. These affairs could last months or years, and in a few cases the couple would have married if they had been able to legally. Police forces did not like the gossip these affairs created, especially since constables often met the women while on duty. To remove the temptation to idle at the homes of their lovers while on duty, constables were occasionally transferred to different parts of the city. But like other relationships between consenting adults, authorities only heard about them if the affair broke down, if the couple was indiscreet or if a disapproving neighbour complained.[38]

Similar to bastardy cases, police forces became less strict about these relationships after the war. Before the war, men were likely to be severely punished. When PC Piltam was discovered having a five-month affair with a woman whose husband was in South Africa, he had to resign,[39] and after PC Murphy was seen sharing a drink with a married woman in a public house before going home with her, he was reduced in class.[40] After the war, the chief source of concern for police forces

37   Gillis, *For Better*, pp. 234, 252; Judith Walkowitz, 'Jack the Ripper and the Myth of Male Violence', *Feminist Studies* 8:3 (1982): 543–74.
38   None of the cases listed husbands as the complainant. In some cases married couples were separated. In others, either the husband never discovered the affair or possibly he did not want to admit its existence to the police.
39   LDRB, 10 February 1911, PCC 288 Piltam, two years' service.
40   LDRB, 17 December 1910, PCE 125 Murphy, three years' service, reduced in class.

was when these relationships became public knowledge. They tended to suspend action until they knew whether or not an affair had public ramifications. When PC Bowe was caught having an affair with Elsie Atkins while her husband was at sea, the case was adjourned 'to see if there is any development in the shape of legal proceedings'. Bowe was told he would have to resign if the case became public and was ordered to keep away from Mrs Atkins.[41] Even in quite serious cases, forces chose to take no action. For at least two years during his annual leave, PC Stokes carried on an affair with Mrs Evans in Southampton and she eventually had a child. Mr Evans had deserted his wife and his ship and the chief constable decided that 'the only thing possible at the moment is to await further developments'.[42] Even though these affairs did not result in automatic punishment, the men were ordered to keep away from the women. PC Fawcett was only cautioned after being seen by a neighbour associating with a married woman in the absence of her husband, but he was also warned to stay away from the woman in future.[43] In a few cases, constables chose the relationship over their job. PC Waldron gave up fifteen years in the force instead of ending his visits to a married woman which had become the source of neighbourhood gossip and letters to the chief constable.[44]

What is apparent from the police evidence is that sexual activity was going on among unmarried couples in spite of oral evidence suggesting that the majority of young women in this period were sexually ignorant and waited until marriage to engage in sexual behaviour. While only about 100 cases of consensual sex exist in the Manchester, Birmingham and Liverpool police records, only exceptional cases came to the attention of police forces. Oral histories revealing working-class parents determined to guard their daughters from premarital pregnancy indicate the disconnect between real fears and assertions that young women had waited until marriage. If the woman got pregnant, a quick marriage somehow negated the premarital status of the sex which preserved the respectability of family but also skewed later memories of events.[45] Police cases indicate a relatively steady rate of consensual sexual activity from 1900 to 1914. In the 1920s when a large proportion of policemen were young, the average number of reported cases doubled. Most probably voluntary activity was increasing at an even faster rate since forces had stopped automatically dismissing men for consensual sexual offences, and the official stigma attached to sexual activity was lessening. During the 1930s, reported cases dropped once the young generation of officers had married, but continuing official

---

41   LCCDR, 30 November 1929, PCA 341 Bowe, cautioned.
42   LCCDR, 5 February 1934, PCF 225 Stokes.
43   LCCDR, 18 June 1932, PCE 194 Fawcett, cautioned, complainant Mrs E. Everden, Rockhouse, Haslingden Lane.
44   LDRB, 24 November 1905, PCB 196 Waldron, fifteen years' service, two defaults, reduced to probationary class, resigned on own request.
45   Beier, '"We Were Green as Grass"', pp. 466–71.

leniency suggests that post-war consensual sexual activity remained more frequent than prewar levels. The change may not have been large but the numbers indicate that postwar society was at least moderately more permissive than before.

At the same time that consensual sexual activity was increasing in frequency, the number of coerced sexual offences was declining. Similar to the voluntary cases, reported unwilling cases remained relatively steady before the war. They increased by about fifty per cent from 1920 to 1924, but then dropped rapidly to half of the voluntary cases and continued dropping in the 1930s. The overall drop happened five years sooner than the drop in voluntary offences. While consensual relationships may have been tolerated, police forces continued to punish coerced sexual contact after the war just as severely as before, and disobedient constables were quickly weeded out. Most involuntary sexual misconduct cases, including verbal harassment, occurred either late at night or early in the morning. It is difficult to establish the class of most of the women, but the majority appear to be working class. A few women were described as 'a young lady' or 'a lady', but that is the only indication that they may have been middle or upper class. Unlike the voluntary cases that were often brought to police attention in complaints by the women, their families or their neighbours, the majority of involuntary cases were reported by police officers who had either witnessed an offence or had one brought to their attention. By their nature, sexual assaults were more likely to attract public and police attention than couples looking for privacy. In the few cases with a civilian complainant, women outnumbered men about two to one. While some were prostitutes angry at constables for taking advantage of them, the rest show that at least some women were willing to speak up for themselves even in sexual cases. Police forces took all of these cases seriously, and the constables accused were likely to lose their jobs.

About a third of the involuntary sexual misconduct complaints made against constables involved verbal harassment. This varied from mild sexual innuendoes to graphic requests. Unlike other forms of sexual misconduct, which declined after the mid-1920s, verbal harassment occurred consistently throughout the period. Like other sexually related cases, the published descriptions of verbal harassment could be vague. PC Hewitt was dismissed after he 'made suggestions to a girl', and PC Reynolds was dismissed for 'whistling after and signalling to a lady'.[46] Perhaps chief constables wanted to avoid giving anyone ideas. The recorded comments were clearly inappropriate and suggestive. They included examples such as when PC Mather told a lady, 'The first opportunity I have I'll pinch you',[47] and when

---

46 LDRB, 10 November 1907, PCC 230 Hewitt, thirteen years' service, three defaults; 8 May 1909, PCE 115 Reynolds, thirteen years' service, seven defaults.

47 LDRB, 23 July 1910, PCB 197 Mather, twenty-three years' service, five defaults, fined 20/- and warned for dismissal.

PC Lane asked Mrs Beresford 'to accompany him to a dark place' when she was walking home from the railway station late one evening.[48] Women alone at night were the most common sufferers of verbal harassment since they were assumed not to be respectable. For similar reasons, nurses in their identifiable uniforms were another frequent target. Nurses had a popular reputation for being 'easy' since their work required contact with naked bodies. One probationary constable had his services dispensed with after shouting at two women on their way to a hospital 'remarks which were of an improper character',[49] and PC Broomfield 'waved his arms and made gestures to nurses in the Liverpool Women's Hospital' on three occasions.[50] Police forces developed little tolerance for these infractions due to the negative image of the police that it created, and men caught making remarks often lost their jobs. Women could not be expected to trust an organization of men which called them graphic names or made sexual suggestions.

One set of women who could not be considered unrespectable were women at home who were visited by constables in the line of duty. Yet they, too, were the targets of unwelcome remarks. Domestic inquiries gave constables a chance to make suggestive comments without witnesses, and the voluntary relationships show that some wives were open to such ideas. But constables who guessed wrong could find themselves reported. While investigating a chimney fire at Mrs Wilkins' house, for instance, PC Binning made 'an improper adulterous suggestion'.[51] On the other hand, someone unhappy about an inquiry could get a little revenge by charging the policeman with inappropriate behaviour. Since these cases tended to involve only the constable and the woman, around fifteen per cent were dismissed for lack of confirmation. This is rather higher than the overall ten per cent case dismissal rate for sexual misconduct charges. In one case, Mrs Brooks accused PC Miller of making 'indecent suggestions to her' while he was checking her dog's licence, but his explanation of the event was accepted.[52] Some women no doubt misinterpreted remarks not meant to be inappropriate, and some were more sensitive than others to comments meant to be friendly.

One detailed complaint illustrates the difficulties in establishing the facts in a case of domestic verbal harassment. Mrs Elsie Jones accused PC Mayer of making advances towards her while she was babysitting a neighbour's children. According

---

48   Birmingham City Police Defaulters Books, 25 August 1903, PC Henry Thomas Lane, to resign, p. 273.

49   BPO, 29 July 1929, PCE 203 Allison Gray, p. 15626.

50   LDRB, 25 April 1933, PCB 121 Broomfield, thirteen years' service, fined 20/-.

51   Birmingham City Police Disciplinary Book 'D' Division, 19 March 1926, PCD 40 Robert James Binning, dismissed, p. 81; BDRB, 22 March 1926, p. 40; BPO, 24 March 1926, p. 11093. He also neglected to report the fire.

52   Birmingham City Police Disciplinary Book 'D' Division, 19 August 1935, PCD 119 Isaac Edwin Miller, pp. 151–2; BOR, 17 October 1935.

to her statement, Mayer came to the door to tell her that the house's chimney was on fire. She had him look around the house but no fire was discovered. Mayer left but came back ten minutes later, saying the chimney was still smoking. He then asked if she would be in later, and she replied that she would. At around eleven that evening, Mayer showed up again and asked for a cup of tea. Jones declined, saying that she was going to bed. She stated that Mayer asked,

> 'Won't you feel lonely without your husband?' I replied 'I'm not man mad. The best thing for you is to go home to your wife and family.' He asked me if I thought he was as bad as all that and I told him I did. He told me he had ten minutes to spare and said 'You don't want rocking to sleep to-night.' and suggested I put out the light so nobody could see us. He said 'Well you'll be quite alright. You won't hear anything more about it' and then left the house.

Mayer denied the entire story, stating that there had indeed been a chimney fire. He argued that Mrs Jones had made up the charge against him so she could explain to the parents why a policeman had been to the house without admitting to any neglect. Mrs Jones entered the Manchester Royal Infirmary for a week and then needed ten days to convalesce after the above events, apparently for a nervous disorder, and Mayer called into question her reliability as a witness. Her nervous condition could have been a reaction to the constable's visits or could have contributed to her turning a simple professional visit into a dramatic delusion. Given her illness, the watch committee took the charge seriously, getting detailed statements from Mayer. In the end, they decided not to charge Mayer with any offence, implying that Mrs Jones' version of events was finally not convincing.[53]

Another third of the involuntary cases did not stop with verbal harassment but involved inappropriate physical contact. Police forces included all uninvited touching in the definition of physical assaults of women by constables. Kissing or embracing a woman against her will was classified as assault, as PC Beddows learned after he was reduced in class for 'assaulting a young woman' after he took hold of Clara Carter, a domestic servant, pushed her against a wall, and kissed her.[54] More often, constables caught 'interfering' with women lost their jobs, no matter how mild the action might appear to them. For example, after 'taking hold of the arm of Lily Bryenton (22) ... and saying to her, "Give me a Kiss"', PC Moss had to resign.[55] One constable who could not keep his hands to himself lost his

---

[53]   MWCM, 29 January, 26 March 1939, vol. 222, no. 26.
[54]   BRB, 14 April 1913, PCE 197 William Beddows, joined October 1909; BPO, 16 April 1913, p. 425.
[55]   BOR, 5 June 1930; Birmingham City Police Disciplinary Book 'D' Division, 25 June 1930, PCD 93 Frederick Moss, pp. 110–11.

job after seventeen years of service. While waiting in Albert Square for election results, three young women had gone to stand near PC Brennan to be safe from some rowdy youths in the crowd. Much to the embarrassment of one woman, Brennan 'placed his hand around her waist and on other parts of her body in a most unbecoming and improper manner'. When she discovered that he had done the same to another of the women, she took his number and they reported him. That the women had approached the constable looking for safety made Brennan's behaviour especially offensive, leading to his resignation.[56]

More serious cases involved constables frightening women into sexual acts. These cases tended to involve women that constables considered to be in already compromising situations. A common group appearing in the records were girls found wandering at night alone. Constables were supposed to take them home or to a shelter, but some took advantage of the situation. When Elvira Eliss complained to PC Wale that she was homeless, he took her into a yard and behaved indecently towards her instead of taking her to a girls' shelter.[57] Any woman out after dark could be vulnerable. In one example, Sarah Murphy and her boyfriend met PC Southwick in a passage late one evening. Southwick told the boy to leave, flattened Murphy against a wall with his body, 'kissing her and putting his tongue in her mouth against her will'. Murphy was terrified that Southwick would rape her, saying that his body was 'trembling'. He finally left when some people walked into the passage. Possibly Southwick targeted Murphy since he assumed that she had gone into the passage with her boyfriend for some private embraces, and so saw her as unrespectable.[58] Married women were just as liable to be assaulted as single women, perhaps since constables considered sexually experienced women to be a better target than single women. While Anna Murphy and her husband were arguing in the street late one night, PC Vaughan came up and told the husband to leave. He gave Murphy a cigarette and told her he would be back. He found her later, and asked 'Can we go somewhere and have a bit properly.' Murphy stated, 'I then stood beside the wall, and he opened his fly-hole and put my hand on his person, and he got me to rub him off ... I would not have gone with him only he said if I did not he would lock me up.' Fortunately for Murphy, two sergeants witnessed all of this, including the fight between the Murphys. Vaughan tried to get the sergeants to overlook it since he was supposed to be getting married and

---

[56]   MWCM, 6 June 1929, PCA 271 Patrick Brennan, seventeen years' service, two defaults, ordered to resign; MGO, 7 June 1929.

[57]   BDRB, 8 February 1923, PCA 163 Alexander Wale, reprimanded, p. 136. Instead of directing two teenage girls to a night shelter, PCA 58 Alexander Bell was found in a room with them (Birmingham City Police Defaulters Books, 24 September 1926, also charged with not reporting that the room was insecure, cautioned).

[58]   MPF, 16 January 1932, PCC 19 William Southwick, appointed December 1926, reduced two classes and transferred.

this 'will spoil it all' but Murphy was more than willing to testify against him.[59] These cases were typical in that constables found women in the streets at night and forced them into sexual acts. More unusually, two of the woman had men with them who left when the constables ordered them to go. Neither man tried to protect the women, perhaps intimidated or unaware of the constables' intentions. The constables may have seen these women as more sexually available since they were already willing to be out after dark with men.

Even policemen carrying out their duties without any intention of harming women tended to assume that women out alone at night must be up to no good and likely to be a prostitute. In a typical case, after Mollie Baillie asked a man for tram fare, a sergeant and constable who had witnessed this began following her around and questioning her about what she was doing, presuming that she must have been propositioning the man.[60] Blameless women suspected by constables could go through frightening experiences, and have a difficult time convincing the police of their innocence. One domestic servant waiting for friends on a street corner was grabbed by a plain-clothes constable who assumed that she was a prostitute. Not knowing who he was, she called for a uniformed constable. Instead of helping, he took her to the station on suspicion of soliciting. Luckily for her, a clergyman who had witnessed the scene bailed her out and swore that the young woman had done nothing wrong.[61] Women could find their reputations damaged and go through the disgrace of being arrested simply through being out after dark.

Women did make spurious accusations of sexual assault against constables for a variety of reasons. In a case where a girl may have been trying to hide her own misconduct, Sarah Jones, aged fifteen, was given money out of charity by PCF 123, and she later accused him of having 'connections with her at a house' nearby. Her charge was found to be without merit but F 123 was warned not to give money to girls.[62] Simple misidentification of the constable probably occurred fairly often, especially since most encounters took place after dark. Nellie Russell charged that PC Harrison had arrested her for being a prostitute and then assaulted her. Fortunately for Harrison, he had been assigned to station duty on the evening in question and could not have arrested her.[63] Possibly a sexual encounter had been

---

59   MPF, 19 December 1937, PCA 231 Alan Vaughan, appointed November 1935, reduced to lowest class, married September 1939 but unknown if to the woman he was to marry in 1937.
60   BPO, 25 April 1934, p. 22064; BOR, 19 April 1934, PSA 8 David Cooper, twenty-six years' service, to resign on pension, PCA 188 William Thornber, nine years' service, severely cautioned.
61   LWCM, 13 May 1901, pp. 59–60.
62   LCCDR, 29 February 1928, PCF 123. This constable was not named in the records, which was unusual. The reason for this can only be guessed.
63   BRB, 13 October 1910, PCC Major Beman Harrison, joined December 1907, later a chief superintendent, case dismissed.

consensual but the woman reported the occurrence as an assault for vindictive reasons. She might have hoped that if she became pregnant, the charge would put the blame onto the man or force him to marry her. About fifteen per cent of all cases did not result in charges, but only in three per cent were constables found innocent. When a constable was exonerated, it can be assumed that evidence supported that verdict since other cases were listed as 'not proven' due to a lack of evidence.

The truth behind some accusations of assault was impossible to discover because of conflicting testimony. If it was apparent that some kind of unseemly behaviour had taken place, the constable would be punished for a less serious default that could be proven. PC Rae was charged with indecently assaulting a nineteen-year-old woman in a field by 'putting his hand up her clothing on to her private parts without her consent', with being in a compromising position with the woman, and with neglecting his duty through gossiping with her. The first and third charges were withdrawn but he was dismissed for the second. Deciding that something inappropriate had occurred, the chief constable used the one charge for which he had evidence to get rid of the constable.[64] Sometimes, it was unclear if inappropriate contact had occurred at all. Mrs Watts accused PC Brown of entering her shop while she was out and remaining to talk with her daughter Mary, aged eighteen. The charge that Brown had 'placed his arms around [Mary] & kissed her, which conduct she resented' was dismissed since testimony conflicted, and Brown was instead cautioned for idling in the shop and for not reporting Mrs Watts' complaint. The chief constable may have concluded that this was simply a flirtation gone wrong or disapproved of by the mother.[65] In a few cases, constables could not be charged due to contradictory evidence. Catherine Cassidy accused PC Maquire of raping her and PC Bolton of saying, 'I don't want to shag you I only want to feel your breasts' after watching Maquire. However, the entries in the constables' notebooks about their location contradicted her statement and no charge could be proven.[66] Records of such cases were kept on file, nevertheless, in case the constables became involved in similar incidents. Their senior officers gave the men advice and kept a close watch on them to ensure that no similar events occurred.

A third of the involuntary cases involved women identified as prostitutes, many of them women who constables met on their beats. These cases have been categorized as involuntary since constables tended to use their authority to obtain favours or bribes from the women in return for not arresting or harassing them.

---

[64] LCCDR, 25 April 1935, PCC 215 Rae, caught by PSC 1 Storey; LDRB, 7 May 1935, PCC 215 Rae, fifteen years' service, appealed unsuccessfully to Home Secretary and ordered to pay costs of appeal.

[65] LCCDR, 17 February 1928, PCC 221 Brown.

[66] LCCDR, 4 December 1923, PCB 92 Maquire, PCB 117 Bolton, complainant Catherine Cassidy, 87 Soho Street.

In typical arrangements, PC Jackson had a deal with a prostitute that in exchange for sex he would not report her, and PC Houghton convinced a prostitute to have 'carnal connection' with him to avoid arrest.[67] But as a rule, policemen left prostitutes alone as long as they were not harassing potential customers or making their activities too public, and prostitutes looked to constables to protect them from unruly customers.[68] Before the war, discipline cases involving prostitutes only appeared about once a year, with the exception of 1913 when ten Liverpool constables were discovered in a raid on a brothel.[69] Similar to other sexual misconduct cases, the number of charges went up during the early 1920s when many constables were young. While off duty in 1921, young PC Jellyman was found in a ladies' lavatory at the Sefton Arms Hotel with a prostitute named Patricia Fegan. After another constable ejected him from the premises for drunkenness, Fegan came out and accused him of stealing her watch. A brawl broke out between Jellyman and men who sympathized with Fegan. He denied taking the watch but was taken with Fegan to a police station, where the watch was found in his pocket. Compounding an offence already leading to dismissal, 'whilst taking part in the above transactions he did improperly use his position as a member of the police force for his private advantage'.[70] The number of such cases dropped rapidly, however, with only one case reported after 1927.

Prostitutes and policemen had each other at a disadvantage, since constables could ruin a prostitute's business through arrest or harassment and the women could get a constable disciplined or fired for sexual misconduct. Simply being caught with a prostitute, on or off duty, in uniform or plain clothes, could get a policeman dismissed for 'association with undesirable ... women'.[71] PC Jones lost his job after three men saw him take a prostitute into a passageway. PC Walsh came

---

67   LCCDR, 22 January 1921, PCD 216 Jackson, resigned before case proceeded; LDRB, 7 April 1907, PCA 100 Houghton, four years' service, dismissed.

68   For police attitudes towards prostitution, see Robert Storch, 'Police Control of Street Prostitution in Victorian London: A Study in the Contexts of Police Action', in *Police and Society*, ed. David H. Bayley (London: Sage, 1977), pp. 49–72; Judith R. Walkowitz, *Prostitution and Victorian Society: Women, Class and the State* (Cambridge: Cambridge University Press, 1980), 'Male Vice and Feminist Virtue: Feminism and the Politics of Prostitution in Nineteenth-Century Britain', *History Workshop* 13 (1982): 77–93.

69   LDRB, 10 January 1913, PCB 184 Jenson, nine years' service, one default, dismissed; PCB 115 Barnett, twelve years' service, one default, dismissed; PCA 234 Hodgkinson, nine years' service, one default, dismissed; 11 January 1913, PCB 146 Hargreaves, two years' service, reduced to probationary class; PCB 234 Edmundson, seven years' service, reprimanded [all married]; PCB 249 Skelton, four years' service, one default, fined one week's pay; PCB 194 O'Connor, one year's service, fined one week's pay; PCB 118 Bebbington, three years' service, reprimanded; PCA 153 Branthwaite, probationary, reprimanded; PCB 152 Warbrick, probationary, reprimanded [all single].

70   LDRB, 30 August 1921, PCE 308 Jellyman, one year's service, to resign.

71   LCCO, 9 December 1921.

upon the men peering around the corner, explaining that 'A Copper has pulled a woman into that passage there and bolted the door after them, he was messing with her here at this corner for over 10 minutes.' Walsh tried the door, which was bolted. After knocking, Jones came out and Walsh found a woman with an arrest record for prostitution hiding behind the door.[72] Official contact between policemen and prostitutes in the line of duty made any other contact open to charges of favouritism, harassment or payoffs. Even so, few prostitutes could afford to report a policeman, since that would leave her labelled as a prostitute and open to retribution. Since many women involved in prostitution did so casually or for short periods, they feared that an arrest would ruin their chances for better or respectable employment. Threatening to arrest prostitutes gave constables an advantage over women, who often found it less trouble to cooperate than to accuse the constable of some crime in return. Nevertheless, constables exploiting prostitutes knew that the women could end their careers if they decided to report them.

Despite examples of constables taking advantage of prostitutes, prostitutes also used the police to protect them from unruly clients and even from corrupt policemen. In one example, Annie Williams, a known prostitute, agreed to go home with a man. When they arrived at her rooms, he declared that he was a detective but offered not to arrest her if she would 'have connection' without payment. She refused and sent a girl for a constable. Williams ran out the back door and hid in a public house. When the man came out later, Williams and two other women chased him, knocked off his hat, and screamed at him. A large crowd joined in. PC Rollit heard the commotion and arrested the man, recognizing him as PC Beaver. The women told Rollit what had occurred and Beaver was taken to the station. The women filed complaints against Beaver, who was subsequently dismissed.[73] It revealed some faith in policemen that Williams immediately sent for a constable to assist her against intimidation by a customer. That Rollit arrested Beaver even after recognizing him as a constable showed that constables were willing to protect prostitutes from other policemen. That prostitutes were aware of this was shown when PC Bowler accosted Floss Blundell, a prostitute, and she asked PC Vonles for help. PC Bowler used obscene language when challenged but PC Vonles got Bowler to leave Blundell alone.[74] Prostitutes cooperated with the police to capture corrupt policemen, including one case where PC Curtiss had extorted money from a prostitute in return for letting her use a section of his beat for her business. Detectives arranged for her to give Curtiss marked shillings which were

---

[72]   MWCM, 20 November 1910, PCB 166 William H. Jones, four years' service, vol. 49, no. 62. The woman made a statement against Jones, who resigned.

[73]   MWCM, 28 December 1904, PCD 98 Frank Beaver, twelve years' service, seven defaults, vol. 26, no. 75.

[74]   Birmingham City Police Disciplinary Book 'D' Division, 26 October 1923, PCD 102 Edward John Bowler, probationary, PCA 23 George Vonles, p. 50.

later found in his pocket.[75] In these cases, the women were known prostitutes so they had less to lose and much to gain from appealing to the police for help. Their willingness to go to the police even to report corrupt policemen suggests that the relationship between prostitutes and constables was not necessarily antagonistic. Policemen could be sympathetic to the plight of these women, reflected in their willingness both to help them and to leave them alone. On seeing a constable arrest one women for prostitution, a sergeant lamented, 'Who is this unfortunate person who is not allowed to live[?]'[76] One constable even recommended that a prostitute do her betting with his brother-in-law and gave her his business card.[77] Though they usually left each other alone, they could become acquainted with each similar to other police and civilian fraternizing and without any improper conduct.

Both the voluntary and involuntary sexual misconduct cases show that more sexual activity was taking place than the working class seemed willing to acknowledge in oral history interviews. Despite recollections that young people remained ignorant or inexperienced until couples were married or at least engaged, police records indicate that by the 1920s a significant sample was experimenting outside of strict working-class boundaries of respectability. While women still assumed that pregnancy would lead to marriage, at least some were risking pregnancy outside of engagements. The cases also illustrate common sexual double standards for men and women. Men could be sexually active outside of marriage without damaging their reputations while women could not be out at night, let alone sexually active, without compromising theirs. Policemen at all levels shared this typical working-class attitude. The primary concern of police forces was with the image and discipline of policemen. Not surprisingly, constables caught with women while on duty or assaulting women at any time faced disciplinary charges. But unlike other working-class men, constables faced interference in their off-duty courtships and relationships if they came to official attention. Even though police forces became more tolerant of voluntary sexual conduct, at least some constables preferred quitting the force rather than put up with having their most intimate relationships under police supervision.

---

75   MWCM, 24 October 1912, PCA 257 Ernest Curtiss, seventeen months' service, one default, dismissed, vol. 56, no. 101.

76   LCCDR, 16 May 1927, PSB 29 Kenworthy, p. 104. A charge of discreditable conduct could not be proved.

77   LCCDR, 30 July 1924, PCA Stanley, to resign. Later he arranged for a friend of his to visit her 'for an immoral purpose'. He also 'approached two naval men in uniform, asked for tobacco & afterwards said that if they wanted two prostitutes named Margaret Roberts and Edna Carson, who were in their company, to take them round the corner, that he could recommend Roberts'.

9

Domestic Life

Every Policeman should marry, for what can be worse for a
man after he has done eight hours out in the rain than to come
home to find nowhere to dry his clothes, and my word! they
do want some drying!

'Happy Wife', *Police Review*, 1928[1]

THE DOMESTIC LIVES of constables and their families, the dynamics of their
marriages, and their interactions with neighbours followed common working-
class patterns. Couples came from similar backgrounds, often from families in
similar professions, and tended to be close in age. They met through family and
friends, at work and at dances. Most married when they were in their early to
mid-twenties and had two or three children. Wives expected their husbands to
hand over their wages, and husbands expected their wives to run the household.
They fought if expectations were not met, if the husband did not earn enough or
spent too much on beer or gambling, or if the wife did not save, did not provide
meals, or did not present a neat family appearance. Unhappy spouses might look
for satisfaction elsewhere, sometimes ending in affairs, separations and unofficial
cohabitation. Since divorce was expensive, the working class could tolerate a fair
amount of marital irregularity. Mostly, families got along with neighbours and,
when they did not, quarrels were often sparked by feuding wives, quarrelling
children and noise. Neighbours asked favours of neighbours with skills such as
plumbing or carpentry, including treating constables living on the street as local
police stations, making it difficult for constables to be off duty and annoying their
wives. If frictions became too extreme, people went in search of better company.
Families moved to new streets and spouses found new partners. Tensions increased
after the war with more families moving and neighbourhoods becoming less stable,
but even then, most couples and neighbours got along reasonably well.[2]

---

1   *Police Review and Parade Gossip*, 13 April 1928, p. 289.
2   For working-class domestic life, see Joanna Bourke, *Working-Class Cultures in Britain*

One critical factor that set police families apart from the rest of their class was the interest police forces took in the private lives, not just of policemen, but of their wives and families. Police wives had early warning of this when their husbands had to apply to get married. Wives learned that their newlywed lives had to be in authorized neighbourhoods and they could not move without permission. They were rarely allowed to live near their families to prevent conflicts of interest, and wives were not allowed to work for the same reason. Supervision could be intrusive: one Liverpool wife complained that when her husband was sick, her house was visited by sergeants and inspectors several times a day to check his condition, unnerving the children and trying her patience.[3] Respectable behaviour was expected of the wife just as much as of her husband to preserve the image of the force. Even disorderly children could attract official attention. This scrutiny had its advantages and disadvantages. Forces helped families with financial problems rather than let them be ruined, particularly if families had medical bills. If wives had problems with husbands, such as men not handing over sufficient wages or being abusive, senior officers intervened. On the other hand, normal arguments could become the subject of embarrassing investigations if neighbours complained. A wife who was too conspicuous or notorious for force standards could delay her husband's promotion, and the police force was possibly the only working-class occupation where a wife's behaviour could lose a man his job.[4]

This domestic interest created records of numerous incidental details of private life and reports into marital problems such as abuse, adultery and marital separation. Yet even after policemen or their families were reported for failing to uphold the image of the force, senior officers remained hesitant to discipline men for their domestic conduct as long as they did not stray too far from working-class

---

1890–1960: Gender, Class and Ethnicity (London: Routledge, 1994); Andrew Davies, *Leisure, Gender and Poverty: Working-Class Culture in Salford and Manchester, 1900–1939* (Buckingham: Open University Press, 1992); John Gillis, *A World of Their Own Making: Myth, Ritual, and the Quest for Family Values* (New York: Basic Books, 1996); Jane Lewis, ed. *Labour and Love: Women's Experience of Home and Family 1850–1940* (Oxford: Basil Blackwell, 1986); Roberts, *A Woman's Place*; Wally Seccombe, *Weathering the Storm: Working-Class Families from the Industrial Revolution to the Fertility Decline* (London: Verso, 1995); Melanie Tebbutt, *Women's Talk? A Social History of 'Gossip' in Working-Class Neighbourhoods, 1880–1960* (Aldershot: Scolar Press, 1997). Portions of this chapter are based on Joanne Klein, 'Irregular Marriages: Unorthodox Working-Class Domestic Life in Liverpool, Birmingham and Manchester, 1900–1939', *Journal of Family History* 30:2 (2005): 210–29; and '"Moving On", Men and the Changing Character of Interwar Working-Class Neighborhoods: From the Files of the Manchester and Liverpool City Police', *Journal of Social History* (2004): 407–21.

3   *Police Review*, 1 November 1901, p. 520.

4   When his wife was arrested and jailed, PC Leonard Fisher had to resign from the service. He asked for the return of his rateable deductions since 'I want to get into a new neighbourhood, so as to give my wife a fresh start in life when she comes from her detention' (MWCM, December 1914, vol. 65, no. 167, eight years' service).

expectations or attract too much public attention. If wives did not have meals ready, keep the house clean or pay bills on time, husbands might be excused for threatening them or even striking them as long as the husbands supported their wives with their wages. Similar to police abuse of civilians, incidents of spousal abuse were often considered explained or only resulted in advice. More serious consequences, including dismissals, resulted if constables became multiple offenders, showing that senior officers accepted the occasional outburst of temper no matter the context but not chronic violence. On the other hand, if wives kept a clean house, provided meals and behaved well, senior officers were less sympathetic with their husbands. If he failed to support his wife, the force garnished his wages and paid her directly. If he became violent, he was fined, reduced in rank and finally dismissed. However, as long as a constable supported his legal wife and was not abusive, many senior officers tolerated affairs and even cohabitation with an unofficial second 'wife' unless relationships attracted unfavourable attention. Overall, senior officers preferred staying out of men's private lives. Instead, they often acted as unofficial family counsellors, advising couples on getting along better. Constables were more likely to get into trouble for quarrels with neighbours than they were for family conflicts since disputes with neighbours were more likely to become public. Here, too, senior officers tried to resolve problems with advice. If necessary, constables with quarrelsome neighbours could be moved, a simple solution compared to resolving a troubled marriage. Yet despite the negative nature of much of the police evidence, the small overall number of serious cases in Manchester, Birmingham and Liverpool suggest that most police families got along with their neighbours and the majority of police marriages were about as enduring and successful as most working-class marriages.[5]

Policemen, like other working-class men, married women with occupational and geographic backgrounds similar to their own. They mostly married women either from their home towns or districts, or from the city where they worked.[6] The fathers of the couples held jobs similar to those of their sons and sons-in-law, such as labourers, weavers, railway workers, miners, watchmakers, locksmiths, clerks, salesman and gardeners, and these changed over time, similar to the patterns of the men who joined the force.[7] The fathers of the husbands and wives held similar jobs, providing no evidence that policemen were marrying up or down the social

---

5   See Weinberger, *The Best Police in the World*, pp. 102–13, for a discussion of police wives. I argue that senior officers were less insistent that families conform to strict ideals of respectability than she contends, most likely the result of my using written versus oral history evidence. Constables who never married were so rare as to be statistically unimportant.

6   BRB, 1900–1939.

7   See Chapter 1 for an analysis of how occupations changed over time and from city to city.

scale but rather marrying women from their own backgrounds. Sometimes, the children of fathers in similar trades married, such as the children of two postmen who married in 1915 and the children of a coach finisher and a coach painter who wed in 1926. Constables occasionally married the daughters of constables, sergeants and inspectors but no more often than they married daughters from other occupations. Fathers and daughters sometimes worked in the same trades, such as in Birmingham's jewellery and chocolate trades. However, while many fathers worked in agriculture, no daughters did, preferring a variety of factory, manufacturing and domestic jobs. Manchester factory jobs tended to be in textiles while Birmingham ones also included Cadbury's chocolates and motor-car plants. During the war, women worked making shells and munitions, and one worked as a postwoman. In both cities, they worked as dress- and hat-makers, hairdressers, book binders, confectioners, and at similar skilled work. Many worked in domestic service, including cooks, parlour maids, and housekeepers, but no more often than they worked in factories. After the war, clerks, typists and secretaries became more common, and a few teachers and nurses appeared, but jobs in manufacturing and domestic service remained common. Shop assistants and waitresses might meet constables on their jobs but they seemed less likely to marry them than women in most other jobs. With the exception of the domestic servants, women did not seem especially likely to have met their husbands while at work unless they met their husbands before the men joined the police. Most constables married after joining the force. Most wives, therefore, knew that they were marrying into the police. Whether they were prepared for the life of a police wife was another matter.[8]

The age at marriage of policemen and their wives was similar to national trends but also reflected the gradual improvement in the quality of recruits. Before the war, most police wives married when they were from twenty-one to twenty-six years old, and constables followed a similar pattern, though with more marrying up to twenty-nine years old. This was higher than averages for unskilled labourers who tended to marry by age twenty-two, supporting the idea that police forces were attracting a better level of recruit after the 1890 Police Act. During the war, nearly a quarter of both husbands and wives married at age twenty or younger, presumably hurrying to marry before men got drafted. Otherwise, men rarely married before they were twenty-one, and only about one in ten women did. Older couples became more common in the 1920s, reflecting the higher level of recruits after the 1919 Police Act, but most still married in their twenties, close to the 1930 national average age of twenty-six for men and twenty-four for women. Most constables married women near their own age. Over half of couples were either the same

---

8   MWCM, 1900–1939 (wives' occupations listed on deceased police officer information sheets). Birmingham City Police Constables Marriage Certificates 1900–1927; 739 couples listed, including ages at marriage, professions at marriage and professions of their fathers.

age or within two years of each other. Another third had a three- to five-year age gap. While larger gaps appeared slightly more often in the 1920s, most remained close in age. Even couples in their thirties and forties were typically similar in age. Husbands were older than wives about half the time, wives were older a third of the time, and they were the same age about fifteen per cent of the time. These proportions held true even for larger age gaps. Wives much older than husbands were no less common than husbands much older than wives. Younger men seemed just as attracted to older women who might have a nest egg as younger women to older settled men. But typical police couples were in their middle twenties, within a couple years in age, and both new to living on their own.[9]

Improving recruitment standards not only affected the age of couples but also created rivalries among police wives that mirrored those between old and new policemen, including similar resentments over pay, pensions and promotion. Just like their husbands, wives often voiced their grievances in letters to the *Police Review*. In a 1927 example, a *Review* article described the essential duties of a wife: running a household on an irregular schedule and taking messages for her husband in emergencies.[10] A young 'Policeman's wife' wrote in reply that she was grateful that someone understood how busy a police wife was, 'why she cannot make arrangements for pleasure like other people, nor take part in the social life of the town'.[11] This led to a series of letters from pre- and postwar wives trying to outdo each other in how stressful their lives were. One 'Pre-war Policeman's Wife' wrote,

> What would 'Policeman's Wife' think if she had to do what I have done – live in a Police Station and be tied there, and not be able to get out at the same time as my husband on account of the telephone and taking in reports. I had offices to clean, cells and corridors to scrub, stray dogs to feed, and all kinds of drunken female prisoners to search and attend to, and all for a small wage. The only time we got out together was once a year ... I think the Policeman's wife of to-day is a very lucky woman, and has a living pension to look forward to, not like we are, practically starving on a pre-war pension and nothing more to look forward to in our old age, after giving the best of our lives to the Police Service.[12]

In a similar 1936 exchange, a 'Pre-war Pensioner's Wife' was glad to see that wives were no longer expected to be policemen, listing her former duties as nearly

---

9   Birmingham Marriage Certificates, 1900–1927; Gillis, *For Better, for Worse*, pp. 232, 289; Lawrence Stone, *Road to Divorce, England 1530–1987* (Oxford: Oxford University Press, 1990), p. 412.
10   *Police Review*, 1 July 1927, p. 496.
11   *Police Review*, 8 July 1927, p. 507.
12   *Police Review*, 15 July 1927, p. 541.

identical to those listed above, but she closed by complaining of the unfairness of prewar pensions not rectified by the 1919 Police Act.[13] In reply, 'P.C.'s Wife' snapped back that the prewar wives could have refused to stay home to take messages or act as matrons or cleaners if they wished.[14] But since working as a police matron or station cleaner was a rare chance for a police wife to earn money, few prewar wives could afford to turn it down. Adding to the acrimony was that after September 1918, police widows received an annual pension of £30, with £10 for each child up to three children. However, widows of constables who had died before this did not receive the benefit.[15] This often-bitter rivalry continued for as long as the prewar wives lived. Wives did agree on some issues. Nothing annoyed them more than women sending in 'perfect budgets' for living on a constable's wages, leading to scathing responses pointing out missing items such as clothing, boots, doctors' bills and insurance.[16] One policeman set off an uproar in 1939 when he wrote to the *Review* warning constables not to marry wives who would not make a good inspector's or superintendent's wife. The wives quickly retorted that few men, no matter how qualified, could attain high rank. One 'Wife of Five Years' Service' replied angrily, 'At the time we married we were looking forward (as I suppose every young couple must) to promotion speeding along on wings. This ... has proved most elusive.' She abused the man for tactlessly assuming that cooks and under-housemaids were not good enough to marry policemen, a stereotype 'just as ridiculous as the manner in which the stage comedian portrays our present-day "Bobby"'. Many wives argued that constables needed good, hard-working wives, not someone with notions above her station. A young wife who had worked as a domestic servant wrote, 'Doesn't he think that a wife who can cook, keep the house clean and look after her husband generally will be far better than a social climber?'[17] The women were united by the challenges of being a police wife, such as keeping fires going at odd hours to dry boots and uniforms or providing two sets of meals depending on work shifts, but they just as easily split over personal and police rivalries, not unlike the sometimes contradictory relationships of their husbands.

Even before they married, police wives learned that their lives would not be quite the same as other working-class wives. Before constables could marry, they had to request permission so their prospective wives could be checked for suitability. Few examples exist of women having problems with this step and no cases were

---

13   *Police Review*, 11 December 1936, p. 554.

14   *Police Review*, 24 December 1936, p. 603.

15   'Report of the Committee on the Police Service of England, Wales, and Scotland', Part II, 1920, Cmd. 574, vol. XXII, 539, p. 18.

16   For examples, see *Police Review*, 8 November 1912, p. 537; 12 October 1934, p. 282, 26 October 1934, p. 317.

17   *Police Review*, 2 June 1939, p. 515; 23 June 1939, p. 590.

reported of constables resigning rather than giving up a fiancée. Either constables were reasonably good at choosing wives or no senior officers felt comfortable challenging a man's choice. PC Jenkins had to resign after marrying without the consent of the chief constable but this was a matter of defying regulations rather than a problem with his wife.[18] Birmingham under the autocratic Chief Constable Rafter was the strictest force, but even he did not stop weddings. An investigation into Lily Dennis produced an adverse report yet PC Bunn was allowed to marry her under the strict observation of his superintendent.[19] Liverpool was more easygoing about marriages, possibly due to the working-class character of the city. Even though PC Corns failed to report the whereabouts of Marie Megann, reported missing from home by her mother, and even though he married Megann three weeks after her disappearance, he was only cautioned.[20] Manchester, a force that did not hesitate to investigate domestic problems, had no records of concerns. Yet even if wives had few problems getting approved, these investigations were an early sign of future intrusions into their private lives.

The first challenge the couple faced was finding housing that combined affordability with force expectations of suitable respectability. Forces placed numerous restrictions on their options. They were not allowed to live too close to their families, they were forbidden to live on premises where their families owned businesses, and constables who met their wives on their beats were often transferred.[21] In Birmingham and Manchester, men had to live in their divisions within a reasonable distance of their stations.[22] They were discouraged from purchasing homes since they could be transferred to new divisions, further limiting their choices. Liverpool men were allowed to live anywhere within city boundaries so long as it did not interfere with their duty, but they still had to live at approved addresses.[23] Acceptable streets tended to attract police families, leading to constables sometimes having police neighbours. This could be good or bad, depending on if a constable wanted to be around colleagues all the time. Streets that had once been acceptable might change in character, such as when Towsen Street stopped being satisfactory in 1906.[24] Rent allowances were meant to compensate

---

18   BPO, 21 July 1937, p. 28,658.

19   BJSC, 28 May 1920, p. 154. The problems remained confidential.

20   LCCDR, 5 March 1923, PCC 80 Corns.

21   Constables could not assume they would live in the same area after marriage and were warned not to take houses until their assignment was known (BPO, 12 October 1906, p. 497; 18 March 1907, p. 22).

22   BPO, 15 December 1921, p. 4430, BJSC, 22 October 1924, p. 843.

23   LSO, April 1919, no. 1, p. 1.

24   A constable's application to lodge on Towsen Street was declined and no more policemen were given permission to live there, though policeman already housed on the street were allowed to stay (Liverpool Watch Committee Orders to the Head Constable, 16 July, 3 September 1906; LWCM, 10 September 1906, pp. 455–6).

for limitations but were rarely enough. Police families had a more difficult time finding housing than other working-class families and often had to spend a higher proportion of their income on rent.

While finding housing was always vexatious it presented an acute problem for police families after the First World War during the national housing shortage. The year 1919 was particularly bad before the adoption of the Desborough pay scale. In Birmingham during the war, for example, some wives had moved in with their parents while their husbands were in the military. About 150 men returning from the war in 1919 were forced to live apart from their families since they could not find housing for them.[25] Facing similar problems in Manchester, the force bought the Alexandra Park Aerodrome from the War Office in 1920 and converted it to house around a hundred police families.[26] All forces began asking constables to give warning when they moved so that other policemen could acquire their old residences.[27] In 1921, in order to receive corporation housing in Birmingham, a married constable with children had to agree to let rooms to another married constable with one or no children.[28] The shortage was still so desperate in December 1922 that Manchester adopted a policy of only promoting men within a division so that they could keep their houses.[29] Corporation houses began to be allocated to policemen, but waiting lists were long.[30] In 1925, over 100 married policemen still could not find houses in Birmingham and the city finally constructed 212 police cottages that also served as auxiliary stations.[31] Liverpool had fewer problems because men were not limited to living within their divisions, but still had more problems than usual for working families. By 1930, the most serious shortages were over but the general problems constables faced trying to find suitable housing remained.[32]

---

[25]   *Police Review*, 27 February 1920, p. 181; DC, Evidence, questions 6262–4, pp. 301–2, Inspector Frederick Walsey, BCP.

[26]   MGO, 17 February 1921. A year later, the Aerodrome was used to house single men. It could house around 500 people.

[27]   MGO, 17 November 1921. Peacock penalized men who did not comply with this request. For more examples, see 'Inspectors of Constabulary report for year ended the 29th September 1920', PP 1921 (39) xvi, 15, p. 11; MGO, 22 December 1920; BPO, 28 November 1921, p. 4350; 12 May 1925, p. 9,886; 11 April 1927, p. 12,702.

[28]   BPO, 3 September 1921, p. 3977.

[29]   MGO, 15 December 1922.

[30]   MGO, 3 January 1924; BWCM, 2 July 1924, p. 32; BPO, 25 September 1930, p. 17120; BPO, 12 May 1925, p. 9886.

[31]   BWCM, 7 October 1925, report no. 7, p. 3. In 1934, occupiers of police cottages were given a two-shilling allowance for their extra duties. In 1935, public exterior phone boxes were added for when the officer was absent (BPO, 8 February 1934, p. 21,761; 12 January 1935, pp. 23,195–6).

[32]   BWCM, 3 October 1934, report no. 3, p. 5; MWCM, 1 September 1932, vol. 162, no. 24. Chief constables commented that housing difficulties had disappeared by the 1930s but a 1936 *Police Review* article disagreed with this conclusion (*Police Review*, 8 May 1936, pp. 433–4).

Police couples might need to move if he was transferred or promoted but they also might need more room for their families. Surviving police records make it difficult to estimate the size of an average police family. Birmingham roster books listed the names of each constable's children but it is uncertain whether every child was recorded, especially before the war. Based on the rosters, such as they are, the average police family was small. They were somewhat larger before the war, averaging slightly over two children per family. After the war, they averaged between 1.5 and two children. A few large families with five or six children existed both before and after the war. Ten to fifteen per cent of families had no children at all. This is slightly higher than the eight to ten per cent found by Elizabeth Roberts but that could be a result of the uncertain evidence. The few adoptions mentioned usually involved relatives, such as when PC Walsh adopted the three daughters of his deceased sister and brother-in-law, also a policeman.[33] Families that had children typically had one to three, and mention of children in other records suggest that two or three children was common. All of this indicates that police families were similar in size to other working-class families, with both getting smaller after the war.[34]

The primary duty of working-class husbands was to provide a weekly wage packet sufficient to support their families. Constables received not only regular pay but also uniform and boot allowances, rent allowances, sick pay and pensions, so they made good husbands in this respect. Like other workers, they risked their earnings if they got into trouble at work that resulted in fines, demotions or dismissal. Married constables tended to be better behaved than single ones because they had families to support, but domestic life could sometimes interfere in a constable's work life. A common result was constables being late for duty, such as when the four-year-old son of PC Rudge played with his father's alarm clock and changed the setting, causing his father to be forty minutes late.[35] Senior officers tended to be sympathetic. PC Elmy fell asleep in a police box after being up all day looking after his sick wife but was not disciplined.[36] The occasional domestic crisis was understandable. However, if a constable had chronic problems balancing home and work life, he got sterner treatment. PC Hamer forgot to tell his wife that his shift had changed before she left to go shopping and found himself home alone

---

[33]   LCCO, 8 September 1919, p. 269. PCB 18 William Lessiter Ackinson adopted the daughter of his wife's sister (MPF, 16 February 1937, appointed July 1925).

[34]   BRB, 1900–1939; fifty per cent of families counted, approximately 1200 men; Roberts, *A Woman's Place*, p. 99. Jeffrey Weeks, in *Sex, Politics and Society*, found that twentieth-century working-class families tended to have three children or fewer which is similar to the national average (pp. 69–70, 202). See Seccombe, *Weathering the Storm*, pp. 157–93, for a thorough analysis of the drop in working-class marital fertility beginning around 1890.

[35]   MPF, 12 June 1925, PCC 80 Leo Rudge, appointed May 1919.

[36]   MPF, 18 October 1928, PCB 117 Henry Elmy, appointed 1923.

with two toddlers when he should have been at work. Since he was habitually late, he was warned about his future conduct.[37] More serious marital strife sometimes disrupted work, and senior officers had to administer stern lessons. The Smiths were a recently married couple in their twenties. Mrs Smith, a member of the British Women's Temperance Association, had fits of temper over her husband's occasional glass of beer. He finally snuck out and drank enough to get reported drunk on duty. Luckily for him, he was only fined twenty shillings and given advice on his home life.[38] Any domestic problem could cause trouble for working men if they interfered with his job. But constables faced the added stress that forces could come down hard on domestic problems if the constable was not supporting his family or if his domestic life attracted persistent unfavourable attention since both reflected poorly on the image of the force.

While earning a living remained his main duty, after the war, examples of young husbands looking after sick wives and children and doing household chores began to appear, reflecting a growing involvement of working-class men in domestic life.[39] These instances always involved a family emergency. Mrs Wallingford wore herself out looking after her sick infant son so her husband took care of the chores for her. A year later, he stayed up all night with the now eighteen-month-old son when he had whooping cough.[40] After Mrs Mighall miscarried, PC Mighall stayed up all night looking after her. Because he was 'demented through worry', he was not charged with insubordination for being rude to a sergeant who came by to check on her.[41] If necessary, constables even took over the household for lengthy periods. Mrs Pickford had a difficult pregnancy and her husband did all the chores as well as attended to his wife for eight months. Even though he missed a swimming exam in consequence, the force allowed him to take it once his wife had recovered.[42] These examples both show that young men were willing to do traditionally women's work if their wives were unable to but also that young families could not always count on mothers or sisters to help them. PC Pickford could not afford hiring someone to look after his wife for so many months and could not find a family member to step in. Family support had by no means disappeared but not all families had it available, requiring husbands to fill the void. The domestic

---

37   MPF, 16 December 1933, PCD 163 Norman Hamer, appointed January 1930; finally warned for habitual lateness.

38   MPF, 18 September 1924, PCB 138 Edward Smith, appointed April 1920, fined 20/-.

39   See Catherine Hall, 'Married Women at Home in the 1920s and 1930s', *Oral History* 5:2 (1977): p. 76; Bourke, *Working-Class Cultures*, pp. 64, 82–8.

40   MPF, 11 April 1924, 22 June 1925, PCD 41 William Ernest Wallingford, appointed May 1919.

41   Birkenhead Disciplinary Report Book, 13 June 1922, pp. 102–3.

42   MPF, 15 February 1937, PCB 217 Charles E. Pickford, appointed October 1934. He passed his swimming exam.

sphere remained the wife's province, but at least some husbands were ready to help out in a crisis. Senior officers were generally understanding if this hindered work, at least within reason.

The duty of the husband was to provide his wages and the primary duty of a working-class wife was to use them to manage the household.[43] She fed, clothed and housed the family, did the cleaning and shopping, and handled the budget. Less typical than other wives, police wives had to cope with her husband's three-shift rotation and unscheduled court attendance and emergency duties, making it difficult to maintain a household routine. She faced unusual restrictions such as not being allowed to work or live wherever she liked, and she was expected to take messages for her husband. But her biggest adjustments were reporting information to her husband that was not normally a working-class husband's business and that wifely failures could get her husband in trouble at work, especially if they attracted public attention. Both of these often had to do with managing the family finances. Living on a budget was a constant struggle but police wives had the extra stress that their husbands faced disciplinary charges if their debts came to police attention. As shown in Chapter 5, prewar budgets were tight. Similar to their husbands, wives were outspoken about low pay, writing to the *Police Review* to vent their grievances. One Liverpool wife sent in her weekly budget in 1901. She figured her weekly expenses to be: rent 7/6d., coal 2/4d., gas 8d., groceries, 8/-, meat and vegetables 4/-, milk 3/4d., insurance, 1/9d., orphanage and burial clubs 2½d. – a total of £1/7/9½d., with only 2/2½d. left over for boots, clothes, doctors' bills and recreation for two adults and four children. She labelled this 'White Slavery'.[44] The First World War made living on a budget hopeless since police earnings remained fixed in a period of inflation. In 1916, one worried Liverpool wife wrote that she had spent 2/6d. over her budget, had used the tontine money to pay a doctors' bill, and had a gas bill she could not pay at all.[45] Of the eight city constables' budgets presented to the Desborough committee in 1919, five spent more than they earned. Wives tried to make up the difference by selling eggs, garden produce, rabbits and furniture, doing without new clothes or boots, and not replacing broken utensils.[46] One Liverpool wife got so into debt that the watch committee stepped in to help clear her account.[47] While the Desborough pay scale relieved this emergency, living on police pay never ceased to be a challenging job for wives.

---

[43] See Roberts, *A Woman's Place*, Gillis, *For Better, for Worse*, and Lewis, *Labour and Love*.

[44] *Police Review*, 1 November 1901, p. 520. This budget is similar to one presented in 1907 by Liverpool men demanding higher wages (LWCM, 14 May 1907, pp. 350–4). See p. 139.

[45] *Police Review*, 3 March 1916, p.99.

[46] 'Report of the Committee on the Police Service of England, Wales, and Scotland', Part I, 1919, Cmd. 253, vol. XXVII, 709, pp. 26–7.

[47] LWCM, 16 May 1916, p. 419. Five shillings of her dependents' grant was paid directly to her husband's superintendent to pay outstanding bills.

One factor hindering police wives' ability to balance their budgets was their being banned from working to avoid conflicts of interest. Even though working-class wives did not generally work full-time after marriage, they could and did work during periods of financial shortfall. Wives who did work often kept shops or worked in a family business. Both policemen and their wives resented this ban. During the 1919 Desborough Committee hearings, Liverpool PC Smithwick complained that wives could not be music teachers or dressmakers without living apart from their husbands.[48] Birmingham PS Clowes pointed out that men could not marry a woman with a business without her being required to give it up. The ban also created problems with housing. He had the opportunity to move to a house with a shop that his wife could run but was forbidden to do so.[49] PC Thorley finally decided that his wife's bakery and confectionery shop paid better than being a constable and resigned from the force rather than have her give it up.[50] Some police wives worked anyway, often to help their families, and faced endangering their husbands' jobs. PC Taylor was told to stop his wife from working at her mother's dress shop or face losing his position, even though she was not being paid and was only helping while her mother was ill.[51] Elise Whittaker was discovered running the bar at her mother's licensed house and was forbidden to do so again.[52] Very rarely, exceptions were made if a financial situation was dire. Since PC Gregory was supporting his parents and mother-in-law, his wife was allowed to continue her work as a typist so the family could live respectably.[53] A few police families lived at stations and the wife served as police matrons, a difficult job with low pay. But for most families, this ban on wives' working limited their financial options, putting more stress on their budgeting skills.

A central part of the wife's budget was paying the rent. That constables remained ignorant of the rent was considered normal and even necessary by both husband and wife, yet could still get him into trouble. Constables reported to the force for delinquent rent routinely stated that they knew nothing about it since it was their wives' responsibility. The newly married PC Gardner, caught twice in one year with large sums of rent in arrears, kept repeating that he was too easy on his young wife and would have to get her to spend less, but he clearly did not see it as his business.[54] Another common problem was changes in rents. Constables were expected to inform senior officers when their rent changed since most received rent

---

48 DC, Evidence, question 3782, p. 193.

49 DC, Evidence, question 6274–80, p. 302.

50 BPO, 1, 4 April 1922, pp. 4868, 4881.

51 MPF, 1, 2, 24 December 1931, PCD 28 Clifford Taylor, appointed June 1926.

52 MPF, 28 November 1927, PSC Reuben Whittaker, appointed 1913.

53 MPF, 22 November 1932, PCA 49 Edmund Gregory, appointed March 1921.

54 MPF, 9 April, 16 November 1934, PCD 221 Francis H. Gardner, appointed April 1931 (in arrears for £7/3/od. and £10/10/od., fined 5/- and warned).

allowances. Men frequently got in trouble for not reporting decreases and, in their defence, they always stated that their wives had neglected to tell them.[55] In April 1924, the Manchester force caught six young constables overdrawing their rent allowance when updating their allowance record books. They all made it clear that the rent was not their responsibility: 'I leave all the domestic affairs to my wife'; 'I leave all my house-hold duties to my wife'; 'I am not in the habit of troubling with the rent book. And my Wife had failed to notify me of the alteration'; '[M]y wife neglected to inform me'; 'I leave [the rent] in my wifes hands'; '[M]y wife ...meets the landlord and pays the rent.'[56] The young wives may still have been learning that the rent, normally not a husband's concern, needed to reported in a police family. Unlike other wives, they could not assume that the domestic sphere was not their husbands' business.

Ideally, wives paid cash rather than used credit since credit could turn into a never-ending debt cycle. However, particularly after the war when many succumb to the allure of hire-purchase schemes, wives sometimes tried to sneak in purchases on account. While most could manage this in a small way, unexpected expenses could doom already-tight budgets for any working-class family. For instance, Mrs Hughes was unable to meet a hire-purchase payment while her husband was in the hospital,[57] and PC Smith had to appeal to his chief constable to pay an overdue doctor's bill of nearly £10.[58] The debts show a willingness of shopkeepers, hire-purchase firms, doctors and others to allow accounts to become months overdue before taking action. This could both help and hurt the wife since debts got progressively out of control. Mrs Ledward ran up a bill of nearly £4 for vegetables supplied over nine months before the shop appealed to the chief constable for payment.[59] Husbands usually had no idea their wives had debts until called before their superintendents to explain them. Unable to pay a doctors' bill, Mrs Burgess went to the extreme of hiding a court summons for the debt from

---

[55]   MGO, 21 September 1920, PCB 204 Morgan; 9 December 1920, PCE 36 Thomas Griffin.

[56]   MPF, 15 April 1924, PCD 221 William Little, appointed September 1920; 15 April 1924, PCD 191 Bertie Arthur Haylock, appointed August 1920; 14 August 1924, PCB 54 Charles Ewen, appointed August 1920; 14 April 1924, PCB 206 John Goodwin Craik, appointed November 1920; 15 April 1924, PCA 31 Edmund Thomas Bryan, appointed January 1921; 9 April 1924, PCE 83 Eli Frederick Brooks, appointed January 1922.

[57]   LCCDR, 22 January 1931, PCG 157 Hughes, complainant The Northern Goldsmiths Co., Blackett Street, Newcastle-upon-Tyne.

[58]   LCCDR, 10 September 1928, PCG 163 Smith, complainant Dr. William Simpson, Bamber Bridge.

[59]   LCCDR, 17 January 1929, PC Ledward, complainant A. Dongherly, 185 Smithdown Road. Mrs Smith had not paid grocery bills for ten months before the grocer complained. She promised to pay the account but repeatedly refused to open her door when they came to collect it (LCCDR, 4 July 1935, PCD 248 Smith, complainant J.H. Owen, 83 Lisburn Lane, The Brook).

her husband.[60] Hire purchases were particularly easy to hide since most companies were out of town and sent letters to remind of payments. Mrs Doyle ignored five letters from a company and was 'highly indignant' when a representative visited her. The company finally appealed to the chief constable and her husband paid.[61] Husbands did not get into trouble if they were able to pay the bills once they came to police attention. At least some constables must have had savings that their wives were either unable or unwilling to use since they were able to discharge bills once they learned about them. If debts were too high to pay immediately, forces often helped out by negotiating new arrangements or with loans, usually accompanied by advice and extra supervision.[62] While this gave police families a safety net, both husband and wife could find it an embarrassing reflection on their domestic abilities.

The most common cause of domestic conflicts in working-class families was financial stress.[63] The husband did not provide enough, the wife did not manage well, some emergency struck, or some combination of these left the family in debt. Financial problems reflected poorly on the couple, contributing to their trying to keep debts secret, often from each other. They borrowed money to pay bills, exacerbating the problem. About thirty-five cases of domestic abuse appeared in police records, reported by wives, family members, neighbours and policemen. Many came from Liverpool where a complete set of reports that mentioned such cases survived, but Manchester and Birmingham had enough examples of domestic discord to suggest that their marriages were not significantly more harmonious. Fewer cases appeared in the 1930s than in other decades, possibly a result of the higher average age of constables. No doubt many instances of abuses were never reported, similar to the working class in general.

In a few cases, all before the war, forces stepped in when police children were at risk. Similar to other abuse cases, the men were put on report to try and resolve the problems. In one Birmingham case, after being summoned by the courts for not sending his children to school, PC Eardley spent six months on report to ensure that his children remained in school.[64] In three Liverpool cases, the men were reported for their homes not being in a satisfactory state. The wives were not mentioned, perhaps because the husbands were considered to be ultimately

---

[60]   MPF, 11 October 1930, PCA 206 George Birtles Burgess, appointed July 1925, paid the debt and a fine as soon as he learned of the summons.

[61]   MPF, 12 May 1928, PCA 288 Arthur Doyle, appointed May 1921.

[62]   Liverpool set up a special fund in 1926 to help families in financial difficulties due to ill health or other emergencies with loans (LCCO, 7 December 1933).

[63]   See Pat Ayers and Jan Lambertz, 'Marriage Relations, Money and Domestic Violence in Working-Class Liverpool, 1919–1939', in *Labour and Love: Women's Experience of Home and Family 1850–1940*, ed. Jane Lewis (Oxford: Basil Blackwell, 1986), pp. 195–219.

[64]   BWCM, 11 February, 14 March, 23 September 1907, pp. 164, 168, 185.

responsible regardless of the wives' household duties. In the first case, in 1906, PC Cartwright was censured after his daughter Florence, age thirteen, died from tuberculosis brought on by neglect. In spite of his inefficiency, the force decided not to punish him further due to his debts and large family.[65] Four years later, they took a stricter stance. PCs Evans and Highman were called before the watch committee for neglecting their children. They spent six months on report but their homes were still considered to be unsatisfactory. Despite their long service, both men were dismissed. Their homes must have been in a deplorable state to take this step, which cannot have helped the children. In these cases, the wives' housekeeping may have played a role in their husbands losing their jobs.[66] Possibly due to better pay after the war, such neglect no longer appeared, or forces may have become better at resolving neglect before it became so serious.

Police forces sent mixed signals in how they reacted to complaints of domestic abuse. Senior officers seemed unwilling to interfere in domestic disputes, and tended to respond to anything from verbal insults to serious physical abuse by putting men on report and giving advice. Verbal abuse was most often reported by wives. Constables accused of harsh words found themselves on probation until they had modified their behaviour. While the number of verbal cases was small, at least a few wives saw making complaints as a way to rein in their husbands. After his wife complained, PC Horton was severely reprimanded and put on report for six months. When he still had not mended his ways, he was put on another three months' report and finally got the message.[67] Investigations into neighbourhood disputes showed that some wives gave as good as they got in verbal wrangles with their husbands. If shouting couples attracted too much attention, senior officers called both of them in for advice on living together more quietly. Physical abuse was more often reported by neighbours or family members, perhaps since abused wives were too afraid of their husbands to complain. What seemed like serious charges could have no real consequences if the constable had an otherwise clean record. Mrs Ashwin took shelter with Mrs Nowell after her husband assaulted and insulted her, and PC Ashwin was then abusive to Mrs Nowell's son. However, Ashwin was only warned to keep away from his neighbour's house.[68] Each case was dealt with on its own merits which could lead to seemingly similar cases having vastly

---

[65]   LWCM, 20 August 1906, p. 422, twenty-two years' service.

[66]   LDRB, 26 November 1910, PCC Evans, twenty-two years' service, seven defaults; PCC Higham, seventeen years' service, one default; LWCM, 6 March, 11 June 1911, pp. 377, 644–5.

[67]   BWCM, 21 January 1918, p. 226; 22 July 1918, p. 348. A complaint that PC Peake was threatening his wife was adjourned for six months to see whether he would modify his behaviour (BWCM, 21 September 1903, p. 35).

[68]   LCCDR, 6 November 1926, PCF 195 Ashwin, complainant Mrs Susan M. Nowell, 22 Dingle Vale, Liverpool.

different results. PC Gee was reduced in class after the 'Constable and his wife had an altercation in the Street, which caused a number of persons to collect',[69] but PC Hone was only cautioned for discreditable conduct for threatening his wife with such violence that she took refuge in a gathering crowd.[70] The constables who found themselves in the most trouble were those who did not limit themselves to one offence. PC Mitchell had been given repeated warnings to improve his behaviour and finally had to resign for ill-treating his wife, throwing her out of the house and grossly neglecting his family.[71] PC Doyle had two previous records for 'persistently and cruelly ill-treating his wife' and was dismissed after his sister-in-law reported him for throwing an open pen-knife at her.[72] The reason usually given for dismissing men for domestic abuse was that such conduct was 'likely to bring discredit on the reputation of the Force'. Yet even quite public offences resulted in minor penalties. In a quarrel over a kettle boiling over, PC Napier called his wife a prostitute, struck her on the head with a brush, and refused to dress the wound. She went to his station to complain, and he abused her for not filing an assault charge and threatened more of the same. He was seen by the chief constable but only cautioned about his behaviour.[73] The haphazard record of forces in dealing with domestic abuse suggests that senior officers remained uncomfortable setting back a constable's career if an incident seemed like an isolated event. However, they did not ignore abuse entirely, putting constables under supervision, advising them about their conduct, and taking more drastic action if constables were impervious to reform.[74]

One detailed 1932 investigation of domestic abuse in Manchester uncovered a marriage that had broken down over about ten years, with confusing evidence over which spouse was more to blame. It showed how problems in marriages rarely stayed confined to the couple, affecting neighbours and children. Unfortunately, the file did not include the wife's perspective, only PC Carlis' statements that she was not a good wife. Despite evidence that Carlis had physically abused his wife, his evidence that she was not fulfilling her duties as a wife saved him from disciplinary

---

[69] MWCM, 29 October 1914, PCB James Gee, five years' service, one default, vol. 65, no. 40.

[70] LCCDR, 30 September 1921, PCC 63 Hone, complainant Mrs L.C. Cafearo, 43a Park Hill Road.

[71] LDRB, 5 July 1901, PCE 246 Mitchell, joined December 1886.

[72] LDRB, 2 October 1909, PCE 278 Doyle, nineteen years' service. PSE 24 Clinton resigned before charges that he habitually beat his wife could be fully investigated (LCCDR, 20 April 1934).

[73] LCCDR, 16 February 1923, PCF 62 Napier.

[74] In a few cases, wives physically abused their husbands. PCC 83 Hewitt had to be treated by the force doctor after his wife struck him on the head (LCI, 6 July 1926), and PCA 50 Fred Carlis lived in fear of his powerful wife and eventually separated from her (MPF, 10, 13, 14, 16 August 1932, appointed September 1922).

action. Carlis had once asked his inspector for advice since 'for years he and his wife had been at loggerheads, that she was dirty, failed to keep the children clean and failed to look after his food'. According to him, she left the rent in arrears and had £8–9 of debts. For three years he had been trying to obtain a mutual separation her since she 'was corresponding with a Steward on the Berengaria', but she refused, though 'she has tried to lose me my job'. Adding to the strain, PS Hall and his wife who lived next door did not get along with Mrs Carlis. Carlis stated, 'I have heard my wife teaching our child to hit the other child, & on a previous occasion my wife – who is a powerful woman – struck Mrs Hall in the face.' Hall confirmed this incident. No doubt Carlis was frustrated at being unable to escape a disagreeable marriage. But the evidence indicates that Carlis handled his marital problems by getting into verbal and physical disputes with his wife. At least one neighbour stated that Carlis hit his wife on more than one occasion. The couple was called before his senior officers twice and advised to live in harmony, the typical response to domestic fights attracting public attention. However bad the marriage seemed to Carlis, the neighbours 'take the side of my wife because she gossips freely with them whereas Mrs Hall minds her own business'. Either their views of her housewifely skills were different from his or her sociability made up for any deficiencies. Matters came to a crisis in August 1932. Carlis heard his wife arguing with the Halls over a fight between their children. Carlis went out but his wife refused to come inside. Here witnesses disagreed. PS Hall stated that Carlis first slapped Mrs Carlis and than Mrs Carlis tried to hit PS Hall. A neighbour's two children told their father that they had been terrified to see Carlis strike his wife on the back of the head and knock her down. The father wrote to the chief constable, adding that it was not the first occasion for such a scene. A slap is difficult to reconcile with Carlis knocking his wife down. Hall may have equivocated, not wishing to lie but sympathizing with Carlis. Carlis denied hitting his wife, then or ever. Possibly, he saw his actions as disciplining his wife for her unsatisfactory behaviour. The chief constable considered the case 'explained'. Even though the couple had been spoken to about their conduct, this was the first time that Carlis had been reported for abusing his wife and his record was clean. The main witnesses against him were children and Mrs Carlis had a bad history with Mrs Hall. The chief constable may have concluded that Carlis had been restraining his wife from hitting Mrs Hall. While PS Hall admitted that Carlis slapped his wife, it was treated as an isolated outburst. Carlis finally separated from his wife and eventually retired with a clean record.[75] Even with these dramatic events, this case illustrates how senior officers hesitated to interfere in men's personal lives. Since a neighbour complained, officers investigated and took statements. But Carlis suffered no consequences in his career and the investigation may even have got him the marital separation that he

---

75   MPF, 10, 13, 14, 16 August 1932, PCA 50 Fred Carlis, appointed September 1922.

desperately wanted. As a rule, only if constables refused to improve their conduct
did they risk serious consequences for domestic abuse.

Police records show that a few husbands and wives unhappy in their marriages
but unable to leave entered into long-term extramarital relationships while still
living with their spouses.[76] Around forty such cases appear in police files. For
constables, separating from their wives meant making maintenance payments which
they might not be able to afford. Wives might not want the uncertainty of leaving
a husband for a man who had no legal obligation to support them, and women
could rarely support their children by themselves. Both may have wanted to stay
with their children or to keep up the appearance of being married. Whatever kept
them in an unhappy marriage, they looked elsewhere for companionship.[77] If they
thought that their spouses were failing to meet working-class expectations, they
might even consider their adultery to be justified. Affairs lasted anywhere from
four months to ten years or more when discovered by police. PC Braddock went
so far as to have two families, his legal family and one with a single woman he was
supporting along with their three children. Their relationship had been going on
for at least four years and probably longer.[78] While sex undoubtedly was part of
these relationships, the constables seemed to be looking as much for a 'home away
from home' that could provide domestic comforts unavailable to them.[79] This need
could be so strong that men were spending their leisure time with women, rather
than the more common pattern of working-class leisure segregated by gender.[80]

Men had affairs more often with widows and married women than with single
women. While single women did have affairs with married men, the problem
became where to meet. Single women were likely to live with families or in
lodgings where entertaining a male visitor was difficult. A married constable could
rarely bring a lover home and evade his wife. Such couples could only meet in
relatively public places such parks, restaurants or hotels, leaving them at the mercy
of sharp-eyed proprietors and nosy passers-by. Married women had more control
over their homes and widows with their own homes faced the fewest obstacles.
Mrs Stevens, a war widow, and PC Rodgers, a married man with four children,

---

76   See Klein, 'Irregular Marriages'.

77   Elizabeth Roberts found that companionate marriages existed in the working class in the
first half of the twentieth century with expectations varying from couple to couple (Roberts,
A Woman's Place, p. 115).

78   MWCM, 20 May 1909, vol. 43, no. 167, PCC 167 Timothy Braddock, twenty-five years'
service, seven defaults, last in 1894. He was not dismissed because of his long record and
instead was reduced to the lowest class, amounting to a drop in pay of 7/4d. He had been
paying the woman 7/- a week to support his children by her. Since he had a family with his
wife as well, the punishment meant that he could no longer afford to support two families.

79   Gillis, *World of Their Own Making*, pp. 32–3.

80   Davies, *Leisure, Gender and Poverty*, for the separation of genders in working-class social and
work life.

had known each other for ten years and carried on an affair for at least two years before they came to the attention of the chief constable as a result of an inquisitive neighbour.[81] Mrs Willets, the thirty-year-old widow of a constable who worked as a cleaner at the main police station, carried on an 'improper correspondence' and 'association' with PC Tandy. Unfortunately for them, being together at work led to their exchange of letters becoming noticed.[82] Any couple involved in an affair risked being discovered by snooping neighbours but women with their own homes could hide affairs for years and many couples were never found out.

If spouses were caught committing adultery, senior officers intervened with warnings, advised couples, and waited to see if gossip resulted before taking strong action. They much preferred reconciling couples to punishing constables or dealing with separations. One case showed the kind of awkward situations with which senior officers could be faced. While PC Pullen was in the army, a Mr Willoughby 'took advantage' of Mrs Pullen and she had a child. Her husband's superintendent advised her to 'write to her husband and tell him what had happened; this she has done and ... he frankly forgives his wife for the wrong she has done him'. Her allowance as a police dependent was not suspended since her husband had forgiven her and since she 'always looked well after her house, and her children are well cared for'.[83] In such circumstances, sympathies might be extended to spouses who kept up marital expectations of household management or financial support regardless of sexual fidelity. The most frequent assumption found in the records was that spouses who did not fulfil their duties should not be surprised if their partners looked elsewhere for companionship. But regardless of any provocation that might lead to an affair, senior officers expected spouses to give up their lovers. In three cases out of four, constables preferred keeping their jobs. Discovered having an affair with Mrs Atkins, PC Bowe was told that 'he must keep away from associations with Mrs Atkins of a compromising nature'. Bowe agreed and was only cautioned.[84] But a few preferred their lovers. After being caught in a three-and-a-half-year affair with Miss Markwell, PC McKeown promised his superintendent that he had stopped seeing her. However, he continued to meet her and finally resigned rather than end the 'improper relationship'.[85] In a few cases, marriages did not survive affairs even if constables gave up lovers and couples ended up separating. Other couples seemed

---

[81]   MWCM, 28 January 1929, no. 1, vol. 130. Rodgers was dismissed in spite of his sixteen years of service with only one default. The chief constable 'caused observations to be taken of the dwelling house' which resulted in Rodgers being caught by two officers with his boots off but otherwise clothed.

[82]   LCCDR, 1 February 1928, PCH 264 Tandy, cpt Supt Gill, no action taken for four months to see if gossip resulted and whether Tandy behaved; finally cautioned.

[83]   LWCM, 24 July 1917, pp. 574–5.

[84]   LCCDR, 30 November 1929, PCA 341 Bowe.

[85]   LCCDR, 8 June 1922, PCB 198 McKeown.

able to reconcile. PC Pullen was able to forgive his wife but otherwise the records were silent on the future of couples in these cases.

Perhaps the strangest form of extramarital relationship was that of a dozen married men pretending to be single in order to court unmarried women. It is uncertain what these men hoped to achieve but they seemed to be looking for a kind of female company missing at home. Possibly, they pretended that these relationships did not count as being unfaithful since no sex took place. The women inevitably assumed that the courtship was a prelude to marriage. Senior officers understood these cases to be deceptive courtship, indicated by charges using phrases such as 'paying addresses' and 'keeping company'.[86] Half of the time, the men used false names. Reggie Ford kept company with the widowed Mrs Sempers and behaved 'towards her as if he were an unmarried man intending to marry her'. In reality, he was PC Cole, a married man with two children.[87] In one of the more detailed cases, William Sumner courted Miss Ada Hopson for six months, passing himself off as a single engineer and seeing her once or twice a week. After a month, he proposed to her, explaining that 'he was going to Brazil for the Firm' and he wished her to accompany him. She declined, saying that she did not know him well enough yet. He then decided to stay home and asked her to marry him at Christmas or at least become engaged. She declined again but they kept seeing each other. One day, she received an anonymous letter warning her that he was married and had three children. She went to the address to check and discovered that the letter was correct.[88] Wives could react violently to their husbands' faithlessness though they often took their anger out on the other women as much as on their husbands. When Mrs Byrne found out that her husband had been taking Miss Muriel Hales, a shop assistant, for walks in a local park, she went to the shop and made a disturbance, calling the girl nasty names even though Miss Hales had stopped seeing the constable once she realized he was married.[89] None of the cases indicate that sex was involved and there is no evidence that the men were considering committing bigamy. Possibly the men were disillusioned with domestic life. They missed the romance of courting someone or courtship fulfilled

---

[86] Typical examples include Thomas Gardiner, 'Behaving in a manner unbecoming a Police Officer and paying addresses to a single woman to whom he falsely represented himself as a single man. To Resign Forthwith' (MGO, 31 March 1911), and William Symms, 'Acting in a manner likely to bring discredit upon the reputation of the Force, viz:- posing as a widower and keeping company with a single woman, he being a married man. Dismissed' (MGO, 20 December 1929).

[87] BDRB, 5 December 1923, PCE 35 Henry Charles Cole; BPO, 5 December 1923, p. 7141, dismissed.

[88] MPF, 15 September 1934, PCB 107 William Sumner, appt November 1924, reduced in class for a year. The letter-writer could have been his wife or a neighbour attempting to warn the girl.

[89] MPF, 11 July 1924, PCD 83 Byrne.

some need for companionship that they craved. Whatever their motives, constables took enormous risks since such courtships were difficult to keep private and the women's families could cause problems if they thought that their daughters were ill-used. Unlike adultery cases, constables caught in these cases either lost their jobs or suffered heavy penalties for victimizing innocent women.

If husbands or wives finally decided that they could not live with their spouses any longer, they could simply leave but most set up separation agreements as well. Some sort of support arrangements were typical though some spouses just walked away, such as when Mrs Warriner left to live with another man and PC Warriner never heard from her again.[90] Separations were not necessarily permanent. PC Groman lived in lodgings apart from his wife for six weeks and then moved back in with his family.[91] Constables' conditions of service required that they support their wives, even if separated, so they usually came to some kind of agreement. Support could be informal or legal arrangements depending on whether the situation met legal grounds for separation or if couples wanted to keep their separation private. Agreements ordinarily involved the husband paying weekly support, typically about a third of the constable's pay and too little for the wife to live on without other income.[92] While normally it was an advantage to have a legal separation agreement to ensure that the husband paid, it could have drawbacks. When PC and Mrs Lloyd separated in 1919, they signed an agreement promising her ten shillings a week. He voluntarily raised this to fifteen shillings when he was promoted to sergeant in 1927 but decreased the allowance by half a crown in 1931. She begged the chief constable to raise her allowance back to fifteen shillings but his hands were tied due to the legal agreement. He could only advise her to put the case in the hands of a solicitor.[93] Many wives lived in suspense over whether or not maintenance would arrive. One advantage of being a police wife was that police forces enforced both formal and informal separation agreements, including garnishing wages. After Mrs Jessie Williams separated from her husband due to his drinking and violence, PC Williams agreed to pay her thirty shillings a week. The chief constable 'warned Con to keep up the payments, otherwise the position would be reviewed again'.[94] PC Williams paid. Police forces took each separation case on its own merits, as they did with any domestic problems. In a 1919 case, a

---

90   BWCM, 5 October 1927, p. 1, report no. 8. He was not penalized for not supporting his wife since he could not find her.

91   LCCDR, 12 November 1927, PCF 107 Groman.

92   The Maintenance of Wives (Desertion) Act, 1886, set support at no more than £2 per week for wives and ten shillings per week for each child. This was not changed until 1949. Roderick Phillips, *Putting Asunder: A History of Divorce in Western Society* (Cambridge: Cambridge University Press, 1988), p. 606.

93   MPF, 5 November 1931, PSB George Norman Lloyd, appointed August 1919.

94   LCCDR, 18 October 1929, PCH 457 Williams.

constable returning from the army was not rehired because of a charge of cruelty to his wife which ended in a separation order.[95] In 1920, however, a man was hired as a constable even though he was separated from his wife since the separation was based on her 'misconduct' while he was in the army.[96] These decisions follow the patterns around other domestic cases; senior officers did not like to interfere but would not tolerate repeated abuse or behaviour that strayed too far from normal gender expectations by either spouse.

Similar to other marital problems, senior officers could go to great lengths to resolve problems between separated couples, attempting reconciliations and negotiating settlements in the hopes of keeping constables' careers on track. They often got involved after receiving letters from wives whose husbands refused to live with them or support them. After months of thought, Annie Macaulay finally wrote to her husband's superintendent:

> I need help very badly as my husband refuses to have me live with him. I have a little girl age five years and I am about to become a mother to a second child[,] this make[s] it very difficult to get a post of any kind or I could keep myself. My husband is impossible to live with, and at times seems almost insane.
>
> It is now the third time my husband has forced me to leave him. I have tried to please him in every way.
>
> My husband [h]as given me to understand that under no conditions would he live quitle [sic] with me. If necessary I would take the case to court. Will you kindly advise me what to do.

Superintendent Lewis met with PC Macaulay and 'pointed out the seriousness of the position to him and ... how important it was for him to get his wife back'. Chief Constable Maxwell also had a private meeting with Macaulay and his wife and gave them a month to reconcile their differences. Lewis kept Macaulay under observation and noted that he had improved in his duties and seemed to be taking the warnings to heart. After a month, Macaulay wrote that he and his wife had 'agreed now to live together in harmony'.[97] The intervention of Lewis and Maxwell was enough to get the constable back on track both in his job and his marriage. But sometimes, even their best efforts failed. The degree of hostility that could be felt towards a spouse can be seen in the acrimonious separation of PC and Mrs Pirie. Who initiated the separation or what caused the marriage to fail was not in the records. When they separated in late 1932, chief

---

95 MWCM, 22 July 1919, vol. 80, no. 14.

96 MWCM, 14 April 1921, vol. 86, no. 102.

97 MPF, 20 August 1928, PCA 163 Aulay Macaulay, appointed August 1920. Macaulay and his wife were probably around thirty years old.

constable Wilson had to step in to negotiate a settlement. He was unlikely to have supported Mrs Pirie's case if she were known to be intemperate or involved with another man, and such matters were thoroughly checked. PC Pirie finally agreed to pay his wife twenty-five shillings a week. However, he soon stopped paying despite two reminders from senior officers in October and November 1933. Instead, he tried to take furniture from her home after agreeing to leave the furniture with his wife. Wilson ordered him to pay the support including an extra five shillings a week until the arrears were paid off. Pirie still refused to pay. In January 1934, he was fined forty shillings and warned that if he did not pay his wife as ordered he would be fired. A month later, he was dismissed for refusing to support his wife. Wilson showed remarkable patience in trying to resolve the situation, knowing that firing Pirie could only hurt his wife. He must have been a decent constable, or Wilson would not have tried so hard to resolve the problem. Unfortunately, there is no evidence to suggest why he refused to support his wife. If she threw him out, perhaps he felt that she was no longer his responsibility. Possibly, losing his wife was more than he could bear. All that is clear is that after a year of struggling with his separation, Pirie preferred losing his job to supporting his wife.[98]

One of the most detailed cases of a failed marriage combines the entire spectrum of domestic problems – the husband's unhappiness over his wife's housekeeping, his affair with a widow with six children, the wife's jealousy, her making disturbances and refusing to accept that her marriage was over, their marital separation, and accusations of cohabitation. At first glance, the case of James and Mary Higgens seemed to be a simple one of a husband committing adultery to the distress of his wife. When events began in 1927, PC Higgens was probably in his early thirties, Mrs Higgens was forty, and Mrs May Jones was thirty-two.[99] After eight years of marriage with no children, PC Higgens met May Jones, a police widow who worked as a cleaner at an inn to support her six sons. Their friendship eventually became an affair. Unhappy with his marriage due to his wife's lack of children and alleged poor housekeeping, Higgens found more congenial companionship with Mrs Jones and enjoyed the company of her sons. Mrs Jones' motives were less clear, though Mrs Higgens later accused her of accepting money from Higgens. In 1934, Mrs Higgens followed her husband to Mrs Jones' house. Possibly, a neighbour of Mrs Jones informed Mrs Higgens of her husband's illicit visits. Mrs Higgens objected to the affair and PC Higgens promised to end it. Mrs Jones even wrote to Mrs Higgens, stating,

---

[98]   LCCDR, 27 November 1933, PCE 129 Pirie, appointed 1926; LDRB, 13 February 1934. Pirie and his wife were probably around thirty years old.

[99]   Higgens joined the Manchester City Police in 1920 when recruits had to be under thirty years old and were usually at least twenty years old. So by 1927, he could have been anywhere from twenty-seven to thirty-six years old.

I daresay when you read this letter, you will think I have got confounded cheek, but think what you will of me. I feel I must write you a few lines, I give you my solemn word that I will never see or communicate with your Husband again, also I do hope that you will try and forgive him, after all said and done, it is human for the best of us to err, and it is up to you to try and help him to forget that he ever went astray. There is not anything more I can say, only that I am more than sorry for it all.

But instead of this apologetic letter calming Mrs Higgens, she went to Mrs Jones' house and accused Mrs Jones of harbouring her husband. Her lack of children while Mrs Jones had so many sons may have added to her insecurities and jealousies. Mrs Higgens then 'tried to do harm' to herself. Neighbours reported to Mrs Higgens that, on hearing this, Mrs Jones remarked, 'it was a pity she didn't b————— well finish herself'. Mrs Higgens believed that Mrs Jones was threatening to blackmail PC Higgens if he stopped seeing her. Higgens stated that he had kept his promise not to see Mrs Jones but every time he went out by himself, his wife taxed him with being with that 'dirty red headed Welsh whore'. He continued,

> On many occasions she has threatened to leave me when we have had little tiffs. She has even accused me of knowing my own sex indecently & also little girls, … I certainly decided to go out as much as I could, as I was afraid I may lose my temper and strike her when she made use of such filthy accusations.

In July 1937, Mrs Higgens finally left her husband to live with a sister and he sent her thirty shillings a week, a typical support payment. At least twice, she returned to her home to take crockery and other items to her sister's house. The separation did not end her jealousy. In August, she sent a letter to Mrs Jones that was written in such 'disgusting terms' that Mrs Jones refused to show it to anyone except Chief Constable Maxwell. It included accusations that the affair still continued, that Mrs Jones had gone on holiday with PC Higgens, and that Higgens was giving money to Mrs Jones, charges which Mrs Jones vehemently denied. In September, 1937, Mrs Higgens wrote to the Manchester Police accusing her husband of cohabiting with Mrs Jones, which both of them denied. The letter concluded, 'I would like, owing to my age – I am 50 years of age, – home life ruined – health shattered – a fair measure of justice from the Manchester City Police Force.' She was invited to see a chief superintendent to whom she told her story. Her motives for writing this letter were not to get support but rather to get back her status as a wife and home-maker.[100] 'I

---

100 See Tebbutt, *Women's Talk?*, p. 108.

would willingly go back to my husband if he gave up this woman.' She could not
tolerate the idea of her husband committing adultery or believe his assertions
that the affair was over. Higgens justified his misconduct by arguing he had been
a good provider but that she had never fulfilled her duties as a wife:

> I am sorry to state that she has not been all a wife should be during our married
> life, on several occasions when I have arrived home from duty I have found
> her missing with no fire or anything to eat ready for me. I also gave her £4
> per week for the past 13 years and she has never saved anything out of it for
> holidays or clothes ... Whenever I asked her what she had done with the money
> she has got into a raving temper and resented my asking her ... A few years
> ago I missed my gold watch & chain, which I had purchased myself, and when
> I asked her what she had done with it, she said that she had lent to a sister to
> pawn owing to her being in a difficulty, I have not seen it since ... I have never
> ill used or been cruel to her ... and she has left me of her own free will and
> she still has her key ... She also said 'I'll soon have you down in front of the
> chief and lose you your bloody job.'[101]

Even though at least some of what he described occurred after his wife learned
of the adultery, he portrayed himself as the injured party rather than his
wife. All three agreed in official statements that the affair occurred; however,
it is difficult to tell if the affair continued after 1934. All of the statements
occurred after the marriage broke down and everyone was trying to justify their
behaviour. The only evidence from before the investigation was the 1934 letter
of Mrs Jones, the tone of which was matter-of-fact and almost kind-hearted. The
letters and statements of Mrs Higgens suggested that she could not control her
jealousy.[102] Senior officers finally concluded that Higgens had a valid grievance
against his wife for her failure to manage her household properly. His regular
paying of support and her persistent temper may have been factors as well. He
was transferred to another division but not otherwise disciplined. No other
disciplinary complaints appear in his personnel file. He must have kept up his
payments to his wife and, if he resumed his relationship with Mrs Jones, he did
so discreetly enough to avoid the attention of meddling neighbours and fellow
officers. While most police marriages followed more ordinary lines, Higgens'

---

101 Ayers and Lambertz, 'Marriage Relations', p. 201. See A. James Hammerton, *Cruelty and
Companionship: Conflict in Nineteenth-Century Married Life* (London and New York: Routledge,
1992), p. 84, for a husband making similar excuses for his own misconduct. Catherine Hall
interviewed a woman who defined domestic happiness in similar words in 'Married Women
at Home'.

102 For a more detailed look at working-class marital jealousy by both husbands and wives,
see Klein, 'Irregular Marriages'.

case showed that senior officers would not insist that men stay in unhappy marriages as long as they supported their families.[103]

The domestic life of constables involved not only couples and their children, but also their neighbours, and senior officers had to appease offended neighbours as often as they counselled married couples.[104] In many ways, the concerns of working-class neighbours did not change dramatically from 1900 to 1939. Getting along was easier when neighbours had similar ideas of space, including noise and boundaries. Streets could be rowdy or quiet, casual or tidy. Neighbours could be gossipy or private, use the front doors or the back doors. Children could be boisterous or restrained. Wives set up local survival networks to help each other from one pay period to the next, but some networks were more gregarious than others.[105] Families protected their respectability, but might have different standards of respectable behaviour. Each street and block developed its own character which evolved as families came and went. Usually this happened slowly as new families both adjusted to and modified local standards but occasionally a sudden change could throw a street into confusion. If a new family was too different from a street's character, neighbours did not suffer in silence, but started campaigns of complaints, arguments and harassment to enforce conformity. If differences became too aggravating, efforts might be made to force families to move. Such sharp conflicts became more common in the 1920s and 1930s when working-class families moved more frequently due to better transportation, new housing and changing job markets. Adding to tensions, men were becoming more involved at home after the First World War.[106] Wives bickering over children now included men protecting their families. Disputes over clothes lines led to men yelling at neighbours' wives, whose husbands then came to their defence. Neighbourhood disputes certainly existed before the war, but wives were more likely to settle matters amongst themselves. After the war, with husbands being drawn into this female arena, conflicts became more acrimonious. The majority of complaints against police neighbours came after the war and were made by men rather than women, though at least some husbands filed complaints at the behest of their wives.

Having a policeman living on the street could be good or bad, depending on circumstances. Neighbours might have to refrain from some activities, though not always, since constables might turn a blind eye to less serious infractions while off duty. Off-duty constables might even participate in minor law-breaking, especially

---

103   All information on this case from MPF, September 1937, PCF 91 James Higgens, appt May 1920.

104   For a detailed study of interwar neighbourhoods, see Klein, 'Moving On'.

105   See Ellen Ross, 'Survival Networks: Women's Neighborhood Sharing in London before World War I', *History Workshop* 15 (1983): 4–27.

106   See Hall, 'Married Women at Home', p. 76; Bourke, *Working-Class Cultures*, pp. 64, 82–8.

if it involved beer or street betting. On the other hand, having a constable handy to deal with problems or give first aid could be useful. Both policemen and their wives had to adjust to neighbours considering their homes to be a sort of local police station. In a typical instance, when PS Smith and his wife were getting ready for bed, a young neighbour came by to tell him that someone had broken into her house. Since the thieves were no longer there, he told her to go to the local station. He complained, 'It is a regular custom for my neighbours to call at my house to lodge complaints of all kinds instead of going to the policeman on the beat or to the station which is a good distance away.' The woman felt that 'Sergt Smith ought to have come with me' since it was late at night.[107] Many neighbours expected police neighbours to act on their behalf whenever they needed assistance. Policemen did not mind this within reason, and certainly responded to emergencies, but they also wanted their own time off. Any neighbours with skills, such as in motorcycle repair or carpentry, might find themselves called upon by their neighbours. Every neighbourhood had its own standard for when asking for assistance was neighbourly and when it became intrusive. Like anyone else, policemen in neighbourhoods with demanding standards had to adapt or educate their neighbours without offending them.[108]

While any family might face neighbourhood pressures to conform, police families were particular vulnerable. Police regulations limited their housing options, and they were dependent on neighbours' good will if they wished to avoid trouble with senior officers. Neighbours knew that they could lodge complaints against policemen, and after the war, mostly neighbourhood men used this as an effective way to force police families to change their behaviour or move.[109] In 1931, Manchester Chief Constable Maxwell protested that he was constantly receiving complaints that on investigation proved to be a result of 'idle and stupid gossip'. However, he could not afford to ignore the complaints, since 'Idle and vindictive

---

[107] MPF, 20 February 1928, PSC Joshua Smith, appointed November 1914, cautioned.

[108] Some Birmingham police families lived in police cottages which served as police stations, a situation more common in county forces. If their husbands were out, wives were expected to answer the phone, take messages and handle inquiries as best they could (DC, Evidence, question 463, PC Herbert Waight, Metropolitan Police Force, p. 26; BPO, 16 April 1931, p. 17,951 – instructions on switching over phone lines when the cottage was vacant).

[109] This was similar to the way in which neighbours threatened each other with summonses to settle disputes, as well as the use of the courts found by Jennifer Davis in *Law Breaking and Law Enforcement*. One reference to a neighbour informing a civilian employer to get another neighbour into trouble was found in police records. William McGuinness and his wife 'were of superior type and excellent address' which aggravated PC Parry and his wife. They began 'continually annoying' the McGuinnesses. McGuinness charged that Mrs Parry had written to McGuinness's employers to get him into trouble (LCCDR, 9 May 1935, PCG 242 Parry, complainant William McGuinness, 400 East Prescot Rd, Parry warned as to his future conduct).

gossip and interference with the affairs of others ... cannot but bring discredit upon the whole of the Force '[110] Liverpool had the same problem. Mr Todd's complaint that PS McLellan and his family had been generally offensive was discovered to be completely unfounded. Nevertheless, McLellan was advised by his superintendent that 'this sort of thing was undesireable & might mean he would have to move if it did not stop'.[111] Neighbours figured out that policemen could be susceptible to the most baseless complaints, and took full advantage since they might get the results they desired. If neighbours persisted, police families might move if only to avoid the aggravation. Senior officers almost never charged constables for neighbourhood complaints but instead constantly gave 'advice about living amicably with ... neighbours'.[112] Within reason, they tended to side with whomever had the more tolerant standards, either the complainant or the constable. They did not see it as their position to be an improving agency. While not a stated aim, promoting mutual tolerance among neighbours contributed in at least a small way to improving public order.

For both police families and their neighbours, public displays of cleanliness had long been a sign of respectability. Wives starched curtains, cleaned door steps and made sure that the appearance of the family was a good one.[113] With more husbands at home, they became drawn into anxieties over appearances, and husbands began quarrelling with neighbouring wives whose husbands then jumped in. When one husband was a constable, senior officers found themselves in the strange position of investigating fights between men over housekeeping. One careless wife infringed on the clean back entry of her neighbour. Mrs Dutch habitually threw her refuse out of her back door rather than into a bin, with much of it landing in front of the Pirie's back door. Finally, no doubt after clashes between the wives, PC Pirie yelled at her. Mr Dutch accused him of bullying his wife, and the situation degenerated into a shouting match between the husbands. After Mr Dutch complained, Pirie was advised to keep on good terms with his neighbours so Mr Dutch got the result he wanted.[114] Front gardens could cause similar trouble. Mrs Mudie let her dog urinate on the Mackay's gate post every day. Frustrated about this 'violation' of his home, PC Mackay protested, leading to an argument between the two husbands.

---

[110] MGO, 9 May 1931.

[111] LCCDR, 24 April 1929, PSA 49 McLellan, complainant R.G. Todd, 35 Sedgewood Road, Norris Green.

[112] LCCDR, PCG 183 Walley, complainant George Abbott, 6 Ashcombe Rd, L-pool, regarding offence taken at abusive language, no charge framed.

[113] See Bourke, *Working-Class Cultures*; Rosemary Crook, '"Tidy Women": Women in the Rhondda between the Wars', *Oral History Journal* 10:2 (1982): 40–6; Roberts, *A Woman's Place*; Ross, 'Survival Networks'; and Tebbutt, *Women's Talk?*, for detailed descriptions of the effort involved in keeping up appearances.

[114] LCCDR, 28 May 1931, PCE 129 Pirie, complainant John Dutch, 109 Chatsworth Ave., Orrel Park.

Mr Mudie complained and Mackay was warned that he would have to move if further complaints occurred.[115] In these and similar cases, the constables were not disciplined but instead their senior officers suggested that they get along with their neighbours, even if that meant putting up with different standards of cleanliness than the police family might prefer.

More tricky could be cases provoked by children. Similar to cleanliness, children's behaviour indicated family status. Different definitions of well-behaved children could lead to neighbours questioning each other's parenting skills. Minor incidents could degenerate into verbal battles such as when PC Baker and Mrs Lord 'exchanged words' after the Lords' son took a fire shovel away from Baker's son and the constable went to get it back.[116] While mothers had always minded both their own and the neighbours' children, after the war men began taking a larger role in child rearing.[117] Men could lose status if they could not control their children so they tended to be strict; but they also came to their families' defence more often. This could create complicated disputes with men protecting their status as heads of families. PC Corlett sent his child to apologize to Mrs Beeney for throwing cabbage leaves into her garden. In response, Mrs Beeney yelled at the child and Mr Beeney both yelled at Mrs Corlett for not controlling her child and complained to police. Corlett's senior officers concluded that the Beeneys had over-reacted and took no action.[118] Fathers could escalate quarrels, perceiving minor squabbles between children as challenges to their standing as fathers. The daughter of PC Tinsley kicked the eight-year-old son of John Ferguson and the boy retaliated two days later. The boy was punished by his own father but Tinsley did not consider Ferguson's punishment good enough. He went to Ferguson's home, 'threatened to kick the boy from one end of the road to the other', and threatened to tell the boy's headmaster. Mr Ferguson complained and Tinsley was ordered to apologize to his neighbour by his chief superintendent.[119] Senior officers had little sympathy with constables or civilians who let childish quarrels get out of hand, especially when efforts had been made to apologize or otherwise resolve the problem.

---

[115] LCCDR, 23 August 1937, PCA 163 Mackay, complainant Edgar L. Mudie, 31 Warnerville Road, no charge framed.

[116] LCCDR, 14 April 1934, PCA 243 Baker, complainant Mrs Louise R. Lord, 5 Aconbury Place.

[117] Bourke, *Working-Class Cultures*, p. 90. See also Ross, 'Survival Networks', p. 12; Carl Chinn, *They Worked All Their Lives: Women of the Urban Poor in England, 1880–1939* (Manchester: Manchester University Press, 1988), p. 43.

[118] LCCDR, 2 October 1934, PCG 130 Corlett, complainant W.L. Beeney, 1 Bramhill Road, West Derby; no action taken.

[119] LCCDR, 2 November 1937, PCA 310 Tinsley, complainant John Ferguson, at 12 Wilberforce Road, no charge framed. It is unknown whether or not the daughter was punished.

The most violent disputes between husbands were also the ones where they had an immediate quarrel with each other, rather than being drawn into disagreements of their wives and children. Gardens and allotments became a growing part of men's responsibilities after the war, and fights over them led to families moving more often than other problems since they involved serious issues of trespassing and physical damage. Men often played out their aggressions in assaulting each other's hedges, the physical barrier dividing their territory. Angry at the Williams children for using his garden as a shortcut, Mr House stopped pruning his hedge. PC Williams responded by cutting the hedge without permission. When Mr House objected, Williams used 'filthy language'. Senior officers warned Williams that he would have to move if he could not learn to live with the Houses, so Mr House made his point that his garden was not a right of way.[120] Mr Grundy was less successful in his complaint against PC Pritchard. A hedge dividing Mr Grundy's garden from Pritchard's allotment had reached a height of eighteen feet and came five feet into the allotment. This stole territory from Pritchard and reflected poorly on the neighbourhood. Grundy complained when Pritchard 'mutilated' the hedge, but since the hedge violated corporation regulations, Pritchard was simply advised to let Grundy know next time he trimmed the hedge.[121] In these territorial combats, the force was careful to remind all sides to respect each other's property. Gardens and allotments could be as tidy or messy as their gardeners desired as long as they did not encroach into territory of their neighbours.

Senior officers perhaps became most exasperated in advising tolerance when it came to complaints over noise. These appeared more frequently than any others, since sound could travel across boundaries more readily than the sources of most other complaints. Ironically, families preferring quiet could be remarkably outspoken in demanding it. Noisy neighbours annoyed people trying to sleep, relax or get work done; talkative neighbours upset those less tolerant of gossip or concerned to protect their privacy. Problems often resulted from people sleeping on different schedules. George Jackson complained that the family of PC Boss made unnecessary noise early in the morning 'poking fires'[122] while an elderly couple complained that PS Charnley made too much noise late at night banging

120 LCCDR, 1 June, 3 September 1937, PCG 94 Williams, complainant Mr. House, 8 Agar Road, West Derby. The Kellys and the Raithbys had a long history of hurling insults at each other. One day, Joseph Kelly cut a hedge dividing their gardens and the Raithby son told him that 'he was making a ———— mess'. Kelly complained to the Liverpool chief constable and Raithby was advised to move.(LCCDR, 15 June 1935, PSE 29 Raithby, complainant Joseph Kelly, 595 Queens Drive, Stoneycroft)

121 LCCDR, 18 June 1936, PCA 93 Pritchard, complainant Mr Grundy, 23 Clinton Place, West Derby.

122 LCCDR, 7 January 1931, PCH 278 Boss, complainant George F. Jackson, 28 Corona Road, Old Swan. 'Div Supt. said complaint was frivolous. CC 6.1.31. I am not disposed to take action.'

doors.[123] The minor yet annoying quality of these disagreements is shown in Mr Peck's complaint that PC Mutch and his wife kept banging on the wall between their homes. Mutch replied that his wife had indeed banged on the wall but only because someone in Peck's home had been playing the piano early in the morning.[124] Demands for quiet could be complicated when some neighbours were enjoying consumer goods such as pianos while others were not.[125] Radio owners experimenting with tuners and volume controls aggravated less fortunate neighbours. The acrimony between PC Turner and two of his neighbours over his wireless set became so severe that Turner began writing abusive letters to them. They responded by turning him in to his senior officers who had to caution him for writing the letters.[126] Status items included gramophones and motorcycles which appealed to men's affinity for tinkering. PC Casson was proud of his air-cooled motorcycle but a neighbour, upset by the noise, complained that its engine disturbed his sleep. His senior officers concluded, 'A little tolerance appears to be needed on both sides.'[127] Noise complaints rarely led to disciplinary action, investigations often finding them to be unfounded or 'frivolous'. Petty complaints were more or less ignored and constables rarely accumulated more than one of them. Nevertheless, neighbours persisted in making them. Senior officers could only advise their men to remember that night shifts required keeping quiet while their neighbours were sleeping and that a little forbearance would save the force a great deal of unnecessary trouble.

After the war, families moved more often, and if new neighbours changed the character of an existing street too abruptly, old residents could have a difficult time adjusting. Some of the more acrimonious complaints involved neighbourhoods in transition. Investigations of an anonymous letter in Manchester discovered older residents on Larch Street fighting a losing battle against an influx of newcomers. Matters came to a crisis on Guy Fawkes Day 1927. PC Wright allowed his three sons and other boys to build a bonfire in his front garden and set off firecrackers. When Eva Kaufman came home from work, her invalid mother complained that the firecrackers were giving her a headache. Making no effort to resolve the problem,

---

[123] LCCDR, 27 June 1936, PSA 5 Charnley, complainant R.H. Lambert, 558 Mather Ave. No charge framed. Charnley stated that 'His own family are in bed & no unnecessary noise has been made.'

[124] LCCDR, PCG 199 Mutch (& his wife), complainant F. Peck, 89 Queens Drive, West Derby, no charge framed.

[125] See Davies, *Leisure, Gender and Poverty*, pp. 42–3, for an exploration of jealousies created by tangible rewards of the economic success.

[126] LCCDR, PCH 219 Turner, complainants J.W. Hughes and R. Bruce, 10 Flaxman Street. Turner denied knowing the men but cautioned for writing the letters. No charge framed.

[127] LCCDR, PCH 64 Casson, complainant Waller Wright, 23 Berwyn Road, L-pool. No charge framed.

Miss Kaufman, a long-time resident of the street, threw a bowl of water on the fire. Mrs Wright came out and argued with her for ruining the boys' fun. PC Wright later explained, 'Hearing an argument was taking place, I went out and saw Eva Kaufman ... She then threw the bowl at my wife. The bowl passed my wife and hit me. She then got hold of my wife and ... she picked the bowl up again and hit my wife with it.' Wright came to the defence of his wife. According to Miss Kaufman, 'Constable Wright ran at me and took hold of me by the throat, and dragged me along a passage ... I screamed ... I admit that I did smack the constable in his face.' This violent encounter brought to the surface the frustrations of older residents on the streets upset at young families such as the Wrights, who were no doubt equally irritated by older families like the Kaufmans for their impatience with the normal activities of children, especially on national holidays.[128]

Competing factions of old and new neighbours tried to drive each other off Larch Street. In an attempt to get rid of Wright and his family, the anonymous letter from one of the older residents brought the brawl to the attention of the chief constable. The illiteracy of the letter suggests that part of the problem may have been tensions between older neighbours protective of their respectability in the face of more educated newcomers. The letter stated, 'I think it is quite time there was A stop to there [sic] carrings [sic] on he is making what was a quite [sic] Street into a very rowdy street he can leave no one alone there we have lived over 40 years in the Street never seen such carrying on untill [sic] he came Disgracefull [sic] to the Manchester police force hoping there will be something done for peace to the neighborrs [sic]'. Yet soon after the investigation was underway, a petition signed by twenty men and women from eight houses on the block arrived, stating that the Wrights were quiet, respectable neighbours and begging that the family be allowed to stay on the street. Clearly, two standards of what constituted quiet and respectability existed. His popularity may have come from his willingness to entertain neighbourhood boys as well as neighbours feeling more secure with a policeman on the street. The petition could also have been a sign of Miss Kaufman's lack of popularity. With an invalid mother, she may have annoyed neighbours with frequent calls for quiet as well as taking out the pressures of dealing with an invalid mother on others. The investigation did lead to Wright being reduced in rank and warned for discreditable conduct; his senior officers could not tolerate his assaulting a woman even in defence of his wife. However, the petition worked to the extent that he was not required to move. Given the extenuating circumstances and the support of so many neighbours, the force decided not to uproot his family.[129]

---

128   Today, police officers will often ignore complaints about noise called in around midnight on New Year's Eve, after dark on national holidays, and on similar occasions, considering such complaints to be unreasonable. My thanks to officers who shared this observation with me.
129   MPF, 6, 7 November 1927, PCB 38 Albert Wright, appointed April 1914. A similar case involving PC Rayner is described at length in Klein, 'Moving On'.

Sometimes newer residents did nothing to provoke older residents and still became the target of accusations. Chief constables kept receiving anonymous letters, often with scurrilous allegations that had to be discreetly investigated. Occasionally letters were based on misunderstandings, but others seemed to have little foundation outside of the imagination of their authors. In 1938, the Manchester chief constable received this anonymous letter:

> Sir, (PC Hughes knows what she does.)
>   There is awful talk of PC Hughe's [sic] wife going out with young Prob. Officers, gambling can be seen from Bus through window of curtains. This has gone on for months, PC Wilson goes with Mrs. Preese, [(]both women are married.) Debt collector after Mrs. Hughes. Them should not live on the Front of Moston Lane. Its the dreadful talk of your men, we think you should know. Have a watch put on them.

The letter was not signed. All such letters were investigated, so a superintendent and chief inspector made careful inquiries. Rather than the den of iniquity described, they learned that PC Hughes and his wife now and then had PC Wilson and his 'young lady' Miss Priest over for 'a friendly game of whist'. Sometimes, Mr Ireland, another friend, joined them. No gambling took place and Mrs Hughes was not in debt. The investigating officer was satisfied that, 'this is a vindictive letter, in all probability written by some person of the household next door, because during my observations I have seen an old lady and another lady which appeared to be her daughter peering through the curtains as if they were watching the movements next door'.[130] It is also possible that the two ladies thought a police investigation might enliven their lives. PC Hughes was not interviewed since the initial investigation found the letter not to be a valid complaint. While anonymous letters did sometimes uncover real problems, more often they did not. They served as a safety valve for neighbourhood frustrations, but also wasted police time investigating their claims.

Strain between old and new residents could be exacerbated by anxiety over respectability, with neighbours upset at real or perceived insults. Families might be seen as flaunting a sense of superiority over others or insinuating that they were too good for their neighbours. Even small differences in pay and employment could create tensions. If stresses became severe enough, neighbours took measures to force families to move elsewhere. Policemen had to live in housing approved by their forces and, in one of the more extreme cases in police records, the Entwistles felt that their new neighbourhood was not up to their standards. They decided to

---

130 MPF, 22 February, 26 April 1938, PCB 48 Charles John Hughes, appointed October 1928.

rid themselves of three neighbours through escalating harassment. They played their wireless set at one and two in the morning. They 'would sit at the kitchen and parlour windows and make faces at the children while they were playing' and ordered away children whenever they played in the street or alley. When Mrs Butler got permission from Mrs Earl to hang washing on her line, PC Entwistle ordered her to take it down since it was blocking his light. More seriously, he tried to get the Earl's son fired from his newspaper delivery job for 'giving impudence to his wife', and tried to get the Butlers evicted for having too many people in their house. But their strategy finally backfired. In what began as a prank, children hoping to cause a little trouble threw a rug belonging to Mrs Entwistle into the back yard of Mrs Smith. Mrs Smith found the rug and hung it on the clothes line. Even though she saw the rug on the line, Mrs Entwistle reported the rug as stolen rather than doing the neighbourly thing and asking Mrs Smith about it. Two police officers appeared at the Smith's house to investigate. To Mrs Smith, who felt she had done the right thing by hanging the rug where it could be seen and claimed, being accused of stealing challenged her respectability. In the face of these intolerable conditions, neighbourhood husbands organized a letter-writing campaign. Mr Smith, writing more in sorrow than in anger, described how, at the bidding of Entwistle, two officers had 'in quite a bullying and offensive manner accused [his wife] of stealing a piece of carpet ... to gratify the personal spite this officer and his wife have against all the neighbours on both sides'. After a thorough investigation, a superintendent concluded that 'the whole of the trouble is a domestic quarrel apparently originating from a little spite and jealousy by the neighbours towards Entwistle's wife who is rather of the superior type and never at a loss for words. Entwistle is undoubtedly guided by his wife who seems to have a domineering influence over him.' The neighbours succeeded in freeing themselves from this abrasive family when Entwistle was told to find a house in a different neighbourhood and advised to reform his domestic behaviour.[131]

Complaints against policemen by their neighbours were often centred on their wives since the wives saw each other every day. Wives helped each other out with errands and chores but they also bickered over children, shared yards and gossip. In more serious instances, they quarrelled, threw insults at each other, and threatened each other with summonses. Frictions usually worked themselves out but could get ugly when combined with other tensions. Unfortunately for her neighbours, Mrs Bramley was 'a woman of tyrannical and overbearing manner who on any and every occasion of a clash with the neighbours, threatens with a wholesale issue of summonses'. Her behaviour was bad enough that she herself had been summoned a few years earlier for insulting words and behaviour. Children were at the root

---

131 MPF, 30 January, 6, 12, 13 February 1935, PCB 82 Albert Victor Bradford Entwistle, appointed August 1920.

of many of the arguments since she incited her children to annoy the neighbours. Her husband, PC Bramley, supported his wife and had recently issued summonses against two neighbour children for kicking a ball in the street. Finally, twenty neighbours signed a petition asking that something be done about the trouble the Bramleys caused on the street. Under the circumstances, the summonses against the children were withdrawn by the chief constable. The investigating inspector concluded that the Bramleys had created enormous resentment and that the trouble was primarily caused by Mrs Bramley. PC Bramley was ordered to move and warned that no repetition of such events would be tolerated.[132] Such complaints against wives show a tendency by both neighbours and senior officers to expect husbands to restrain their wives' behaviour. Yet despite this perception, police records clearly show that few husbands, police or civilian, were able to do so. In marriages such as the Bramleys and the Entwistles, husbands supported their wives rather than restrained them.

The presence of husbands in neighbourhood disputes after the war left them open to questions regarding their masculinity if they were perceived as not controlling their wives. Many neighbours complaining about wives stated that they did not want to get the husbands into trouble but did want them to stop their wives' unacceptable behaviour. It is clear from the investigations that many husbands had a difficult time managing their wives but a policeman unable to control his wife was particularly open to ridicule. PC Thompson admitted having little influence over his wife who enjoyed antagonizing her neighbours, including accusing one wife of having bugs in her house to that woman's distress. After neighbours complained, a police inspector spoke to her about her behaviour in the presence of her husband but even this authority figure had no effect. Finally, a year later, eight families, including another police family, sent a petition to the police force, stating that 'it would be to the very great benefit & satisfaction of all, if the family living in number 12 were removed'. After interviewing the families, senior officers agreed and moved the Thompsons. The only complaint about PC Thompson was 'that he has no control over his wife', a fairly typical remark in cases where wives were seen as the primary source of trouble.[133] In spite of husbands being more involved at home, they remained absent much of the time and their wives still dominated the domestic sphere. When a police wife simply could not get along with her neighbours, even the police force had no choice but to move the family.

Despite the evidence of neighbours clashing with each other, even the conflicts illustrated that generally amicable streets could cope with one or two troublesome

[132] MPF, 30 August, 2 September 1932, PCD 243 Wilfred Leslie Bramley, appointed June 1921, dismissed and reinstated October 1928 for drinking on duty (see Chapter 3).
[133] MPF, 31 May; 3, 5, June; 4 September 1935, PCA 126 Richard Stonehouse Thompson, appointed April 1926.

families. Intense battles were fairly unusual. Neighbours helped protect compatible neighbours, perhaps more than they tried to move the incompatible. One such instance made it into police records by accident after neighbours tried to stop a domestic assault out of concern for the family rather than out of anger at the husband. PC Wilkinson, in his mid to late twenties, had lived on Elsie Street for years and was well liked except for his drinking problem. Coming home drunk one night after a sports event, Wilkinson attracted the attention of two Hulme families when he broke a pane of glass, shouted at his wife, and grabbed her by the hair. The Hulmes ran towards his house to stop him.[134] Wilkinson shouted out the window, 'I will show the bloody lot of you what I can do', ran into the street and challenged the men to fight. Both Hulme men advised Wilkinson to go home and sleep it off. Unfortunately for Wilkinson, two other police families lived on the block. The wife of PC Davenport heard the ruckus, and PCs Davenport and Hawley arrived on the scene. They managed to get Wilkinson back into his house in spite of his struggles against them. Concerned about his drinking, they reported him to the local station. When an inspector showed up, Wilkinson had passed out and his young wife was 'greatly distressed'. The next day, Wilkinson could not remember anything and apologized profusely to his wife, the constables and his neighbours. Wilkinson remained on the block but was ordered to keep his drinking under control. Here, neighbours had tried to defuse a nasty situation, protecting Mrs Wilkinson, without getting her husband into trouble. In none of the interviews was there any hint of animosity towards him, even by the two constables, but rather concern for his welfare and hope that his drinking problem could be resolved. Perhaps appreciating this support, his senior officers allowed him to remain on the street and Wilkinson managed to get his career back on track.[135]

Finding good neighbours could make all the difference for a comfortable life, but this became more challenging after the war with more families on the move. The increasing presence of men in family life exacerbated misunderstandings, adding frictions over masculinity. When differences became too extreme, neighbours did not suffer in silence, but started campaigns of arguments, complaints and harassment. Ultimately, families might be forced to move. Policemen were particularly susceptible to this pressure since police forces could not afford to have their men in conflict with their neighbours. Overall, police domestic life followed working-class patterns both with their neighbours and within their marriages. Senior officers tolerated a certain amount of irregularity as long as husbands continued to support their families and wives ran their households. Constables had

---

134 Roberts found that neighbours would physically restrain men abusing their wives or children (*A Woman's Place*, p. 194).
135 MPF, 19 July 1923, PCB 130 William Wilkinson, appointed January 1920, reduced to lowest class and transferred for being 'mad with drink' and striking a constable.

to endure sometimes-intrusive attention being paid to their private lives and a good deal of unsolicited advice. Yet while police forces could demand that constables move to new neighbourhoods, they did not insist on constables staying in unhappy marriages. Despite the lament of Chief Constable Maxwell that it was 'a pity that neighbours cannot live in amity with each other',[136] neighbours generally managed to get along with each other without too much commotion. Senior officers kept advising toleration and providing opportunities for reformed conduct, both within police marriages and with police neighbours.

---

[136] MPF, Entwistle.

10

Taking off the Uniform

Cause of Leaving: At own request (To assist Parents in business).
At own request. To return to Merchant Service as Engineer.
Own request (To join another Police Force nearer to his home).
Died in Hospital as the result of motor cycle accident. At own
request (Domestic Reasons). At own request (For betterment
of his future). At own request (To take up other employment).
At own request (Obtained position in Canada). At own request.
(Lack of interest). At own request (to join Air Force).[1]

THE PRECEDING CHAPTERS have described men entering the police
force and living with its conditions and restrictions. Some did not make
beyond their probationary year. Quite a few were dismissed or asked to resign for
committing defaults, though fewer as force discipline improved after the war. But
outside these cases, a significant minority of qualified constables left the police
force before reaching retirement age. Some left voluntarily. Their reasons for
leaving, and for losing the supposedly irresistible police pension, fell into two basic
categories.[2] First, men in their first years of service discovered that they did not
care for or could not cope with police life. Restrictions were too severe, the job was
different than expected, or the physical requirements were too great. Second, as
men got older, they left for domestic reasons. Their families disliked the constantly
shifting schedules, parents wanted sons to enter a family business, or promotions
did not arrive as hoped. The senior officers of these discontented constables did
everything they could to dissuade the men from leaving. Forces suffered from
chronic shortages of suitable recruits and could ill afford to lose experienced and

---

1   Birmingham City Police Resignation Register, 1930–1939, diverse entries.
2   Portions of this chapter relating to voluntary resignations are based on Joanne Klein,
'"Leaving at His Own Request": les démissions volontaires d'agents de police britanniques
(1900–1939)', in *Métiers de police: être policier en Europe, XVIIIᵉ-XXᵉ siècles*, ed. Jean-Marc Berlière,
Catherine Denys, Dominique Kalifa and Vincent Milliot (Rennes: Presses Universitaires de
Rennes, 2008), pp. 189–99.

satisfactory men. No doubt, some men were convinced to remain; but every year capable policemen quit the force due to discontent with the police life or in search of better opportunities elsewhere.[3] Other men may have wanted to remain but had to resign for health reasons, brought on by exposure to weather, constant walking or job-related injuries. When possible, forces found them desk jobs or other duties within the force that they could manage. A few unlucky men died from injuries and illnesses often linked to police work. Finally, men left to serve in the military in the First World War and did not return. They died in service, they suffered injuries that prevented their returning to the force, or they chose new occupations after demobilization.

As men reached retirement age, they began to balance retiring sooner to protect their pensions with hanging on longer to increase its size, but even the early leavers might take their pension money into consideration when resigning from the force. Every week, men had part of their wages paid into a pension fund. Under the 1890 Police Act, this averaged two and a half per cent of their wages; under the 1919 Police Act this doubled to five per cent. Both acts allowed policemen to retire after twenty-five years of service but before 1919, watch committees often added age minimums to extend service to avoid paying pensions as long as possible.[4] The 1919 Act disallowed these minimums, awarding a half-pay pension at twenty-five years with increments up to two-thirds pension at thirty years' service. The 1890 Act gave a partial pension after fifteen years on medical grounds; the 1919 Act gave medical pensions after ten years. Men who left voluntarily often asked to have their deductions returned but forces had no obligation to comply. Manchester tended to grant requests automatically but in Birmingham and Liverpool, men needed to combine their appeals with the projects that they wanted the money for, such as opening a business or travelling abroad for a new career. He got his money if a watch committee considered the constable and his request worthy. Birmingham granted men deductions around three or four times a year.[5] Since medical retirement was not allowed until ten or fifteen years of service, forces also routinely granted deductions to men disabled on duty.[6] But

---

[3]   A handful of 'voluntary resignations' were noted in records as disciplinary cases where men resigned before defaults could be proceeded with against them. To get another position, it helped to have at least technically a 'clean book' with the police force. It is impossible to know whether additional 'voluntary resignations' took place under similar conditions but were not so noted in the records.

[4]   See pp. 140–1 for details.

[5]   BAR, 1900–1939. Refusal rates were not reported. Some deductions were returned due to ill health but reasons for returning deductions were not given in annual reports in most cases.

[6]   See BAR, 1900–1939. Some deductions were listed as returned due to ill health; others had no reason listed. One rare refusal to return deductions in a medical case involved doubt regarding the illness. After making arrangements to buy a farm, PC Wright stated that he

occasionally watch committees denied returning deductions if the constable was found to be unworthy, usually through excessive drink. In some cases, deductions might be granted to other family members to ensure that police children were looked after or if a constable left behind dependent parents or siblings.[7] Even after retirement, policemen did not gain complete control over their money. Pensioners who thought that they were finally free from police regulation could find that part of their pensions were paid directly to estranged wives over their protests. Men who took advantage of retirement to set up irregular households could not lose their pensions, but they still had to support their wives. A pensioner could never quite leave behind the force and its interest in his personal life.

The two basic categories of voluntary leavers remained constant, but rates of voluntary resignation decreased from the prewar to the postwar period, reflecting changes in police conditions of service. Prewar low wages and low prestige made it difficult for forces to keep men if other opportunities beckoned. In Liverpool, an average of forty-four men voluntarily resigned every year from 1900 to 1914. In Manchester, just over half of the men who joined before the war left, either voluntarily or involuntarily, before serving twelve years. At least some of those men must have served in the war. After the war and the 1919 Police Act, the better wages and growing professionalism of the police force encouraged men to stay, and the higher education standards prevented many casual workers from joining. In Liverpool, thirty-four men left voluntarily each year in the 1920s. Only seventeen a year left from 1930 to 1935, no doubt partially influenced by the Great Depression. The total of Manchester men leaving with under twelve years' service between 1919 and 1939 dropped to thirty-five per cent. Birmingham was an exception, with a fairly steady rate of around fifteen to twenty resignations a year. Perhaps under the iron hand of Chief Constable Rafter, conditions did not vary enough to affect the numbers. Yet similar to Liverpool, resignations climbed

---

had to resign due to ill health resulting from getting wet while on duty. When the surgeon did not understand the symptoms Wright described, he arranged to send him to the hospital for observation. Wright refused to go, fearing 'that the doctors would experiment upon him'. Since the surgeon could find nothing wrong with him, Wright's request for a medical gratuity or his rateable deductions was declined (LWCM, 15 November 1915, pp. 608–9).

7   The City of Birmingham Police Force looked after the children of PC Snipe, 'who met with his death in the execution of his duty' (BAR, 1907, p. 6; 1908, p. 6; 1909, p. 6; 1910, p. 6). A mother and four sisters were awarded a constable's gratuity of £66 and the father of another £15 (BWCM, 25 November 1907, pp. 191–2; 25 July 1910, p. 293). They awarded the father of PC West £12, the mother of PS Tansell £33 and the mother of PS Midwinter £94 (BWCM, 6 June, 25 July 1923; BJSC, 28 January 1931, p. 12). Though objecting to William Maloney's accusation that onerous duties had killed his son, the chief constable allowed him a small grant (LHCWC, 14 August 1905, p. 274). When PC Capper died, his sister with whom he had lived for twenty-two years was given his gratuity of £108 (MWCM, 20 December 1928, vol. 128, no. 29).

during the high emigration before the war and in the midst of the heavy hiring after the 1919 police strike when recruits were rushed into uniform, and dropped from 1931 to 1933, the worst of the Depression. In Birmingham, resignations climbed again in the late 1930s as the economy recovered. The peaks suggest that men were more likely to leave for civilian life when the economy looked promising. For the entire period in all three cities, men were more likely to leave before they completed twelve years of service and were still young enough to begin another career. Men continued to resign after twelve years but in significantly lower numbers.[8] By then, constables understood what was required of them and could balance the expectations of their job with other employment options. The lure of the pension took on a more concrete existence, especially if they had families, and made it more sensible to stick it out in the force. Nevertheless, perfectly suitable constables with years of experience still opted to leave the force despite all the efforts of their senior officers to convince them to remain.

Most young men joined the police without any clear idea of what they were getting into and without any particular calling to be a constable.[9] They dropped in and out of policing, particularly before the war, but even during the Great Depression one man left after a day, policing being 'different to what he has been accustomed to', another left after two months because he did not like Birmingham, and another left after six months because he did 'not like the work'.[10] Both before and after the war, men leaving within the first three years tended to be unable or unwilling to adjust to police life. They were still learning how to balance contradictory expectations such as being told never to neglect their beats under threat of disciplinary action, yet also instructed never to ignore complaints even from another beat.[11] Constables needed to work out police regulations and discipline and often became frustrated with the unfamiliar level of supervision. Caught up in the fervour at the beginning of the First World War, PC Wright was shocked to discover that the local recruiting office had been specifically instructed not to

---

8   Manchester City Police roster cards show fifty-three per cent of constables leaving within the first twelve years of service from 1900 to 1914. After 1919, this dropped to thirty-five per cent. Between 1900 and 1914, seven per cent left with thirteen to twenty-one years' service; between 1919 and 1939, nine per cent. These per centages include both voluntary and involuntary leavers. Liverpool numbers from Liverpool City Police Annual Reports, 1900–1935. Birmingham numbers from Birmingham City Police Annual Reports, 1902–1939. A 1905 Liverpool report listed around 120 men joining and leaving the force every year but this number included both voluntary and involuntary departures (LHCWC, 3 June 1905, p. 228).

9   See Chapter 1.

10   BRR, 29 July 1931, PCE 185 John Edward Southern, one day's service; 28 July 1937, PCE 44 Leslie A.K. Harris, two months' service; 11 August 1934, PCD 243 Arthur Jack Thorogood, six months' service.

11   BPO, 10 August 1905, order to attend to all complaints regardless of location, pp. 169–70.

allow him to enlist.[12] Despite a successful start in his career, Thomas Smethurst left after feeling 'victimized' by a sergeant with a 'swelled head'. The sergeant reported him for neglecting his duty and gossiping after Smethurst had run into a relative and talked with him for a moment. Smethurst decided, 'Such rigid discipline I had not been used to, and did not intend to put up with, for it was unreasonable and unenglish; so I looked out for something else, made my arrangements accordingly, and then sent in my resignation.' His chief constable tried to talk him out of this but Smethurst persisted, leaving to work in his native village.[13] Constables became fed up with economies that never seemed to favour them. One Manchester constable complained, 'we do not know what to make of a man being made a defaulter for failing to attend to a certain thing because he has not yet paraded, and then when a man meets with an accident whilst cycling to duty to be regarded as off duty and his full pay stopped'.[14] Men genuinely concerned with being good policemen left the force out of frustration that police headquarters seemed more concerned with statistics than reality and that magistrates let prisoners go that the constable knew to be guilty due to what often seemed like capricious considerations.[15] The reality of violence was more than some men could face. Witnessing another constable being assaulted by a prisoner, PC Rice ran away rather than risk being beaten himself.[16] The difference between their pre-police notions that the job required little more than walking a beat and arresting the occasional drunk and the actuality of policing required a change of thinking that some men simply could not or would not make.

For some constables, the best reaction to police life was to flee. Both before and after the war, the tedium of beat work combined with bad weather and rough conditions prompted men to disappear without bothering to resign. PC Tyler 'absconded' from Birmingham, never to be seen again.[17] Many such fugitive policemen came from Liverpool, perhaps linked to their bad morale problems. Before the war, after five years' service, PC Smith took to his heels, and after one year, PC Droogan ran away. Both made the mistake of withdrawing from duty without returning their uniforms which lead to warrants being issued for their arrest.[18]

---

12   BWCM, 30 November 1914, p. 133.

13   Smethurst, 'Reminiscences', pp. 88–95.

14   *Police Review and Parade Gossip*, 12 May 1911, p. 226.

15   *Police Review*, 18 October 1901, 'Should Policemen Be Truthful?', p. 496.

16   BPO, 8 September 1903, PCC 160 Stephen Rice, charged with cowardice and asked to resign, p. 562.

17   BPO, 25 September 1909, p. 124. He was finally dismissed for failing to report to work.

18   LDRB, 4 April 1913, PCH 91 Smith, five years' service, sentenced to forfeit all pay due to him; 8 August 1913, PCE 253 Droogan, one year's service, one default, struck off the strength, fined 10/- and costs by the courts.

After the war, a constable could 'remember at least three who disappeared and nipped home. I remember one Welsh fellow up from the Valleys – he run home at night-time. It broke his nerve. Went home to Wales and he had the police uniform on. That's where he made his mistake. They sent up to bring him back.'[19] Even after years in the force, men walked away from the job without bothering to resign. PS O'Hare, with eighteen years' service, and PC Morris, with fourteen, simply vanished and were 'struck off the strength'.[20] All of these men forfeited their pension deductions, but getting away from policing seemed to outweigh that consideration. Failing to resign properly may have been their final rebellion against force regulations.

Some young constables did not necessarily mind police life but they did not like the local force or the location itself; they left hoping to find a better situation in another police force in another place. Men sometimes tried out two or three forces before they settled down, looking for better conditions or better officers. They might miss home or want to try a bigger city. In 1911, Birmingham Chief Constable Rafter did a special five-year report finding that three men had resigned and since rejoined, eight men had left for other forces, and thirty-nine men had applied from other forces, seven being accepted. The eight who had left had given 'special, personal, or family reasons'.[21] A 1930s Birmingham resignation roster listed numerous young constables leaving for London and Glasgow forces as well as joining forces closer to home. Others arrived to try Birmingham after starting their careers elsewhere. Even older men thought they might like a change, such as PC Croft who transferred to the Plymouth City Police after eight years in Birmingham. Fourteen months later, Croft rejoined the Birmingham force, Plymouth apparently not living up to expectations.[22] A few constables found that their original force was better than they realized after trying policing somewhere else. After four years in Manchester, Reginald Borthwick begged to be transferred to the Gateshead force so he could live with his ailing parents. He did not add that he wanted to live near his fiancée as well but his transfer was allowed. In less than a year he returned to Manchester, finding it difficult to police people where he had 'youthful associations'.[23] After five years in Liverpool, Walter Bailey transferred to the Hants County Constabulary. After only a month, he applied to return to Liverpool, finding Hampshire different from what he

---

19   Brogden, *On the Mersey Beat*, p. 58.

20   LDRB, 11 July 1908, PSH 22 O'Hare; 13 June 1913, PCE 59 Morris, two defaults.

21   BAR, 1911, p. 6.

22   BRR, 20 June 1936, PCD 260 Frank Charles Croft, eight and a half years' service; BRB, PCD 260 Frank Charles Croft, joined January 1928, left for Plymouth force June 1936, rejoined October 1937, retired January 1953.

23   MPF, 8, 17 April 1930, January 1931, PCD 233 Reginald Borthwick, appointed May 1926.

had expected.[24] Some men left policing entirely only to return later. Thomas Smethurst resigned from the Bolton police force but five years later joined the Stalybridge Borough Police where he remained until he retired.[25] While these men had not left policing, these moves nevertheless signalled dissatisfaction with their work and unhappiness with their location. They 'force hopped' looking for better conditions. Some men eventually found a force they could live with, but others finally realized that it was policing rather than the location that was the problem.

For some constables, changing forces within Great Britain was not enough to satisfy their search for better opportunities. An adventurous few emigrated to join police forces abroad, ranging across every continent except mainland Europe. Some emigrated to join colonial police forces. Two young Manchester men joined the Ceylon police,[26] Hugh Service joined a force in New Zealand[27] and Stanley Scott joined a force in Tanganyika.[28] Moving abroad often included significant promotions, most likely ones not available at home. Three Birmingham men given a choice between remaining constables at home and advancement abroad chose emigration. Two went to Australia, one to become the governor of a jail and the other a chief constable; another became a chief constable near the Klondyke in Alaska.[29] Manchester PS John Rabbitt was appointed chief inspector of police in Buenos Aires.[30] Losing motivated men could be a blow to English forces, however much senior officers understood the opportunities available abroad. But constables learned that only so many openings for promotion existed at home, no matter how many men might qualify. Options became settling on remaining a constable, looking outside of England for promotion, or leaving the force.

Most of the voluntary leavers left the force altogether, attracted by better prospects in terms of locations, pay, conditions and advancement. Constables well thought of by senior officers left, sometimes despite efforts of chief constables to convince them to remain. With five years' service and against the wishes of his chief constable, Thomas Silvester thought he could do better in another profession after the war.[31] The Birmingham resignation roster included regular cases of

---

24   LWCM, 20 December 1932, p. 838. This application was denied since he 'was making a convenience of the service' but he quit the Hants force and returned to Liverpool anyway. He applied again five months later and was accepted back into the force.
25   Smethurst, 'Reminiscences'.
26   MWCM, 5 August 1910, PCA 46 Daniel Lloyd, two years' service, PC Thomas Caine, four and a half years' service, vol. 48, no. 117.
27   BJSC, 27 April 1927, PCB 171 Hugh Service, p. 57.
28   BRR, 29 June 1930, PCB 66 Stanley Scott, four years' service.
29   *Police Review*, 23 September 1904, p. 459.
30   MWCM, 18 September 1919, DS John Rabbitt, seven years' service, vol. 80, no. 99.
31   BRB, 13 July 1919, PCC Thomas Leonard Silvester, joined May 1914, 'Resigned at own request against the wishes of the Chief Constable.'

men leaving in search of more agreeable employment. Younger men left to look for 'more suitable' occupations.[32] Men with substantial service left, tired of being constables and seeing few prospects for advancement in remaining. Often around ten to twelve years of service, they left for 'civilian employment'.[33] A surprising number of such men left during the Great Depression to find civilian work, suggesting a great dissatisfaction with the police. Though some men took over businesses left to them or in response to offers of employment elsewhere, others left to find a different job without any firm options. After fifteen years' service, Daniel Manton left for the 'betterment of his future', and after eleven years, Robert Gately decided that he was tired of working for someone else and went into business for himself.[34] By the 1930s, many of the better-educated men hired immediately after the war had to accept that hoped-for promotions were not going to materialize. If advancement did not seem likely, men might finally decide to try something besides the police force.

Many constables came from another part of the country when they joined the police, and a desire to return home was a common reason to resign. Many were recruited from small towns and rural areas. Some could not adjust to city life and some missed their families. Such homesickness tended to affect younger men. After only ten days, one young recruit fled home to Bath, a not unusual reaction with at least a few new recruits resigning within days.[35] During their first years of policing, once the novelty of the work and the city wore off, men might feel the pull of home. After four years, Frank Lloyd desired to 'leave district' for home and after six years, John Griffiths moved back to the Channel Islands.[36] When Thomas Smethurst quit after five years, he went home. Other men might leave not because they disliked policing or the city but because of family problems back home. After his father became ill, Cecil Paget resigned in order to return home and Dennis Tanner resigned on 'compassionate grounds' related to

---

32   After two years in the force, PCC 63 Raymond Hickman decided he could find more suitable employment elsewhere (BRR, 8 July 1934). PCE 250 Frederick Wright left to 'obtain occupation more suitable' after two years (BRR, 27 May 1936). PCE 203 Victor John Dunleavy changed occupations after six years (BRR, 12 April 1936).

33   PCC 143 Archibald Stokes gave up ten years' service to 'take civilian employment' (BRR, 26 June 1938). With eleven years' service, PCA 71 William Horatio Inwards left 'to take up other employment' (BRR 7 October 1930). PCA 53 William Edward Gifford left 'to enter business' after eleven years in the police (BRR, 10 April 1938). PCC 41 Robert Henry Harcourt had fourteen and a half years' service when he left for civilian employment (BRR, 12 September 1938).

34   BRR, 5 August 1934, PCD 40 Daniel Manton; 24 June 1934, PCB 142 Robert William Gately.

35   BRR, 10 April 1932, PCD 119 Paul Macdonald, ten days' service.

36   BRR, 28 February 1932, PCB 137 Frank Lloyd; 25 January 1931, PCC 76 John Griffiths.

family matters.[37] As they got older, men might face pressure from families to return closer to home to look after relatives or to take over businesses. A family business also could be an attractive option for a constable starting to wonder about his future.

Some constables leaving the force did so not to go home but in order to emigrate, usually to some part of the Empire or to America, and begin a new life altogether. Most men going abroad tended to have two to eight years' service. These men were still young enough to begin life elsewhere and experienced enough to make an informed decision to move abroad. Some were single but others already had young families. In the years immediately before the First World War, emigration became so pervasive that it put a strain on police forces; experienced men were resigning and men were taking their pensions as soon as they qualified to go overseas.[38] In Liverpool and Birmingham, the number of voluntary resignations jumped, and from 1910 to 1914, the Manchester Watch Committee received regular letters from men asking for the return of their pension deductions so they could go abroad. The married PC Cully needed the money to move his family to Canada,[39] while the single PC Jackson left for South America.[40] Liverpool PC Parr received a year's pension in advance so he could emigrate to Australia with his family.[41] Reasons for going were generally vague, such as going with friends or joining relatives, though PC Ainsworth left for Australia on account of the health of his wife and child, using his deductions to pay the fares.[42] Both PC Lishman and his wife came from the countryside and, having relatives in Canada, decided to emigrate since she had 'never settled to town life'.[43] Requests for returns of

---

[37]   BRR 14 December 1934, PCC 40 Cecil John Paget, three months' service; 23 April 1933, PCA 146 Dennis Carl Tanner, one and a half years' service.

[38]   'Inspectors of Constabulary report for year ended the 29th September 1912', PP 1913 (76) lii, 663, p. 57.

[39]   MWCM, 30 March 1910, PC Thomas W. Cully, five and a half years' service, moved to Canada with wife, children and friends, received £9, vol. 46, no. 131. PCE 23 Archibald Irving, eight years' service, and PCE 104 James Beavies, four and a half years' service, left for Canada four months later (MWCM, 5 August 1910, vol. 48, no. 117). PCA 148 William Williams needed his deductions back to 'make arrangements for my wife before leaving' to go abroad (MWCM, 26 July 1912, thirteen years' service, received £23, vol. 56, no. 31).

[40]   MWCM, 5 October 1912, PCD 48 Fred Jackson, seven years' service, received £12., vol. 56, no. 98. PCA 63 John Forrest left for Australia (MWCM, 12 June 1912, four years' service, received £7, vol. 55, no. 40e). PC Harold Shaw went to Australia after five years' service, receiving £8 (MWCM, 14 January 1913, vol. 57, no. 51).

[41]   LWCM, 21 November 1910, PCC 185 Parr, p. 105 (the pension advance was paid on the condition that he be insured).

[42]   MWCM, August/July 1912, PCA 30 James Ainsworth, nine years' service, received £16, vol. 56, no. 30.

[43]   LWCM, 16 February 1914, PCA 182 F. Lishman, four children under four years old, request for return of pension contributions declined, pp. 328–9.

deductions tended to be made only weeks or days before leaving. After eight years as a policeman, PC England asked for a return of his deductions on 25 March 1913, officially resigned on 31 March, and sailed for Australia on 10 April. Men no doubt wanted to stay in the police until the last moment in order to keep earning but these requests put a strain on the force both to come up with the money and to replace experienced men. In 1913, Manchester had four constables move to Australia, one to New Zealand, and two to New York; all but one had eight to nine years' experience and all received full refunds. The low wages and pension were no incentive to remain, particularly if they had relatives or friends who could help them settle in the new country.[44] Fewer men emigrated after the war but the basic pattern continued. After two years in the force, PC Sutcliffe decided to move to Australia in 1921 and, with four years' service, PC Miller left for South Africa in 1925.[45] In the 1930s two Birmingham constables went abroad with five and six years' service and one went to Canada with two years'.[46] About half had families and generally moved to places where they had relatives or connections. In 1920, Albert Gilbert returned to America to rejoin his brother's business after six years in the Manchester force.[47] Most years, emigrants only made up a handful of men, but in the years before the war, emigration created a particular hardship for forces which could ill afford to lose experienced men when wages were low and recruitment difficult.

As men settled down and created homes of their own, they began to leave policing for domestic reasons, often resenting interference in their private lives. Not only did men have to follow rules while on the job, their off-duty lives were subject to police approval touching on everything from their choice of wife to their choice of pub. Constables were forbidden to take on outside work, even during the war when wages were particularly inadequate, could not join a political society or party and, after the war, could not be members of a union. They could not even

---

[44]   MWCM, 25 March 1913, PCA 182 Thomas England, received £13, vol. 58, no. 160. PC Frederick Metcalfe resigned on 27 March, asked for his deductions on 31 March and left for the US on 4 April, giving the force only four days to give him his £5. He did provide a mailing address in case the notice was too short (MWCM, 31 March 1914, three years' service, vol. 63, no. 4).

[45]   MWCM, 13 July 1921, PC Harold T. Sutcliffe, two years and three months' service, received £11, vol. 88, no. 17; 12 December 1924, PC John Miller, received £22, vol. 105, no. 4. After about a year in the police, PCB 197 Walter Woodcock moved to Australia (MWCM, 6 May 1927, joined January 1926, received £12, vol. 117, no. 5).

[46]   BRR, 15 February 1931, PCC 58 David Aeron Mathias, five years' service; 24 January 1937, PCD 205 Walter John Cartwright, six years' service; 30 June 1935, PCB 195 Arthur George Chesmer, two years' service.

[47]   MWCM, 19 November 1920, PSF Albert Gilbert, received £21, vol. 85, no. 6, asked for certificate of service from the force, presumably in case he wished to join an American police force.

volunteer in many cases. Having a friend who ran the Liverpool zoo, PC Messenger did him the favour of performing a free show with his dog after the scheduled act quit suddenly only to be ordered by his senior officer immediately to desist in his public performance.[48] Some men tried to evade regulations. David Kirk continued running his cab proprietor's business[49] while PC Kirkwood worked as a motor dealer for over a year.[50] When forced to choose, both men resigned rather than give up their lucrative civilian occupations. Their unwillingness to give up second jobs also showed an unwillingness to conform to police expectations. Men who left for 'domestic reasons' tended to be a little older, after experiencing a few years of the affect of policing on their family lives. They finally decided that they did not care to commit their entire lives, on and off duty, to the police force. The Birmingham resignation roster included many entries of constables leaving for 'domestic reasons' or, more ominously, for 'domestic trouble'.[51] PC Hill's wife threatened to leave him unless he quit the force.[52] 'Domestic reasons' often included a need to get a job with a regular schedule and one that did not include constant interference with domestic life.

Men had more positive reasons for leaving the force, often connected to taking over family businesses. Resigning to help with parents with their business appeared regularly in the Birmingham roster and sporadically in other records. After four years as a constable, Horace Coxhead resigned to 'relieve parents in business', William Deakin left after ten years to join his mother in her business, and Ronald Brown left after five years 'to enter business with father'.[53] There is no way of knowing if the men had planned to step into the family business all along when parents got older or if circumstances changed since joining the force. Wilfred Smith left after only sixteen weeks to assist his parents in their business which suggests either quick dissatisfaction with police life or a sudden change in his parents' situation.[54] Generally, men shifting to a family occupation did so in their thirties when parents wanted the next generation to help with the burden of running a business. Men without family businesses to step into left 'to take up other employment' and to move into 'another position in civilian life'.[55] They tended to be in their early to mid-thirties. All of these constables had reached a point in their

---

48   LCCDR, 30 August 1933, PCE 245 Messenger, no charge framed. The father of the previous act complained that Messenger had taken his son's job away but it was proven that the son had quit first.

49   MGO, 24 January 1901, PCB 159 David Kirk, resigned.

50   LCCDR, 1 June 1922, PCB 230 Kirkwood.

51   See BRR, various dates.

52   Emsley, *The English Police*, pp. 214–15.

53   BRR, 9 July 1934, PCE 256 Horace Robert Coxhead; 9 October 1934, PCE 201 William George Deakin; 6 May 1934, PCC 158 Ronald Wheaton Brown.

54   BRR, 9 February 1930, PCB 199 Wilfred Smith.

55   BRR, various dates.

careers where they could make an informed decision regarding their futures and were still young enough to start a new occupation.

However frustrating these voluntary resigners were for their senior officers, at least their numbers dropped by about a third from the early 1900s to the 1930s. In part, this reflected a change in how long it took to change a civilian into a policeman. The transition from recruit into fully fledged constable took longer before the war than afterwards, since prewar recruits were less educated and more casual joiners. This left men vulnerable for longer to the temptation to leave the force. Once these men adjusted to police life, most remained until retirement age or until their health gave out. After the 1890 Police Act, policing experienced a gradual improvement over the nineteenth century at keeping men in the force, even with more than half weeded out or leaving before twelve years of service. After the 1919 Police Act, the improvement was more dramatic. The decrease in attrition rates was connected to the decline in policing as a casual occupation, and its improved conditions of service and pay. Yet good men kept leaving for both negative and positive reasons, to get away from the force or to seek new opportunities elsewhere. They made up only one or two per cent of their force strength in any year, but in police forces struggling to find and keep quality recruits, such men remained a constant nightmare.

A few men left forces not by choice but for health reasons, often physical ailments such as respiratory complaints and joint problems brought on by walking beats in all kinds of weather. Illness could hit men at any point in their career. PC Richards had to resign after only thirty months for health reasons, PC Heath after seven years, and PC Matthews after thirteen years.[56] After twenty-three years, PC Burgess left for Canada for his health, arranging for his pension to be paid to his wife who remained in Manchester.[57] However, according to Birmingham annual reports, only a handful of men were discharged on medical report or given medical pensions. Even if all Birmingham men receiving their pension deductions were considered to be medical resignations, they only averaged three a year.[58] What this suggests is that only men too disabled to work in any way were resigning. In other cases, men were finding ways to hang on. When possible, forces moved these men into jobs they could manage, such as handling lost property or answering phones, especially if they were close to earning their pensions. Many men hid illnesses to try to make it to their pensions. They also worked when ill since if they took too many sick days, these were added to the length of service they needed to qualify for pensions. On rare occasions, they hid their ailments so well that they died in

---

[56]   BRR, 5 November 1939, PCB 253 David Samuel Richards; 19 November 1933, PCE 45 Albert Henry Heath; 13 August 1939, PCD 179 Leonard Ernest Frederick Matthews.

[57]   MWCM, 29 May 1924, PC John Robert Burgess, joined May 1901, vol. 102, no. 40.

[58]   BAR, 1902–1939.

service. Though clearly sick, PS White took regular leave instead of going on the sick list to limit his number of sick days. Suffering from influenza but refusing to see the doctor, he finally collapsed in his kitchen and died.[59] While designed to stop men from malingering on the sick list, adding sick days to length of service no doubt contributed to breaking down the health of at least some men who persisted in working while ill. Nevertheless, whatever toll policing took on the health of the men, most could manage to qualify for their pensions with help from their senior officers, through their own persistence, or both.

At least according to annual reports, dying on the job was more likely than a medical resignation. In Birmingham, an average of four men a year died while in uniform, and in the larger Liverpool force, eight men died a year before the war, and six a year after.[60] While some men died from traffic collisions, from falling into the Irwell and Mersey rivers and from similar work-related misfortunes, most deaths resulted from illnesses. Thirty years of records listing Liverpool constables injured gave only two fatalities, one killed when a police horse fell on him and another who died of tetanus after he was blown down the steps of a warehouse in a gale and had to have his leg amputated.[61] The 1930s Birmingham resignation register listed twenty-three men dying of illnesses, one killed in a motor accident while off duty, three killed in motorcycle accidents, and one 'killed whilst on duty'.[62] Ill health was more dangerous than accidents, probably exacerbated by men concealing illnesses to stay off the sick list. Nearly half of the men who died listed in the register had fewer than ten years' service. While only in their twenties, PC York died of pneumonia, PC Robinson died of a 'disease of nerves', PC Mole of tuberculosis and PC Miller of gastric ulcers.[63] Respiratory illnesses such as pneumonia, pleurisy and tuberculosis were common.[64] Excessive walking could

---

59   BPO, 1 November 1922, p. 5618.

60   BAR, 1902–1939; LAR, 1900–1935.

61   LCI, 31 July 1916, p. 148, PSH 43 Sant, died 5 August; 11 January 1921, p. 248, PCD Peers, sustained compound fracture of leg, leg amputated, died of tetanus 22 January.

62   BRR, 23 November 1938, PCE 130 Sidney Owen, two years' service; 17 August 1936, PCC 49 Ronald George Dawding, five years' service; 25 June 1931, PCD 273 Joseph Shipton, one year's service; 10 November 1935, PCC 54 Robert Holmes, eleven years' service; 27 Dec 1930, PCE 143 Hugh Miller, ten years' service.

63   BRR, 30 December 1932, PCE 268 Leonard York, two and a half years' service; BRB, 20 August 1934, PCD 79 Charles Arthur Robinson, joined May 1930, married 1933, 3–6 March 1934 suffered from stomach trouble, also BRR 20 August 1934; BRR, 14 December 1931, PCB 12 Arthur Mole, four and a half years' service, 29 September 1930, PCD 174 Herbert Stanley Miller, five years' service.

64   PCE 82 Francis Noblett, ten and a half years' service, died of pleurisy (BRR, 27 February 1931). PCE 84 Thomas Victor March, fifteen years' service, died of pneumonia (BRR, 1 March 1935). PSD 10 Thomas John Griffiths, fifteen years' service, died of pthisis (BRR, 15 May 1935). PCD 103 William Henry Burton, nineteen years' service, and PCC 219 William Rose, twenty-six years' service, died of tuberculosis (BRR, 18 April 1932, 24 November 1931). For a

lead to death, such as when PS Johnson died of an abscess in the popliteal artery while in his thirties.[65] Walking also had a tendency to lead to kidney problems, generally but not always in older men.[66] Stomach ailments brought on by stress and walking after heavy meals killed men such as PC Heydon who died of enteritis.[67] Constables also died from scarlet fever, splenic anaemia, cerebral haemorrhage and appendicitis.[68] Four to eight men dying in uniform a year was not a significant number. However, at least some of these deaths may have been prevented if men had not ignored illnesses to stay on active duty, partly to protect their pensions and no doubt in part due to a masculine culture that encouraged disregarding medical problems.

The most tragic cases were men who committed suicide or tried to, often as a result of job-related stress.[69] They were usually experienced men, in their thirties and above, and frequently had families. Some of these men may simply have had mental illness. PC Armstrong lost his mind and had to be forcibly removed to an institution, and PC Capewell was found guilty but insane on a charge of arson.[70]

---

summary of police illness, see Dr J.M. Webster, 'Health Factors in the Modern Police Force', Chief Constables' Association Annual Report, 11 June 1936, pp. 42–57; for the duties of force surgeons, see Dr Hoyland Smith, 'Police Medical Services', Chief Constables' Association Annual Report, 7 June 1928, pp. 31–42.

[65]   BRR, 11 July 1935, PSE 1 Ralph Johnson, fourteen years' service.

[66]   PCD 136 Harry Birks, five years' service, died at home of kidney trouble (BRR, 20 February 1939). PCD 232 Herbert Edward Williams, twenty-four years' service, died of heart trouble, high blood pressure and kidney trouble (BRR, 5 September 1937). PCA 139 John King, thirty years' service, died of bronchial catarrh, nephritis, chronic kidney inflammation and cardiac debility (BRR, 12 May 1931).

[67]   BRR, 2 May 1939, PCB 220 Reginald Ernest Heydon, seventeen years' service.

[68]   PCD 267 Patrick Ruddey, ten and a half years' service, died of a combination of scarlet fever and pneumonia (BRR, 17 December 1931). PCB 241 George James Cann, seventeen years' service, died of splenic anaemia (BRR, 7 December 1937). PCD 65 Percival Summers Smelling, eighteen years' service, and PCB 128 Henry Thomas Deakin, twenty-five years' service, died of cerebral haemorrhage (BRR, 2 September 1939, 9 March 1933). PCB 170 Gilbert Humphrey Wright, twenty-one years' service, died following an operation for acute appendicitis (BRR, 6 September 1932). PCC 199 William David Taylor, twenty years' service, died in the Ear and Throat Hospital without the illness specified (BRR, 23 September 1931).

[69]   The police force forms an occupational 'suicide cluster' related to stress. In London suicide statistics for 1921–1923 and 1930–1932, suicide rates were higher at the upper end of the social scale and tended to rise again in the poorest classes. This makes police suicide against the pattern for their class which tended to have the lowest suicide rate. Peter Sainsbury, *Suicide in London: An Ecological Study* (New York: Basic Books, 1956), p. 19. Modern US policemen go through periodic suicide waves, with victims tending to be more experienced or even retired officers suffering from 'burn out'. Loren Coleman, *Suicide Clusters* (London: Faber and Faber, 1987), pp. 31–3.

[70]   LCI, 19 August 1928, PCE 263 Jones was 'struck in the Stomach when assisting to remove Con 100 E Armstrong from his home ... to Mill Rd Institution'; BJSC, 1 April 1921, PC 125

Some mental illness resulted from injuries. PC Capper suffered from the after-effects of a war wound, and finally drowned himself in a pond in 1928.[71] One Liverpool constable was badly beaten by a group of men while trying to arrest one of them. His serious head wounds brought on melancholia and he cut his throat, leaving behind a widow and four children.[72] But other men seemed overcome by stalled careers, failed cases or a perceived job blunder. Senior officers did what they could to help troubled men. One way to ease stress was to transfer men to less tense locations, which ironically could exacerbate fears over lack of advancement. Ideally, a sergeant talked to his constables and taught them to cope with the ups and downs of the job. Yet no one apparently noticed that PC Woods was under strain. He went home one night and, after quarrelling with his wife, turned her out of the house. When she managed to get back in, she found him with his throat cut. Woods survived but was asked to resign from the force since no 'man who so loses his self control as to attempt to take his own life can be safely trusted to perform the duties of a constable'.[73] Such a result could only have persuaded other men to hide their anxieties in a culture that already discouraged men from admitting to stress. Recorded suicides rarely included reasons; it is impossible to tell if the force did not know or kept the reason private. PC Durrant killed himself after five years on the force with a clean record, reasons not given.[74] With eight years' service, thirty-two year old PC Heath disappeared from duty and wrote a letter to his superintendent stating that he was going to Bristol to commit suicide, but no details from the letter were stated. Luckily for him, the Bristol police were informed and brought him back to Birmingham two days later.[75] The few cases that provide details describe anxiety about promotion and discipline that led men to become obsessed and depressed, ending in suicide or suicide attempts. Liverpool PC Lockwood gave evidence in a case which resulted in a proceeding against him and other constables for false arrest. He became obsessed that the accusation would

---

Arthur Capewell, received £7, p. 284; BWCM, 2 February 1921, p. 16, 6 April 1921, report no. 3, p. 2. He caused £150 damage to either the parsonage or church of the Rev. Henry Gilbert. He was dismissed and his rateable deductions given to his legal representative. The city did not admit any liability for Capewell's actions.

71   MWCM, 20 December 1928, PCB 168 Arthur Capper, joined August 1904, vol. 128, no. 29. Capper lived with an unmarried sister who acted as his housekeeper. She was awarded his full gratuity of £109.

72   17 October 1933, p. 234. He had been rescued by civilians. He left a widow and four children, ages thirteen, eleven, seven and one month.

73   LHCWC, 16 March 1903, pp. 254–5; Liverpool Watch Committee Orders to the Head Constable, 16 March 1903. His wife wrote to the watch committee asking that her husband be reinstated without success.

74   BRB, 22 November 1926, PCB 202 William George Durrant, five years' service.

75   It was not stated how the matter was dealt with by the police authorities (BOR, 17 October 1933, PCE 45 Albert Henry Heath).

ruin him, telling his wife that he was going mad and had no friends any more. After four months, the case was decided in favour of the police and he appeared to cheer up. But days later, he complained of pains in his head and hanged himself while his wife was out shopping.[76]

The suicides who took everyone by surprise were the men close to or past retirement age, sometimes of sergeant or higher rank, who had kept their problems to themselves for so long that they finally broke under pressure. In 1932, after twenty-three years on the force, Birmingham PC Beddowes committed suicide, the only reason given was 'whilst of unsound mind'.[77] In 1905, Manchester PS Petler, age forty-six, disappeared from duty, taking with him £117 belonging to prisoners. The next day he visited his brother, giving him £65 for his family, which the brother later returned to the force. A month later Petler poisoned himself in a hotel room seventy miles away with twopence in his pocket. He had a bedridden wife and no family; his reasons for either the robbery or the suicide were never discovered.[78] Stress continued to affect men beyond retirement. A year after taking his pension, a Birmingham sergeant committed suicide by jumping in front of a train with no explanation given in 1921.[79] In 1926, a Manchester inspector, age fifty-one, disappeared from home a year after his retirement, telling his wife he was going for a walk. Traced to a boat to Ireland, he was found drowned six weeks later, apparently having thrown himself into the sea. He was suffering from an undefined nervous complaint.[80] Every man committing suicide had his own story but the known cases include job stress and anxiety that finally overwhelmed him.

Constables who adapted to life in the police force, stayed healthy enough to keep working, and experienced no intractable family pressures qualified for half-pay pensions after twenty-five years of service, and two-thirds pay after thirty years, under the 1919 Police Act. Before 1919, required service for half-pay varied from force to force anywhere from twenty-six to thirty years of service or more, with similar variations for two-thirds pay.[81] Between 1905 and 1914, Birmingham supported around 163 pensioned constables a year, about eighteen per cent of active constables.[82] This reflected the gradual improvement that the 1890 Police

---

[76] *Police Review*, 25 April 1913, p. 201. George Fancourt remembered a detective inspector committing suicide by shooting himself in the head with a revolver after 'something went wrong' with a murder case leading to the prisoner being discharged ('The Police Service of George Frederic Fancourt', p. 7).

[77] BRR, 5 May 1932, PCE 197 William Beddowes.

[78] *Police Review*, 15 December 1905, p. 597. The rest of the money was apparently given to friends, who returned it to the police. His widow was looked after by the Manchester police.

[79] BWCM, 26 October 1921, p. 4.

[80] MWCM, 8 July 1926, vol. 112, nos. 82, 89.

[81] See pp. 140–1 for more on local variations in retirement age and pensions before 1919.

[82] BAR, 1905–1914.

Act had on police retention, with more men making it to retirement age.[83] However, prewar conditions of service prevented dramatic gains and constables tended to retire at half pay. Men had two primary reasons for not trying to increase their pensions. The first was fear of losing the pension altogether through a disciplinary dismissal. Prewar men tended to have more defaults, making dismissal for repeat offences a real possibility.[84] The second was simply a matter of health. Lower wages meant poorer diets than available for postwar men and prewar medicine could not compete with postwar medicine. On reaching pension age, many prewar men had little choice but to retire or break down entirely. Conditions improved with the 1919 Police Act. From 1919 to 1924, Birmingham supported 252 pensioners a year, twenty-one per cent of active constables. This jumped to 320 pensioners and twenty-six per cent from 1925 to 1929. The climb continued steadily from 1930 to 1934, with 389 pensioners and twenty-nine per cent, and from 1935 to 1939 with 428 pensioners and thirty-one per cent of active constables.[85] Manchester experienced a similar improvement. Of men who joined between 1900 and 1914, under pre-1919 Police Act qualifications but benefiting from its pension, nearly forty per cent made it to retirement age. However, less than three per cent made it to the two-thirds pension at thirty years' service. Over fifty-five per cent of the men hired during the first ten years of the Act made it to their pensions, and nearly fifteen per cent lasted thirty years. Overall numbers dropped during the 1930s, with about fifty per cent of men hired earning their pensions but twenty-two per cent made it thirty years with men's overall health improving and concern over dismissal declining.[86] The drop in pension rates resulted from men hired in the 1930s leaving to join the armed forces during the Second World War and men leaving after the war to

---

[83]   In a study on the nineteenth century, S.J. Davies wrote that 'Low wages may explain another marked feature of Victorian police forces, in Manchester as elsewhere: the very high turnover of recruits. Between 1858 and 1869 less than 2% of those recruited into the police force endured to draw superannuation. The average length of service up to 1865 was just over five years.' S.J. Davies, 'Classes and Police in Manchester 1829–1880', in *City, Class and Culture*, ed. A.J. Kidd and K.W. Roberts (Manchester: Manchester University Press, 1985), p. 34. W.J. Lowe came up with a similar average length of service for the Lancashire Constabulary between 1845 and 1870, finding that 82.4 per cent of recruits left with fewer than ten years' service. Lowe, 'The Lancashire Constabulary', p. 55. Carolyn Steedman found that, between 1857 and 1880, after only five years, constables were more likely to remain until pensioned. However, only approximately twenty-five per cent of recruits made it five years and only fifteen per cent made it to pension age. Lowe had similar figures. Steedman, *Policing the Victorian Community*, p. 93.

[84]   See LHCWC, 10 July 1905, p. 213.

[85]   BAR, 1919–1939.

[86]   Length of service numbers are based on approximately 5500 Manchester City Police roster cards, 1900–1939.

take advantage of new career opportunities during the postwar economic boom. Overall, the first half of the century saw a dramatic improvement in the per centage of constables who made it to retirement, particularly after 1919, a result of improving pay and conditions attracting better recruits and convincing them to stay once they joined.

Most constables took their pensions in their late forties or early fifties, with their age gradually increasing into the 1930s as more men stayed to take their pensions at thirty years' service. Their children were typically old enough to be working, though they often still lived at home until they married. Depending on their economic situation, their ambitions and their health, pensioners might find another job. They became security guards, worked at public houses, opened betting shops and went into business with family members. Their wives sometimes took the opportunity to work now that their husbands were no longer constables, setting up shops, giving music lessons, doing dress-making and joining family businesses. Some men were too broken down physically and retired altogether, concentrating on gardening, carpentry or other hobbies. In these cases, their wives might need to work to balance the family budget. Half pay or even two-thirds pay did not necessarily pay the bills, especially when men used to receive rent allowances and other perks. Nevertheless, with good budgeting and now free to live wherever they wished, retiring on a pension made policing better than many working-class occupations. Many pensioners could simply choose to retire.[87]

While most constables took their pensions and went on with their lives, a few needed to be reminded that they still had to support their wives and children. Policemen could never entirely retire since the police force remained interested in their domestic lives. This was an advantage in many ways since police widows and orphans were looked after as much as possible. However, senior officers also continued to step in to resolve domestic disputes, including creating and maintaining separation agreements, since abandoned wives and children could be just as detrimental to the image of the force after policemen retired as before. Forces had to deal with nearly three times as many pensioners who refused to support their wives as active duty men.[88] Couples may have stayed together while the husband was working in order to protect his job, or because they still had children at home, only to separate once his pension was secured. It is possible that suddenly being together all the time was more than some couples could bear. Most came to mutually acceptable arrangements, but some pensioners refused to

---

[87]   If a police pensioner was found guilty of an offence against the law, they forfeited their pension. The police felt this amounted to punishing a man twice for the same offence and requested unsuccessfully that it be removed (DC, Evidence, questions 3769–70, p. 192).

[88]   See Klein, 'Irregular Marriages', p. 211.

support their families adequately or to support them at all now that their pensions were safe. In typical cases, Mr Law was irregular in paying his wife legally ordered support of ten shillings a week and Mr Morecroft paid his wife and children only seven shillings a week when they had agreed to nine.[89] Wives finally wrote to chief constables begging for help. Forces generally paid a third or half of the pension directly to the wife, but sometimes awarded as much as the entire pension if children were involved. If the husband failed in his responsibilities, the force became a kind of surrogate husband providing for the family.[90]

Even though wives had the power to appeal to chief constables for help, this only worked if they were perceived to be good wives. Double standards existed, since a pensioner could cohabit with another woman and keep his pension, but a wife lost her pension if she cohabited with another man. Mrs Connor lost her husband's pension when she left him to live with a man in County Meath, but Mr Geddes kept his pension after he left his wife to live with Mrs Walling, a police widow.[91] In Geddes' case, the watch committee's main concern was to prevent Mrs Geddes from harassing her husband since the marriage had irrevocably broken down and reconciliation was not an option. They awarded part of Geddes' pension directly to his wife on the condition that she stay away from her husband after she followed him to his new residence and created a scene. Geddes and Walling then left Liverpool and his wife began hounding the man who was drawing Geddes' pension for him, asking for his address. The watch committee then arranged that Geddes' pension be paid to him by post.[92] As long as Geddes supported his wife, his marital irregularities were not the force's problem. Ironically, if Mrs Walling had been receiving a pension as a police widow, she almost certainly lost it for cohabiting with Geddes.

Similar double standards applied to 'intemperance', a common factor undermining marriages.[93] The intemperate husband did not lose his pension rights though he did lose control over how it was distributed to support his dependents. Louisa Bainbridge informed the chief constable that her husband's drinking habits had become so violent that he had threatened to 'do her in', forcing her to leave him. The chief constable at first attempted a reconciliation, but when this failed he awarded her fifteen shillings a week for herself and the two children.[94] Mrs

---

89   LHCWC, 14 August 1905, p. 264; 17 April 1905, p. 110.

90   The 1890 and the 1919 Police Acts included the requirement to support wives and dependent children, and gave forces the power to pay pensions directly to police dependents if necessary.

91   LHCWC, 27 April 1903, p. 306.

92   LWCM, 26 April 1909, pp. 35–6, 22 August 1910, p. 640. The affair between Geddes and Walling had been going on for some time prior to his retirement.

93   Hammerton, *Cruelty and Companionship*, pp. 36–41; Phillips, *Putting Asunder*, pp. 496–7.

94   LWCM, 10 May 1927, p. 454.

Williamson legally separated from her intemperate husband and finally took her children to live at an address kept secret from him to evade his abuse and prevent him from spending their money on drink. The watch committee awarded her half of her husband's pension after he only offered four shillings a week for the support of the children.[95] However, if wives were intemperate, they forfeited their pension rights. Mrs Porte complained that her husband, a retired constable, had left to join the army without giving her any allowance so the watch committee awarded her and her four children seven shillings a week. The chief constable then learned that Mr Porte had removed the children from his wife's custody. Since she was of 'intemperate habits' and 'otherwise not worthy of any help', her share of his pension was cancelled.[96] The different standards for husbands and wives were clear in the case of the Murrays. When pensioner Murray became an inmate of a workhouse due to his intemperate habits, the watch committee paid his pension to his wife on the condition that she pay the parish charges for her husband. When the chief constable discovered that Mrs Murray was 'of intemperate habits and quite unfit to have the disbursement of the pension', the pension was assigned back to Murray. Mrs Murray was left with nothing.[97] Even though a pensioner was required to support his legal dependents, this obligation was considered void if his wife's behaviour did not meet a reasonable standard of propriety.

In spite of the double standards, senior officers tried to be fair and assign pensions depending on individual circumstances. When PC Blinkhorn retired in 1909, his entire pension was paid directly to his wife for unknown reasons. In 1923 he became destitute and the pension was split between them. Two years later, he found a good job but now he wanted his entire pension. He argued that his wife was living with a married daughter so she no longer needed his support. However, the force kept dividing the pension since husbands, not daughters, were expected to support wives, even if long separated.[98] When PC Church retired, he moved to the country where he rented out three bungalows and did odd jobs. However, his wife refused to join him, having been advised by her doctor to stay in town. Church offered her thirty shilling a month, a low amount of support, but she applied to the Liverpool force for £4 a month, about two-thirds of his pension. He then offered

---

95   LHCWC, 16 November 1903, pp. 6–7; LWCM, 4 January 1904, p. 472. See Roberts, *A Woman's Place*, pp. 120–1, and Tebbutt, *Women's Talk?*, p. 129, for similar cases.

96   LWCM, 11 November 1915, p. 601; 11 January 1916, p. 82. On the other hand, watch committees would award money to wives with no legal claim if they considered her case to be a deserving one. A wife of an ex-constable dismissed on a disciplinary charge was awarded his rateable deductions when they learned that she was 'a striving woman' who had 'done her utmost to keep her husband straight'. She used to money to leave her husband and return home to Anglesey (LWCM, 8 December 1925, pp. 606–7).

97   LWCM, 10 October, 20 November 1905, 8 January 1906, pp. 513, 571, 685–6; LHCWC, 16 October, 20 November 1905, 8 January 1906, pp. 352, 395, 472.

98   LWCM, 16 June 1925, p. 379.

her £3, a more typical settlement. She must have been convincing because she got the £4. Mrs Church was not content with this. Six months later, she claimed two of the bungalows as her own property and rented them for £4 a month. The force then reduced her share of his pension to £2 a month. Mrs Church still came out ahead in her monthly income, showing herself to be a shrewd businesswoman.[99] Pension cases could drag on for years. In 1902, William and Mary Connor separated and their two sons were sent to live with Mrs Connor's father. Mr Connor neglected to support his children so part of his pension was sent to his father-in-law in February 1903. In April 1903, Mrs Connor lost her share of her husband's pension when the chief constable learned that she was living in adultery. Between 1903 and 1908, the elder son lived with an uncle and the younger son became an inmate of an industrial school. In 1908 the elder son died and younger son returned to live with the uncle. For the next five years, the boy moved between various relatives and then disappeared. In 1913, the entire pension was paid to his father. The watch committee reallocated the pension each time the situation changed.[100] Watch committees even skirted the law when appropriate. Retired PC Clowes had lived apart from his wife for nineteen years and had custody of their two children. He lived with another woman as his wife who raised the children and had one of her own. This arrangement was not discovered until the watch committee tried to award his pension funds to his second 'wife' after his death only to discover that she was not official. Since the unofficial marriage was of such long standing, they awarded the pension to the unofficial wife.[101]

A few cases of marriage breakdowns, similar to the suicides, hint at the mental stresses that constables could endure. Once no longer held together by their work routines, neither could they keep their home lives together. Some men simply walked away after they retired with no explanation. In 1925, Walter Wall left home one day, advising his wife to sell the house, and moving to the Isle of Man where he worked as a barman. He agreed to pay her £5 a lunar month but only paid once. He failed to send his baffled wife any more support or to answer her registered letters. Trying to support herself keeping lodgers, she could not make ends meet. The watch committee awarded her the £5 a lunar month from his pension.[102] One pitiable case revealed a man who could no longer grasp reality. PC Hasledine retired from the police after twenty-three years as medically unfit. He also somehow concluded that this meant retiring from supporting his family, even

---

99   LWCM, 28 April 1925, pp. 311–12; 13 October 1925, p. 551.
100   LWCM, 23 February 1903, p. 504; entries around 1 and 29 March 1903 removed to file from minute book; 27 April 1903, p. 306; 24 July 1911, pp. 746–7, 17 June 1912, p. 295; 5 May 1913, p. 376.
101   MWCM, May 1904, vol. 24, no. 78. The first wife's whereabouts were not mentioned and she apparently made no claim to the pension.
102   LWCM, 8 September 1925, p. 496.

though he continued to live at home. His bewildered wife wrote to Chief Constable Maxwell on September 12, 1930 about her husband:

> He has been very indifferent since his retirement … he tells me he has finished with me not only by not speaking to me, but does not intend to give me any money. On Sept 1st he received his Pension & went away until the thursday [sic] following, he comes home and then he tells me he has no money for me and does not intend to give me any more. Sir I do hope you will give me help in this matter. The Children do not think it fair that he should have a good home and food and not pay for it. The home is very much upset. I am afraid if there is not something done for a betterment the Children will be leaving the home. I do not quiet [sic] know the reason for it, I keep a good clean home …

Maxwell granted Mrs Hasledine an interview but her husband refused to be interviewed, writing, 'I do not wish to discuss my private affairs with anyone. As for my pension, this was granted to me … and any question of re-assignment does not arise, unless and until I commit myself in some way or other.' Since he continued to live with his wife, he did not consider it fair that she be paid part of his pension. On 21 November 1930, he claimed that a reconciliation had occurred but when a police woman went to the house, she found conditions as Mrs Hasledine had described them. The only change was that her husband occasionally spoke to her and their three children. On 27 November, she was awarded thirty-two shillings per week, an unusually high award, leaving him with only sixteen. The chief constable and watch committee clearly did not approve of his behaviour. Mr Hasledine wrote to the watch committee,

> I cannot imagine what kind of a tale my wife told to the Chief Constable … I think it very unjust that I should be condemned without being given an opportunity of presenting my side of the matter. I might say that I was only away from home for four days … Since then we have removed to a better neighbourhood, and as my three children [ages 26, 23, 14] are all working, we are all living together very happily. The question of my wife and I living apart has never arisen, and as I informed the Chief Constable last week my wife did not wish to go any further with her complaint as we had arrived at a mutual arrangement. I suppose I shall have to abide by the decision of your Committee but I can assure you that I feel very grieved at the humiliation, as it will not tend to make my home any happier.

In reality, he turned down invitations to be interviewed. The watch committee resolved to let the letter 'lie on the table'. Mr Hasledine felt the degradation of not being considered capable of supporting his wife in spite of his own refusal to do so. Evidence showed that he was not contributing any money to the housekeeping. Since she kept a 'clean home', Mrs Hasledine could not understand her husband's behaviour. The reasons for Mr Hasledine's medical discharge were not given but somehow his mental balance became thrown off. It is difficult to explain his behaviour otherwise. No further information appeared in his file so the matter seems to have remained there. The watch committee had little choice but to act as they did in order to keep the family together.[103]

Forces continued their responsibility for a policeman's family after his death though double standards continued to apply. Before 1919, police widows did not receive a pension but instead received what was left of their husband's pension funds at the discretion of the watch committee. This might only amount to £10–20 by the time the pensioner died, a sum that did not last a widow long. If the policeman died while still serving, the gratuity could be much higher depending on his length of service. Before the war, widows tended to take in lodgers, do cleaning or open a small shop, using the gratuity to get a start. If the widow was living apart from her husband and was not being supported by him, she received nothing. When pensioner Hinton died, his £75 gratuity was given to his sister who had the care of his two children, and his widow did not receive anything.[104] Only after September 1918 did widows automatically receive an annual pension of £30, and £10 for each child with a maximum of three children allowed. Widows became more likely to do 'home duties' and not work at all. Even after 1918, if the couple was living apart without the husband having deserted his wife and the husband was not contributing to her support, the widow would not receive a pension. She also lost it if there was evidence of misconduct or lack of good character.[105]

Prewar gratuities to widows were generally doled out in weekly lots, but it was common for Liverpool widows to request advances in times of special need. Records of any similar practice in Manchester or Birmingham have not survived. If the widow was considered respectable, and she almost always was, the request was granted. These requests shed some light on the lives of working-class widows. Advances were paid for children's clothing and doctors' bills, to open businesses, and for resettlement outside of Liverpool. Businesses tended to be related to domestic skills. Margaret Henry, Mrs Gregson and Sarah Burrows were each advanced £10 so they could buy furniture to take in lodgers.[106] Margaret Henry was

---

103   MPF, 12, 19 September, 27, 29 November 1930; PS Hasledine, twenty-three years' service, retired medically unfit.
104   BWCM, 26 February 1901, p. 112.
105   'Report of the Committee on the Police Service of England, Wales, and Scotland', Part II, 1920, Cmd, 574, vol. XXII, 539, p. 18.
106   LHCWC, 6 March 1905, p. 44; 26 June 1905, p. 202; LWCM, 1 March 1909, p. 647. Numerous additional examples exist in both the LHCWC and LWCM.

later given her balance of £157 so she could open a small drapery business.[107] Annie Mary Power received £5 to buy a sewing machine and to put a railing around her husband's grave.[108] Similar to constables who left the city and emigrated, widows left to take jobs and to live with relatives, sometimes both. Mary Smith, 'a very respectable and careful woman', took a situation as a housekeeper and caretaker in Dorset.[109] Mary Fry resettled in Ireland with her married daughter,[110] and Mrs Martin and five of her children emigrated to Toronto, Canada, to work with her sister in a large laundry business.[111] Mrs Moore and her two children moved to Cumberland with her brother to carry on a small general shop. She was 'very respectable and ... will use the money to the best advantage'.[112] The 1918 Act was a great improvement in giving widows a regular pension but it did remove this option of granting advances on pensions. Unfortunately, widows of men who died before September 1918 did not benefit from the new pension law; they continued to be paid often tiny gratuities under the old system.

Police forces looked after police widows and orphans in both formal and informal ways similar to their many other charity undertakings.[113] Many widows still had children at home since constables tended to die of various work-related ailments within ten years of retirement. Forces frequently employed sons of deceased constables as telephone operators or in other odd jobs and widows as warders or charladies as one way to look after them.[114] To compensate for shortfalls in widows' pensions and to help orphans, policemen took regular voluntary collections and set up payment schemes. To help widows left out of the new pension plan, in the 1920s and 1930s, Liverpool men collected £46 for Mrs Brown, £35 for Mrs Scott, £37 for Mrs Whitlow, and many others received similar sums.[115] In 1930 Birmingham tried to set up a Widows' and Orphans Scheme to make such collections more systematic but was unable to get it working.[116] In 1933, Liverpool had better success with their voluntary benevolent scheme where one penny was deducted from members' pay on the death of a policeman or pensioner to benefit his widow.[117] Liverpool also created a Necessitous Widows' Fund in the

---

[107] LHCWC, 10 July 1905, p. 226; LWCM, 10 July 1905, p. 285.
[108] LWCM, 30 September 1912, p. 564.
[109] LHCWC, 29 August 1904, p. 304.
[110] LHCWC, 19 August 1901, pp. 203–4.
[111] LHCWC, 5 September 1910, p. 670.
[112] LWCM, 25 January 1915, p. 380.
[113] For police charity work, see pp. 215–21.
[114] For example, see LAR, 1907–1910, p. 6.
[115] LCCO, 26 April, 25 August, 1919, 15 June 1928, 25 February, 16 March, 17 June 1929, 19 March, 7 April, 8 May, 4 June 1930; BPO, 29 December 1931, p. 18923, 15 November 1935, p. 24563.
[116] BPO, 23 August 1930, pp. 17023–4.
[117] LCCO, 1933.

late 1930s that made special Christmas appeals.[118] Police orphans who could not be kept by their mothers or relatives could go to public orphanages at Harrogate or Redhill, operated by the International Christian Police Association, founded in 1883.[119] Birmingham policemen made regular contributions to the Redhill Surrey Orphanage,[120] and after the war, Liverpool policemen had money deducted from their pay every week to support their orphanage.[121] Special collections were made, such as when Birmingham policemen raised £33 to buy an orphan an artificial leg, £57 to form an orphans' boy-scout troop, and £12 for an adult orphan destitute through illness.[122] All forces sent special Christmas boxes and treats to their orphanages every year.[123] For all of the force's intrusions into their personal lives, policemen could be reasonably assured that their widows and orphans would be looked after by their colleagues in uniform.

---

[118]   LCCO. It received £70 on 16 December 1937, £80 on 12 December 1938 and £90 on 27 December 1939.

[119]   *Police Review*, 4 May 1906, p. 207.

[120]   BPO, 4 August 1900, p. 238; 20 October 1900, pp. 285–6; 30 June 1902, p. 140; 7 February 1903, p. 352; 3 October 1904, pp. 358–9; 15 October 1907, p. 162; 14 October 1908, p. 449;13 October 1909, p. 128; 28 June 1913, p. 507; 5 June 1914, p. 160; 4 June 1915, p. 563; 3 June 1916, p. 310; 10 July 1917, p. 112; 15 October 1919, p. 1284; 12 July 1922, p. 5211; 10 July 1923, p. 6603; 26 July 1924, p. 8693; 6 October 1924, p. 8944; 8 July 1925, p. 10101; 10, 13 February, 1926, pp. 10912, 10927; 13 August 1926, p. 11607.

[121]   LCCO, 7 November 1921, 25 May, 17 November 1927, 21 March 1928.

[122]   BPO, 23 October 1931, p. 18701, 17 July 1936, May 1937.

[123]   An account of Christmas celebrations at force orphanages, including pantomimes given by policemen, is in *Police Review*, 19 January 1934, p. 36.

Conclusion

IN MANY WAYS, the prospects of a constable joining in the 1930s had changed considerably from a constable joining in the 1900s. The 1900s recruit had one chance in three that he would take off his uniform within three years, while the 1930s recruit had only one chance in seven. Policemen perceived the 1933 drop in recruits pay to sixty-two shillings[1] as a setback from the 1919 Police Act standard of seventy shillings, even during a period of deflation, but overall pay and conditions were a vast improvement over prewar standards. However, even with better educational standards and recognition as a skilled occupation, men applying to the force after 1919 still did not have clear ideas about the reality of the job, and forces continued to have problems finding quality recruits. Formal training improved but was never very good, and probationers still learned most of their policing from veterans. Both pre- and postwar constables needed to unravel the differences between their own expectations, formal and informal training, and the reality of walking a beat, and to adapt to the culture of supervision. Probationers never ceased to be held to a higher standard than veterans, weeding out potential problems quickly. This rather haphazard system could not create the ideal police constable presented to probationers in their instruction books but did produce working-class constables suited for the realities of their jobs.

Their most important skill remained exercising discretion, deciding how to prioritize their attention and what to ignore. Even with the introduction of traffic duties, constables ordinarily worked alone; therefore 'the responsibility for Police work rests primarily on the individual constable and not on his superior officers'.[2] They learned the normal patterns of their beats so they could recognize unusual sights, sounds and individuals. Much beat work remained routine and unnoticed, such as checking doors, but the postwar constable had to contend with more traffic and public safety problems. Constables grappled with soaring numbers of first aid

---

[1]   'Report of the Committee on Police Pay (New Entrants)', 1932–1933, Cmd. 4274, vol. XV, 379. Constables now reached seventy shillings pay after three years' service.

[2]   'Report of the Royal Commission on Police Powers and Procedure', 1928–1929, Cmd. 3297, vol. IX, 127, p. 7.

cases and lost objects at the same time that men were shifted from patrol beats to traffic duty to keep both vehicles and pedestrians moving safely. To cover regular patrol beats, all three cities eventually created police-box or pillar systems that relied on telephones, rather than hire more men. Both senior officers and the public could now easily summon constables, and civilians developed the habit of calling the police for annoyances rather than only for emergencies. The new technologies meant more specialized departments and opportunities for promotion but also frustration if left on beat duty. Traffic duty and telephone demands put traditional beat policing under increasing stress in the 1930s with fewer men covering more ground.

Despite getting busier, a 1930s constable generally broke fewer regulations than his 1900s counterpart as policing became a more stable occupation and working-class drinking declined. Constables still had to follow a myriad of rules, and most struggled with at least a few of them. Constables persisted in being late, avoiding paperwork, and smoking on duty. Sergeants and inspectors tended to handle such minor problems informally, giving constables advice and warnings. Constables had to figure out which regulations they could ignore with a little practice, such as smoking, and which they had to be careful about, such as bothering women. They could lose their tempers at just about anyone, including each other, senior officers, civilians, neighbours and wives, as long as it only happened once. The key was to avoid chronic problems at work or at home, especially ones that caused talk. Most constables had few serious disciplinary problems though it might only take one bad report to end a man's career. Most reported defaults were minor, involving neglect of duty. Insubordination, exceeding duty and corruption made up a quarter of defaults but the number of serious cases remained small. Before the war, constables were more likely to get into trouble for drinking; afterwards, drinking became less common in the police and the working class in general, and the total number of defaults dropped substantially. The improvement in discipline lead to an improvement in policing both since constables were better behaved and because senior officers could spend time on matters besides constables on report.

Postwar constables got into less trouble but the strange medley of internal camaraderie and factions persisted. Favouritism networks up and down the police hierarchy based on religion, nepotism or simply friendship tended to be worse where chief constables were more out of touch with their men. Liverpool never entirely rid itself of corrupt promotion and discipline practices but Birmingham and Manchester were also not completely free from problems of undue influence. Antagonisms could be exacerbated by sometimes bitter generational conflicts pitting experience against education, often with men split by whether they were hired before or after the 1890 and 1919 Police Acts. Even their wives could be drawn into factional and generational feuds. Despite all the friction, constables looked out for each other on a daily basis, protecting each other against default charges and helping each other get through another shift. They tended to be united in their contempt for the police office staff, whom they considered not to be real policemen, and in their envy of the detective branch, whose duties seemed more rewarding than street patrol. New technologies added new departments, new opportunities for favours and new jealousies. But most constables remained constables for their entire careers, no matter how many connections they had, and it made sense to be on friendly terms with their colleagues.

The greatest accomplishment of the prewar policemen was the 1919 Police Act, but it was also the event that most divided them from the postwar men. From the 1890s onwards, constables became more likely to remain in the force, creating more experienced and professional policemen. However, they struggled to get policing recognized as a skilled career and they lacked any real influence with watch committees reluctant to grant them better pay or conditions. The economic stresses created by the First World War finally convinced many to join the Nation Union of Police and Prison Officers. Police strikes in London, Liverpool and Birmingham in 1918 and 1919 were largely the fault of police authorities and watch committees who had refused to take seriously years of police petitions for better pay and conditions. The hearings of the Committee on the Police Service of England, Wales and Scotland finally provided a forum for policemen to be heard and resulted in the 1919 Police Act. The Desborough Committee recognized policing as a skilled profession and improved pay, but the problem of representation was never satisfactorily resolved. Policemen remained sceptical of the Police Federation, which remained moribund in Liverpool and Birmingham and had limited success in Manchester. Policemen might exercise the authority of law on the streets but watch committees could still ignore them. The postwar constable still did not have the right to confer that his prewar colleagues had fought for.

Ironically, despite policing improving its image as a profession after 1919, increasing its education standards, and seeing a decline in drinking and defaults, postwar constables were much more likely to be involved in outbreaks of incivility due to indignant drivers, unstable neighbourhoods, and husbands more involved at home. Whenever necessary, their senior officers offered them advice on getting along with the public, with neighbours and with wives. By the 1900s, constables and the rest of the working class had settled into a reasonably stable relationship that did not change substantially into the 1930s. Disputes might break out, but rarely serious ones, especially when drinking declined. Prisoners struggled and friends lent assistance, but injuries tended to be kicks, bites and blows. When constables turned their attention to bad drivers, they discovered that middle- and upper-class law-breakers were just as unhappy with official police attention as anyone in the working class, and were often patronizing and rude. As police attention to the higher classes increased, so did working-class rescues of constables, perhaps signalling approval of this crackdown on dangerous drivers. The 1920s and 1930s became an era of incivility, with middle- and upper-class drivers complaining and writing letters to chief constables, and the working class and constables keeping up their customary insults.

Despite these occasional outbursts, most police and civilian interaction remained neighbourly. Though traffic might raise tempers, constables helped both drivers and pedestrians of all classes navigate busy intersections and find their way through city streets. Most fraternizing went on between constables and the working class simply because they made up the majority of the city populations and shared the same class identity. Nothing chief constables could do stopped constables from gossiping, loitering and sharing refreshments with civilians, and senior officers overlooked it unless constables exercised poor judgment. Constables participated in local perk and tip networks, even though banned, since it was seen as common custom. They joined benevolent schemes, contributed to charities and passed the hat during emergencies. Overall, constables tended to be a sociable group, and many constables defended this as necessary to get to know the regular patterns of their beats. Both constables and civilians appreciated the company, and benefited from the give and take of social networks. Constables just needed to use common sense to avoid taking it too far on duty.

One area where constables needed to exercise caution was in their treatment of women, and mostly they did. Despite force concerns over constables getting into trouble with women, it remained a minor problem. Before the war, constables were reported more often for objectionable attention to women and after the war for voluntary relationships with women, but the number of cases was never high. Before the war, forces were strict with all cases, frequently dismissing constables. But as working-class standards shifted, so could force discipline. After the war, voluntary relationships with women became more likely to be handled on a case-by-case basis. The main concern became whether or not relationships became public. However, to preserve the reputation of the force, any unacceptable behaviour towards women continued to get constables fired, including verbal harassment. Inappropriate language was one default which did not decline; men succumbed to the temptation throughout the period even though it could lead to dismissal as much as serious assaults. Both the voluntary and involuntary discipline cases brought out double standards, particularly the assumption that women out late after dark could not be respectable. Men could indulge in premarital sex without losing respectability but women could not unless quickly married. Nevertheless, Manchester, Birmingham and Liverpool senior officers insisted that all women be protected, regardless of status and constables were expected to treat even the lowliest women with courtesy.

Police domestic life continued to follow working-class patterns, with the major difference remaining that constables and their families had to tolerate the intrusion of force interest, even if everything was going well. Most constables got married in their mid-twenties to a woman a year or two younger from a similar background, and they had one to three children. If problems did occur, either within marriages or with neighbours, senior officers advised toleration on all sides. If necessary, they negotiated separation agreements but they did not insist that unhappy couples stay together. If appealed to by abandoned wives, they made sure that constables supported their wives and children. Neighbourhood upsets were investigated, and, if unhappy neighbours could not be appeased, police families might be moved. After the war, husbands were more likely to be involved at home. They looked after sick wives, played with their children and got drawn into neighbourhood disputes, making them more acrimonious. Neighbourhoods also became less stable as working-class families moved more often. Both changes contributed to constables getting into more quarrels with their neighbours. But only if constables had chronic problems with their tempers or attracted public attention did domestic problems threaten their careers. Despite any bickering, similar to other frictions both within the force and with civilians, most families and neighbours got along reasonably well.

Police forces did a better job of keeping constables until retirement after the war both due to the 1919 Police Act improvements and better discipline. Nevertheless, hundreds of constables left before pension age. Some did not make it through probation, either leaving by choice or not having necessary police qualities. Many left for disciplinary reasons, some minor according to civilian standards and others more serious. Many left during the First World War and never came back, either casualties of war or choosing new occupations. A significant minority left because they decided that they did not like the job, they did not like the interference in their private lives, or they thought they could do better in another occupation. This group decreased in size after the war to the relief of their senior officers. Ill health also contributed to constables leaving the force early. Between 1900 and 1939, about half of constables returned to working-class occupations with anywhere from a few months of service to ten years or more. Even if they did not keep up their police friendship, they took their memories and stories which many no doubt shared with new colleagues in new jobs. Former constables stayed in Manchester, Birmingham and Liverpool, they returned to their original homes or they moved to new regions entirely. They went back to old occupations, or started new ones, sometimes using connections they made as constables. Police records rarely mentioned these men, except for a few employees at the Birmingham Cadbury plant, and owners of shops. What impact these hundreds of former constables had outside of the force, it is impossible to know. Before the war, the constables making it to retirement age tended to retire as soon as they qualified for the half pension, often for health reasons. After the war, while their chances of reaching retirement age only increased from forty to fifty per cent, they were seven times more likely to reach thirty years of service and the larger two-thirds pension. Even after retirement, the force could intrude into their private lives since they still had to support their wives and families. On the other hand, they were reassured to know that their widows and orphans were looked after, especially after the 1918 Pensions Act. Wives also had this comfort, though they suffered under the double standard that they would lose their pensions if they did not live respectable lives whereas their retired husband did not have these constraints.

What perhaps had changed the most from the 1900s to the 1930s was that policing was improving as a choice of occupation. The primary duty of a working-class man was to earn a good living, and, even before the war when pay was low, policing had certain advantages. Policemen received clothing and rent allowances, they got sick pay and the services of force doctors if their sickness was work-related, and they received pensions. While annual leave was shorter than men might like, at least they got leave, and it improved after the 1919 Police Act. Promotion into the higher ranks or the detective branch was a possibility for men sufficiently talented, well connected and lucky, and after the war, new departments created new options. If they joined before 1918, their widows usually received what was left of their pension contributions, and after 1918, their widows received a regular pension. Their orphans were looked after in orphanages, with pensions and with job prospects. After the 1919 Police Act, pay improved enough to make policing one of the better working-class occupations. If they got into debt, forces usually helped out with loans or other assistance. If they had a good record and decided to resign from the force, they got a good reference and often their pension deductions returned, and if they retired they got help finding a new job if they wanted one. So, from the perspective of pay, allowances, prospects and pensions, policing was a decent option before the 1919 Police Act, and a good one afterwards.

Police work itself could be acceptable or not, depending on the character of the man and of the force, and when he joined. Beat work, particularly traffic beats, could be boring and miserable in bad weather. No doubt many shifts were uneventful and dull but not every man minded that. Every day held a certain sameness, but they also brought their own variety and unexpected incidents. Moving from morning shifts to afternoon shifts to night shifts upset their sleep, but constables may have been among the few people to be familiar with the regular patterns of early-morning life, afternoon life, late-night life and the rest of a day's pockets of time. They met all sorts of people, shared cups of tea in kitchens and got into brawls outside public houses. Constables were surprisingly talkative, gossiping with each other, with residents of their beats, with anyone they met at any time and any place. Senior officers did not try to enforce rules against it and Chief Constable Charles Rafter himself could not stop it at his own doorway. With the growth in traffic, telephones and other technologies, constables had opportunities for jobs as mechanics, technicians and drivers, though traffic also meant the dreaded point duty. They exercised considerable discretion but lived with a high degree of supervision of their work and domestic lives. They experienced a sense of camaraderie with their fellow constables but also suffered from factionalism and internal force strife. Problems with neighbours or transfers to new divisions could mean uprooting their family, finding new housing and schools, as well as adjusting to new colleagues and senior officers. Policing was a curious mixture of boredom and excitement, solitude and company, independence and restrictions. Men unable to make this work got themselves into disciplinary trouble or left voluntarily for other jobs. But strange as the combination of impossible expectations and contradictions could be, a growing number of working-class men found policing agreeable enough to wear the uniform.

Appendix

Chief Constables in Birmingham, Liverpool, and Manchester, 1900–1939

Birmingham

1899–1935 Charles H. Rafter, Royal Irish Constabulary 1883–1899

1935–1941 Cecil C.H. Moriarty, Royal Irish Constabulary 1902–1918, Birmingham Assistant Chief Constable 1918–1935

Liverpool (called 'Head Constable' until 1919 Police Act)

1881–1902 John William Nott Bower, Royal Irish Constabulary 1872–1878, Chief Constable Leeds 1878–1881, Chief Constable City of London 1902–1925

1902–1912 Leonard Dunning, Royal Irish Constabulary 1882–1895, Assistant Chief Constable Liverpool, 1895–1902, HM Inspector of Constabulary 1912–1930

1912–1925 Francis Caldwell, Junior Clerk 1876–1879, Police Officer and Office Staff 1879–1906, Assistant Chief Constable 1906–1912, all in Liverpool City Police

*1925–1931 L.D.L. Everett, Police Officer Wiltshire 1895–1908, Chief Constable Preston 1908–1925

*1931–1940 Archibald Kennedy Wilson, Police Officer Cardiff 1909–1928, Chief Constable Carlisle 1928–1929, Chief Constable Plymouth 1929–1931

Manchester

*1898–1926 Robert Peacock, Police Officer Bradford 1878–1882, Police Officer Rotherham 1882–1886, Police Officer Bacup 1887–1888, Chief Constable Canterbury 1888–1892, Chief Constable Oldham 1892–1898

*1926–1942 John Maxwell, Police Constable 1901–1910, Police Sergeant 1910–1914, Police Inspector 1914–1920, Police Superintendent 1920–1926, all in Manchester City Police

* Began career as beat constable.

Bibliography

Parliamentary Papers

'Report from the Select Committee on the Amalgamation of Police Forces', 1931–1932 (106), vol. 123.

'Report of the Committee Appointed to Consider Possible Readjustments in the Standard Conditions of Service of the Police Forces in Great Britain', 1924, Cmd. 2086, vol. XII, 61.

'Report of the Committee on Police Pay (New Entrants)', 1932–1933, Cmd. 4274, vol. XV, 379.

'Report of the Committee on the Claims of the Men Dismissed from the Police and Prison Services on Account of the Strike in 1919', 1924–1925, Cmd. 2297, vol. XV, 265.

'Report of the Committee on the Police Service of England, Wales, and Scotland', Part I, 1919, Cmd. 253, vol. XXVII, 709; Part II, 1920, Cmd. 574, vol. XXII, 539; Evidence, 1920, Cmd. 874, vol. XXII, 573 (*abbreviated as DC throughout: see List of Abbreviations*).

'Report of the Royal Commission on Police Powers and Procedure', 1928–1929, Cmd. 3297, vol. IX, 127.

Reports of the Inspectors of Constabulary: 1900–1939.

Unpublished Official and Personal Papers

Birmingham

Birmingham City Library
Birmingham Branch, National Union of Police and Prison Offices, four leaflets: August 1919, 19 October 1919, 24 October 1919, December 1919.
Watch Committee Minutes: 1900–1903, 1917–1939.

West Midlands Police Authority
Birmingham City Police Annual Reports: 1900–1939.
Constables' Marriage Certificates: 22 October 1900 – 18 December 1926.
Conditions of Service: Scales of Pay, 1936.
Conduct Book: 7 July 1890 – 16 March 1904.
Defaulters Books: 1878–1908; 5 December 1924 – 20 June 1956.
Discipline Book 'D' Division: 27 September 1920 – 8 December 1948.

Discipline Report Book Index and Abstract: 1924–1933.

Discipline Report Books: 1 October 1920 – 13 November 1924; 31 December 1926 – 22 February 1927.

Minutes of the Judicial Sub-Committee: 3 March 1919 – 12 December 1934.

Orderly Room Books: 1928–1933, 1933–1938.

Police Roster: 1900–1939.

Resignation Register: 1930–1951.

Superintendent's Reports and Confidential Letters R Div: 21 October 1901 – 4 April 1923.

Watch Committee Minutes: 11 February 1890 – 5 February 1919; 7 January 1925 – 3 November 1948.

Liverpool

Liverpool City Local History Library and Archives

Instructions for the Liverpool City Police Force. Liverpool: W.H. Lloyd, 1896.

Instructions for the Liverpool Watch. Liverpool: Rockliff & Duckworth, 1834.

Liverpool City Police. Instructions. Liverpool: C. Tinling and Co., 1903.

Liverpool City Police. Instructions. Liverpool: C. Tinling and Co., 1911.

Liverpool City Police. Instructions. Liverpool: C. Tinling and Co., 1926.

Orders of the Watch Committee to the Head Constable: September 1899 – March 1909; January 1910 – June 1915.

Reports of the Head Constable to the Watch Committee: April 1899 – January 1905.

Watch Committee Minutes: 1900–1939.

Merseyside Police Authority

Anon., *Short History of Members of A Div. during First Ten Days of Police Strike August 1st to 10th 1919*. n.d.

Birkenhead Disciplinary Report Book: 1920–1930.

Chief Constable's Disciplinary Reports: August 1923 – January 1925; July 1926 – January 1928; January 1928 – May 1930; May 1930 – December 1932; December 1932 – April 1935; April 1935 – October 1938; October 1938 – January 1943.

Chief Constable's Order Books: July 1918 – March 1920; September 1921 – September 1922; May 1926 – May 1931; May 1933 – December 1939.

Daily Reports Books: September 1896 – September 1901; January 1905 – November 1908; November 1908 – January 1913; January 1913 – March 1919; March 1919 – June 1927; July 1927 – March 1936.

Head Constable's Special Reports: January 1905 – January 1906.

Liverpool City Police Force Annual Reports: 1900–1939.

Liverpool City Police Standing Orders.

Pension Books Liverpool City Police: 1894–1968.

Police (Liverpool Inquiry) Act, 1909, Commissioner's Report; Liverpool Police Inquiry before Mr. Arthur J. Ashton, K.C., Commissioner., 6 vols.

Police Strike 1919: Original Documents, Reports and Memoranda.

Reports of Constables Injured: September 1903 – June 1911; June 1911 – February 1924; February 1924 – May 1930; November 1936 – December 1944.

Manchester

Greater Manchester Police Museum
Appointment Roster Cards: 1858–1941.
Chief Constable's Annual Reports: 1900–1913, 1927–1939.
City of Manchester. *Police Instruction Book.* Manchester: John Heywood, Ltd., 1908.
City of Manchester. *Police Instruction Book.* Manchester: Co-operative Wholesale Society's
  Printing Works, 1923.
City of Manchester. [For the consideration by the Watch Committee, Thursday, 8 December
  1927.] *Reports Relating to the Police 'Box' System.*
Crime Busters. *Police Strike.* Pamphlet, n.d., pp. 2067–70.
Fowler, Joseph, MCP: 1908–1933. 'From a Convict to a Parson', 1912; 'The Gentleman's
  Letter Writer', 1931, unpublished notebooks.
General Orders: 1900–1901, 1910–1937.
Manchester City Police. *'Police Box' System Instruction Book. 'C' Division.* Manchester: Henry
  Blacklock and Co., 1931.
Manchester City Police. *'Police Box' System. Reorganization of the 'C' Division.* Manchester:
  Henry Blacklock and Co., 1929.
Manchester City Police. *Telephone Pillar System 'B' Division.* Chief Constable's Office, January
  1938.
Manchester City Police Force. *Supplementary Instruction Book.* Manchester: Henry Blacklock
  and Co., 1931.
Manchester Constabulary Force. *Constables' Guide.* Manchester: Henry Blacklock and Co., 1898.
Police Federation of England and Wales. *Annual Report of the Manchester City Police Joint Branch:
  for the Year 1933–1934.*
Police Personnel Files: 1900–1939.
Smethurst, Thomas, Bolton Police (1888–1890), Stalybridge Police (1895–1922), '"Mems."
  from My Notebook (finished 15 April 1914)' and 'Reminiscences' (1922), unpublished
  manuscripts.
Watch Committee Minutes with Documents: 1900–1939.

Manchester City Local History Library and Archives
*In the Matter of an Inquiry re. the Efficiency and Discipline of the Manchester Police Force. Before J.S.
  Dugdale, Esq., Q.C., Commissioner. At the City Sessions Court, Minshull Street, Manchester, On
  May 24th, 25th, 26th, 27th 28th, 29th, and June 14th, 15th, 16th, 17th, 18th, 1897. From the
  Shorthand Notes of Mr. Frederick William Baber, York Chambers, 27, Brazenose Street, Manchester.*
  Manchester: John Heywood, Typo., 1897.
Manchester Police-Aided Clothing Association for Needy Children Annual Report,
  1903–1904.

Open University Police Archive, Milton Keynes
Chief Constables' Association Annual Reports.
Dixon, Arthur L. *The Home Office and the Police between the Two World Wars.* London: Home
  Office, 1966.
Fancourt, George. 'The Police Service of George Frederic Fancourt: Birmingham City Police
  1929–1960', unpublished manuscript, n.d.
'Interview with George Frederick Fancourt Who Served in the Birmingham City Police from
  1929 to 1961', conducted on 3 December 1986 by Clive Emsley, unpublished hand-
  corrected transcript.

Published Primary Sources

Anon. 'The Police and the Thieves', *The Quarterly Review* (1856): 160–200.

Branthwaite, J.M., Constable. 'The Genesis, Aims and Scope of the Police Federation System of England and Wales', *Police Journal* 1:1 (1928): 19–30.

Chesterton, G.K. 'The Problem of Policemen', *Police Review and Parade Gossip* (30 September 1904).

Coppersmith, Alexander. 'The Policeman: An Appreciation and Criticism', *Police Journal* 5:1 (1932): 80–4.

Daley, Harry. *This Small Cloud: A Personal Memoir*. London: Weidenfeld and Nicolson, 1986.

Jervis, Constable T.E.H., Liverpool City Police. 'The Betting Dilemma', *Police Journal* 9:4 (1936): 473–8.

Mark, Sir Robert. *In the Office of Constable*. London: Collins, 1978.

Metropolitan Police. *Instructions to the Force*. London: J. Hartnell, 1829.

Moriarty, Cecil C.H. 'The Making of an English Policeman', *Police Journal* 2:1 (1929): 1–9.

———. 'The Police Recruit', *Police Journal* 2:2 (1929): 453–66.

Nemo. 'The White Paper: A Criticism', *Police Journal* 6:3 (1933): 288–94.

Nott-Bower, Sir William. *Fifty-Two Years a Policeman*. London: Edward Arnold and Co., 1926.

Peacock, Sir Robert. *Police Constables' Duties. Addresses by Robert Peacock, Chief Constable, City of Manchester*. Manchester: Henry Blacklock and Co., 1900.

'The Police and the Thieves', *The Quarterly Review* (1856): 171: 160–200.

Police Review and Parade Gossip, 1900–1939.

'Rate of Constables' Pay in English Borough', *Police Review* (12 January 1900): 15–16.

Reynes, Clifton. 'The Police as a Career: A Review of the Past, with Suggestions for the Future', *Police Journal* 7:3 (1934): 292–320.

Tarry, F.T. 'Mechanization as an Aid to Police Duties', *Police Journal* 6:2 (1933): 210–35.

Tripp, H. Alker, 'Police and Public: A New Test of Police Quality', *Police Journal* 1:4 (1928): 529–39.

Troup, Sir E. 'Police Administration, Local and National', *Police Journal* 1:1 (1928): 5–18.

Wood, Captain S.A. 'The Police Mutual Assurance Society, a Notable Achievement', *Police Journal* 3:2 (1931): 242–9.

Secondary Sources

Allen, V.L. 'The National Union of Police and Prison Officers', *Economic History Review* 2nd ser., 11:1 (1958): 133–43.

Ayers, Pat and Jan Lambertz. 'Marriage Relations, Money and Domestic Violence in Working-Class Liverpool, 1919–1939', in *Labour and Love: Women's Experience of Home and Family 1850–1940*, ed. Jane Lewis. Oxford: Basil Blackwell, 1986, pp. 195–219.

Baines, D.E. and R. Bean. 'The General Strike on Merseyside, 1926', in *Liverpool and Merseyside*, ed. J.R. Harris. London: Frank Cass, 1969, pp. 239–76.

Bean, Ron. 'Police Unrest, Unionization and the 1919 Strike in Liverpool', *Journal of Contemporary History* 15:4 (1980): 633–53.

Beier, Lucinda McCray. *For Their Own Good: The Transformation of English Working-Class Health Culture, 1880–1970*. Columbus: Ohio State University Press, 2008.

———. '"We Were Green as Grass": Learning about Sex and Reproduction in Three Working-Class Lancashire Communities, 1900–1970', *Social History of Medicine* 16:3 (2003): 461–80.

Benson, John. *The Working Class in Britain 1850–1939*. New York: Longman, 1989.

Berlière, Jean-Marc. 'The Difficult Construction of a "Republican" Police: The Experience of the French Third Republic', in *Policing Interwar Europe: Continuity, Change and Crisis, 1918–1940*, ed. Gerald Blaney. London: Palgrave Macmillan, 2007.

Bessel, Richard and Clive Emsley, eds. *Patterns of Provocation: Police and Public Disorder*. New York: Berghahn, 2000.

Bourke, Joanna, *Working-Class Cultures in Britain 1890–1960: Gender, Class and Ethnicity*. London: Routledge, 1994.

Broady, Duncan. *The Police! 150 Years of Policing in the Manchester Area*. Runcorn: Archive Publications, 1989.

Broady, Duncan and Dave Tetlow. *Images of England: Law and Order in Manchester*. Stroud: Tempus, 2005.

Brogden, Mike. *On the Mersey Beat: Policing Liverpool between the Wars*. Oxford: Oxford University Press, 1991.

———. *The Police: Autonomy and Consent*. London: Academic Press, 1982.

Buckley, Anthony, 'Neighbourliness – Myth and History', *Oral History Journal* 11:1 (1983): 44–51.

Chinn, Carl, *They Worked All Their Lives: Women of the Urban Poor in England, 1880–1939*. Manchester: Manchester University Press, 1988.

Clegg, H.A., et al. *A History of British Trade Unions since 1889*, vols I and II. New York: Clarendon Press, 1964, 1985.

Cockcroft, W.R. 'The Liverpool Police Force, 1836–1902', in *Victorian Lancashire*, ed. S. Peter Bell. Newton Abbot: David and Charles, 1974, pp. 150–68.

Coleman, Loren. *Suicide Clusters*. London: Faber and Faber, 1987.

Conley, Carolyn A. *The Unwritten Law: Criminal Justice in Victorian Kent*. Oxford: Oxford University Press, 1991.

Critchley, T.A. *A History of Police in England and Wales, 900–1966*. Letchworth: Garden City Press, 1967.

Crook, Rosemary, '"Tidy Women": Women in the Rhondda between the Wars', *Oral History Journal* 10:2 (1982): 40–6.

Davies, Andrew, *Leisure, Gender and Poverty: Working-Class Culture in Salford and Manchester, 1900–1939*. Buckingham: Open University Press, 1992.

———. 'The Police and the People: Gambling in Salford, 1900–1939', *Historical Journal* 34:1 (1991): 87–115.

Davies, Andrew and Steven Fielding, eds. *Workers' Worlds: Cultures and Communities in Manchester and Salford, 1880–1939*. Manchester: Manchester University Press, 1992.

Davies, S.J. 'Classes and Police in Manchester 1829–1880', in *City, Class and Culture*, ed. A.J. Kidd and K.W. Roberts. Manchester: Manchester University Press, 1985, pp. 26–47.

Davis, Jennifer. 'From "Rookeries" to "Communities": Race, Poverty and Policing in London, 1850–1987', *History Workshop* 27 (1989): 66–85.

———. *Law Breaking and Law Enforcement: The Creation of a Criminal Class in Mid-Victorian London* (Ann Arbor, MI: University Microfilms, 1986).

Dingle, A.E. 'Drink and Working-Class Living Standards in Britain, 1870–1914', *Economic History Review* 2nd ser., 25:4 (1972): 608–22.

Dixon, David. *From Prohibition to Regulation: Bookmaking, Anti-Gambling and the Law* Oxford: Clarendon Press, 1991.

Dunnage, Jonathan. 'Mussolini's Policemen, 1922–43', in *Policing Interwar Europe: Continuity, Change and Crisis, 1918–1940*, ed. Gerald Blaney, London: Palgrave Macmillan, 2007, pp. 112–35.

Emsley, Clive. *Crime and Society in England, 1750–1900*. New York: Longman, 1987.

———. 'The English Bobby: An Indulgent Tradition', in *Memory, Myths and Monuments*, ed. Roy Porter. Cambridge: Polity Press, 1992, pp. 114–35.

———. *The English Police: A Political and Social History*. 2nd edn. New York: Longman, 1996.

———. *Hard Men: The English and Violence since 1750*. London: Hambledon and London, 2005.

———. '"Mother, What *Did* Policemen Do When There Weren't Any Motors?" The Law, the Police and the Regulation of Motor Traffic in England, 1900–1939', *Historical Journal* 36:2 (1993): 357–81.

———. *Policing and Its Context, 1750–1870*. New York: Schocken, 1983.

———. '"The Thump of Wood on a Swede Turnip": Police Violence in Nineteenth-Century England', *Criminal Justice History* 11 (1985): 125–49.

Emsley, Clive and Mark Clapson, 'Recruiting the English Policeman c. 1840–1940', *Policing and Society* 3 (1994): 269–86.

Emsley, Clive and Barbara Weinberger, eds. *Policing Western Europe: Politics, Professionalism, and Public Order 1850–1940*. Westport, CT: Greenwood, 1991.

Ewen, Shane. 'Civic Identity and Police Leisure in Birmingham during the Inter-war Years', *International Journal of Regional and Local Studies* 2nd ser., 1:1 (2005): 44–62.

Frost, Ginger. *As Husband and Wife: Cohabitation in Nineteenth-Century England*. Manchester: Manchester University Press, forthcoming.

———. 'Bigamy and Cohabitation in Victorian England', *Journal of Family History* 22:3 (1997): 286–306.

———. *Living in Sin: Cohabiting as Husband and Wife in Nineteenth-Century England*. Manchester: Manchester University Press, 2009.

Gatrell, V.A.C. 'Crime, Authority and the Policeman-State', *The Cambridge Social History of Britain 1750–1950*, vol. III. Cambridge: Cambridge University Press, 1990, pp. 243–310.

———. 'The Decline of Theft and Violence in Victorian and Edwardian England', in *Crime and the Law*, ed. V.A.C. Gatrell, Bruce Lenman, and Geoffrey Parker. London: Europa, 1980, pp. 238–337.

Geary, Roger. *Policing Industrial Disputes: 1893–1985*. Cambridge: Cambridge University Press, 1985.

Gillis, John R. *For Better, For Worse: British Marriages, 1600 to the Present*. Oxford: Oxford University Press, 1985.

———. *A World of Their Own Making: Myth, Ritual, and the Quest for Family Values*. New York: Basic Books, 1996.

Hall, Catherine, 'Married Women at Home in the 1920s and 1930s', *Oral History* 5:2 (1977): 62–83.

Hammerton, A. James. *Cruelty and Companionship: Conflict in Nineteenth-Century Married Life*. London and New York: Routledge, 1992.

Hewitt, Eric J. *A History of Policing in Manchester*. Manchester: E.J. Morton, 1979.

Hoggart, Richard. *The Uses of Literacy*. New York: Penguin, 1958.

Holdaway, Simon. 'Changes in Urban Policing', *British Journal of Sociology* 28:2 (1977): 119–37.

Howard, R. 'The Tardis', *Journal of the Police History Society* 5 (1990): 98–100.

Humphries, Stephen. *Hooligans or Rebels? An Oral History of Working-Class Childhood and Youth 1889–1939*. Oxford: Basil Blackwell, 1981.

———. *A Secret World of Sex: Forbidden Fruit: The British Experience 1900–1950*. London: Sidgwick and Jackson, 1988.

Jenkins, Philip. 'Into the Upperworld? Law, Crime and Punishment in English Society', *Social History* 12:1 (1987): 93–102.

Johnson, Marilynn S. *Street Justice: A History of Police Violence in New York City*. Boston, MA: Beacon Press, 2003.

Jones, D.J.V. 'The New Police, Crime and People in England and Wales, 1829–1888', *Transactions of the Royal Historical Society* (1983): 151–68.

Jones, J. Mervyn. 'The Man on the Beat', *Policing* 2:2 (1986): 114–28.

Joyce, Peter. 'Recruitment Patterns and Conditions of Work in a Nineteenth-Century Police Force: A Case Study of Manchester 1842–1900', *Police Journal* 64:2 (1991): 140–50.

Judge, Anthony. *The First Fifty Years: The Story of the Police Federation*. London: Police Federation, 1968.

King, Joseph F. 'The United Kingdom Police Strikes of 1918–1919', *Police Studies* 11:3 (1988): 128–38.

Klein, Joanne. 'Blue-Collar Job, Blue-Collar Career: English Policemen's Perplexing Struggle for a Voice in the Early Twentieth Century', *Crime, Histoire & Sociétés/Crime, History & Societies* 6:1 (2002): 5–29.

———. 'Invisible Working-Class Men: Police Constables in Manchester, Birmingham and Liverpool 1900–1939', PhD diss., Rice University, 1992.

———. 'Irregular Marriages: Unorthodox Working-Class Domestic Life in Liverpool, Birmingham and Manchester, 1900–1939', *Journal of Family History* 30:2 (2005): 210–29.

———. '"Leaving at His Own Request": les démissions volontaires d'agents de police britanniques (1900–1939)', in *Métiers de police: être policier en Europe, XVIIIe-XXe siècles*, ed. Jean-Marc Berlière, Catherine Denys, Dominique Kalifa and Vincent Milliot. Rennes: Presses Universitaires de Rennes, 2008, pp. 189–99.

———. '"Moving On", Men and the Changing Character of Interwar Working-Class Neighborhoods: From the Files of the Manchester and Liverpool City Police', *Journal of Social History* (2004): 407–21.

———. 'Traffic, Telephones and Police Boxes: The Deterioration of Beat Policing in Birmingham, Liverpool and Manchester between the World Wars', in *Policing Interwar Europe: Continuity, Change and Crisis, 1918–1940*, ed. Gerald Blaney. London: Palgrave Macmillan, 2007, pp. 216–36.

Lewis, Jane, ed. *Labour and Love: Women's Experience of Home and Family 1850–1940*. Oxford: Basil Blackwell, 1986.

———. *Women in England, 1870–1950: Sexual Divisions and Social Change*. Bloomington: Indiana University Press, 1984.

Lowe, W.J. 'The Lancashire Constabulary, 1845–1870: The Social and Occupational Function of a Victorian Police Force', *Criminal Justice History* 4 (1983): 41–62.

Lowndes, G.A.N. *The Silent Social Revolution: An Account of the Expansion of Public Education in England and Wales, 1895–1965*. Oxford: Oxford University Press, 1969.

Maclure, Stuart. *A History of Education in London, 1870–1990*. London: Allen Lane, 1990.

Marsh, David C. *The Changing Social Structure of England and Wales, 1871–1961*. London: Routledge, 2002.

Martin, J.P. and Gail Wilson, *The Police: A Study in Manpower*. London: Heinemann, 1969.

McKibbon, Ross. 'Working-Class Gambling in Britain 1880–1939', *Past and Present* 82 (1979): 147–78.

Morgan, Jane. *Conflict and Order: The Police and Labour Disputes in England and Wales, 1900–1939*. New York: Clarendon Press, 1987.

Palmer, Stanley H. *Police and Protest in England and Ireland, 1780–1850*. Cambridge: Cambridge University Press, 1988.

Pelling, Henry. *A History of British Trade Unionism*. 4th edn. London: Macmillan, 1987.

Perkin, Harold. *The Rise of Professional Society: England since 1880*. London: Routledge, 1989.

Petrow, Stefan. *Policing Morals: the Metropolitan Police and the Home Office in London 1870–1914*. Oxford: Oxford University Press, 1994.

Philips, David. *Crime and Authority in Victorian England: The Black Country, 1835–1860*. London: Croom Helm, 1977.

———. '"A Just Measure of Crime, Authority, Hunters and Blue Locust": The "Revisionist" Social History of Crime and the Law in Britain, 1780–1850', in *Social Control and the State*, ed. Stanley Cohen and Andrew Scull. New York: St Martin's Press, 1983, pp. 50–74.

Phillips, Roderick. *Putting Asunder: A History of Divorce in Western Society*. Cambridge: Cambridge University Press, 1988.

Prochaska, Frank. 'Philanthropy', in *The Cambridge Social History of Britain 1750–1950*, vol. III. Cambridge: Cambridge University Press, 1990, pp. 359–70.

———. *The Voluntary Impulse: Philanthropy in Modern Britain*. London: Faber and Faber, 1988.

Punch, Maurice and Trevor Naylor. 'The Police: A Social Service', *New Society* 24:554 (1973): 358–61.

Rawlings, Philip. *Policing: A Short History*. Cullompton: Willan Publishing, 2002.

Reilly, John W. *Policing Birmingham: An Account of 150 Years of Police in Birmingham* Birmingham: West Midlands Police, 1989.

Reiner, Robert. *The Blue-Coated Worker: A Sociological Study of Police Unionism*. Cambridge: Cambridge University Press, 1978.

———. *Chief Constables: Bobbies, Bosses, or Bureaucrats?* Oxford: Oxford University Press, 1991.

———. 'The Modern Bobby: The Development of the British Police', *Policing* 2:4 (1986): 258–75.

———. 'The Police in the Class Structure', *British Journal of Law and Society* 5:2 (1978): 166–84.

———. 'Political Conflict and the British Police Tradition', *Contemporary Review* 236:1371 (1980): 191–200.

———. *The Politics of the Police*. New York: St Martin's Press, 1985.

Reinke, Herbert. '"Armed as if for a War": The State, the Military and the Professionalisation of the Prussian Police in Imperial Germany', in *Policing Western Europe: Politics, Professionalism, and Public Order 1850–1940*, ed. Clive Emsley and Barbara Weinberger. Westport, CT: Greenwood, 1991. 55–73.

Reynolds, Gerald and Anthony Judge. *The Night the Police Went on Strike*. London: Weidenfeld and Nicolson, 1968.

Roberts, Elizabeth. *A Woman's Place: An Oral History of Working Class Women 1890–1940*. Oxford: Basil Blackwell, 1984.

Roberts, Robert. *The Classic Slum: Salford Life in the First Quarter of the Century*. Harmondsworth: Penguin, 1974.

Robinson, Cyril D. 'The Deradicalization of the Policeman: A Historical Analysis', *Crime and Delinquency* 24:2 (1978): 129–51.

———. 'Ideology as History: A Look at the Way Some English Police Historians Look at the Police', *Police Studies* 2 (1979): 35–49.

Ross, Ellen. '"Not the Sort That Would Sit on the Doorstep": Respectability in Pre-World War I London Neighborhoods', *International Labor and Working Class History* 27 (1985): 39–59.

———. 'Survival Networks: Women's Neighborhood Sharing in London before World War I', *History Workshop* 15 (1983): 1–27.

Sainsbury, Peter. *Suicide in London: An Ecological Study*. New York: Basic Books, 1956.

Seccombe, Wally. *Weathering the Storm: Working-Class Families from the Industrial Revolution to the Fertility Decline*. London: Verso, 1995.

Sellwood, A.V. *Police Strike – 1919*. London: W.H. Allen, 1978.

Shackleton, Richard. 'The 1919 Police Strike in Birmingham', in *Worlds of Labour: Essays in Birmingham Labour History*, ed. Anthony Wright and Richard Shackleton. Birmingham: University of Birmingham, 1983, pp. 63–87.

Shpayer-Makov, Haia. 'The Making of a Police Labour Force', *Journal of Social History* 24 (1990): 109–34.

———. *The Making of a Policeman: A Social History of a Labour Force in Metropolitan London, 1829–1914*. Aldershot: Ashgate, 2002.

Silver, Allan. 'The Demand for Order in Civil Society: A Review of Some Themes in the History of Urban Crime, Police, and Riot', in *The Police: Six Sociological Essays*, ed. David J. Bordua. New York: Wiley, 1967, pp. 1–24.

Stead, Philip John. *The Police of Britain*. New York: Macmillan, 1985.

Steedman, Carolyn. *Policing the Victorian Community: The Formation of English Provincial Police Forces, 1856–80*. London: Routledge and Kegan Paul, 1984.

Stone, Lawrence. *Road to Divorce, England 1530–1987*. Oxford: Oxford University Press, 1990.

Storch, Robert D. 'The Plague of the Blue Locusts: Police Reform and Popular Resistance in Northern England, 1840–57', *International Review of Social History* 20 (1975): 61–90.

———. 'Police Control of Street Prostitution in Victorian London: A Study in the Contexts of Police Action', in *Police and Society*, ed. David H. Bayley. London: Sage, 1977, pp. 49–72.

———. 'The Policeman as Domestic Missionary: Urban Discipline and Popular Culture in Northern England, 1850–1880', *Journal of Social History* 9:4 (1976): 481–509.

Tebbutt, Melanie. *Women's Talk? A Social History of 'Gossip' in Working-Class Neighbourhoods, 1880–1960*. Aldershot: Scolar Press, 1997.

Thompson, F.M.L. *The Rise of Respectable Society: A Social History of Victorian Britain 1830–1900*. London: Fontana Press, 1988.

Walkowitz, Judith R. 'Jack the Ripper and the Myth of Male Violence', *Feminist Studies* 8:3 (1982): 543–74.

———. 'The Making of an Outcast Group', in *A Widening Sphere: Changing Roles of Victorian Women*, ed. Martha Vicinus. Bloomington: Indiana University Press, 1977, pp. 72–93.

———. 'Male Vice and Feminist Virtue: Feminism and the Politics of Prostitution in Nineteenth-Century Britain', *History Workshop* 13 (1982): 77–93.

———. *Prostitution and Victorian Society: Women, Class and the State*. Cambridge: Cambridge University Press, 1980.

Weeks, Jeffrey. *Sex, Politics and Society: the Regulation of Sexuality since 1800*. New York: Longman, 1989.

Weinberger, Barbara. *The Best Police in the World: An Oral History of English Policing*. Aldershot: Scolar Press, 1995.

———. *Keeping the Peace? Policing Strikes in Britain 1906–1926*. Oxford: Berg, 1991.

———. 'Police Forces and Public Order in England and France during the Interwar Years', in *Policing Western Europe: Politics, Professionalism, and Public Order 1850–1940*, ed. Clive Emsley and Barbara Weinberger (Westport, CT: Greenwood, 1991).

———. 'Police Perceptions of Labour in the Inter-war Period: The Case of the Unemployed and of Miners on Strike', in *Labour, Law and Crime: An Historical Perspective*, ed. Francis Snyder and Douglas Hay. New York: Tavistock Publications, 1987.

Williams, Chris. 'Constables for Hire: The History of Private "Public" Policing in the UK', *Policing and Society* 18:2 (2008): 190–205.

Wolcott, David. *Cops and Kids: Policing Juvenile Delinquency in Urban America, 1890–1940*. Columbus: Ohio State University Press, 2005.

Wrigley, C.J., ed. *A History of British Industrial Relations 1875–1914*. New York: Harvester, 1982.

Index